, Victor Gollancz 9. Professor E. R. Dodds 10. The Boy Scouts 11. The Fabian Soc
otary International 19. The British Music Society 20. The Museums Association 21.
28. Picture Post 29. E. M. Forster 30. Harry Pollitt 31. Sylvia Pankhurst 32.
John Baker White 43. Passport Office 44. Home Office 45. Arthur Steel-Maitland
Patterson 54. Jakob Makhonin 55. Dr Arnold Toynbee 56. Sir John Hope Simpson 57. L
r 68. Lord Linlithgow 69. Sir Robert Vansittart 70. Sir Samuel Hoare 71. Winston C
Workers' Union 79. Ernest Bevin 80. Bakers, Confectioners and Allied Workers 8
, Neville Laski 89. Sir Cecil Kisch 90. Sir T. E. Guggenheim Gregory 91. Thomas
F. Franklin 101. C. M. Franklin 102. Saemy Japhet 103. Paul Lindenber 104. Max
113. Sir Lionel de Rothschild 114. Lord Bearstead 115. Lord Roseberry 116. Sir Ge
126. Professor Dr Lord Christopher Addison 127. Sir Bertrand Dawson 128. Baron Da
Plesch 138. Dr Otto Prausnitz 139. Carl Prausnitz-Giles 140. Dr Harry Fischgold
149. Peace Pledge Union 150. Sir Norman Angell 151. George Barnes 152. Fenner Brockw
160. Elizabeth Fox Howard 161. Philip Noel-Baker 162. Bennie Smith 163. Friends of N
ofessor Alfred Zimmern 173. Professor Gilbert Murray 174. Austrian Centre 175. The
Smallbones 182. Arthur Dowden 183. Doreen Warriner 184. Jewish Refugees Commit
rine Stuart-Murray, Duchess of Atholl 193. Dame Elizabeth Cadbury 194. League of Na
nica Whately 204. Aldous Huxley 205. Jacob Epstein 206. David Low 207. Wilfred Ro
216. Hon. Harold Nicolson 217. Stephen Spender 218. Professor J. B. Trend 219. H.
man 228. Oscar Kokoschka 229. Methuen 230. Marconi 231. Midland Bank 232. John
a Street 242. Francis Aldor 243. G. R. Kaye 244. Stanley Unwin 245. William Bl
Selwyn and Blount 255. Professor Lascelles Abercrombie 256. Noel Coward 257. Sto
gen 266. Fritz Gottfurcht Felix Langer 269. Karl C
gs 279. A. V. Alexander . Megan Lloyd George 282
Haldane 292. John Haldane 294. The Daily Express
J. A. Spender 303. Henry W roke Stephens 305. Harme
lli Frischauer 316. Hans Loth hin 318. Siegfried 'Sieg
ru 328. Birnbaum 329. Blaazer 331. Colonel Claude Dansey 332. Leonard
William Edward Hinchley-Cooke 341. Theodore Felstead 342. Robert Hamilton Bruce
dler 351. Herr zu Putlitz 352. Countess Moura Budberg 353. Bertrand Russell 354.
363. Captain Stanley Howard 364. Major Humphrey 365. Colonel Julius Guthlac Birc
on-Macfarlane 373. Major-General Sir Edward Louis Spears 374. Captain Kenneth Kille
Victor Stopford 383. Glyn Hearson 384. John Glanville Hearson 385. Captain Oscar
any 393. Wolseley 394. Federation of British Industry 395. Atlas Steel and Iron
n, later Lord Cadman of Silverdale 404. William Hulme Lever, Second Viscount Lever
413. Clement Davies 414. Sir Thomas Royden 415. Sir W. Charles Wright 416. Lon
426. Frederic d'Erlanger 427. Westminster Bank 428. Stern Bros 429. Imperial
countess Samuel 439. Samuel Montagu 440. Isidore Ostrer 441. Petschek family
berg 451. Pastor Herbert Friedrich Friess 452. Hildegard Friess 453. Carl Gunthe
461. Rev. Paul Stacy 462. Rev. E. Schomberg 463. H. F. Peerless 464. Church
ic World Union 473. B'nei B'rith 474. Jewish Colonisation Association 475.
r 483. Dr Edgar Wind 484. Dr Rudolf Wittkower 485. Dr Alfred Scharf 486.
tz Heichelheim 495. Hermann Kantorowicz 496. Dr Elise Baumgartel 497. Dr L
as Bonn 506. Fritz (later Frank) Burchardt 507. Adolph Lowe 508. Jacob Mar
516. Professor Sir Hans Singer 517. A. D. Lindsay 518. Dr Professor Elisabe
ard Pares 528. Professor Eileen Power 529. R. W. Seton-Watson 530. Jan Mas
8. Dr Reinhold Aris 539. Franz Xaver Aendrl 540. Raymond Klibansky 541. Wa
wich 549. Alfred Kerr 550. Kurt Maschler 551. Albert Malte Wagner 552. C
detsky 562. Professor Hyman Levy 563. J J S. Haldane 564. Sydney James Cha
Rosin 573. Dr Adolf Schallamach 574. Hans Krebs 575. Ernst Joseph Friedmann

THE BLACK BOOK

THE BLACK BOOK

Britons on the Nazi Hit List

SYBIL OLDFIELD

PROFILE BOOKS

First published in Great Britain in 2020 by
Profile Books Ltd
29 Cloth Fair
London
EC1A 7JQ

www.profilebooks.com

Extract from W. H Auden's Twelve Songs from
W. H. Auden *Selected Poems* (Faber & Faber, 2010).
Reproduced with permission of Curtis Brown.

1 3 5 7 9 10 8 6 4 2

Typeset in Swift Neue by MacGuru Ltd
Printed and bound in Great Britain by Clays Ltd, Elcograf S.p.A.

A CIP catalogue record for this book is
available from the British Library.

ISBN 978 1 78816 508 2
eISBN 978 1 78283 697 1

In memory of my husband Derek Oldfield, 1924–2008
and my companion Gwen Shaw, 1923–2018 – two rare spirits.

We are adult because we have behind us
the silent presence of the dead.

Natalia Ginzburg, 'Human Relations', in *The Little Virtues*

Contents

Acknowledgements

Whom to thank first?

My dear companion, the late Gwen Shaw, was an indispensable support right into her nineties, with her unfailing belief in the project. All her seven children took a more than polite interest in the book, but I owe special thanks to Daniel, Phil, Martin and Cathie Shaw who went out of their way to help me with research questions and computer knowhow.

I am indebted to my friend Dr Elspeth Knights for her many helpful comments and for tracking down material in the British Library and to the late Professor Edward Timms, Professor Rod Kedward, Professor John Roehl, Professor Cedric Watts and Nicholas Tucker, all former colleagues at Sussex, who read parts of the manuscript or else encouraged me to keep going. As did my friends, the historian Lyn Smith and her late husband Peter Smith. Abhinav Kumar and Andrew Huggett were indispensable word-processing buffs and, as always, I owed a lot to the patience and knowledge of the librarians at the University of Sussex.

Finally, my agent, Maggie Hanbury found me my publisher and Ed Lake of Profile Books found me my assiduous, skilled editor Natasha Lehrer. My copy editor, Penny Gardiner, was superb.

Thank you all.

PART ONE

WHY CARE ABOUT WHAT DID NOT HAPPEN?

Introduction: Why Resurrect These Dead?

Few people nowadays know very much about the Gestapo's 'Black Book' and its implications. Even fewer know of more than a dozen of the most famous English names that it included. Anonymous, with no publisher, and stamped *GEHEIM!* (SECRET!), it was compiled in German by the Gestapo and their informants at some time between 1936–7 and July 1940, in readiness for a German invasion of Britain.

This is the first serious attempt to identify, classify and analyse a significant sample of the hundreds of anti-Nazi men and women, both British-born and refugee, targeted by the Nazi secret police in the Black Book.[1] I deliberately include as 'Britons' those Jewish refugees who, stripped of their German or Austrian citizenship, would become 'naturalised' British and who comprise the majority of those on the List. I also include those of them who contributed indispensably to the British war effort but who did not become permanent British citizens after the war. Some would go to West or East Germany, others to the United States or Palestine.

This book is not a comprehensive study of the Gestapo. Nor is it a survey of all refugees in Britain from 1933 to 1945, nor of British anti-fascist organisations and activity from 1925 on. Rather, it is a study of the Nazis' plan to perpetrate '*selective* terror' in an occupied Britain.[2]

How did I come to embark on this project? From July to October 2014 an exhibition of portraits, 'Virginia Woolf, Art, Life and Vision', curated by Frances Spalding, was shown at the National Portrait Gallery in London. In its last room was the facsimile of a page from the 'Black Book – the List of Britons Most Wanted for Arrest by the Gestapo' which said:

> **Woolf, Leonhard** (sic), 1880 geb. (born), *Schriftsteller* (male writer) **Woolf, Virginia**, *Schriftstellerin* (woman writer) (accompanied by the relevant Gestapo dept. ref. no. RSHA [*Reich Sicherheit Haupt Amt* – State Security Head Department], V1G [Foreign Intelligence North-West – including Great Britain]).

Why ever, I wondered, had the Gestapo targeted Virginia Woolf, the modernist novelist? And whose were the names above and below her on that page? To my surprise I recognised very few of them, though it was clear that almost all were foreign. Who were they and why were they listed there with the Woolfs? It was sheer curiosity that first made me try to trace the Gestapo's 'Most Wanted' people in Britain in 1939–40.

I had little idea what I would discover. Very soon, however, I realised that almost every one of the Gestapo's targets about whom I was now learning – whether British-born or refugee – had been a hero of humanity. 'Great ones have been among us ... ' as Wordsworth wrote. I am resurrecting them so that they may become once more an essential part of our collective memory, exemplifying at least part of what it can mean to be 'British'. Nationalism in every country is always appropriated by the far right – but patriotism need not be. I have come to understand that these British anti-Nazis made a collective, indispensable contribution to victory in the Battle of Britain.

By April 1934 the Gestapo had already been handed over by Goering to Himmler, the head of the SS. Himmler had appointed Wilhelm Mueller, whose subordinate was Eichmann, to direct the Gestapo. Mueller answered only to Heydrich, who answered only to Himmler, who answered only to Hitler.

The Nazis idealised themselves as the only good Germans – brave, patriotic crusaders whose thousand-year Reich would save not only Germany but also Britain and the whole world from international Jewish-capitalist/Bolshevik/Masonic domination. The Nazis would not trouble any Briton who cooperated – but they would be forced to hunt down everyone in occupied Britain who threatened their project. As the Prussian military theorist Carl von Clausewitz had taught in *On War* (1832), the object of war is to render the enemy incapable of further resistance and resistance is constituted by the values that are antipathetic to those of the conqueror. However, the Gestapo hardly ever labelled their enemy prey 'anti-Nazi'; instead they accused them of being *deutschfeindlich* – 'enemies of Germany' – out to encircle the Fatherland.

The bitter irony is that it was they themselves who were the true 'enemies of Germany'. For it was the Nazis who made the word 'German' stink for generations, synonymous with torture and sickening massacres, including the deliberate murder of more than a million Jewish children. And it was the Nazis' unleashing of a hubristic world war that led to Germany's nemesis – her own beautiful old towns and cities reduced to smoking rubble just four years after the secret publication of this Black Book. It is currently estimated that over 5 million German soldiers and civilians were killed in the Second World War. But even that was not enough for Hitler. After his scorched earth 'Nero Order' of 19 March 1945, he demanded the forced evacuation of *all* Germans west of the Rhine, without food, without trains, without shelter – and with all males aged between 14 and 45 to be enlisted for a last, suicidal armed stand – or else face summary execution. 'German industry, infrastructure, culture and lives were all to end in an orgy of destruction.'[3] It was Hitler who decreed the destruction of defeated Germany as the Germans' only fitting punishment for having been defeated, proving themselves unworthy of their Führer – and not the *Herrenvolk* after all. In a contrasting irony, many of the alleged 'enemies of Germany' in the Black Book were being excoriated in Britain for *not* being 'enemies of Germany' – because they urged the cessation of the bombing of German civilians, the feeding of starving Germans after the war, and support for a new, revived, democratic and humane Germany. For example **Arthur Ponsonby, Vera Brittain, Bishop Bell, Richard Stokes, Eleanor Rathbone, Victor Gollancz** and **Professor E. R. Dodds**. (Names in **bold** throughout are of those individuals and organisations on the *Sonderfahndungsliste GB*.)

Death-bringing Nazism, as well as being the true enemy of Germany, was also of course the enemy of the peoples of Austria,

Czechoslovakia, Poland, the Netherlands, Norway, Denmark, France, Yugoslavia, Greece, Romania, Hungary, the Soviet Union, European Jewry – and Britain. Nazi Germany was accountable for well over 40 million violent non-German deaths – at the very least – as well as for innumerable blighted lives. And wherever they waged war they tried to destroy each resistant civil society.

The two parts of the Gestapo's Black Book that I focus on consist of:

1. The Gestapo's *Sonderfahndungsliste GB*, i.e. 'Most Wanted List for Arrest in Great Britain' compiled *c.*1937–*c.*September 1939, popularly known ever since as the 'Black Book', which is in turn divided into two sections: first, the alphabetical listing of some 2,619 names of men and women, mostly with their addresses, to be arrested and interned in camps or placed under house arrest at once, if not executed; and second, the more or less alphabetical listing of the names and addresses of nearly 400 British '*Behoerden*', '*Firmen*' and '*Vereinigungen*' (institutions, businesses, organisations and associations) – all of which were to be proscribed, their papers seized and their mostly British-born leaders arrested.[4]

2. The Gestapo's *Informationsheft GB*, compiled May to July 1940 as an introductory handbook on Britain for the occupation troops, including the SS, and mentioning many additional leading individuals who would require surveillance and probable arrest.

Compiling alphabetical lists of suspects to be arrested, interrogated and imprisoned in special 'camps' was what the Gestapo spent much of their time doing:

> [Producing] or updating index cards, working through the flood of instructions and regulations, filing documents ... collecting and working through information was the normal sense of affairs ... At the beginning of 1939, the central records office of the Gestapo is said to have comprised around two million personal index cards.[5]

220

33. **Weber, Editha**, 27.10.05 Düsseldorf, Erzieherin, vermutl. England, RSHA IV E 4.
34. **Weber, Ludwig**, 22.5.02 Pfungsstadt/Darmstadt, RSHA IV A 1, IV A 2.
35. **Wechselmann, Kurt**, 3.2.88 Mieckobitz, Kaufmann, zuletzt: Den Haag, vermutl. England, RSHA IV E 4, Stapoleit Breslau.
36. **Weck, Kurt**, 20.11.92 Werdau/Sa., vermutl. England, RSHA IV A 1 b.
37. **Weckel, Kurt**, 15.3.77 Schedewitz, Volksschullehrer, RSHA IV A 1 b.
38. **Wedgwood, Josiah Clement**, 1872, brit. Oberst, RSHA VI G 1.
39. **van Weegen, Wilhelm**, 1.2.04 Uden/Holland, zuletzt: Renkum b. Arnheim, vermutl. England, RSHA IV E 4.
40. **Weidmann, Friedrich Wilhelm**, 8.11.02 Erlangen, Arbeiter, London, RSHA III B 3, Stapo Nürnberg.
41. **Weil, Hans, Dr.**, 1905 geb., Assistent, Emigrant, Newcastle-on-Tyne, RSHA III A 1.
42. **Weiler, Gerhard, Dr.**, 1899 geb., Emigrant, Oxford, RSHA III A 1.
43. **Weinberger, Martin, Dr.**, 1893, verh., Emigrant, London, Dozent a. d. Universität, RSHA III A 1.
44. **Weinhart, Josef**, 17.6.97 Gfell, Glan Y Mor, Y. M. G. A., Barry i. Glam, RSHA IV A 1 b.
45. **Weinmann, Fritz**, Emigrant (Jude), London, RSHA III D 4.
46. **Weinmann, Hans**, Hauptaktionär d. Westböhmischen Bergbauaktienvereins, London, RSHA III D.
47. **Weinstein, Alexander, Dr.**, geb. 1897, London, Privatdozent a. d. Universität, Emigrant, RSHA III A 1.
48. **Weisenfeld, Nathan**, Arzt, London, RSHA IV A 2.
49. **Weiß, Bernhard**, 30.7.80 Berlin, ehem. Pol.-Vize-Präs., RSHA IV A 1, VI G 1.
50. **Weiß, Harry, Dr.**, 1906 geb., Emigrant, London, RSHA III A 1.
51. **Weiß, Joseph, Dr.**, 1905 geb., London, Emigrant, Assistent an der Universität, RSHA III A 1.
52. **Weißenberg, Karl, Dr.**, 1893 geb., Emigrant, a. o. Professor, Southampton, RSHA III A 1.
53. **Weizmann, Chaim**, 1873 oder 1874 in Motyli bei Pinks, Professor der Chemie, Führer der gesamten Judenvereine Englands, London S. W. 1, 104 Pall Mall, Reform-Club, RSHA III B 2, VI G 1.
54. **Welker, Helene**, 13.12.04 Berlin, RSHA IV A 2.
55. **Wells, Herbert George**, 1866 geb., Schriftsteller, London N. W. 1, Regents Park 13, Hanover Terrace, RSHA VI G 1, III A 5, II B 4.
55a. **Welsh**, brit. N.-Agent, zuletzt: Kopenhagen, vermutl. England, RSHA IV E 4.
56. **Welter, Charles Joseph Ignace Marie**, 6.4.80 Den Haag, ehem. holl. Kolonialminister, zuletzt: Den Haag, Statenplein 10, RSHA III B.
57. **de Werdestuyn, de Wijkersloot, Robert**, 21.9.12 Utrecht, Student, zuletzt: Nymwegen, vermutl. England, RSHA IV E 4, Stapoleit Düsseldorf.
58. **Wenzel, Johann**, Deckname: Hermann und Bergmann, 9.3.02 Niedau, Schlosser, Schmied, RSHA IV A 2.
59. **Werner, Heinz, Dr.**, 1890 geb., Cambridge, Emigrant, a. o. Prof. an der Universität, RSHA III A 1.
60. **Werner, Hermann**, 27.9.93 Buckwa, vermutl. England, RSHA IV A 1 b.
61. **Werner, Paul Robert**, 16.5.15 Scheidelwitz, Gefreiter, RSHA IV E 5, Stapoleit Breslau.
62. **Wertheimer, Lydia**, Mitarbeiterin d. Merton, London, RSHA III D.
63. **West, Rebeca**, 1892 geb., Journalistin, RSHA VI G 1.

210. **Quarrymen's Group,** Leiter R. W. Williams Carnarvon, gewerkschaftl. marx. Organisationen, Sitz: London, Westminster Smith Square, RSHA IV A 1, Stapo Bremen.
211. **Record Dept., Leiter J. Gill,** Sekretariate der General-Worker Union, Sitz: London, Westminster Smith Square, Ort: London, RSHA IV A 1, Stapo Bremen.
212. **Relief Committee for the victims of German and Austria Fascism,** kommunistisch eingestellt, Ort: London (Marxismus), RSHA II B 4.
213. **Relief Committee of Victims of Fascism,** RSHA VI G 1.
214. **Rotary-Club,** International, London W. C. 1, Tavistock Sq., RSHA IV E 4, VI G 1.
215. **Royal Institute of International Affairs,** internat. Auskunftsbüro im brit. Sinne, deutschfeindl. Material, steht in enger Zusammenarb. mit d. Foreign Office u. d. Informationsmin., Sitz: London, RSHA IV E 4, III A 1, IV A 5.
216. **Royal Society of Arts,** Internationale Tätigkeit gegen Deutschland gerichtet, Ort: London, 18 and 19, John St. Adelphi, W. C. 2, RSHA III A.
217. **Scottish Farm Servants — Union Dalmacoulter, Airdrie, Lanarkshire,** engl. Gewerkschaften auf marx. Grundlage, RSHA IV A 1.
218. **Scottish Headquarter, Sekretary Boy Scout,** Sitz: Edinburgh, 44 Charlotte Square, Ort: Edinburgh, RSHA III A (ZB).
219. **Scottish Unionist Association,** Ort: Edinburgh, 9 Atholl Crescent, RSHA VI G 1.
220. **Smith Square,** Unterstützuungsorg. f. Emigranten, Sitz: Transport House, Ort: London S. W. 1, RSHA IV E 4.

National Worker's Sport Association, britische Sektion der briti- [illegible] Street, RSHA VI G 1.

[illegible] **League (S. L.),** sozialistische Organisation, Sitz: London S. W. [illegible], Victoria Street (Marxismus), RSHA II B 4.

Socialist Party of Great Britain (S. P. G. B.), sozialistische Organisation, Ort: London S. W. 1, 42 Gr. Dover Str. (Marxismus), RSHA II B [illegible], VI G 1.

Society for Cultural Relations between the British Commonwealth and the USSR, Ort: London W. C. 1, 98 Gover Str., RSHA VI G 1.

225. **Society for the Protection of Sciende and Learning,** betreut Akademiker, Ort: London W. C. 1, 6 Gordon Square, RSHA IV A 5.
226. **Society of Friends, Quäker,** Ort: London N. I., RSHA IV E 4.
227. **Society of Jews and Christans,** Ort: London W. 8, 31 Philli more Gardens, RSHA VI G 1.
228. **Schriftsteller-Internationale (Britische Sektion),** kommunistisch eingestellt, Ort: London (Marxismus), RSHA II B 4.
229. **Studentische Bewegung,** kommunistisch eingestellt, Ort: London (Marxismus), RSHA II B 4.
230. **Talmud Torah Trust,** London E 1, 9 Mulberry Street, The Jewish Institute, RSHA II B 2 (jüdisch).
231. **The Academic Assistance Council,** bringt emigrierte Wissenschaftler aus Deutschland unter, London W. C. 2, 12 Clement's Inn Passage Clare Market, RSHA III A 1.
232. **The British Council,** Britische Auslandspropaganda, London, Hanover Str., RSHA III A 1.
233. **The British Music Society,** Internationale Tätigkeit gegen Deutschland gerichtet, London, 18 Great Marlborough Street, RSHA III A 42.

Black Books were compiled not just for Britain but first of course for Germany itself and then for Austria, the Sudetenland, Czechoslovakia and Poland – in the case of Poland with 60,000 names.

The plan to Nazify the whole of Britain is clear from the Gestapo's list of proscribed '*Vereinigungen*' ('Associations') in Part Two of their 'Most Wanted' list, the *Sonderfahndungsliste GB*. How British would Britain still have been without any of her political parties or trade unions – from the **Amalgamated Societies of Bakers and Confectioners** to **Boot and Shoemakers**, **Ship Builders** and the **Transport and General Workers' Union**? And without any of the following – **the Boy Scouts, the Co-operative Movement, the Fabian Society, the Society of Friends (Quakers), Esperantists, the Fellowship of Reconciliation, the Jewish Board of Guardians, the National Council of Civil Liberties, the National Council of Women, the Navy League, the Public Record Office, Rotary International, the British Council, the British Music Society, the Museums Association, the PEN Club, the Student Christian Movement, the United Grand Lodge of Freemasons, War Resisters International, the Waterways Group, the Women's International League for Peace and Freedom, the World Fellowship of Faiths, the Workers' Educational Association (WEA), the World Union of Progressive Judaism**, and **the YMCA**? To name but a few. (Names of Blacklisted associations and institutions listed in the *Sonderfahndungsliste GB* are also in **bold** throughout.) Some of these Gestapo-targeted British organisations were tiny and looked upon as cranks, others were massive and mainstream, but together they had helped to weave the social fabric of Britain over generations. Wherever they were on the political or religious – or non-religious – spectrum, all these associations shared a basic humanism that was the antithesis of Nazism.

Similarly, almost all the named individuals in Part One of the *Sonderfahndungsliste GB* and in the *Informationsheft GB*, were, without being plaster saints, compassionate altruists who totally rejected the Nazi doctrine of righteous cruelty – '*Haerte*' ('hardness'). Here we find, cheek by jowl, anti-communists and pro-communists, Conservatives and East End activists, secularists haranguing passers-by at Speakers'

Corner as well as eminent churchmen. We discover the passport officers as well as diplomats who defied the Foreign Office's orders by issuing thousands of illegal visas to desperate Jews; we see aristocrats and poor men's lawyers, indefatigable Quakers, dissident pastors and atheist philosophers, trade union leaders who had left school at 10 and refugees who were some of the most eminent scholars and academic researchers in the world.

As for the influence of the mass media, we should not overlook the BBC's 14 million listeners to **J. B. Priestley**, or the million buyers of Penguin Specials or the 50,000 **Left Book Club** subscribers to millions of anti-fascist books, pamphlets and leaflets by 1940, let alone the readers of the weekly anti-fascist ***Picture Post***, estimated as comprising almost half the adult population. All these people, no matter how different from one another, were united in their commitment to anti-authoritarianism, anti-racism, anti-militarism and, above all, to fellowship with persecuted fellow humans. 'To me, anti-Semitism is now the most shocking of all things', **E. M. Forster** said in his BBC talk 'On Jew-consciousness' in 1939. Ironically, some of the British anti-Nazis were so committed to left-wing activism that they were simultaneously under the surveillance of both the Gestapo *and* MI5. For example **Harry Pollitt, Sylvia Pankhurst, Ivor Montagu** and **Sidney Bernstein**. As for anti-Nazi German and Austrian refugees, they were not particularly popular for trying to warn their hosts that Hitler definitely meant another war, and many of them in 1940 were even arrested as 'enemy aliens' and interned indefinitely without trial behind barbed wire by a reluctant fiat of the British Home Secretary at the behest of the British military and media. It would need an **Eleanor Rathbone** and a **George Bell** and a Maynard Keynes, among others, to have most of them released.

But the refugees won out. For refugees carry with them their years of past experience, their knowledge of another culture, language and education, their areas of expertise, their natural gifts and their determination to start again. Their situation demands immense courage, perseverance, adaptability, and responsiveness to the positives in a new, unfriendly world. The wealth of intellectual gifts that the German, Austrian, Czech, Hungarian and Polish, mostly Jewish, refugees from Nazism brought with them to Britain after 1933 is attested in the rest of this book.

Why resurrect the contribution of British anti-Nazism from 1933 to 1940 now? Immediately after the defeat of Nazism and the unspeakable revelations of the exterminatory concentration camps in 1945, anti-fascist resistance was claimed to be an *essential* part of British DNA, ignoring the fact that it had also had to combat some 'appeasing' pro-fascists in 1930s' Britain.

> [In] Britain anti-fascist attitudes became central to constructions of national identity, with animosity towards Nazi Germany and the heroic struggle against Hitler functioning as major sources of national loyalty and patriotic pride … [This] fusion of anti-fascism with nationalism reinforced perceptions … that fascism was essentially an alien creed inimical to British culture and traditions.[6]

However, all our anti-fascist forebears are dead and we cannot live off the moral fat of their endeavour. That self-serving myth of Britain as an eternally anti-fascist nation leaves our society blind to the danger of ultra-right extremism here and now. For the uphill struggle of anti-fascists to make Britain face the reality of Hitler between 1933 and 1940 is no longer common knowledge. The anti-fascists' actions, speeches and writings are not taught in schools; their very names are forgotten – '[Anti]-fascism is a little studied area … [even though] far more people supported the anti-fascist cause than ever supported fascist organisations.'[7]

And not only has the anti-fascists' vital contribution to the Battle of Britain and to the subsequent war effort been erased or even denied; the huge contribution made by hundreds of thousands of 'foreign' Allied servicemen from all over the world has been largely forgotten, even though many of them perished in the struggle. The population of Britain had never been as diverse as it was between 1939 and 1945. 'But when the war ended, awareness of the diverse wartime population in Britain was lost and has played little part in public memories of the war.'[8] The myth that Britain's 'finest hour' was achieved by native British citizens *on our own* soon emerged and still wreaks great damage.

However hard it is to acknowledge it, nationalistic, xenophobic, militaristic and misogynistic populism – even leader-worship – have resurfaced today in Britain.[9] A dormant quasi-fascism is being resurrected that yet again demonises the outsider – whether migrant or Muslim or East European or Jewish.[10] But if fascism – in Rolf Dahrendorf's words, 'the authoritarianism of the threatened class' – or classes – can re-emerge, so can anti-fascism. That is why I needed to write this book *now*.

*

There is also a personal motive. I was born in London, half German, half English, in 1938. My parents would never have met had the Nazis not come to power. In spring 1933, my German grandparents, who were socialists and pacifists, told my then 18-year-old mother that she must leave the country for the good of the rest of the family. Skilled at languages, she would be able to acquire a work permit abroad and make a safe base for her young brother so that he would never have to kill for Hitler. They had already realised from *Mein Kampf* that the new German dictator would be determined to trigger an expansionist world war.

My mother met my father at the Bosch headquarters in London while she was working there as a trilingual personal assistant – to my grandmother's delighted relief: 'He's an Englishman, a gentleman, a socialist, you'll be safe! Marry him.' In 1936 my father filled out the required form telling the Nazi authorities that, as a British citizen, he was exempt from having to prove Aryan descent in order to marry a German woman. On the day I was born, 23 April 1938, Viennese Jews were made to scrub the streets with their toothbrushes, taunted by laughing onlookers. In Britain, after the war broke out, my mother became 'an enemy alien, naturalised by marriage', while my 17-year-old uncle, whom she had got out to Britain, was interned by the British for the next six years in POW camps. And in Germany my grandparents became secret resisters. My grandmother kept a diary from 1940 to 1945, any page of which if discovered would have had her beheaded.[11] She survived to initiate West Germany's first law permitting its citizens, on conscience grounds, to refuse to bear arms. My grandmother's example of resistance helped to inspire this book and the many stories of courage it contains.

1

The Black Book in Context: Nazi Plans for the Invasion 1939–40

On 14 September 1945 the ***Manchester Guardian*** announced:

NAZIS' BLACK LIST DISCOVERED IN BERLIN
Booklet of over 2,300 Names
GESTAPO'S FIRST VICTIMS IF BRITAIN HAD BEEN INVADED

There follows a hasty Associated Press report[1] on the discovery in the Gestapo's Berlin HQ, which, after naming some of the targeted British institutions and newspapers, focuses almost exclusively on English men and women on the list, from the worlds of politics, arts, literature and education – as well as members of the peerage and journalists. There is a reference to some of the listed members of the exiled governments operating in London in wartime, and to 'large numbers of refugees from Germany', 'too long to be published in full', who are neither classified nor named. The Associated Press report says, inaccurately, that '[The list] was originally compiled *after* [my italics] the fall of France', but, possibly more accurately, that it 'appeared to have been revised, probably yearly, thereafter'. It is therefore possible that this particular copy of the *Sonderfahndungsliste GB* found in Berlin is a different one from the one now held in the Imperial War Museum, London, which is used in this work and in which there is no evidence of subsequent revisions or additions. A selection of *almost exclusively English* names follows, with names beginning with A to S, which was complemented the following day by additional names beginning with P to Z.

The ***Manchester Guardian*** commented on 15 September 1945, under the heading (with its echo of Gilbert and Sullivan's *Mikado*) 'The Little List':

> We are indebted to the Associated Press for its enterprise in letting the public have the Gestapo's little list for Britain. We can look at it now with amusement, but we may be sure that the handy booklet had no frivolous purpose. It was the fruits of Nazi research into pre-war Britain and was the invaders' guide to dangerous persons who should be put under lock and key or rather in the new concentration camps to be opened. Presumably the theory was that if the better-known anti-Fascists were safely put away, the rest of Britain would be docile.

Thus the ***Manchester Guardian*** initially shared the English reflex reaction of indulging in superior laughter – 'amusement' – but immediately retracted that reaction, given the hideous revelations from the recently liberated 'camps'. The ***Manchester Guardian****'s* commentary continues:

> [Here] the list is, the painstaking collection of names of men and women who during the years of the Hitler regime had spoken against it and for freedom ... How diligent the Nazi note-takers must have been searching through newspapers, listening to gossip, scrutinising German passport visas and keeping track of the poor exiles who had fled from persecution in their homeland.

Unlike the Associated Press, the ***Manchester Guardian*** *did* recognise right away that 'the larger part of the list is given up to German Jewish exiles. They were to be followed and exterminated.'

The Gestapo's selection of potential resisters is deeply revealing, since it tells us not only a good deal about the nature of Nazism but also much about who Britain's outstanding anti-Nazis were, as picked out by Nazi eyes. And to all the named individuals in the Black Book, I add many *un*named British-born men and women who were leading figures in the hundreds of institutions and societies which *are* named, with their addresses, on the supplementary lists of '*Vereinigungen*' – 'associations', whether in the Black Book or in the *Informationsheft GB*, and who would have been arrested in their offices or tracked to their homes by the SS. My principal aim is to understand *why* all those particular native Britons, and those particular Jewish refugees who became British, were singled out by the Gestapo as their 'Most Wanted for Arrest'. Why were they suspected above all others of having the potential to obstruct the successful Nazification of Great Britain? The targeted men and women on the lists were to be arrested by the 20,000 members of the SS deployed in Britain, each issued with their own copy of the Black Book or Arrest List, and the Gestapo's invasion Handbook, the *Informationsheft GB*. I can only suppose that the prisoners would then have been placed under surveillance and house arrest or, more often, taken into the new, purpose-built camps. '"Protective detention" was ... an important feeder for [Himmler's] concentration camp system.'[2] For most, this would have meant mistreatment or disappearance into '*Nacht und Nebel*' – otherwise known as death.

Some commentators consider the *Sonderfahndungsliste GB* to have been of little significance. Peter Fleming in his *Operation Sea Lion* (1957, 1975), wrote: 'Men and women of every political persuasion are included and there is little to suggest that the list was a "Black List" or that any action was necessarily intended against the individuals whose names – freely misprinted – appeared on it' (p. 195).

William Shirer in *The Rise and Fall of the Third Reich* (1960) maintained that 'The Most Wanted (*die Sonderfahndungsliste* GB) was among the more amusing "invasion" documents found in the Himmler papers' (p. 783); and Norman Longmate, in *If Britain had Fallen* (2004), is equally dismissive:

> [The] Black List is ... a document of interest rather than importance, for no evidence exists that those on it were marked down for permanent detention, much less liquidation. The Jews and anti-Nazi refugees might indeed have been lucky to emerge

> from the wine-cellars of the Reform Club, or wherever it was the Gestapo kept its prisoners, but most of those mentioned would either have gone underground before the occupation began or have been released once the Gestapo had satisfied itself they were not a potential threat. (p. 196)

But I believe that the opposite was true. 'Most' people on the Black List would not have had a chance to 'go underground' successfully in time, and both the refugees, who actually made up well over half of those on the list, *and* the British-born anti-Nazis, would certainly not have been released, for they were seen by the Gestapo and the SS as posing an ideological threat whose resistance and indeed existence would have to be neutralised immediately in September 1940 through 'protective custody'.

Shirer and Longmate seem to have forgotten that the Nazi Reich had already shown criminally brutal 'form' when dealing with anyone whom they anticipated might resist. It is only necessary to remember what the Nazis had done to their own German opponents from the very outset. 'The first official concentration camp in Nazi Germany [Dachau] opened its gates on 22 March 1933.'[3] Three hundred thousand non-Jewish Germans – communists, Social Democrats, trade unionists, pacifists, including Jehovah's Witnesses – not to mention their wives – are now estimated to have been sent to concentration camps by 1939. And ever since 1922, many other opponents had of course been summarily killed, often assassinated or shot down in street battles.

Moreover, in October 1938 the German annexation of the Sudetenland had been instantly accompanied by demands that the Czech government hand over for arrest all anti-Nazi Czechs named on lists supplied by the Gestapo. And already from September 1939 to 1940 in Poland, through *Operation Tannenberg* and *Intelligenzaktion*, the German *Einsatzgruppen* were brutally 'eliminating' much of the Polish intelligentsia, as well as the Polish officer elite, and members of the priesthood and the upper classes, working from a similar *Sonderfahndungsbuch Polen* – in that case with 61,000 names.

> The genocidal policies of the Nazis resulted in the deaths of about as many Polish Gentiles as Polish Jews. [The methods included] execution, [or] forced labour and Germanisation. The German policy of destroying the Polish nation focused … upon eliminating anyone with even the least political and cultural prominence. Hitler gave the green light, placing responsibility for this campaign on Himmler's SS and police forces.[4]

Shirer acknowledges that 'The Nazi German occupation of Britain would not have been a gentle affair … [the] real terror was to be meted out by Himmler and the SS. For this the dreaded [*Reichssicherheitsdienst*/Gestapo] under Heydrich, was put in charge.'[5] Heydrich, when 'Reich Protector' of Bohemia, had already tried to eliminate all Czech opposition to Nazi occupation by suppressing Czech culture and deporting or shooting any resisters, using *Einsatzgruppen*, SS execution squads. The Gestapo was above the law and its interrogation methods included 'threats, blackmail, flattery, torture, [and] producing genuine or fake … statements from other prisoners'.[6]

The late Professor John Erickson in his introduction to Walter Schellenberg in *Invasion 1940* (St Ermin's Press, 2000), concludes categorically that the Black Book ' … was a manual for total occupation, for the ruthless elimination of any who stood in its way or who had shown any hint of a propensity to opposition, resistance to or revulsion at the sights and sounds of National Socialism, with a candidate list for the *Knickschuss* [bullet in the back of the neck]'.

The Nazi invasion of Britain, of course, never took place. Britain was saved by the young fighter pilots (of many nationalities) in the 'Battle of Britain',[7] by the defeat of the U-boats in the Atlantic, by the decoding of German Ultra/Enigma signals at Bletchley, by the Land Army and the factory workers doing long overtime shifts in order to produce all the food, weaponry, planes, and defence infrastructure essential to win, by the merchant seamen bringing still more food to Britain across the submarine-infested Atlantic, *and*, as I shall try to show, by the 'mental fight' waged by anti-fascist Britons, both native and refugee. So why bother with what did not happen but only nearly happened? Much speculative 'alternative history' is vitiated by the plethora of all the different might-have-beens that branch out from a great number of initial variables. But in this case we *do* know exactly what was intended to happen following a Nazi occupation of Britain. And from that evidence I am able to consider three questions:

1. What would a Nazi Britain have been like?
2. Who were the anti-Nazis most feared by the Nazis?
3. How did they contribute to Britain before, during and after the Second World War?

Attempting a statistical analysis of the individuals listed in the Black Book cannot be a scientific undertaking because of the Gestapo's own ignorance and inconsistencies. The duplication and even triplication of some entries has been addressed, however, and brings the total of entries down from an earlier estimate of *c.*2,830 to 2,619. Of these 2,619, 2,353 were men and 266 were women – roughly 89 per cent to 11 per cent. Out of the total 2,619, at least 1,657, i.e. well over half, were refugees. And of those *c.*1,657 refugees, at least two-thirds, 1,072, were Jews – 'at least' because many Jews had altered or anglicised their names. (For instance **H. W. Wilson** was really H. Maurice Wilson, born Cohen, the producer of the film about a Welsh mining disaster, *The Stars Look Down.*) Although 1,657 seems like a lot of refugees to be promptly arrested, it must be remembered that they were only a selected few, roughly 1.1 per cent, out of the total number of refugees then in Britain. '[The] Home Office estimated that the total number of refugees in Britain in 1943 was around 150,000'[8] – 78,000 of them from Austria, Germany and Czechoslovakia, mostly Jews. The Jews from these countries listed in the Black Book comprised roughly 2 per cent of that number.

But all the above Gestapo figures can only be approximations because of the vagueness and unreliability of some of their data. In the case of Austrian and German *academic* Jewish refugees, the listing is usually detailed and precise, giving surname, full forenames, date and place of birth, occupation and current address in Britain – as well as the Gestapo filing reference such as Amt RSHA IVA – 'Combating ideological opposition, Emigrants'. Clearly the Gestapo had been tracking these particular distinguished refugees even after they had been forced out of Germany. But all too often an entry may consist only of a last name and a last known city – Copenhagen, Amsterdam, Istanbul, or even Kabul, ending with a vague 'British agent thought to be in England' (*'vermutlich in England'*). Moreover the Gestapo were often ignorant when any one of their 'Most Wanted' , e.g. '**Sigmund Freud, *Jude*,**' had died, or when, like **Einstein**, **Paul Robeson** (*'Negersaenger'*) and the nuclear physicist **Leo Szilard**, they had already left Britain for the United States. Indeed many of the listed had never even tried to reach Britain, preferring Sweden, Canada, Palestine or the United States.

And others of those listed who had tried to find asylum in Britain had failed. We should not forget those tragic few who were denied sanctuary in Britain – the communist trade unionist and sailor **Werner Lehmann** for example, who ended up betrayed by Vichy France and died a brutal death in a Nazi prison in Berlin in 1942. The Gestapo believed he was in London, but in fact he had never made it. Or **Lina Wertheimer**, who was the devoted Jewish secretary of the boss of German AG Metall, exiled **Richard Merton**. He could not get her a British visa as his housekeeper and she, along with her sister, the great refugee child rescuer Martha Wertheimer, died, probably in Sobibor concentration camp in June 1942.

It should also be noted that most of the *c.*585 *non*-Jewish wartime refugees on the Black List were Czech, Austrian, Polish, Belgian, Dutch, Danish and Norwegian politicians, spies, diplomats, trade union leaders or military men. They were part of their respective occupied countries' governments in exile, now based temporarily in London. They had no intention of applying for British citizenship but lived to return to their homelands and so they are not relevant to this book about native and adoptive 'Britons'.

The compilation of British names, organisations and associations had at first been collated by an SS Major Walter zu Christian, a functionary in the Gestapo's foreign intelligence, Amt RSHA VI in Berlin, who claimed to have had his early education in Britain and to have visited the country several times since in order to gather information. Zu Christian had then been superseded in late 1939 by his superior, the SS colonel Walter Schellenberg, as overall supervisor in readiness for the planned imminent invasion of Britain, 'Operation Sea Lion'. Walter Schellenberg was a law student from a modest family background who had wasted no time in joining the SS on 1 April 1933, soon after Hitler's takeover. Personable and plausible, clever and 'cultured', Schellenberg considered himself worthy of attaining a high position in Nazi Germany, and his own account of his choice of the SS as his favoured career option reveals his deeply unserious nature: 'The SS was already considered an "elite" organisation. The black uniform of the Führer's special guard was dashing and elegant ... In the SS one found the "better type of people" and membership of it brought considerable prestige and social advantages' (*Memoirs*, 1956). While many of his fellows in the SS spent the best part of a decade arresting, torturing and killing, on an industrial scale, their fellow Europeans, including women, children and the elderly, Walter Schellenberg's only serious concern was the career progress of Walter Schellenberg. After the war, in the dock at Nuremberg as a war criminal, he would claim to have been kept in the dark about Nazi mass murder. In fact, however, Schellenberg had actually accompanied his mentor figure Himmler in Nazi-occupied Poland in September 1939. He was also a favoured junior officer under Heydrich – and a colleague of Eichmann. Despite those unsavoury connections, he, just like Eichmann, had persisted in seeing himself as merely a dedicated, patriotic administrator whose military duty had demanded uncritical obedience. He was apparently too absorbed in overseeing the efficient completion of the Gestapo's enormous bureaucratic listing task to note with any disquiet that the goal of those lists was incarceration or execution, without trial. Like his Gestapo informants '[The] individual agents are often not aware of any moral guilt, but are rather convinced that they are doing the right thing.'[9]

Schellenberg, a careerist Nazi, was not himself a fanatical anti-Semite, unlike Himmler and Heydrich. As soon as he realised that

Germany was losing the war, already in late 1942, he tried to ensure his own safety by making contacts for a possible eventual safe haven in Switzerland or Sweden, and a few weeks before the end of the war he aimed to improve his profile by negotiating the survival of some Jews, through the good offices of the Swede, Count Bernadotte. It appears to have come as a genuine surprise to Schellenberg that he himself should have to face the charge of having been a war criminal. As long as Hitler appeared to be victorious, Schellenberg had been happy to claim that he was at the centre, and in the know about everything. After 1945 he would claim to have known nothing. But the very fact that he finally helped to rescue some Jews is proof that he knew perfectly well that Jews under the swastika desperately needed rescuing. And he was finally indicted and condemned at Nuremberg to six years' imprisonment for having belonged to the security service (i.e. Gestapo) of the SS –'an organisation declared to be criminal by the International Military Tribunal'.[10]

Not surprisingly, the informants have remained in the shadows.[11] An example of a Gestapo agent and assassin who 'passed' as a refugee in London, but reported back to Berlin on genuine left-wing refugees, is cited by **Fenner Brockway** àpropos of the mysterious fate of Berthold Jacob in Switzerland and of the Social Democrat Marie Wurm and her socialist friend Dora Fabian in London in 1938.[12] And there were more than a few pro-Nazi Germans then resident in England, belonging to the *Ausland* Association who filed reports home. Moreover, as Robert Hutton wrote in *Agent Jacob: The True Story of MI5's Secret Nazi Hunter*, there were also *British* Nazis who were would-be traitors in the Second World War,[13] as well as Britons who simply admired Hitler. Already in 1935 a pro-Nazi Anglo-German Fellowship was founded. It was estimated to have 600–800 members by 1938, including Conservative MPs and leading businessmen eager for commercial contracts with the Reich, as well as British fascists and pro-Hitler German nationals in Britain. They too could have provided much useful, unofficial information. In addition, a few German post-graduates at Oxbridge, the London School of Economics and Manchester universities, sympathetic to Nazism and strongly anti-communist, may also have informed the Gestapo in Berlin about the names, addresses and writings of prominent anti-Nazi intellectuals, including Jewish refugees, then teaching at universities in Britain.

As will be seen in the chapter on 'The Secret Service', the counter-intelligence section of the Gestapo under Schellenberg had mounted a highly successful 'sting' in Venlo, Holland, in October 1939, resulting in the exposure of almost the whole of Britain's network of spies, some of whom were then promptly added to the Black Book. Another probable source was the double agent Colonel C. H. ('Dick') Ellis who later confessed that he had been selling information to the Germans ever since 1923.[14] As for the **Communist Party of Great Britain**, it had been infiltrated at the outset by British right-wingers reporting to MI5 from 1920 on (see **John Baker White**, in 'The Secret Service', p. 168 below). Some of those informants could have also become a source of information about British Communists and trade union activists in the later 1930s for the Gestapo. Prior to September 1939, however, the Gestapo did not have the 'octopus tentacles' in Britain that it did in Germany, or as Bocchini's secret political police OVRA did in Italy, where they saw to it that 'there were spies and informers in restaurants, hotels and cafés; in brothels, factories and military barracks; in schools and universities, where teachers denounced their colleagues and students their teachers, and, sometimes, their parents and their parents' friends.'[15]

As Howard Caygill pointed out, von Clausewitz's *On War* had stressed already in 1832 that the object of the application of force was 'to render the [enemy] incapable of further resistance [*zu jedem ferneren Widerstand unfaehig zu machen*]'.[16]

> The concept of resistance is … constituted by its [values] … and antipathy [to] other concepts … [It] is shaped by that which it opposes. [Nazism has since revealed] the possibility of the *extinction* of the capacity to resist … the enemy, precisely defined by their capacity to resist … is transformed into prey.[17]

There then begins a manhunt.[18]

Thus, in keeping with its development of the Clausewitzian concept of war, aimed at total, permanent domination, the Nazi war machine, above all its Gestapo, had always to anticipate resistance by any persons who could be suspected of holding an anti-Nazi *Weltanschauung*. They would all have to be hunted down. The man selected by Heydrich to do the hunting and implement the British operation based on this Black Book was SS Colonel Professor Dr Franz Six, a professional Nazi ideologue and another future war criminal. Coming from a poor family, Six had succeeded brilliantly in the German academic system, studying sociology and politics and becoming a doctor of philosophy in 1934 and professor of politics at Koenigsberg University in 1936. He had been an early convert to Nazism, having already, unlike Schellenberg, joined the Nazi Party in 1930, before it had actually won power, and he chose to join the SS in 1935. A fanatical anti-Semite and anti-Freemason, Six was put in charge of disseminating Nazi ideology in Germany before Heydrich ordered him to implement the elimination of anti-Nazism in Britain. Six's SS and Gestapo orders for the occupation of Britain were, in a letter from Heydrich, 17 September 1940: '[Seize] and combat effectively the numerous important organisations and societies in England which are hostile to Germany.'

Instead of managing to 'cleanse' Britain of anti-Nazism in 1940, however, Six would order notorious selective massacres and political executions in the occupied territory of the Soviet Union. *Einsatzgruppe B*, after 'purging' Belorussia of communist functionaries and Jews, was also allocated the *Vorkommando* Moskau under the Head of Office V11 – Ideological Enemy Research – of Professor Dr Franz Six. According to its own records, *Einsatzgruppe* B murdered over 140,000 people by 31 March 1941, the overwhelming majority of them Jews. 'The Vorkommando Moscow was forced to execute another 46 persons, amongst them 38 intellectual Jews who had tried to create unrest and discontent in the newly established Ghetto of Smolensk.'[19] Six was, according to his interrogator Otto John, 'one of the worst of the lot'.[20] He was sentenced at Nuremberg to twenty years' imprisonment but was released in 1952 and was employed by Porsche, while secretly working for West German and US anti-Soviet intelligence thereafter. Both Walter Schellenberg and Franz Six 'lacked the kind of moral and political compass that would have helped them recognize the nature of the Nazi regime and prevented them from working for it.'[21]

The secret Gestapo orders for an occupied Britain would hardly have been life as normal, given that the *Wehrmacht* was simultaneously issuing its own orders for the Occupation of England signed by its Chief of General Staff, Franz Halder. The German army commanders were to have 'supreme judiciary power over the civilian population' and their 'Economic Defence' officers were to 'seize, secure and remove raw materials, semi-finished products and machinery of military importance'.[22]

As von Brauchitsch, designated future Commander-in-Chief of the Army of Occupation in Britain, spelled out in his 'Most Secret Direction for Military Government in England':

> The main task of military government is to make full use of the country's resources for the needs of fighting troops and requirements of the German war economy ...
>
> The able-bodied male population between the ages of 17 and 45, will ... be interned and dispatched to the Continent with a minimum of delay [i.e. for slave labour] ...
>
> The Chief Supply Officer for England would 'be responsible for seizing such stocks of food, petrol, motor transport, horse-drawn vehicles, etc ... as have not already been taken over by the armies' ...
>
> [The following articles were to be requisitioned]: Agricultural products, food and fodder of all kinds, ores, crude metals, semi-finished metal products of all kinds including precious metals, asbestos and mica, cut or uncut precious or semi-precious stones, mineral oils and fuels of all kinds, industrial oils and fats, waxes, resins, glues, rubber in all forms, all raw materials for textiles, leather, furs and hides, round timber, sawn timber, timber sleepers and timber masts.[23]

General von Brauchitsch then warned in his *Proclamation to the People of England*:

> … All thoughtless actions, sabotage of any kind, and any passive or active opposition to the German armed forces will incur the most severe retaliatory measures.
>
> I warn all civilians that if they undertake active operations against the German forces, they will be condemned to death inexorably …

The country would be under German *military* law, which forbade, among other things:

> Any communication with prisoners of war
> Any insult to the German armed forces or their commanders
> Assembling in the street, circulating of pamphlets or holding of public meetings without previous authorisation from a German commander …
> Incitement to stop work … strikes or lockouts …

It would also be forbidden to listen to 'non-German wireless transmissions publicly or in the company of others' and all wireless transmitting apparatus would have to be surrendered. Anyone who ignored this order would 'be condemned to death [or] in less serious cases to penal servitude or imprisonment'.[24]

All British citizens attempting armed resistance or sabotage, whether men or women, would, von Brauchitsch warned, be executed. In the event, after September 1940, von Brauchitsch was despatched to invade the Soviet Union instead. In his case the first Russian winter defeated him.

David Lampe, in his important pioneering study in 1968, *The Last Ditch: Britain's Secret Resistance and the Nazi Invasion Plans*, believed that 'if Hitler's Army had occupied Britain, Western civilization as we knew it in 1940 … would have been at the last ditch'.[25]

2

What was Wrong with Britain in Nazi Eyes? – The *Informationsheft GB*

The copy of the *Informationsheft GB*[1] now held in the British Library has a handwritten inscription:

> This book was found by me in the ruins of the Gestapo HQ,
> Prinz Albrechtstr., Berlin, September 1945.
> [signed] H. R. Trevor-Roper [British Intelligence Officer in 1945]

The Nazis saw themselves as embattled patriots of a hard-done-by, encircled Fatherland. They had no alternative but to be ruthless, for it was Britain who was the aggressor. German public opinion blamed Britain first for having declared war on Germany in September 1939, and then for having rejected the Führer's generous peace offer in his Reichstag speech of July 1940. On 29 March 1941 a German in Stuttgart would be heard saying, àpropos of the London Blitz:

> We are Germans, we are to educate the human race, to chastise them, to impose a new order, they have to submit to us just as children and servants have to subordinate themselves to our will. What we undertake succeeds! We are chosen by God to be a rod of iron, we must carry out our mission, and the easier England makes it for us, the better it will be for that country. But if they resist, we must show them no mercy![2]

Similarly General Doenitz, Commander-in-Chief of U-boats, in reissuing Standard Order 154 in September 1942 concerning the crews and civilian passengers who were being torpedoed in the Atlantic, gave the order: 'Rescue no one ... We must be hard in this war. *The enemy started this war in order to destroy us, therefore nothing else matters*' (my emphasis).

The *Informationsheft GB* (or *Handbook GB*) regards Britain as a guilty, hostile, morally inferior nation that needs to be totally refashioned for its own good. In September 1940, SS Colonel Professor Dr Franz Six, who had been appointed the future head of the Gestapo in Britain to eliminate anti-Nazi elements, had received his order from Goering, countersigned by Heydrich. The full text ran:

> Your task is to combat, with the requisite means, all anti-German ['*deutschfeindlich*'] organisations, institutions, opposition, and opposition groups which can be seized in England, to prevent the removal of all available material, and to centralize and safeguard it for future exploitation ... and I authorize you to set up small action groups *Einsatzgruppen* [execution squads] in other parts of Britain as the situation dictates and the necessity arises.[3]

In fact the Gestapo had already brought out their hastily printed *Informationsheft GB* for their Britain-destined military staff by July 1940. It is therefore more up to date than the Black Book's list of names and addresses, both of individuals and of organisations, which it complements and to which it refers. That *Sonderfahndungsliste GB* had been completed in March 1939, but was not actually printed until July 1940, when its front page refers to the later *Informationsheft*. This updated overview of Britain in the *Informationsheft* was intended to inform Gestapo and SS officers about the British Army, the British police and the British Secret Service. But it was also concerned to describe British political and cultural institutions and attitudes, highlighting those organisations and people most prominent in the Establishment whom the German forces would immediately have to investigate and very possibly arrest – in addition to those already listed in the earlier Black Book. Thus the *Informationsheft* also anticipates a British resistance that would have to be neutralised from the start. It is 'a substantial compendium covering virtually every aspect of British life … indispensable to those setting up a German-dominated administration and an occupation regime'.[4]

Although the name of SS General Walter Schellenberg is given as its author, in fact in the early summer of 1940 Schellenberg was for much of the time either in hospital or else in Portugal trying – and failing – to kidnap Edward, Duke of Windsor and his wife before they left for the Bahamas. Moreover '[It] is obvious from the style and the contents that many hands had been at work'[5] on the Handbook, which was clearly based on publicly available reference books and gazetteers as well as on the Gestapo's own massive project of counter-espionage. In many cases an academic had been hired for the historical background, but the intermittent 'warped, derisive and malignant'[6] commentary on the facts may well have been added at the last minute by Schellenberg himself.

What was it about Britain and the British in general that the Nazis so detested? The British Empire naturally aroused deep, jealous resentment, but so did what was seen as British humbug. The British proclaimed to the world that they were a democratic, liberal, civilised, humane society – morally superior to Germany after 1933. But the anonymous compilers of the *Informationsheft GB* saw the Britain of 1940 rather differently, pointing out that, as in the First World War, the British had now actually suspended their democratic constitution by cancelling the general election due in 1940 and by forming an unelected coalition government. The author of this section of the *Informationsheft GB* then exposes Britain's inbuilt conservatism, given its largely hereditary House of Lords with its Conservative Party connections and close involvement in capitalism. In the House of Commons, the compiler alleges, the Conservatives were split between the moderates and the 'die-hard' warmongers around **Churchill**. As for the leaders of the Labour Party, they were in no way revolutionary, being themselves often products of the feudal public schools and soon absorbed into collusion with the social and even the political outlook of the Conservatives. Moreover all political freedom in England had actually been suspended for the duration of the war through the imposition of Emergency Powers (*Standrecht*): 'An Enabling Act at the beginning of the war has allowed the government to impose military law on the entire country, which, in its dictatorial application, defies all acknowledged democratic principles.' After listing all the members of Churchill's new War Cabinet (as of 13 May 1940) the *Informationsheft*, or Handbook, goes on to survey the British Civil Service establishment. Special attention was to be paid by the Gestapo not only to the **Passport Office** within the **Home Office** and to the Office for Passport Control, but also to the **Department of Overseas Trade** – ***Arthur Steel-Maitland*** (all names of individuals and organisations in the *Informationsheft* are in ***bold italic.***)[7] was alleged to be 'Head of Trade espionage', the **Commission of Inland Revenue** for individual and corporate tax records, the **Public Record Office** for births, deaths and marriages, and **His Majesty's Stationery Office** for printing public documents. The **Ministry of Information** is specially linked, without evidence, to **Bristol** and **Oxford universities** and to University College London.

The universities identified in the *Informationsheft* as being especially hostile to Germany are London, Bristol and Oxford, which began in spring 1939 to publish a new series of 'Oxford Pamphlets' beginning with *Mein Kampf* by ***R. C. K. Ensor.***[8] In addition, those academics with expertise in East European and Slavonic Studies, some of them in London, Cambridge, Liverpool and Nottingham and not already on the *Sonderfahndungsliste*, are now named for the first time – ***Dr B. Manilowski, Professor W. J. Reddaway, Dr Alexander Boswell, Dr Kenneth Edwards*** and ***Dr Eric Patterson.*** Other suspect academic institutions highlighted as needing to be searched include the Scottish, strongly Christian ***Newbattle Abbey College,*** the internationalist and pacifist Quaker college ***Woodbrooke***, at Selly Oak, Birmingham, which took in refugee students, the University of London's **School of East European and Slavonic Studies** and the ***Cambridge Slavonic Society.*** In contrast, the Ukrainian experts and émigrés in Britain, except for the suspected US spy **Jakob Makhonin**, were *anti*-Bolshevik and could make promising collaborators with the German occupation, being '*durchaus deutschfreundlich*'.

Next comes **Chatham House – the Royal Institute of Foreign Affairs**, in close contact with the Foreign Office and allegedly wielding huge influence on world public opinion to the disadvantage of Germany, especially in central and eastern Europe, as well as in the British colonies. It held extremely important political materials which must be seized. (***Dr Arnold Toynbee***, ***Sir John Hope Simpson***, ***Lionel Curtis*** and ***Margaret Cleeve*** are singled out for special interrogation and private house searches.) The liberal **Cobden Club** with its motto 'Free Trade, Peace, Goodwill among Nations' is Blacklisted as '*deutschfeindlich*' as is the **Institut Français** for being a centre promoting French cultural propaganda throughout Britain and for having close connections with British universities. The **Academic Assistance Council** (see p. 215 below), which 'finances propaganda for émigré German scholars', was also flagged as needing to be searched and for its records to be seized.

The *Informationsheft* goes on to point out how the British public schools, attended by fewer than 1 per cent of school-age children have, for centuries, produced Britain's rulers and formed their political attitudes, enabling them to fill roughly 80 per cent of all important social and political positions. Even the leadership of the Labour Party, which traditionally appointed someone who had risen through the ranks of trade unionism, was now, the Gestapo alleges, in the hands of former public school boys – **Attlee, Greenwood, Dalton** and **Stafford Cripps.** On the Conservative side, **Chamberlain, Lord Hankey, Lord Halifax, Anthony Eden, Oliver Stanley, Duff Cooper, Lord Linlithgow** and **Sir Robert Vansittart** were products of Rugby or Eton and **Sir Samuel Hoare** and **Winston Churchill** had gone to Harrow. These boarding schools, notes the *Informationsheft* with a hint of envy as well as condescension,

> have done England the great service of inculcating in each younger generation the traditions of the English ruling class. Here the future English gentleman who has no interest in

> philosophical problems or much knowledge of foreign cultures, who sees Germany as the living embodiment of evil but regards English imperial power as untouchable, is reared. The whole system is designed to bring up men of the most determined will and an energy *uninhibited by morality* [my emphasis], for whom spiritual/intellectual problems are a waste of time but who have a knowledge of people and understand how to be ruthlessly dominant.

Immediately following that assessment of the role of British public schools comes the Gestapo view of the **Boy Scouts movement**, founded by **Baden-Powell** in 1907 and which by 1940 had branches over much of the world. At its headquarters in London, its international office, according to the *Informationsheft,* had been until recently headed by a 'half-Jew', Mr Martin, who was simultaneously head of the Passport Office. Each Scouting branch was accused of being almost exclusively concerned with pre-military youth training while also being a powerful medium of English cultural propaganda abroad and an excellent domestic intelligence source for the British Secret Service. **Lord Baden-Powell,** it points out, had himself been a spy in the First World War against Germany. Therefore the International Office of the Scouts, based in London, is believed to be now active in the English Secret Service through its numerous foreign contacts. Ominously,

> [the] liquidation of the Austrian Boy Scout movement [has] provided evidence of the connection with the Secret Service … The Boy Scout Movement shares many values of '*buendisch*' German youth groups [i.e. banned non-Hitler Youth groups like the *Wandervoegel*], which had included members of minorities [i.e. Jews] in their membership and had had close contact with émigré youth leaders.[9]

Part Two of the *Sonderfahndungsliste,* on '*Vereinigungen*' or 'Associations' had already Blacklisted the **National Adult Schools Union** and the

WEA – Workers' Educational Association – as well as the 'Marxist educational propaganda' of the **Fabian Society**, and the **League of Nations Union.** The **National Adult Schools Union,** focusing on adult literacy and strongest in the North of England, had long been associated with one of the Gestapo's bêtes noires, the **Quakers**. The secular and often left-wing **WEA** had, by the 1930s, become a radical, questioning, mind-expanding British institution. By 1938–9 its national network comprised 2,172 branches, providing one-year and shorter courses in the social sciences, philosophy, psychology and the arts, with 39,844 students in all. Closing the **WEA** down under German occupation would have had an incalculably deadening effect.

When the *Informationsheft* turns its attention to England's most important museums and art galleries, including the priceless manuscripts in the **British Museum**, it claims that their outstanding collections were of great interest to the Reich, given that all their documents and art objects relating to German history were really treasure that had been looted from the rest of the world ('*zusammenrauben*'). The **New Burlington Gallery** is castigated for its 'anti-German exhibition of [banned] "degenerate art"' in 1938, and the **National Gallery** is criticised for including among its 4,000 portraits of well-known English personalities, '*eine Reihe von Juden*'. The director of the National Museum of Scotland at the time, however, 'Direktor Edwards', is praised for having been consistently sympathetic to Germany.

As well as alerting attention to all the main museums and galleries not only in London but also in the Oxford and Cambridge colleges, the *Informationsheft* lists the following libraries and learned societies that held the most important documents relating to Europe and above all to *German* cultural history and which, allegedly, 'have supported the fight against Germany': ***the Royal Society of Arts, the International Society for Contemporary Music, the British Music Society, the Museums Association, University College Arts Libraries, the Royal Academy of Music Library***, and ***the Library of the Royal Academy of Arts.***

The *Informationsheft GB* has two sections on the press, apparently written by different hands. The first gives much background information on the ownership and political slant of the *'Pressewesen'*. All the British press magnates are listed with the various newspaper titles they owned, as is Oswald Mosley's *The Black Shirt, Action* and the *British Union [of Fascists] Quarterly.* This section in the *Informationsheft* stresses that Lord Rothermere, owner of the *Daily Mail,* was the exception among the British press barons in having a 'friendly to Germany' stance. He is the brother of the late Lord Northcliffe, founder of the *Daily Mirror*, the *Evening News* and the *Sunday Dispatch.* Despite Britain's claim to have a free press, the mass circulation tabloids are, it is pointed out, run by Conservatives out for big commercial profit through sales and advertising. Only the ***Observer***, the ***Manchester Guardian*** and ***The Times*** are said to be 'independent'. (It should be noted that the *Informationsheft* does not duplicate the list of thirty-five suspect British newspapers, already published in the second part of the *Sonderfahndungsliste* including ***Picture Post***. Only the *Daily Mail* and *The Times* are not on that list of to-be-banned national newspapers because at the time of compilation before March 1939, those newspapers were still in favour of appeasement.) The second section on the British press, by a different hand, is inserted into the *Informationsheft*'s overview of the activities of British-born Jews (see p. 41).

The following section, '*Radio*', on the structure and organisation of the elements of English broadcasting that 'has supported anti-German agitation and propaganda' seems surprisingly brief and superficial – until one remembers that listening to non-German broadcasts would be forbidden and that all wireless transmitters were to be handed in under the occupation.

Whereas the *Sonderfahndungsliste* had named very few religious leaders, most of them Bonhoeffer's dissident German Protestant colleagues now in exile in Britain (see p. 35 below), the later *Informationsheft* decided that it was in fact vitally important to scrutinise the various churches in Britain because of their disquieting 'hostility to Germany' in the name of Christianity. Thus the *Informationsheft* highlights the British **Ministry of Information's** special 'Religious Division' and alleges that it 'attempts … to ignite anti-German sentiment' throughout neutral nations, identifying the British government's war policy as a *Christian* matter and hence a religious task. 'Taking possession of this department's material would be absolutely necessary.'

The *Informationsheft* describes the Church of England, its membership in England calculated as 2.3 million, as the long-established church of the British state, its bishops being appointed by the Crown via the prime minister. The Gestapo alleges that it constitutes a powerful factor in the exercise of British imperialism and takes a leading role in global Protestantism. They were especially interested in the phenomenon of Buchman's evangelical Moral Re-Armament Movement as being strongly represented among English diplomats and 'readily accepting anti-German propaganda'.

What the Gestapo most strongly disliked, however, was the Church of England's international and *internationalist* contacts. Among other suspicious Anglican organisations, the *Informationsheft* instances the ***Anglican and Eastern (Orthodox) Churches Association***, the pacifist ***Church Esperantists League***, the ***Church of England Council of Empire Settlement***, the ***Church of England Council on Foreign Relations***, the ***Church Socialist League*** and the ***Modern Churchmen's Union for the Advancement of Liberal Religious Thought***. Above all the *Informationsheft* anathematises the recent ***World Conference of Churches*** in Oxford where the ***Archbishop's Commission on Relations of Church and State*** 'strongly criticised national socialism and indicated that the totalitarian state and Christianity are incompatible. Germany should therefore be seen as enemy of all Christian states.'[10]

The ***Student Christian Movement*** is accused of having a 'democratic pacifist character ... it pretends to work for the spread of Christianity among students. But from the past few world conferences it has become clear that the World Union under English leadership has strong political tendencies and at different times members have sharply criticised Germany.'

The other Protestant sects and organisations mentioned include the ecumenical ***Methodists,*** likened to the **Freemasons** for their internationalism, the ***YMCA***, 'entirely in the hands of the **Freemasons**' and the ***Salvation Army*** with its headquarters in London and covering 'the whole globe'.

The *Informationsheft* has relatively little to say about Catholics, clearly not expecting much resistance from that quarter. Estimated at about 3 million adherents in Britain, including Scotland and Northern Ireland, and of predominantly Irish background, the ***Roman Catholics*** are seen as a distinct cultural and educational sector, with their own press outlets and an allegedly disproportionate representation in the Diplomatic Service, the Foreign Office and the Privy Council. The Gestapo was particularly opposed, however, to the Catholic Archbishop of Westminster, ***Cardinal Hinsley***.

Immediately following that section on British Churches comes what some consider to have been an alternative religion in the 1930s – communism. Between 1928 and 1932, Nazi activists in Germany had participated in bloody street fighting against German communists, followed in 1933 by the mass arrest of German left-wingers, their imprisonment in concentration camps and the torture and/or death of their leaders, such as Ernst Thaelmann and Johanna Melzer.[11] Why should the Nazis see any reason to be more tolerant of communists in the German-occupied territories outside Germany now?

Therefore the *Informationsheft* pays an inordinate amount of attention to British Communists and Marxists, including trade unionists, from whom they did expect resistance. While admitting that actual **Communist Party** membership numbered under 18,000, they saw 'entryists', subversives and undercover organisations at work everywhere in Britain. The Nazis had always labelled all their opponents 'Bolsheviks', in the pay of the Kremlin. Hence not just the **Society for Cultural Relations with Russia**, the **Fabian Society,** the **ILP** and the **National Council for Civil Liberties** are labelled 'Marxist', but even the most unlikely people, from **War Resisters International,** the **Quaker Friends of Europe**, **Socialist Freethinkers**, the British sections of **Artists' International Associations** and **Writers' Associations (PEN)** to the **Labour Party** itself – as is every single British trade union, large or small. Over ten pages are devoted to the Communist Party and the trade unions in the *Informationsheft*, while eight pages in the *Sonderfahndungsliste Part Two* were already allocated to every branch of the single largest British union, the **Transport and General Workers' Union** alone, with each branch called a 'Marxist workers organisation'. Their leader, the fiercely anti-communist **Ernest Bevin,** would have been surprised.

The other English trade unions said to be 'Marxist', listed with their addresses, in the *Informationsheft* are **Bakers, Confectioners and Allied Workers, the Distributive and Allied Workers, the Building Trades, the Woodworkers, the Pottery Workers, the Journeymen Felt Hatters, the Leather Workers, the Boot and Shoe Operatives, the Diamond Trade Workers, the Civil Servants, Tailors and Garment Workers, Lithographic Printers and Artists, Designers, Engravers, the Engineers, Firemen and Electrical workers, the Miners, the House Painters and Decorators, Quarry Workers, Bookbinders, General and Municipal workers, Cigar makers, Scottish Farm servants, Textile Workers, the National Union of Railwaymen, Glass Workers, Shop Assistants,** and **Mental Hospital and Institutional Workers.** All these had already been Blacklisted, with their addresses, in the *Sonderfahndungsliste,* but the *Informationsheft* now includes a few more for good measure – ***the Packing Case Makers, the Metal, Chemical and Engineering Workers, the Shipbuilding Draughtsmen, the Gold and Jewellery Workers, the Coal Trimmers*** and ***the Ship Decorators***, together with their addresses. All culminating in the blacklisting of the **TUC** itself – together with the **International Federation of Trade Unions** – at Transport House. The most prominent leaders of the 'communist cover' organisation, the **Anti-Fascist League,** are said to be 'mainly Jews'. According to the *Informationsheft*, British **Communist Party** members had been (unofficially) instructed in the Moscow party line via the international Communist Central HQ in Paris until the very recent collapse ('*Zusammenbruch*') of France in June 1940.

One of the fiercest of irrational Nazi obsessions was their conviction, shared by the papacy since 1870, that Freemasonry was evil. After 1917 the ultra right in Europe believed that Bolsheviks and Jews were in a joint world conspiracy *with* **Freemasons**. One begetter of this conspiracy theory, which in his mind also encompassed machinations by the Jesuits, was General Erich Ludendorff, former head of the German general staff in the First World War and hence an unimpeachable national hero. Ludendorff, a Social Darwinist, believed war to be the natural state of mankind, and military dictatorship, therefore, the necessary form of government. He had maintained, like Hindenburg and other military leaders, the myth that the German army had been 'stabbed in the back', treasonably betrayed in 1918 by a secret conspiracy of pacifist Jews, Bolshevik revolutionaries, Social Democrats, Catholic clergy – and **Freemasons**.[12] In 1929 Ludendorff published his influential best seller, *Destruction of Freemasonry through Revelation of their Secrets*. He had been a leading Nazi in the 1920s but he and Hitler had later fallen out over the general's increasingly wild mystical obsessions, once he had become a devotee of Wotan (the supreme Teutonic god of pre-Christian Germany corresponding to the Norse god Odin).

After 1933 the Nazis had clamped down on secretive German Freemasonry, closing the Lodges and forbidding Masons from joining the Nazi Party or the *Wehrmacht* – until manpower shortages led to a partial amnesty. In 1935 Heydrich 'counted the Masons, along with the Jews … as the most implacable enemies of the German race, [stressing the need] to root out from every German a Jewish, liberal and Masonic infectious residue that remains in the unconscious of many'. He created a special section of the SS's SD 11/111 to deal specifically with Freemasonry, which later became RSHA Section V11 B1 when the SD and the Gestapo were amalgamated in 1939.[13]

The ideology of Freemasonry remained highly suspect, and therefore the *Informationsheft* has a lengthy section on Freemasonry in Great Britain, for '*England ist das Land der Freimaurerei*'. Not only was England indicted as the country of origin of Freemasonry, it also, according to the Gestapo, exploited the British connection with Freemasonry as a tool for its international power politics, and its attempted economic and cultural world dominance. Even worse, it was the British-backed spread of Freemasonry throughout Europe that was seen by the Gestapo to have caused the 'Enlightened' emancipation of the Jews. With its adherence to a rational world religion in which all men, without regard to difference of race or nationality, were equal brothers, Freemasonry had given Jews unconditional entry into the English Lodges and supported the social emancipation and political citizenship of English Jews – who had thereby gained entry to the British 'Establishment' ('*den tragendenden Schichten der englischen Gesellschaft*'). The commentator in the *Informationsheft* suggests that the British had used the non-racist, non-nationalist principles of Freemasonry in order to further their own imperialist project. Thus under the cloak of 'humanity', the colonised natives of the British Empire had been bound ever closer via Freemasonry to the 'Motherland' and the native élites had been depoliticised from their own nationalist struggles. Although Freemasonry in the British Empire had begun with a 'Whites Only' policy in its Lodges, during the later nineteenth century their doors had been opened, according to the Gestapo, not only to leading Indians but also to outstanding, British-educated black men ('*Schwarzen*') some in black and some in mixed Lodges in the British colonial possessions in Africa. The Bible is laid open on the **Freemasons**' altar, symbolising both the ancient Jews' claim to be the Chosen People and the British Puritan belief that *they* were the Chosen Nation of the world.

The Handbook goes on to claim that the **Freemasons** had penetrated all the highest and middle ranks of British society from the Royal family and commanding officers in the army and navy down, through the learned professions, businessmen, politicians and journalists, and finally to the rank and file of the male middle class – constituting a powerful weapon in the alternative, secret, plutocratic governance of Britain with its opposition to German National Socialism. Although purporting to be 'unpolitical' and simply devoted to philanthropic welfare projects, it is in fact, according to the Handbook, the ***British Freemasons*** who are manipulating British politics behind the scenes and who are at the core ('*Kernzelle*') of British imperialism throughout the world. The British Freemasons' enlightened invocation of 'Humanity' has become a propaganda tool used against any country standing in the way of British global domination. The First World War was, according to the British press and the British

Freemasons, a struggle for liberation between democracies and autocracies; now they substitute 'Authoritarian' for 'Autocratic'.

The German occupation forces in Britain are then directed by the *Informationsheft* to check the *Sonderfahndungsliste* for the detailed listing of all the Grand and Provincial Lodges in Britain and Ireland, including their schools and publishing outlets as well as Lodges connected with the Royal Family and the aristocracy and the '*Judenlogen*' – together with all their secretaries' addresses. Both the **Oddfellows** and **Rotary International** are included in this section of '*Logen*'.

As early as the 1920s in fascist Italy, the **Freemasons**, who had initially supported Mussolini, withdrew their approval and Mussolini promptly called on fascists throughout Tuscany to 'strike at the **Freemasons** in their persons, their property and their interests'. On 3 October 1926, *Battaglie Fasciste* had declared: 'Freemasonry must be destroyed and to this end all means are good: from the cudgel to the revolver, from the smashing of windows to the cleansing fire.'[14] In 1937, during the Spanish Civil War, Franco was interviewed in the Catholic weekly review, *The Tablet*, where he declared: 'In my opinion Freemasonry, with all its international influence, is the organisation principally responsible for the political ruin of Spain.' Large numbers of Spanish Masons were arrested and executed. Throughout occupied Europe the Nazis would mount anti-Masonic exhibitions, and within German army propaganda the Jews and the **Freemasons** were charged with having provoked the Second World War.[15] It is estimated that almost a thousand French Masons who had participated in the Resistance died in concentration camps.[16]

In the occupied Channel Islands the Lodges were looted and locked up but no action was taken against individual Masons, despite an order from Hitler in 1943 that all Jews and high-ranking **Freemasons** be deported to Germany, suggesting that the Bailiff of Jersey himself might have had Masonic connections. Given the huge importance and influence that the Gestapo believed **Freemasons** to wield in Britain, and via Britain throughout the world, there can be little doubt that, come the invasion, all the most active Lodge office-holders would have been arrested and deported.

The number of Jews in Britain is said in the *Informationsheft* to be 300,000 – an underestimate. Where the later *Informationsheft* differs most from the earlier *Sonderfahndungsliste* is in its 'outing' of prominent *British-born* Jews with powerful roles in politics, finance, banking, business and the media, as well as in the World Zionist movement. However, its first mention of Jews in Britain was in an earlier section titled '*Émigré* Organisations' (my emphasis) (See Appendix 1). The Gestapo never called Jewish refugees 'refugees', preferring the term 'emigrants' as though they had left their native Germany or Austria of their own unpatriotic volition. The official total of the German Jewish 'emigrants' in Britain in 1940, the Gestapo estimates, stood at 62,244, with the Austrian Jewish 'emigrants' numbering 11,989. This whole 'emigration' is labelled '*deutschfeindlich*' but with no explanation given as to why the migrants had had to leave Germany and Austria – and later Czechoslovakia. Bizarrely, it makes the groundless accusation that the Quaker 'Friends of Europe' are engaged in *military* espionage. It also singles out the Committee for the Relief of Victims of German Fascism for having publicised the incarceration in concentration camps of Frau Seeger and Frau Seifert.[17] That was '*Greuelpropaganda*', mere 'atrocity peddling' – but true.

The *Informationsheft* later devotes nearly twelve pages to the long-established British-born Jews, settled century after century since c.1650, including yet another long consolidated list, complete with addresses and key personnel, under the heading 'Jewish Organisations' (See Appendix 2). It does not, however, duplicate the *Sonderfahndungsliste's* naming of hundreds of the individual *refugee* Jews then in Britain, mostly intellectuals and professional men and women. And the irony should be noted that still, in 1936, both the Anglo-Jewish **Board of Deputies of British Jews,** whose president was the lawyer **Neville Laski,** and the British **Jewish Chronicle** refused to collocate anti-Semitism with fascism. Instead they foregrounded the former and absolutely *opposed* the anti-fascist militancy of the radical left wing in Britain, which included more and more militant East End working-class Jews.[18]

Under the heading 'Politics', ***Sir Cecil Kisch, T. E. Gugenheim Gregory, Thomas Levy*** MP, ***Sir Isidore Salmon,*** and ***Sir Samuel Joseph***

(Lord Mayor of London) now make their first appearance as a supposedly sinister part of the British Establishment. Under the heading 'Finance' there are ***C. J. Hambro*** and ***Lord Goschen***, both alleged to be influential directors of the Bank of England; ***Sir Albert Stern*** is important at the Westminster Bank and at Stern Bros; **F. D.** and **Peter Montefiore-Samuel (Viscount Bearstead)** are named as directors of the Bank of Samuel and Co., as are ***E. L. Franklin, S. F. Franklin*** and ***C. M. Franklin*** at Samuel Montagu and Co., ***Saemy Japhet, Paul Lindenberg, Max Frontheim*** and ***Gottfried Loewenstein*** at Japhet and Co., and the ***d'Erlanger family*** at Erlangers Ltd. Finally, **Sir Osmond Elim d'Avigdor-Goldsmid** MP is named as chairman or director of at least seven different trading companies. Almost all of these are here 'outed' as Jews for the first time – only the **Rothschilds** and **Lord Swaythling** had already appeared in the earlier *Sonderfahndungsliste*. In many cases the relevant bank's capital is quoted as though it constituted the personal assets of the directors.

Under 'The Economy', **Peter Montefiore-Samuel, Lord Bearstead** and **Sir Robert Waley** (i.e. **Waley Cohen**) are mentioned as directors of Shell and ***B. Maisel*** and ***Johanna Maisel*** as directors of Petroleum Trust and Orient Oil. **Sir Lionel de Rothschild, Lord Bearstead** (i.e. Colonel Walter Horace Samuel) and ***Lord Roseberry*** are directors of Alliance Insurance, and **Sir George Schuster**, together with ***Sir Charles Seligman,*** is director of Commercial Union as well as being chairman of Allied Suppliers, Home and Colonial, Maypole Dairies and Lipton in the retail food industry. Lyons and Co. Ltd, with its chairman ***Sir Isidore Salmon,*** are named as the owners of huge food and catering interests including restaurants and big London hotels. The gold and diamond business is alleged to be almost exclusively Jewish, with ***Sir George Albo*** the chairman of the General Mining and Finance Corporation, ***Geoffrey Joel*** director of De Beers and ***Sir Ernest Oppenheimer*** chairman of twenty-four branches of the gold and diamond industry in South Africa. ***Sir Henry Strakosch***, from an Austrian banking background, naturalised British since 1907, made his fortune as managing director of some of the richest gold mines on the South African Rand as well as of Rhodesian copper mines. The clear implication of this whole section of the *Informationsheft* intended for German occupation forces was that, behind the scenes, Britain's economy was really being controlled by very rich, assimilated British Jews.[19]

After this comes the second section on the press, radio and film, placed in the section 'The Jews in Britain', which states:

> The anti German attitude of these instruments of propaganda is mainly due to the large number of Jews working for them ... [In all of the six corporations dominating the English press] Jews either hold leading posts or finance the enterprises ... Lord **Beaverbrook** ... is a close friend of the Jew **Melchett** and is completely pro-Jewish ... **Lord Roseberry**, a half-Jew, has a large interest in the Westminster Press ...

The Jewish press magnate **Lord William (Levy-) Lawson Burnham** (1864–1943), who still had an interest in the *Daily Telegraph*, formerly owned by his grandfather Joseph Moses Levy, had already been put on the Black List. In the other British media – radio and film – British Jews are also said to have a great influence, above all ***Ivor Montagu*** and ***S. Bernstein***, who are named as the men chiefly responsible for the production of recent '*deutschfeindlich*' films and acting as unofficial 'film censors'. This is ironic because until September 1939 the British Board of Film Censors had been instructed (by appeasers high up in the Home Office and the Foreign Office) to tell film-makers 'to avoid not only criticism of Germany, but also any plot-lines that could ... [involve Nazi] persecution and refugee movements'.[20] **Isidore Ostrer**'s brothers ***Mark*** and ***Maurice Ostrer*** are named here for the first time as the owners of many film businesses. And a great part of the British film industry, now welded into one, is claimed to be under the control and ownership of '*dieser Jude*', **Oscar Deutsch**. 'This Jew controls 500 cinemas [including the merged Gaumont-British and Odeon].' Once again, it is the Jews who are said to be pulling all the strings behind the scenes; in fact Deutsch's holdings were about to be bought by the English, and very committed Christian, J. Arthur Rank.

The last sections of the *Informationsheft* describe the structure of the British police force and of the British Secret Service with its network of 'Passport' offices in all its consulates. Given Schellenberg's personal involvement with the 'Venlo incident' in October 1939,[21] it is not surprising that the German occupation forces should have been initiated into a very full and accurate summary of sensitive British Secret Service information that was still being kept from the British public by MI6 – and would not be released until 1966.

The *Informationsheft* fails to give close attention to the Ministry of Information and pays no attention to the Mass Observation Project, founded in 1937, with its unprecedented first-hand information on British social attitudes and morale – about which the Gestapo may not even have known. As for the vital efforts to crack Germany's Enigma code at Bletchley Park, these had still been successfully kept a secret from the Gestapo. Nevertheless the overwhelming impression given by the *Informationsheft* is, in John Erickson's words, just 'how much and exactly what they did know'.[22] The last sentences of the Handbook are very significant. The British of all classes, unlike the Germans, are praised for being quite willing to spy for their country, thinking of spies not as criminal informers or paid traitors, but as soldiers in an army. The Handbook's final editor, Walter Schellenberg, plainly envies this separation of patriotism and morality and hopes that Nazi Germany will emulate it. He ends: 'The motto "My country, right or wrong" does not have to be a British monopoly and, having been adopted to suit our ideology, it can and must be transferred to Germans.' As indeed it was then being transferred, most murderously, in Poland.

It is not surprising that John Erickson concluded that the *Informationsheft* 'was a manual for total occupation, [and] for the ruthless elimination of any who stood in the way or who had shown any hint of a propensity to opposition, resistance to or revulsion at the sight and sounds of National Socialism, with a candidate list for the *Knickschuss* [bullet in the back of the neck].'[23]

PART TWO

GUNNING FOR THE KINDEST

3

Medical Men and Women

What wisdom can you find that is greater than kindness?

Rousseau, *Emile, Book ii*, 1762

The poet Keats defined the humane as those ' … to whom the miseries of the world / Are misery and will not let them rest' (*The Fall of Hyperion*, 1819). But such humanism in action made no sense at all to the Nazis, who believed that what had hitherto been judged good – compassion, succour, fellowship, kindness – was inapplicable to the new Germany. Their pity was only for their Fatherland now so unfairly attacked on all sides – and for themselves as its embattled defenders. Himmler said that: 'The SS man's basic attitude must be that of a fighter for fighting's sake; he must be unquestioningly obedient and … emotionally hard; he must have contempt for all "racial inferiors" and for those who do not belong to the order.'[1] It was not only the SS who were now commanded to be 'emotionally hard'. A German woman lecturer in December 1942 declared to young women trainee teachers 'Hardness [*Haerte*], pitilessness and mercilessness: these must be the outstanding qualities of German women, of German people in general … We must finally recognise our mission and become true members of the German master race!' (Quoted in Timms, Edward, *Anna Haag and her Secret Diary of the Second World War*, Peter Lang, Oxford, 2015, p. 171.)

Nazi school biology textbooks were illustrated by the cartoon of an upright German worker carrying two disabled people with the caption: 'How long must he carry this burden?' The secret Nazi 'euthanasia' regime, 'Aktion T4', authorised by Hitler on 1 September

1939, targeted the senile, the mentally handicapped and mentally ill, epileptics, the physically disabled, and children with Down's Syndrome. Between September 1939 and August 1941, 70,000 people were murdered in Germany and Austria for being 'useless eaters' – unfit to live. That policy could not in fact be kept secret because of the impact on the victims' families and the involvement of charities and nuns who tried to thwart it. Bishop Count von Galen preached against Nazi euthanasia on 3 August 1941.

Prominent British humanitarians who would be most likely to resist Nazi inhumanity were, however unbelievably, listed for immediate arrest in the *Sonderfahndungsliste GB* – usually on the grounds of their left-wing, internationalist politics. They included medical men and women, pacifists, refugee rescuers and social reformers.

Those doctors who reach out to people whom the majority of us are reluctant to touch – the homeless, the socially neglected, the incurable, the mentally ill, foreign immigrants who do not speak our language – have to be exceptionally humane. If they were also left wing, they came under special Gestapo suspicion. On the first page of the 'A's on the *Sonderfahndungsliste*, we find listed, without his titles or degrees, **Professor Dr Lord Christopher Addison**, FRCS, over 70 years old in 1940, and now considered the most eminent doctor ever to have entered parliament. He had been a leading anatomist, teaching at Charing Cross Hospital; '**Addison**'s plane', a method of identifying the shape and position of the pancreas, was named after him. **Addison** realised that the health of the poor was dependent on the action of governments rather than of doctors. As a reforming Liberal MP he had supported Lloyd George's 1911 National Insurance Bill and he had also worked for the improved welfare of children. In 1919 he was the first ever minister of health, responsible for the **Addison** Act for Housing and Town Planning, the great, controversial housing reform act, providing state-subsidised, low rent, high-quality 'council' housing, because he realised that medicine could do little to help people condemned to homelessness – or else to live in 'slums'. One hundred years later, his housing reform was commemorated as transformative and revolutionary in *The Big Issue* (no. 1369, July/August 2019).

It was also in 1919 that **Addison** commissioned the physician to the king, **Sir Bertrand Dawson, Baron Dawson of Penn**, FRCP (1864–1945), himself also eventually on the Gestapo hit list, to draft a report on a new system of medical and other health provision for peacetime Britain. (It was probably **Dawson**'s signing of the September 1939 'Warning: A Message from Great Britain – a leaflet to the German People', that accounts for his inclusion in the Black Book.) In 1920, **Dawson**, who had served on the Western Front and had been appalled by the physical unfitness of British troops, produced his Interim Report on the Future Provision of Medical and Allied Services, with detailed plans for a network of primary and secondary health centres, which would later be influential in planning the National Health Service.

Addison joined the Labour Party in 1922, writing *The Betrayal of the Slums* (1922) and *Practical Socialism* (1926). In the 1930s he was active in the Socialist Medical Association (SMA) and helped to organise medical aid for the anti-fascist Spanish Republicans in the civil war, being elected president of the Spanish Medical Aid Committee in 1936. Having been a fiercely anti-appeasement Labour peer from 1937, **Addison** was made Labour's leader in the House of Lords by **Attlee** after 1945, and it was he who would steer Labour's welfare state reforms, especially Bevan's National Health Service, through a reluctant second chamber. In 'What Sort of Men Get to the Top?' in the ***Observer***, 7 February 1960, **Attlee** called **Addison** 'one of the most influential men in my time … No orator. No art. Patience, friendliness, commonsense – these were his virtues.' Although a vigorous partisan when he chose, **Addison** always felt that, in his biographers' words, 'progressive objectives were more important than party ties … A future generation was to build on foundations laid … by this unassuming doctor-statesman to help create a more humane and compassionate society.' (Morgan, Kenneth and Jane, *Portrait of a Progressive: The Political Career of Christopher, Viscount Addison* (OUP, 1980, conclusion.) It was **Addison**'s humanitarianism, expressed in part through his consistent anti-fascist political activism, that put him in the Gestapo's Black Book.

The chemical pathologist and nutritionist **Professor Dr John R. Marrack**, DSO, MC, MD (1886–1976), was, like **Addison**, always deeply concerned to apply science, especially medicine, to social needs. His article on diphtheria toxin had been published in 1930 and in 1934 he published his seminal, authoritative work in immunology, *The Chemistry of Antigens and Antibodies.* The other focus of **Marrack**'s work was nutrition. His essay on the social implications of biochemistry in *Perspectives in Biochemistry* (1936), pointed out that it was only in the last thirty years that the discovery of vitamins and the body's need for minerals and proteins meant that it had at last become possible to draw up minimal standards for a healthy diet. Most people in Britain in the 1930s needed a better diet, he wrote in *Nature*, 141, 15 June 1938; but the adequacy of a family's sustenance was, of course, dependent on that family's income.

Why should an immunologist and nutritionist be in the Black Book? Quite simply, **Marrack** had joined **the Communist Party of Great Britain** in the 1930s and always remained a friend of **Harry Pollitt**, the party secretary. During the Spanish Civil War **Marrack** served with **Addison** on the Spanish Medical Aid Committee, and had actually been with the International Brigade at the siege of Barcelona. On 11 February 1939 he co-signed a letter to the *British Medical Journal* asking Londoners to support the children's food ship leaving for Valencia and the convoy going to Catalonia.

Before the Second World War, **Marrack** had agitated for a national British food distribution policy, writing 'A National Food Policy' in *Labour Monthly* 10, 1938, anticipating the food shortages in Britain that would definitely accompany the coming war against Nazism. During the war he would advise the Ministry of Food on rationing, writing 'Food in Wartime: Free Rations – or Higher Wages' in *Medicine Today and Tomorrow* in 1940. He also accurately predicted Britain's – and not just Britain's – post-war food needs in his essay, 'Food and Politics' in **Leonard Woolf**'s *Political Quarterly*, July 1942: 'Over all, at the very least, some 470 million people in Europe [after the war] will need to be supplied with 700 calories a day; in terms of food between two and three million tons per month. Relief will not be needed in Europe only. Parts of China ... suffer already from serious scarcity or complete famine.' What is notable here is **Marrack**'s breadth of prophetic vision. He was already anticipating, in 1942, the need to establish a UN Food and Agriculture Organisation as well as a UN World Health Organization. He would continue to be a consultant on food provision after the war before returning to immunology and being hailed as 'a giant in immunology'.[2]

Forbidden to follow her father, a veterinary surgeon, because of the continued ban on women as veterinary students, **Dr Esther Rickards**, MB, BS, LRCP, MS and FRCS (1893–1977) had to content herself with treating humans. She was one of very few women surgeons then in Britain and specialised in gynaecology and obstetrics. Only five feet tall, but with a strong voice, **Rickards** had a tremendously powerful, dynamic personality and was a passionate advocate for maternal welfare, even being evicted from the gallery of the House of Commons for loudly protesting against a statement that underestimated maternal mortality rates in childbirth. Elected in 1928 as a Labour member of London County Council, then the largest provider of hospital beds in Britain, **Rickards** became a prominent, tireless campaigner for socialised medicine, both preventive and curative. From 1930 she was a founding member of the Socialist Medical Association, which in 1939 published a detailed plan for a future National Health Service.[3] The reason for **Rickards**' inclusion on the Black List was most probably her public support for **Medical Aid for Spain,** assisting the Spanish Republicans in the civil war after August 1936 via the SMA.[4] It is unlikely that the Gestapo would have known that she was also a non-observant Jew.[5] She always lived with her sister, their private passions being breeding cocker spaniels and the music of Haydn. A prominent figure in her day, **Rickards** has since been totally forgotten.

Dr Rickards' younger colleague, **Dr Janet Vaughan**, FRS, MD (1899–1993), had also 'decided very young to become a doctor in order to fight the results of poverty and injustice'.[6] Her medical research had focused on blood disease, especially pernicious anaemia then prevalent among underfed, child-bearing women. A committed anti-fascist,

Vaughan also became passionately involved in raising money for Spanish medical aid, eventually giving refuge in her own home to the defeated Republican director of the Barcelona blood bank from whom she learned how to store and use anti-coagulated blood for transfusions in wartime. She then pioneered the use of plasma for wound shock after the evacuation of Dunkirk. And she would herself direct blood transfusion depots during the Blitz.

In May 1945, **Vaughan** went with an (unauthorised) anti-starvation team into liberated Belsen where she used her solutions of milk powder to enable the recovery of inmates with any chance of survival – instead of killing them with injections of protein impossible to digest. That discovery she then applied successfully to countless other victims of near-starvation in post-war Holland and Norway, before it was used by the War Office for released British prisoners of war in the Far East. In the 1960s and 1970s, **Vaughan** would research radiation pathology, becoming a world authority on the biological effects of plutonium. At the end of her life she experimented on herself to see whether strontium-90 and plutonium were carcinogenic, thereby demonstrating the official underestimates of the effects of radiation. 'I considered myself too old to worry about developing the cancers.'[7] (She published *The Effects of Irradiation on the Skeleton* at the age of 74 and died at 94.) It was no doubt **Vaughan's** public commitment to anti-fascist politics from 1936 that had damned her in Nazi eyes and caused her to be listed by the Gestapo.

The British medical profession offered two contrasting responses to the plight of German and Austrian Jewish refugee doctors eager to work in Britain after 1933. The Socialist Medical Association firmly supported them, lobbying the Ministry of Health and the Home Office on their behalf, both as part of their own anti-fascist witness and out of their wish to see medical provision in Britain improved and enlarged.[8] But the much larger and more influential British Medical Association (BMA) – or an élite directing it – attempted to run a closed shop and was intransigent in its opposition to allowing refugee doctors into Britain, let alone to their professional acceptance once they were here. Even the president of the Royal College of Physicians,

Lord Dawson, sought cover in condescending superiority: '[The] number [of refugee physicians] who could be usefully absorbed or teach us anything could be counted on the fingers of one hand.'[9] The medical profession was under pressure in Britain in the 1930s to reform the provision of medicine, and that hardened the defensiveness of the BMA. They used the Aliens Acts and Aliens' Order as a regulatory control from the Home Office to keep selective admission of refugee doctors down to a minimum. 'After the *Anschluss* [in 1938] it actually vetoed a Home Office scheme to bring five hundred Austrian Jewish doctors to Britain.'[10]

Widespread anti-Semitism also reared its head: '"The way stateless Jews from Germany are pouring in from every port of this country is becoming an outrage ..." In these words Mr Herbert Metcalfe, the Old Street magistrate, yesterday referred to the number of aliens entering the country through the "back door" – a problem to which the *Daily Mail* has repeatedly pointed.'[11]

Nevertheless some refugee doctors did manage to fulfil the stringent requirements for requalification and registration after entering Britain in the 1930s. **Dr Stefan Engel** for example (1878–1968), was among those who did practise successfully in Britain. He was a paediatrician and pioneering specialist in the treatment of children with TB, and he advocated fresh air sanatoria for his young patients. After having been forbidden to head the German Children's Hospital in 1933, he had worked without pay for the Jewish Children's Hospital in Berlin until he left Germany in 1936 and took up a post at Great Ormond Street Hospital for Sick Children.[12]

Then there was **Dr Alfred Loeser** (1887–1962), who, despite having performed emergency surgery on German soldiers on the battlefields of the First World War, even winning the Iron Cross, was later forced to flee to London in 1934 for being a Jew. Tall and slim, he had in fact recently been photographed as an example of a 'Typical German Doctor' in the *Deutsche Aerzteblatt*. In Britain he became a gynaecologist in private practice, having made fundamental discoveries on the therapeutic effect of testosterone on breast cancer and on other women's cancers, which have since become standard interventions.

Another cancer researcher was **Dr Lorenz Michaelis** (1902–1979), who gained a medical postgraduate degree from Glasgow University. He specialised in bone pathology, radiology, orthopaedics and child surgery. From 1950 he would work at Stoke Mandeville Hospital with Sir Ludwig Guttmann, the great instigator of sport for the disabled, skilfully operating on spinal cord injuries and cerebral palsy and winning 'the respect and love of all his patients'.[13] Intervening to improve the lives of people with paraplegia and quadriplegia, **'Laury' Michaelis** was an outstanding example of a medical man who reached out to those whom the Nazis believed ought to be disposed of.

The Hungarian-born polymath **Janos**, later called **Johannes** or **John Plesch** (1878–1957), was yet another quite extraordinarily gifted refugee doctor. After studying many different branches of medicine from physiology to bacteriology in Budapest, Vienna, Berlin and Strasbourg, including work on radium treatment with the Curies in their Paris laboratory, **Plesch** had finally settled in Berlin in 1903. He then served with the German army as a medical consultant on several battle fronts in the First World War and afterwards became a professor of internal diseases. His specialities were blood pressure, the hardening of the arteries influenced by high cholesterol, and cardiac disease. Despite his eminence, wealth and many famous cultural contacts, **Plesch** had to emigrate to Britain as soon as the Nazis took power. He obtained British medical qualifications within a year and by 1934 set up a private practice – as well as being cardiac consultant at St George's Hospital and Edward VII's Hospital, London. He was granted British citizenship in 1939 – the Nazis naming him an 'enemy of the state' in 1940. His publications in English included *Physiology and Pathology of the Heart and Blood-vessels* (1937), *Blood Pressure and its Disorders* (1944), *Blood Pressure and Angina Pectoris* (1947), *Janos, the Story of a Doctor* (1947) (a bestseller), and a work on how to recognise genuine Rembrandts, in 1952.

A pioneer in bacteriology and immunology **Dr Otto Prausnitz**, later **Carl Prausnitz-Giles** (1876–1963), was another outstanding refugee medical practitioner.[14] He was a specialist in cholera diagnosis, rabies prevention, pollen allergy (hay fever) and other allergies such as peanut allergy – he had experimented on himself in order to develop the **Prausnitz**-Kuestner blood test for allergic reactions. A professor of bacteriology and hygiene at the University of Breslau, he had also served actively in the League of Nations health organisation in the late 1920s – which would not have recommended him to the Gestapo. Despite his international eminence and his responsibility as director of public health for Breslau, **Prausnitz** was forced to resign under racist pressure in 1933. His first work in Britain was to study cotton-spinners' asthma ('respiratory dust disease') in Manchester in 1933–5. He lectured at the University of Manchester until 1936 and was given British citizenship in 1939. Then, at the age of 64, and reverting to his English mother's name of **Giles**, he started to practise as a GP at Ventnor on the Isle of Wight where he set up an advanced clinical pathology laboratory in his own home. Known to many as 'Father Giles', he would finally retire from the NHS at the age of 84. '**Prausnitz [Giles]** loved his fellow-men and was beloved by them. Never shall we see his like again.'[15]

One medical field which was absolutely transformed by the advent of German and Austrian refugee doctors was psychiatry.[16] Here again we find physicians who deliberately reached out to help people deemed to be hopeless cases and who therefore, in Nazi eyes, 'deserved' to be killed. For example **Dr Harry Fischgold** (later Fisher), MD Berlin, MRCP Edinburgh (1903–*c*.1992), had originally been a research biochemist at the Charité Hospital in Berlin before he was driven to resettle in Britain in 1933 where he worked as a researcher at University College Hospital, London. In 1936 he was appointed assistant medical officer at Mapperley Mental Hospital, Nottingham, where he played an important part in 'the Nottingham experiment', pioneering open wards, and humane therapeutic intervention as well as offering work and education for psychiatric patients. In the 1950s he would become consultant psychiatrist and deputy physician superintendent at Mapperley Hospital.[17] Another refugee neurologist was **Dr Hans Fleischhacker** (1898–1965), who worked as a researcher at the Maudsley Hospital, London, from 1936. He later moved to the Middlesex County Council's new, progressive, experimental Shenley Mental Hospital in Hertfordshire. He was 'naturalised' at last in 1947.

Yet another eminent psychiatrist, **Dr Rudolf Karl Freudenberg** (1908–1993), had left Berlin for Vienna in 1933 where he had undertaken research on the physiology of insulin coma. He was invited to work in Britain in 1936 at Moorcroft House where he was one of the pioneers of new physical treatments for schizophrenia. With the establishment of the NHS after the war, **Freudenberg** went to Netherne Mental Hospital in Surrey, becoming physician superintendent in 1951, and making great changes to the conditions of patients suffering from schizophrenia by reducing overcrowding in the wards, as well as by providing more individual care and attention, occupational therapy and better clothing. He was one of the first to recognise the social and emotional aspects of mental illness. In 1961 he became head of the Medical Mental Health Section of the Ministry of Health and, after retirement, he served on the management committee of Cheshire Homes for the severely disabled. No one could have been a more committed opponent of the Nazis' compulsory 'euthanasia' programme, both practically and ideologically.[18] Freudenberg's wife, **Dr Gerda Freudenberg** (1908–1993), qualified to practise in Britain almost twenty years after having first qualified in Germany, and worked alongside her innovative husband at Netherne Hospital in Surrey.

Another innovator in psychiatric treatment, **Dr Erich Guttmann** (1896–1946), pioneered creative art therapy for mental patients at the Maudsley Hospital, London. He was especially interested in the art produced by some of his patients suffering from schizophrenia, and, together with his colleague Dr Walter Maclay, he assembled the Guttmann-Maclay art collection that also included work by contemporary surrealist artists who allowed themselves to be experimented on with the hallucinatory effects of mescalin. (That collection can be seen now in the Bethlehem Museum of the Mind, Beckenham.) **Guttmann** was interned as a suspect German 'enemy alien' for a year in 1940–41 but was then released to work at Oxford's Radcliffe Infirmary for the rest of the war. In 1943, he published, with Desmond Curran,

Psychological Medicine: a Short Introduction to Psychiatry – with an Appendix – *War-Time Psychiatry*.

For other indispensable contributions to medical research made by refugee doctors in Britain in the 1930s, 1940s and beyond, see 'Medical Researchers' pp. 281. But here are two last examples of outstanding humanitarian intervention by refugee medical men placed on the Black List. **Franz Bergel**, FRS (1900–1987), had worked for many years as a researcher for La Roche pharmaceuticals. An Austrian working at a German university, he had not been subject to the new racist laws, but had left Germany of his own volition because he could not stomach the inhumanity of Nazism. He had been 'naturalised' in 1938 after working in Britain since 1936 on the synthesising of vitamin E and later of other vitamins, analgesics, and anti-bacterials. From 1952 until 1966 **Bergel** was appointed professor at the Research Institute of the Royal Cancer Hospital in London where he worked on developing chemotherapy and especially on the diminution of tumours through enzyme therapy. 'A kind, compassionate and gentle man',[19] **Bergel** worked indefatigably on his medical research, despite himself suffering from rectal cancer and having undergone a colostomy.

Finally, there was the specialist in tuberculosis, **Dr Ernst Brieger** (1891–1969). Until 1933, **Brieger** had been the only German member of the International Tuberculosis Committee. After 1933 he had initially been protected from dismissal from his University of Breslau post because of his service in the First World War, and had continued to work as chief doctor at the city's tuberculosis hospital, but in 1934 he had to emigrate. (It would not have helped him that he had married into the dissident Protestant Bonhoeffer family.) **Brieger** was appointed as a researcher at Papworth Hall tuberculosis hospital, at the same time as he was working on tissue culture with Dame Honor Fell at the Strangeways research laboratory at Cambridge, where he was one of the first to use the electron microscope.[20] Nevertheless, 1940 still saw him interned in Britain as an 'enemy alien'. On his release, **Brieger** extended his interest in cell biology and bacteriology from tuberculosis to that most 'untouchable' of all diseases, leprosy, inspired by a 'deep compassion for those suffering from the diseases to the study of which he devoted his life'.[21] 'He was the first [medical scientist] to show by cytochemical and electron-microscopical studies that lysomes were involved in cellular defence in leprosy.'[22] **Brieger**'s publications in English included *After-care and Rehabilitation: Principles and Practice* (1937) and *The Papworth Families: a 25 Years Survey* (1946).

All in all, the findings of refugee medical researchers in Britain covered an extraordinary range of afflictions.[23] By August 1941, the British Medical Association began to lessen its intransigence and recognise that in the war situation, given the shortage of doctors and the terrible under-provision of medical care in all the deprived areas of Great Britain, every doctor and nurse was now at a premium, regardless of his or her nationality, statelessness, religion or 'race'.

4

Pacifists

> [Of course] the people don't want war … neither in Russia nor in England, nor in America, nor for that matter in Germany. That is understood … But the people can always be brought to the bidding of the leaders. That is easy. All you have to do is tell them they are being attacked and denounce the pacifists for lack of patriotism and exposing the country to danger. It works the same way in any country.
>
> Goering interviewed in prison during the Nuremberg Trials, 18 April 1946[1]

It was German pacifists who had warned most urgently against the militarist expansionism behind *Mein Kampf.* 'Never again War!' (*'Nie wieder Krieg!'*) the famous Käthe Kollwitz poster had exhorted in 1924. So strong was the depth of German mass feeling against another war that Hitler knew that he had to lie to the electorate and pronounce himself a bringer of peace. After he had gained power in January 1933, however, he immediately targeted German pacifists as nothing but defeatist traitors, unfit to influence German youth in its hour of destiny. The leader of the German Peace Movement, Carl von Ossietzky, who had long denounced secret German rearmament and the bloodstained, profiteering armament manufacturers, was sent to Papenburg concentration camp, where, despite being awarded the Nobel Peace Prize in 1935, he died in 1938 of TB and mistreatment in terrible prison conditions.

Ossietzky's successor as the leading German pacifist spokesman was **Otto Lehmann-Russbueldt** (1873–1964), founder of the German

League for Human Rights. He had published attacks on the armaments industry, both multinational and German, and on Germany's secret aggressive rearmament – especially her air force – 'Hitler's wings of death'. He had campaigned for reconciliation between France and Germany and had championed the idea of a disarmed, united Europe. This earned him the reward of being one of the thirty-three Germans who were the very first to be stripped of their nationality and made stateless in August 1933. After being imprisoned with von Ossietzky in January 1933, **Lehmann-Russbueldt** escaped to Holland disguised as one of a group of psychiatric patients in the charge of Catholic priests. On settling in Britain he tried in vain to warn the British of the Nazis' threat to world peace and of Germany's secret experiments in airborne gas and bacteriological warfare. During the Second World War **Lehmann-Russbueldt** helped his fellow refugees and worked with like-minded Germans such as the lawyer **Alois Ernst** – also placed on the Gestapo Black List – to plan for the reconstruction of a new post-war Germany that would reject every aspect of Nazism in a peaceful Europe. He had a 'prodigious and unquenchable spirit'.[2]

The great German anti-war novel, *Im Westen Nichts Neues* (*All Quiet on the Western Front*), published in 1929, was, of course, banned in both fascist Italy and Nazi Germany. It had been publicly burned in May 1933 on Goebbels' orders and its author, Erich Maria Remarque, fled Germany for Switzerland. In 1943 Elfriede Scholz, Remarque's youngest sister, was denounced for saying that foreigners were not such bad people as one was being told and that Germany had lost the war. She was charged with undermining national morale. The judge at her trial declared: 'Your brother has unfortunately escaped, but you will not escape', and she was beheaded.

German *women* pacifists had long been a particular bête noire of the Nazis. As early as 1932 their *Illustrieter Beobachter* had made the Party's feelings known:

Pazifistinnen
Vom Kopf bis Plattfuss pervers dekadent!
Bolschewistische Furien und Gaense! …

Hysterische Weiber, maskulin und blasiert! …
Pazifistische Friedenshyaenen!
Eine juedische Clique fein organisiert
In Ligen und Frauenverbaenden,
Um allen Voelkern franzoesisch frisiert,
Die 'Friedensbotschaft' zu senden …

(Women Pacifists – perverted and decadent from their heads to their flat feet! Bolshevik furies and geese! Hysterical females, masculine and smug! … Pacifist peace hyenas! A Jewish clique, well-organised in Leagues and Women's Groups to send the French styled 'Peace Message' around the world.)

In 1932, 1,500 women from all over Germany attended a women's peace conference in Munich, which the Nazi press attacked: 'Peace Scandal in Munich! Women Traitors!' The leading women in the various branches of the German peace movement – Erika Mann, Constanze Hallgarten, Lida Gustava Heymann, Dr Anita Augspurg and Helene Stoecker – knew that they were prime targets and in 1933 they all went into exile. Jewish German women pacifists, like the writer Anna Seghers, also fled. The non-Jewish pacifist artist Käthe Kollwitz, aged nearly 70, was arrested and interrogated by the Gestapo and she and her husband carried suicide pills ever after. Despite huge international protests and pleas to Hitler for clemency (including from British women), in 1937 the pacifist socialist young German mother Liselotte Herrmann was beheaded as a traitor for having sent abroad undeniable technical evidence of Nazi Germany's rearmament and its preparations for aerial warfare. As for the Jehovah's Witnesses in Germany, their pacifism led to their deportation to concentration camps, while the mothers who had tried to hide their sons to keep them from killing for Hitler were also beheaded.

But why should the Nazi occupation-planners have been quite so determined to round up leading *British* pacifists in 1940? Who could have been more harmless? Throughout the preceding twenty years British pacifists had been stigmatised in Britain as 'pro- Germans', speaking up for defeated Germany, protesting against the Allied blockade, deploring the punitive Treaty of Versailles, founding small Quaker meeting houses in Germany and setting up Quaker 'feeding stations' in the hungry 1920s in German universities and in working-class districts of Berlin, Leipzig and Hamburg, as well as in Vienna. Meanwhile the British pacifists had also campaigned tirelessly for *general* disarmament. Even after 1933 they still tried to see Germany's point of view in their desperate attempts to prevent a Second World War. *Peace News*, the weekly organ of the **Peace Pledge Union** after 1936, was so pro-appeasement that it could seem pro-Nazi; indeed the Union had in fact been infiltrated by a handful of British fascists.

Nevertheless, the Gestapo still classed all British peace groups as '*gegen Deutschland*' – by which they meant '*gegen Hitler*' – and anticipated resistance from them. For British pacifists did indeed constitute an awkward squad – they were a troublesome lot who would never have cooperated with an exterminatory, racist, military dictatorship running a thousand-year Reich. For they incarnated the ultimate alternative to Nazism, rejecting the very concept of an 'enemy' and substituting for war-waging 'patriotism' a universal humanist vision, hoping to the end for all people to be brothers – '*Alle Menschen werden Brueder*'. The Gestapo sneeringly categorised the Quakers, in particular, as being '*edelkommunistisch*' ('nobly communistic').

The second section of the *Sonderfahndungsliste GB*, '*Behoerden* and *Vereine*' ('Institutions and Associations') includes, cheek by jowl with the Boy Scouts, the Conservative and Unionist Central Office and the Docks Group, the names and often the addresses of all the many British peace organisations still active in 1939 that were to be immediately banned, their membership lists seized and their leaders arrested. They include, inter alia, **The Arts Peace Campaign, the Council of Christian Pacifist Groups** and **the Jewish Peace Society**. Behind the door of each of these offices the SS would have found the dedicated foot soldiers of the British peace movement, still sending out leaflets. (See Appendix 3 for the full list of peace organisations to be banned.)

If this seems to be overstating the danger that British pacifists would have faced in a Nazi-occupied Britain, one should remember the wartime fate of leading members of the proscribed **Women's International League for Peace and Freedom (WIL)**, founded at the Hague in 1915 to 'demand that international disputes shall in future be settled by some other means than war [and] to claim that women should have a voice in the affairs of the nations'. In Nazi-occupied Prague, the Czech MP Frantziska Plamenkova was hanged, together with six fellow women members of the **WIL**; Rosa Manus, the Dutch pacifist and co-founder of the **WIL** in 1915, was deported from the Netherlands and perished in a German concentration camp. That was also the fate of the president and the secretary of the Hungarian section of the **WIL**, Eugenie Meller and Melanie Vambery. In late 1940, behind the door of the **WIL** at 5 Gower Street, London, the SS would have found Mrs Katherine Innes, Ada Salter and Barbara Duncan Harris – among others.

Many leading British pacifists were actually singled out by name as 'Most Wanted' for immediate arrest in the alphabetical *Sonderfahndungsliste*. They include: **Sir Norman Angell** (1872–1967), '*Praes. d. Weltkommittee gegen Krieg u. Fascismus*' ('President of the World Committee against War and Fascism') who had won the Nobel Peace Prize in 1933. **Angell**, aged nearly 70 in 1940, had written indefatigably about ways of preventing war. His first famous work was *The Great Illusion* (1909), which had demonstrated the false economics of having a war between trading partners, because bankrupting one's chief supplier or one's chief customer could only hurt oneself.[3] Forced to recognise that his rational argument against war in a modern, economically interdependent world was not enough to convince his irrational fellow humans, **Angell** focused during the 1930s on the need for collective security through international alliances, in order to counter and curb the emotion-grounded, expansionist nationalism of the newly fascist states. In 1940, with Hitler the opposite of uncurbed, **Angell** renounced his lifelong pacifism and went to the United States to plead for American war support for Britain.

A former leader of the Labour Party, **George Barnes**, CH (1859–1940), was the next pacifist on the list, despite the fact that he was 80 years old and dying. In his retirement he had supported the League of

Nations' International Labour Organisation and had co-founded the international 'New Commonwealth Society', which advocated 'pacifism, disarmament and multilateral resolution of conflicts'. By 1937 it was advocating an international League of Nations police force, including an air force, to keep global peace. (**Churchill**, in a speech to the society, said in May 1937: 'We are one of the few peace societies that advocates the use of force, if possible overwhelming force, to support public international law.')

The anti-militarist **Vera Brittain** (1893–1970), author of the devastating, best-selling autobiography *Testament of Youth* (1933), her elegy for the destroyed lives of her brother, fiancé and close friend, was targeted by the Gestapo as a '*Journalistin*'. Ironically, it was her experience of nursing dying German prisoners in November 1917, near the fields of Passchendaele, which planted the seed of her lifelong absolute pacifism. The sheer universality of the suffering and young death that she witnessed initiated her into a profound internationalism that led her eventually to convert to Christian pacifism in 1936 and to supporting the Peace Pledge Union in 1937.[4] Predictably, she then found herself extremely unpopular in wartime Britain when she doggedly – and unsuccessfully – wrote that Britain must not, by indiscriminately bombing German civilians, perpetrate atrocities worthy of the Nazis. Her daughter, Shirley Williams, wrote later: 'Church leaders and politicians denounced her … obscenities and dog faeces were put through her letter box.'[5] It was a great relief for **Brittain** to discover, in September 1945, that she too had been on the Black List – that the Nazis had recognised that non-violent women resisters, whose values were the opposite of their own, would be as implacably anti-Nazi as any resistant, armed, British men. 'Himmler's addition of conspicuous pacifists to the list of Nazism's arch-enemies showed … how clearly the Gestapo realised that the advocates of non-violent resistance were at least as dangerous to their authority as the belligerent politicians who fought fascism by its own methods.' (**Vera Brittain**, *Testament of Experience*, 1957.)

A former conscientious objector in the First World War, who had suffered years of imprisonment with hard labour, was the anti-imperialist, socialist editor of the **ILP**'s *Labour Leader*, **Fenner Brockway** (1888–1988). He supported **War Resisters International** and the **No More War Movement** – the 1920s' successors of the No Conscription Fellowship of the First World War (1916–19). A Labour MP and later chairman of the Independent Labour Party (1931–3), **Brockway** had taken part in the last doomed public socialist campaign against Hitler in Germany in 1932. However, he moved away from absolutist pacifism in the Spanish Civil War – 'I felt I couldn't want them [the Republicans] to win without doing something to help them win.' And he helped recruit volunteers for the **ILP** contingent fighting Franco. By September 1939 he was in a mental no man's land: 'I was too conscious of the evil of Nazism and Fascism to be completely pacifist. Yet I could not be pro-war …'[6]

From a very different social and political background, **Lord Robert Cecil** (1864–1958), aged 76 in 1940, the Conservative son of the 3rd Marquess of Salisbury, was in a similar dilemma. He had been converted by the First World War to an unshakeable belief that civilisation could only survive by developing an *international* system to keep the peace. Already in September 1916 **Cecil** had advocated the formation of a body he called the 'League of Nations'. He was president of the British **League of Nations Union** from 1923 until 1945 and a leader of the **International Peace Campaign**, advocating multinational disarmament. In 1935 he had initiated the National Peace Ballot, helped by **Dame Adelaide Livingstone** (1881–1970),[7] when half a million people went from door to door eliciting the responses of over half the British electorate (11 million) to questions on peace and war and the League of Nations. (The Gestapo, of course, took Hitler's line that the League of Nations and therefore all its supporters in the British **League of Nations Union**, with its 400,000 British members in the early 1930s, were 'hostile to Germany'.) In 1938 **Cecil** was awarded the Nobel Peace Prize, but he felt a failure. He had become less and less of a Conservative and was now strongly anti-appeasement, feeling deeply bitter about Munich and himself 'a miserable worm' because he had been unable to do anything to save Czechoslovakia. All his internationalism, his life's work since 1916, had proved futile. But at the final meeting of the League of Nations in Geneva, in spring 1946, 82-year-old **Cecil** would still be enough of an optimist to declare: '[The] League is dead, long live the United Nations.'

Willoughby Dickenson, 1st Baron Dickenson ('*Pazifist*') former Liberal MP and still Privy Councillor, at 81 years old was on the Black List because in 1914 he had founded – and was later secretary-general of – the 'World Alliance for International Friendship'. This alliance was an ecumenical church body working chiefly for international peace via arbitration; it linked up with secular educational bodies in the pursuit of just settlements and collective security. Between 1933 and 1938 it published the bulletin *The Churches in Action.* One of its supporters in Germany had been the anti-Nazi pastor, Dietrich Bonhoeffer, who was executed in Berlin in 1945 after the German generals' 1944 plot had tried and failed to assassinate Hitler.

But it was the Quakers, as always, who formed the bedrock of British pacifist resistance. **War Resisters International (WRI)**, had been co- founded in Holland in 1921 by the Quaker **H. Runham Brown** (1879–1949), a nature-loving, pioneer environmentalist. In the First World War **Brown** had been imprisoned for two and a half years with hard labour for being an absolutist conscientious objector. He later wrote *Spain: a Challenge to Pacifists* (1936), *War is a Crime Against Humanity* and *Why Hitler?* (1942). The **WRI**'s founding declaration was, and still is, 'War is a crime against humanity. I am therefore determined not to support any kind of war and to strive for the removal of all causes of war.' It adopted the broken rifle as its symbol, in contrast to the SS's death head, and became a world movement for conscientious objection supported by **Einstein** – (who was also in the Black Book as **Dr *Alfred* Einstein,** despite being by then safe in the United States).

Another quintessential exemplar of Quaker pacifism, both in his mildness of aspect and in his firmness of spirit, was **William Ravenscroft Hughes** (1880–1966) ('*Taeterkreis von der Ropp*' – i.e. alleged by the Gestapo to be an anti-Nazi plotter with the Polish archbishop who had died in 1939). An early conservationist and ecologist in Welwyn Garden City, Hertfordshire, during the mid to late 1930s, **Hughes** was also secretly active as a Quaker emissary in Germany and Holland. He had carried – and concealed – large sums of Quaker money to support endangered Germans, both Jewish and non-Jewish and including pacifists and left-wing activists. And he also worked closely with Corder Catchpool, an English Quaker based in Berlin's Quaker centre. Both men aroused suspicion. Forced to leave Nazi Germany, **Hughes**, a fluent German speaker, returned clandestinely under a false identity at the end of 1938, in order to report on the terrible danger threatening Jewish Germans after *Kristallnacht.* In 1940 he travelled daily to London from Hertfordshire to attend meeting after meeting at Friends' House, Euston Road, serving on the Committee of Meeting for Sufferings, the **Friends Service Council** and the (Friends') Executive **Committee for Refugees and Aliens.** It was no wonder that he was 'Most Wanted' by the Gestapo. In 1941 **Hughes** visited interned Germans behind barbed wire on the Isle of Man to demonstrate that they had not been forgotten and that Quakers did not see them as 'the enemy' but were, instead, agitating for their release. So committed was he to their welfare that he moved to the Isle of Man during their internment. At the end of the war **Hughes** visited German POW camps in Britain and then worked for the Friends' relief service in the British zone of hungry, occupied West Germany.

Other British Quakers on the 'Most Wanted' list included 62 year-old **Ruth Fry** (1878–1962), the heroic famine relief organiser in Poland and Soviet Russia after 1919. By the 1930s she had become secretary of the National Peace Council, chair of the **Society for Cultural Relations with the USSR** from 1936 and treasurer of **War Resisters International.**[8] Her colleague, **Elizabeth Fox Howard** (1873–1957), '*Leiterin [womanleader] d. Engl. Quaeker*', worked for years in Germany after the First World War on relief and reconciliation projects, including at the Quaker centre at Bad Pyrmont, which offered 'recuperation to some 800 people, Jews, Catholics, Lutherans, Communists and other victims of [Nazism].'[9] Finally, she had the difficult task of interviewing and sorting out in Nazi Germany which would-be German refugees the British Quakers would be able to help with guarantors and visas – 'It was heart-breaking to have to refuse so many.' She was arrested by the Gestapo on the German border with Belgium in 1938 and taken for interrogation to Berlin where 'it needed some ingenuity to avoid incriminating other people'.[10] After her release she surprised the Gestapo by returning voluntarily next day to their Berlin HQ in order to intercede for a woman whose case she had taken on. She left Germany just before September 1939, returning after the Second World War to work with 'displaced persons'.

The most politically prominent Quaker in the 1930s and after was **Philip Noel-Baker** (1889–1982), who had been a Quaker conscientious objector in the First World War, but not an 'absolutist'. Instead, he had organised and led the Friends' ambulance unit, first on the fighting front in France and then in Italy, and he never ceased to grieve for all his friends and fellow students from King's College, Cambridge, the young officers mown down on the Western Front. Having helped to found the League of Nations, **Noel-Baker** became professor of international relations at the London School of Economics, University of London from 1924 to 1929 and then a Labour MP. He assisted **Arthur Henderson** when Henderson was president of the unsuccessful World Disarmament Conference, Geneva from 1932 to 1933, and he was elected to the Labour National Executive in 1937, where he remained until 1948. A supporter of international disarmament overseen by the League of Nations, **Noel-Baker** spoke in the House of Commons in June 1938 against any future aerial bombardment of German cities by Britain. With a terrible, impotent idealism, he said: 'The only way to prevent atrocities from the air is to abolish air warfare and national air forces altogether.' In the mid 1940s **Noel-Baker** helped to draft the UN Charter. He wrote *Disarmament* for the **League of Nations Union** (1934), *Hawkers of Death: The Private Manufacturer and Trade in Arms* for the Labour Party (1934), and *The Arms Race, a Programme for World Disarmament* (1958). At the age of 90, in 1979, he co-founded, with **Fenner Brockway**, the World Disarmament Campaign.[11] **Noel-Baker** also bears the distinction of being the only person in the world so far to have won both an Olympic medal (in 1920 for the 1,500 metres track) as well as the Nobel Peace Prize (in 1959).

A former Labour MP from 1924 to 1931, a **WEA** lecturer and anti-militarist journalist, **Rennie Smith** (1888–1962), was Blacklisted for his work for '**Friends of New Europe**' at St Stephen's House, Westminster, accused by the Gestapo of 'Marxism' and supporting 'emigrants'. (In the First World War, St Stephen's House had been the Quaker headquarters of the emergency committee for Germans, Austrians and Hungarians who were stranded and in distress in Britain.) Between 1933 and 1940, **Smith** was responsible for translating and publishing the **Friends of Europe** pamphlets on Nazi Germany, and he also brought out *Peace Verboten*, a *Fight for Freedom* publication. 'Wherever we find him – his task [is] peace and international understanding' was the comment in *Fight for Freedom*. **Smith** would become a civilian adult education officer in the British zone of occupied West Germany after the Second World War. Though he is not well remembered, his papers are now held in the Bodleian Library in Oxford.

The even more uncompromising Christian pacifist and left-wing Labour MP, **George Lansbury** (1850–1940), was, at 90, one of the oldest people named in the Black Book, and a steadfast opponent of both world wars. His idealistic eloquence brought tears to the eyes of **Virginia Woolf** when he spoke at the 1935 Labour Party conference. However, he had then felt obliged to resign as leader of the Labour Party when **Ernest Bevin** mauled him for 'touting his conscience around to find a home'. Recently it has been argued that it would have been fatal for Britain had **Lansbury** not resigned and had still been the Labour leader in 1940 when it needed **Clement Attlee** and **Arthur Greenwood** to back **Churchill** against **Halifax** and **Neville Chamberlain** in favour of fighting on against Hitler. There would have been no VE-day in 1945 had that vote in 1940 gone the other way.[12] Nevertheless, in spite of **Lansbury's** age and the fact that he no longer held any office, the Gestapo still wanted to arrest the 90-year-old in 1940 for 'supporting German emigrants and the encirclement [of Germany]'.

A possibly surprising opponent of Nazism was the confectioner **Sydney Pascall** (1890–1949), who was targeted for having co-founded **Rotary International**. At first **Pascall** had concentrated on **Rotary's** civic functions within Britain's communities, but he then became increasingly outspoken about **Rotary**'s role as a secular, non-racial, internationalist organisation, contributing to peace and fellowship throughout the world. His obituary, proclaimed in *The Rotarian*, October 1949: 'Only his deep passion for world understanding and accord transcended perhaps his crusade for harmony and justice in the world of work.' In 1942, **Pascall** chaired a world conference of ministers of education, including those from the many governments in exile then in London, as well as delegates from the United States and the Soviet Union, looking ahead to post-war reconstruction. They all recognised the urgent need for the youth of the world to be educated in internationalism and that conference's insight that 'wars begin in the minds of men' because the inspiration behind the founding of UNESCO in 1946. **Rotary International** was banned in Nazi Germany and all over occupied Europe. It would have been a banned organisation in occupied Britain also and was listed by the Gestapo alongside the abhorred **Freemasons**. Clearly the Gestapo had earmarked **Pascall**, a tireless planter of trees worldwide, not to mention of ideas, as a dangerously influential man. (Similarly, British individuals and groups attempting to spread the international language of **Esperanto** in the furtherance of peace were also targeted – and they too, like **Rotary International**, have survived to this day.)

Arthur, Lord Ponsonby (1871–1946), once a page-boy of Queen Victoria, was another unexpected idealist in the Black Book. He was an absolutist pacifist and a Labour peer who continued to advocate unilateral disarmament ('disarmament by example') even after the rise of Hitler, opposing his own Labour Party's policy of 'collective security'. He backed the Peace Pledge Union and was committed to appeasement in his desperation to avoid another world war. **Ponsonby** never got the measure of Hitler's manic dream of world dictatorship; at the beginning of 1940 he was still hoping that the war could be stopped by negotiation. But by May 1940 even he realised that the **Peace Pledge Union** had had its absolutist day and he was left in utter despair: 'I used to think that the diabolical brutality of modern warfare might impress people sufficiently to make them hesitate to support such a method of attempting to settle international disputes; just as I used to think that decent men in high positions would have learnt that this was not the way of establishing peace in the world. But in both cases I was quite wrong.'[13] All that **Ponsonby** could then do was plead for his own country not to commit atrocities. Therefore, ironically, he who was to have been one of those arrested by the Germans in 1940, in 1941 signed the programme of the British Committee for the Abolition of Night-Bombing of Germany.

One of the very few Anglican clerics named in the Black Book was **Canon Charles E. Raven**, DD (1885–1964) – '*Geistlicher*' ('Priest'). He had been a military chaplain in the First World War but had been converted to Christian pacifism in 1920. A distinguished theological scholar and an eminent naturalist, as well as a charismatic, if outnumbered, male advocate for the ordination of women priests in the Anglican Church, **Raven** had chaired the **Fellowship of Reconciliation** from 1931 and co-sponsored the **Peace Pledge Union** from 1936. His eloquent but unpopular pacifism before and during the Second World War may have cost him preferment in the Church of England – he did not become a bishop let alone archbishop – but he never wavered.[14]

His great fellow-campaigner for the ordination of women in the Anglican Church was **Maude Royden**, CH, Hon. DD (1876–1956), labelled '*Publizistin*' by the Gestapo. She was so great an orator that she was always billed to speak last at radical political demonstrations; no one would leave until they had heard her. 'How she would blaze at injustice and cruelty!' wrote **Sybil Thorndike**. A Christian socialist, pacifist and feminist, **Royden** was the first person ever to call for non-violent direct action against the twentieth-century war machine in her pamphlet *The Great Adventure* (1915): 'We [should] have called for the peace-lovers in the world to fling themselves – if need be – in front of the troop trains. If millions of men will go out to offer their lives up in war, surely there are those who would die for peace and if not men, we could have called out women.'

After the Japanese invasion of Manchuria in 1931, **Royden** developed an extraordinary project – she proposed the formation of an

'International Peace Army' of unarmed, middle-aged or older volunteers to interpose their bodies between the fighting divisions in a war zone – and was disappointed that only a thousand people in Britain volunteered. In the event, the British government did not allow them to sail to Japanese-invaded areas of China. Naturally, before his death in 1937 **Royden** became Dick Sheppard's right-hand woman behind the **Peace Pledge Union**. But Hitler's treatment of the Jews and the real prospect that, if he conquered all Europe including Britain, the next generation would be brainwashed and terrorised into fascist racism, forced her to re-think. After a tremendous inner struggle, she, the best known, most beloved of all British pacifists, publicly renounced her pacifism in October 1939. In 1941 she went to the United States on a speaking tour to try to bring over Americans to enter the war on the Allied side, and 1942 would see her driving an ambulance car in London air raids.[15]

Royden's friend **Dame Sybil Thorndike** (1882–1976), the classical actress famous for her Hecuba in Euripides' anti-war tragedy *The Trojan Women* and for her embodiment of Shaw's *Saint Joan* in the 1920s and 1930s, was Blacklisted by the Gestapo for supporting the **National Council for Civil Liberties**. A committed pacifist, she was also a reliable bastion of many other left-wing causes.[16] She had been one of the British women signatories, together with **Eleanor Rathbone**, **Ellen Wilkinson**, **Lady Rhondda** and **Violet Bonham Carter** – all therefore also on the *Sonderfahndungsliste* – pleading in vain to Hitler for clemency for Liselotte Herrmann, and she had spoken in public throughout the 1920s and 1930s on behalf of striking miners, Indian independence, anti-racism, civil liberty and, most of all, advocating the pacifism she never renounced. On the outbreak of war, together with **Vera Brittain** and **Maude Royden**, **Sybil Thorndike** wrote to **Neville Chamberlain** urging that Britain should not bomb German women and children in open cities and she was a co-signatory with **Haldane**, Shaw and the **Webbs**, urging Britain not to attack Soviet Russia, despite the Nazi-Soviet pact.

The last British pacifist to be singled out by name, **Professor Alfred Zimmern** (1879–1957), born in Britain to 'naturalised' German

Jewish parents, had been, in 1921, the first professor of international politics in the world at the University College of Wales, Aberystwyth, and from 1930 to 1944 he was inaugural professor of international relations at Oxford. Together with **Professor Gilbert Murray**, **Zimmern** was possibly the best-known British idealistic internationalist in academia – but he would soon be mocked as a hopelessly utopian theorist.[17] A founding supporter of the **League of Nations Union** in Britain, **Zimmern** wrote *The League of Nations and the Rule of Law 1918–1935* (1936) and 'The Ethical Presuppositions of a World Order' in *The Universal Church and the World of Nations* (1938). He coined the word 'Commonwealth' to replace 'British Empire' and was the first to use the concept and words 'Welfare State'. After 1945, **Alfred Zimmern** would contribute to the founding of UNESCO.

Can one generalise about such a heterogeneous collection of unheeded would-be saviours of the world? The unsympathetic view is that they were just cranks, headless chickens hopelessly divided among themselves, running in contradictory directions. Even before 1933, **Ponsonby** had discovered that the **No More War Movement** over which he was president was split into at least four groups – the Tolstoyan/Gandhian enthusiasts for non-violent non-resistance; the communists taking their orders from Moscow; the socialist revolutionaries urging class war in Britain; and the more conservative Christian pacifists deeply suspicious of the left, including the Labour Party. Initially, in the wake of Hitler's rise to power, the temptation for the British peace movement was to underplay that menace and concentrate on saving their own souls – becoming isolationist war-refuseniks in all circumstances. But then came the pressure to attempt a collective international effort to build armed alliances that would both contain fascism *and* prevent a Second World War. But ought that 'common front' to include Stalin's Russia? And did the Germans have some valid post-Versailles Treaty grievances which should be appeased? **Ponsonby** was an appeaser, and **Fenner Brockway** wanted to send arms to Republican Spain. And what about the goal of *dis*armament? Was the way ahead through multilateral agreement **(Noel-Baker)** or through unilateral 'disarmament by example' (**Ponsonby**)?

A few pacifists like **Norman Angell**, **Fenner Brockway** and **Maude Royden**, not to mention the philosopher **Bertrand Russell** and the novelist **Virginia Woolf,** when faced by Hitler's invasion of non-fascist Europe, eventually felt compelled to renounce their pacifism. But most British pacifists continued to be conscientious objectors to war as late as 1940. Was it ridiculous of the Gestapo to worry about British pacifists as anti-Nazi resisters? They might not have presented any overt opposition but they would most certainly have secretly obstructed many Nazi occupation measures, for instance by hiding political dissidents and Jews.

Dissidents are by nature driven by their own individual thinking and conscience; hence they are also bound to differ, one from the other. But the fact that British pacifists so desperately ran hither and yon in the late 1930s as they chased the chimera of an anti-fascist victory without a war, reveals the real hopelessness of their situation. They were faced by a dictator with whom it was impossible to reason and to whose sick, damaged psyche it was impossible to make a moral appeal. What were they to do, up against this deranged, racist megalomaniac intent on world dictatorship, who was followed at that particular historical moment by almost an entire people, so bitter at their defeat in 1918, and so convinced by Hitler's populist, lying oratory that they believed, irrationally, that they now had a Führer who would give them prosperity, world power *and* peace?

E. M. Forster's disheartened conclusion in 1939 was that for a very long time it had been too late to prevent the Second World War. The rise of Nazism itself should have been prevented, for it could not be 'contained', and once Hitler had insisted on having his war, 'we must become Fascist to win'.[18] However, after that competition in savagery had at last been won by the anti-fascist armies, it was time to listen to the voices of the pacifists once more. Hence **Victor Gollancz**'s 'Save Europe Now' movement fed the defeated Germans rather than starved them through an Allied blockade – as had been done in 1919. **Adelaide Livingstone**, **Philip Noel-Baker** and **Professor Alfred Zimmern** were given new roles in support of a United Nations that avoided some of the mistakes of the League of Nations, and their thinking helped in the formulation of the Universal Declaration of Human Rights. **Sydney Pascall**'s ideas for the cultural and psychological prevention of war through UNESCO would be fleshed out and **Noel-Baker's** argument for agreed multilateral disarmament could at least be put on the table. **Vera Brittain**, **Fenner Brockway** and **Philip Noel-Baker** used their freedom to spell out to their own side, the victors against fascism, just what it was that they had now given humanity – a potential world-destroyer in the atomic bomb. They begged Britain – and the world – to see the necessity for nuclear disarmament before it was too late.

5

Refugee Rescuers

Say this city has ten million souls
Some are living in mansions, some are living in holes:
Yet there's no place for us, my dear, yet there's no place for us ...
Came to a public meeting; the speaker got up and said:
'If we let them in, they will steal our daily bread';
Thought I heard the thunder rumbling in the sky;
It was Hitler over Europe, saying: 'They must die'...
Saw a poodle in a jacket fastened with a pin,
Saw a door opened and a cat let in:
But they weren't German Jews, my dear, but they weren't
German Jews.

W. H. Auden, *Twelve Songs*

If the Nazis disliked and despised pacifists, they abominated refugee rescuers. 'Assisting refugees is often interpreted by refugee-producing countries as a hostile act.'[1] For were not such people supporters of those unfit to live in the Reich, whom their foreign champions insisted on calling 'victims of Fascism'? On the other hand, helping thousands of such refugees was also unpopular in Britain, both with the government and with an electorate that dreaded the prospect of more unemployment. But many of the British pacifists and socialists who were failing to save the world either from war or from fascism after 1933 felt all the more compelled to try to save at least some of the desperate individual victims now being driven out of Germany, Austria, Spain, Czechoslovakia and Poland. One such pacifist who became a refugee rescuer was **Norman Angell** who wrote *You and the Refugee*, as a Penguin Special in 1939 with Dorothy Buxton.

There were many others working for the British emergency organisations offering help in the refugee crisis before September 1939, the names and addresses of which are interspersed, like those of the many peace movement groups, in the alphabeticised second part of the *Sonderfahndungsliste GB*, under *'Vereinigungen'*– ('Associations'). The Gestapo could thereby kill two birds with one stone. Not only could they weed out some of the most determinedly active *English* anti-Nazis but they could also discover, when arresting them and searching their headquarters, the lists of the names and addresses of German, Austrian, Czech and other anti-Nazi refugees now living in Britain, the so-called *'Emigranten'*.

Refugee-supporting organisations included **the Austrian Centre, the Catholic Committee for Refugees from Germany and Friends' Service Council.** (See Appendix 4 for the whole list.) From the duplication of their references to **Friends of [New] Europe, Friends' House, Friends' Service Council, Quaeker** [sic] **Union, Society of Friends**, etc. it is clear that the Gestapo recognised the very significant, if sometimes confusing, role played by British Quakers in the rescue of refugees driven out of Germany. 'There were [only] 20,000 Quakers in Britain in the 1930s [but] at least that number of refugees from fascism would not have been able to get into Britain without Quaker support.'[2]

Quaker support included not just the initial financial sponsorship of £50 (£2,500 in today's money) per head, but often hospitality in their own homes, domestic employment vouchers and free educational placements in Quaker schools, as well as business loans. The *Kindertransport* of 10,000 children, for example, could not have happened without the Quakers. Three out of the five-strong deputation that successfully lobbied the Home Secretary in November 1938 were Quakers.

The first trainload of children set off from Berlin just three weeks after *Kristallnacht*, on 1 December. But the British government merely *permitted*, they did not finance, the temporary emergency entry of these 'non-Aryan' children, including children from secular, socialist and pacifist families, from Germany, Austria and Czechoslovakia, from December 1938 to September 1939. All the essential organising and financing had to be voluntary, and much of it was Quaker.[3]

Whom would the Gestapo have found working for German and Austrian Jewish refugees at the Friends' various listed London offices? Quaker work with refugees in the 1930s was guided, organised and led by three women – Bertha Bracey, Edith Pye and **Dr Hilda Clark** who all had impressive records in practical international relief work and in international policy-making.[4] The redoubtable Bertha Bracey (1893–1989), secretary of the **German Emergency Committee** (later **the Friends Committee for Refugees and Aliens**) was the Quaker director of almost *all* Quaker humanitarian projects to do with refugees. In December 1938, after *Kristallnacht*, she had been part of the delegation of five that had persuaded the Home Secretary, Sir Samuel Hoare, to allow the '*Kindertransport*' trains to come to Britain. (The other two Quakers were Graham Greene's cousin Ben Greene and the MP **Philip Noel-Baker**.) Bertha Bracey's motives were passionately political as well as humanitarian – she could not bear 'the poison of fascism'. She would most certainly have been arrested in 1940 doing her daily work either at **Friends' House** or at Bloomsbury House, the HQ of the **Refugee Children's Movement**. In August 1945 she masterminded the airlifting – in the stripped-out bomb racks of ten British bombers – of the 732 child survivors from Theresienstadt concentration camp to Windermere in Cumbria,[5] and after the war she became a consultant for UNRRA.

As early as 1933, the Quaker Edith Pye (1876–1975) had co-founded **The German Emergency Committee for assisting Jewish and anti-Nazi refugees** from her base in **Friends' House.** The president of the British Midwives' Institute, a brilliant organiser and worldwide expert on the welfare of mothers and children, she became a veteran refugee rescuer. During the Spanish Civil War she had set up the Geneva office for the assistance and feeding of tens of thousands of child refugees from Spain. After Franco's victory she worked in France from January 1939 to June 1940, struggling to accommodate more than 100,000 defeated Spanish Republicans who had fled across the border. Now that she was back in London, after escaping on the last boat from Bordeaux before the fall of France, she served from July 1940 as one of the lynchpins of the **Friends Executive Committee for Refugees and Aliens** in London. She too would certainly have been picked up by the SS at the **Friends' House** in Euston Road, in September 1940. In 1944 she followed the British tanks back into France, organising bulk food supplies for malnourished children first in Normandy and then in Paris, after which, at the age of nearly 70, she organised relief operations in starving Greece.[6]

The only individually named Quaker refugee rescuer on the Black Book list besides **William Ravenscroft Hughes**, was **Dr Hilda Clark** (1884–1955), Edith Pye's lifelong companion. Edith Pye would write to her from the refugee camps, letting her know whom she was trying to reach at the Foreign Office in order to secure more funding. **Clark** would then back her with judicious lobbying in London. Having helped pregnant French refugee women in the First World War by setting up, together with Edith Pye, a successful emergency maternity hospital near the fighting lines under the auspices of the Friends' War Victims' Relief Committee, **Clark** went on, again with Edith Pye, to tackle child starvation in post-war Vienna; after which she dealt with the hunger and dysentery among the displaced in post-war Poland. Subsequently she went on to call for international government assistance for the million Greek refugee women and children 'transferred' from Turkey after 1923. From 1936 on she had helped Edith Pye on the **International Committee for the Assistance of Child Refugees**, beginning with the child refugees arriving from Spain. In September 1938 she went back to Vienna, this time to help to organise the exodus from the city now under Nazi control – from where she wrote to Edith Pye: 'Clearly no Jew is safe.'[7] The summer of 1940 saw **Clark** back in London serving on the **Friends' Refugees and Aliens Committee.** The Gestapo had probably earmarked her ever since she had returned to Vienna following the *Anschluss* and had helped Jews. '**Dr Hilda Clark** and Edith Pye had the right attitude to the people they were helping – respect, sympathy and unsentimental affection, and they were – as far as is possible in human beings – quite selfless in their attitude to their work ... They were pure in motive and quite incorruptible.'[8]

Among the leading Christian, but not Quaker, refugee rescuers in Britain, the **Rev. Henry Carter**, CBE (1875–1951), pacifist and temperance campaigner, stands out. A Methodist minister for fifty years, he was an ardent pacifist who pioneered the Methodist Refugee Fund and thereby earned Gestapo condemnation. Described as having 'the biggest mouth in Methodism, his blend of passion and logic was utterly compelling'. In 1950 he would become a patron of the Pestalozzi Children's Village Association.[9]

The youngest Briton mentioned by name in the Black Book was **Alec Dickson,** born in 1914. A budding journalist in 1937, he was sent to Czechoslovakia as foreign correspondent for the *Daily Telegraph*. But when the Germans invaded first the Sudetenland and then the rest of Czechoslovakia, **Dickson** threw up his job in order to work in Prague for the socialist Sudeten German refugees as well as for the threatened Czech and German Jews trying to escape to Britain. The Gestapo would have noted his activities there, where he remained until spring 1939, and then tracked him to London where he began working for the British **Committee for Refugees from Czechoslovakia.** In the event it was a very good thing that **Alec Dickson** did survive the war for, together with his wife Mora, he would go on to found both Voluntary Service Overseas (VSO) – the inspiration for America's Peace Corps – and Community Service Volunteers (CSV). The *Guardian*'s 2002 obituary for Mora remarked, '[Much] of the current thinking in citizenship and social responsibility, both in Britain and internationally, stems from their work.'[10]

Before one can become a refugee living in another country, one has to have a visa. **Captain Frank Foley** (1884–1958), passport officer in Berlin, used every possible means, legal and not quite legal, to issue thousands of British visas between 1938 and 1939. Small, bespectacled, unassuming-looking, in his mid fifties, **Foley** worked fifteen hours a day in the British embassy, trying to deal with the needs of the hundreds of desperate Berlin Jews queueing seemingly endlessly outside. He would go out to see them, apologise for their long wait, take them cups of tea and eventually produce the necessary (often forged) documents enabling them to go to Britain or Palestine. He took a few endangered Jews into his own home; and went to rescue others in concentration camps, bringing them the vital visa.

A mere passport officer, he was not protected by diplomatic immunity, and neither was he obeying the immigration regulations of his own Foreign Office. Perhaps the British government had to turn a blind eye to **Frank Foley**'s refugee rescue activity. given that he was also the most useful secret agent they had in Germany. For it was **Foley** who persuaded leading German scientists *not* to reveal to one another essential information for the Reich's atomic weapons project.[11]

Why did **Foley** take such risks and work so tirelessly to get people out of Germany in time? '[The] basic fact was – he was a *Mensch* … **Foley** was a real Christian for whom help to others was the first commandment … he wanted to prove how little the "Christians" governing Germany had to do with real Christianity.'[12] Foley's nephew agreed: '**Foley** did what he did as a witness to the Christian churches to show what they should have done at that time but did not do.' Posthumously, **Foley** was honoured as one of the Righteous Among the Nations at Yad Vashem and as a British Hero of the Holocaust.

Similarly, **Robert Smallbones**, and his deputy **Arthur Dowden**, both working in the British consul office in Frankfurt and both listed by name in the Black Book, rescued thousands of Jewish would-be refugees by issuing them with temporary visas to enable them to enter the British Protectorate of Palestine, if not Britain itself. **Smallbones** successfully stood up to the Gestapo officers' attempts at intimidation and shouted back at them. After *Kristallnacht*, his deputy **Arthur Dowden** drove round Frankfurt with food for the Jews who were forbidden to buy groceries. When asked in old age why he had gone out of his way to help so many unwanted, persecuted people, **Smallbones** said: 'I was just trying to be a good Scout.'[13]

The MP associated above all others with the ever-unpopular cause of admitting refugees into Britain was Blacklisted **Eleanor Rathbone** (1872–1946), Independent MP for the Combined Northern Universities:

> Benign and yet menacing, she would stalk through the [Commons] lobby, one arm weighed with the heavy satchel

> which contained the papers on family allowances, another arm dragging an even heavier satchel in which were stored the more recent papers about refugees and displaced persons; recalcitrant Ministers would quail before the fire of her magnificent eyes.[14]

It would take a whole book to do justice to **Rathbone**'s championing of the refugees from fascism, and that book has been written: *Rescue the Perishing: Eleanor Rathbone and the Refugees*, by Susan Cohen (2010). Here it is only possible to attempt the briefest summary. Alert to the menace of Hitler from the start, **Rathbone** immediately took up the cause of his political and racial victims within Germany. She also became active on the National Joint Committee for Spanish Relief and on the Basque Children's Committee in 1937. In 1938 and 1939 she pressed the government time and again in the House of Commons to assist the evacuation of political and racial refugees from Spain, Austria, the Sudetenland and Czechoslovakia. 'More and more … of her insistent Parliamentary questions concerned their finances, their passports, their immigration conditions, their visas.'[15]

> [Never] have I dwelt in such a Heartbreak House as the Refugee Problem. It is just as though one stood hour after hour, day after day, with a small group of people outside bars behind which hordes of men and women and children were enduring every kind of deliberately inflicted physical and mental torture. We scrape at the bars with little files. A few victims are dragged painfully one by one through gaps. And all the time we are conscious that streams of people are passing behind us unaware of or indifferent to what is happening …[16]

In 1940 **Rathbone** went to Huyton, the British internment camp for 'enemy aliens', and told the anti-Nazi refugees as she stood in the rain with them: 'You have not been forgotten.' Then she went back to the Home Office, armed with the necessary lists of names and anti-Nazi credentials, to secure their release. But when, in December 1942, she asked to give a talk on the BBC about the genocide then being perpetrated against European Jews, the director general said: 'She must be refused.'[17]

An anti-fascist humanitarian to her core, at the end of 1945 **Rathbone** was working for the Poles against Stalin, for the Greek communists against the monarchists and with **Victor Gollancz** to feed the starving Germans and thus 'Save Europe Now'. Like **Gollancz**, she refused to condemn *all* Germans after 1945, reminding the British instead of martyred German anti-Nazi resisters like Hans and Sophie Scholl, and challenging her compatriots with the question: 'Ask yourselves what you would have done had you been German.' Aged 73 she collapsed and died from exhaustion – it was world news.

The last British refugee rescuer named in the Black Book, **Doreen Warriner** (1904–1972), was a dynamic young lecturer in economics at University College London when, in October 1938, she threw up her prestigious travelling Rockefeller Fellowship and flew to Prague instead. 'I had no idea at all of what to do, only a desperate wish to do something.' Her desperation arose from the recent British complicity in the annexation of the Sudetenland by Hitler – **Chamberlain**'s Munich Agreement. **Warriner** was mainly concerned with political refugees, especially the tens of thousands of socialist anti-Nazis from the Sudetenland with their families, now seeking refuge in a Prague that did not want them. (After all, were they not Germans and Reds?) From the end of November 1938, she was responsible for administering the ***News Chronicle*** British Committee Refugee Relief Fund for all the different anti-Nazis now stranded in Prague – Zionists, German and Austrian Socialists, Sudeten Liberals, Social Democrats and Communists. She spelled out in the *Daily Telegraph* that it was not blankets or chocolate that was urgently needed but British visas. The Lord Mayor's Relief Fund tried to have her sacked from the ***News Chronicle*** committee.

Like **William Hughes**, **Alec Dickson** and **Frank Foley**, **Doreen Warriner** was an exemplar of heroic humanitarianism. She personally – and illegally – risked taking hundreds of refugee Sudetenland women and children across the German frontier and into Poland on their way to rejoin their socialist menfolk in Britain before emigration to Canada. It was a race against time, given the Nazis' imminent attack on the rest of Czechoslovakia in March 1939, and **Warriner** worked morning and night, fabricating false passports, feeding and sheltering the last desperate ones left behind and undergoing Gestapo accusations of protecting 'Communist *Dreck*' – ['rubbish']. She left Prague only in April 1939 on one of the last refugee trains into Poland, having received warnings that she was next in line for arrest. The papers of the **Czech Refugees' Trust Fund** and the **British Committee for Refugees from Czechoslovakia**, both named with their London addresses in Part Two of the Black Book, would have revealed all **Warriner**'s allies at the British end – including Nicholas Winton and Trevor Chadwick.[18] **Warriner** survived to serve as chief of UNRRA's food mission to Yugoslavia from 1944 to 1946, after which she worked on land reform in underdeveloped countries, reporting to the UN in 1954.

For the tireless, too little supported, efforts of the **Bishop of Chichester**, **George Bell**, to get the Church of England and the British government to rescue 'non-Aryan', i.e. Jewish, German Christians, including pastors and their families, see chapter 14, ' The Church'.

Naturally, many British Jews, whether Orthodox, Liberal or freethinking, also felt impelled to do all that they could to help endangered German and Austrian Jews escape to a new life in Britain – either by collective fundraising, personal sponsorship and/or taking refugees into their own family homes. Equally naturally, the Gestapo Blacklisted all the leading Jewish names associated with such efforts, as well as the addresses of the various Jewish refugee rescue organisations, both in Part Two of the Black Book and in the *Informationsheft GB's 'Emigrantenorganisationen'*.

Among the 'Most Wanted' individual Jewish refugee rescuers listed by name was **Norman Bentwich** (1883–1971), barrister, champion of Liberal Judaism, and an idealistic Zionist who wanted a peaceful, two nation solution in Palestine – where, as Attorney General for Palestine, he had been shot at by Arabs for being pro-Jewish and shouted down by Jews for being pro-Arab. A distinguished academic, eventually professor of international relations at the Hebrew University of Jerusalem and a former British public servant, **Bentwich**, on Hitler's coming to power, immediately became one of the foremost fighters for the rescue of Jews in danger. He travelled widely to plead with governments to increase their migration quotas and to investigate possible places of refuge, becoming director of the League of Nations High Commission for Refugees from Germany from 1933 to 1935, and of the Council for German Jews. He was indefatigable in his commitment to 'help the perishing' and proudly recorded the amazing intellectual contribution made by continental Jews to Britain after 1933 in *They Found Refuge: An account of British Jewry's work for victims of Nazi oppression* (1956).

The leading Jewish ally of **Bentwich** in Britain was the Frankfurt-born British banker and stockbroker **Otto Schiff**, CBE (1875–1952), 'An outstanding figure in every enterprise on behalf of the refugees'.[19] **Otto Schiff** had first worked on behalf of Jewish refugees already in Britain in 1914 after the German invasion of Belgium. It was then that **Schiff** became known to the Home Office as a dependable authority on 'aliens', a position he consolidated when president of the Jews' Temporary Shelter from 1922, providing short-term accommodation for immigrants and ensuring observance of UK immigration controls. In March 1933 **Schiff** was ready to help establish the **Jewish Refugees Committee** as a subsidiary of the **Central British Fund for German Jewry**, liaising with the Home Office on funding, re-training, employment and possible re-emigration for Jews fleeing Hitler. By September 1939, 80 per cent of all the refugees in Britain had registered with the **Jewish Refugees Committee**, chaired by **Schiff**. His personal intervention supported 'the admission of innumerable immigrants whose case he made his own'.[20]

After *Kristallnacht*, the attention of refugee rescuers focused on the project of taking in thousands of unaccompanied German and Austrian Jewish children (the British government would not contemplate taking in their parents as well, and the US government did not accept child migrants without parents). The ensuing *Kindertransport* was a model of constructive cooperation between Quakers and Jews, with help from some church and refugee organisations and individuals.

The Jewish, but not exclusively Jewish '***Inter-Aid Committee for children from Germany***' is listed in the *Informationsheft* in 1940, but there is of course no explanation as to why these Jewish German children were in need of immediate rescue. Predictably, it was women who took on most responsibility for saving the 'parentless' children.[21] The Black Book lists two Jewish women child-rescuers for immediate arrest. **Eva Violet Mond Isaacs, 2nd Marchioness of Reading** (1895–1973), was chairwoman of the aftercare section of the **Refugee Children's Movement** (RCM) and came into the Bloomsbury House HQ almost every day. She felt all too sure that the children faced a hard future, so she encouraged them to be tough and independent, while tempering her realism with personal generosity.[22] The second Jewish woman targeted by the Gestapo was the British Zionist and humanitarian **Rebecca ('Becky') Sieff** (1890–1966), whose concerns for Hitler's victims, according to Jennie Lee's tribute in *Jewish Woman's Review*, February 1966, included not only Jews but 'liberals, socialists, trade unionists and Christian dissenters'. She set up a committee to work with the **Central British Fund for German Jewry**, especially for women and child refugees, and she personally facilitated the escape of a thousand Jewish children from Germany to Palestine via *Youth Aliyah*.

Other leading Jewish women child-rescuers who would assuredly have been picked up as daily volunteers at the Bloomsbury House HQ for refugee Jewish children were Elaine Laski, wife of Blacklisted **Neville Laski,** Lola Hahn Warburg, wife of the Blacklisted publisher **Simon Warburg** and Helen Bentwich, LCC councillor, wife of **Norman Bentwich**, all of whom served the myriad needs of the thousands of the *Kindertransport* children then trying to find their bearings in wartime Britain.[23] Their 'chief' was the **Refugee Children's Movement**'s outstanding 60-year-old general secretary, Dorothy Hardisty, always at the Blacklisted London head office of the **German Jewish Aid Committee**, at **Bloomsbury House** (originally the **Bloomsbury Palace Hotel**), keeping a file on every child.[24] She too would certainly have been picked up.

The vital non-sectarian Refugee Rescue and Relief Organisation for displaced university teachers and researchers, was the **Academic**

Assistance Council, also targeted in the Black Book under its later name, ***Society for the Protection of Science and Learning***. This organisation concentrated on rescuing and supporting the most gifted of the university lecturers, researchers and professors who had been booted out from Germany and Austria in the cause of 'racial cleansing'. 'The universities form a kingdom of their own, whose intellectual autonomy must be preserved.'[25] The Gestapo took a rather less elevated view of the attempt by British academics to offer practical solidarity – both money and employment or research openings – to their persecuted colleagues. The council's influential backers included not only the Nobel prizewinners Lord Rutherford and Professor A. V. Hill, MP for Cambridge University, but also Professor William Beveridge at LSE. However, the one person really running the show at the **Academic Assistance Council** was Esther ('Tess') Simpson (1903–1996). She became a one-woman reception centre, accommodation bureau and specialist academic re-employment exchange for around 2,600 refugee German and Austrian Jewish intellectuals between 1933 and 1940. Tess Simpson started work in 1933 and did not stop for sixty years, still helping persecuted intellectuals from all races and from all over the world. Being the only person manning the **Academic Assistance Council**'s offices at Clement's Inn, she certainly would have been arrested there after a Nazi invasion.[26]

Finally, the Gestapo were very interested in the work of the **International Student Service**, later the World University Service, which had branches in every British university and operated from its (Blacklisted) London headquarters at 49 Gordon Square. Its original purpose had been to enable British students to assist desperately needy students abroad. But the most desperate between 1933 and the 1940s were of course the 'alien' refugee Jewish students now trying to survive in Britain. The *Informationsheft GB* names the **ISS** chairmen ***Dr Tissington Tatlow*** and ***Sir Walter Moberly*** and the treasurer, **Professor Sir Ernest Barker** – whom the Gestapo had also listed in the earlier *Sonderfahndungsliste*. Once a university branch had been raided, the names and addresses of all the staff and student supporters of Jewish refugee students in Britain, plus the names and addresses of those young refugees, would have been discovered. In Manchester, for example, the leading figure who supported the **International Student Service** was the philosopher and radical thinker Dorothy Emmet.

There is no need to labour the point that all these Britons who were active in refugee rescue from 1933 to 1940, whether they were native or 'naturalised' British, were committed anti-fascists whose politics had to find an outlet in action. Like **Eleanor Rathbone**, they were driven to do whatever was in their power to help save at least some of Hitler's victims. From the Nazis' point of view, their enemy's friend was their enemy, and all would face retribution should Germany invade.

6

Social Reformers

It happens that nearly all of the social reformers named in the Black Book were women. The humane reforms they pioneered reached out to the deprived, the disabled and even to the criminally convicted. The rebellious daughter of a Chief Rabbi, **Nettie Adler**, CBE, JP (1868–1950), for example, had defied her father by insisting on living an 'unwomanly' life of public, political action – while never denying her Jewish heritage. She championed poor Jewish girls and women in the East End of London and campaigned against the use of child labour – especially in 'sweated' conditions. A pioneering woman London county councillor for many years, **Nettie Adler** battled for the needy in the East End, but her chief crime in Gestapo eyes was her 'ideological opposition' ('*Weltanschauliche Gegner*'), as a fearless Jew.

Her younger contemporary **Margery Corbett Ashby** (1882–1981) ('*Führerin der Lib. Partei*'), was also a feminist; in her case, however, she championed not only the British women's movement but also the emancipation of women throughout the world. She worked for the International Woman Suffrage Alliance for over seventy years, from its foundation in 1904 until 1976. Hers was a humanistic feminism that wanted all people, including men, to be able to fulfil themselves. In 1933 she began coordinating efforts to oppose the setback to the position of women under the new fascist governments, and in 1939 she declared, as president of the International Alliance of Women, that 'a world governed by force, brutality and fraud will find no place for women, save as breeders of men and forced labourers'. She had consistently supported the League of Nations and eventually, as a British delegate to the United Nations, she would play an important role in the UN's focus after the Second World War on the new horrific crime that the international community must now forever try to prevent or combat – genocide.[1]

Whereas **Corbett Ashby** had tried and failed seven times to become a Liberal MP, always being assigned to fight an 'impossible' constituency, **Katharine Stuart-Murray, Duchess of Atholl** (1874–1960) held a 'safe' Conservative seat. But 'The Red Duchess' turned out to be a very unusual, and finally an impossible, Conservative MP. Her first social intervention had been to investigate the lack of medical and nursing services in the Highlands and Islands. Her second was on behalf of gypsy and Scottish traveller (known at the time as 'tinker') children deprived of adequate winter housing and education. First noted by the Gestapo for her personal publication (in 1933 in English) of the most alarmingly aggressive passages in *Mein Kampf*, all of which had been omitted from the more sanitised translations, the **Duchess of Atholl** went on to earn increasing Nazi disfavour. Her fact-finding parliamentary delegation to Czechoslovakia, Yugoslavia and Romania in 1936 had enlightened her about the virulent anti-Semitism and pro-fascism already present in central and eastern Europe. As soon as the Spanish Civil War broke out, she joined **Eleanor Rathbone** MP and **Ellen Wilkinson** MP in founding an all-party Committee for Spanish relief with which she visited war-torn Spain. The duchess was in Barcelona and Madrid while those cities were being shelled and she was aghast at the plight of the Spanish children she saw. On her return to Britain she wrote the Pelican Special *Searchlight on Spain* and worked energetically – together with the Salvation Army, the Quakers, the TUC and the Save the Children Fund – to win temporary asylum in Britain for 4,000 Basque children. In April 1938 the prime minister, **Neville Chamberlain**, withdrew the Party whip from her for being too staunch an anti-appeaser, and she was de-selected from her 'safe' Conservative seat. She took in a refugee from Prague at her home at Blair Castle, and she never stopped championing the ever-growing number of 'displaced persons' after 1945 – whether from western Europe or from Stalinist eastern Europe. The **Duchess of Atholl** 'had a nerve peculiarly sensitive ... to cruelty and oppression'.[2]

The oldest woman on the *Sonderfahndungsliste* at 82, **Dame Elizabeth Cadbury** (1858–1951), mother and stepmother of ten children, was a well-known Quaker philanthropist active in the cause of disabled children. She had co-founded Birmingham's Royal Orthopaedic Hospital, built a large holiday home for children from the Birmingham slums and pushed for medical inspections in schools. Possibly the greater crime in Nazi eyes was her pacifist devotion to the war-prevention role of the **League of Nations**. (Similarly, **Dorothy, Viscountess Gladstone**, was almost certainly listed for arrest not only because of her campaigning for the welfare of the disabled, especially the blind, and for district nursing in poor districts, but also because she was a long-standing member of the executive committee of Britain's Blacklisted **League of Nations Union**.)

Although Jewish himself, the publisher **Victor Gollancz** (1893–1967) rejected the concept of German collective guilt for Nazism. It was in that spirit that in 1945 he founded the 'Save Europe Now' movement to feed starving Germans, especially German children. It was a cause that would strike some as a humanitarian step too far. Damned as 'Marxist' by the Gestapo, **Gollancz** considered himself a Christian socialist and an internationalist, who said: 'I hate everything that is pro and anti different peoples. I am only one thing: I am pro-humanity.' After the Second World War he went on to co-found both War on Want and the Campaign for Nuclear Disarmament, and he finally crusaded, this time more successfully, together with **Violet Bonham Carter** and **Sydney Silverman**, for the abolition of capital punishment in Britain.

Gollancz's great predecessor as a penal reformer, Quaker-born **Margery Fry** (1874–1958), had begun her life of humane social intervention by attempting, unsuccessfully, to abolish caning in British schools. She went on to help found the Howard League for Penal Reform. She visited British prisons, remand homes and borstals, but above all she worked to abolish capital punishment throughout the whole world, beginning with Britain. She could never forget going into the cell of the condemned murderer Edith Thompson to help her pass some of the hours before her hanging. **Margery Fry** reported to the League of Nations with her study *The Prison Population of the World*, published in 1936, although she was of course only too aware of having been refused permission to visit either the Nazi concentration camps or Stalin's Gulag. Her attempts to make the League of Nations bring about the abolition of torture and to ensure the basic civilised treatment of all prisoners – as well as her defence of civil liberty in Britain – brought her to the hostile attention of the Gestapo before 1940. Her nephew, in an unpublished memoir, remembered how she, a committed anti-fascist, co-founded **For Intellectual Freedom** in 1938. **Margery Fry** did not live to see the abolition of capital punishment in Britain but she did see the success of her campaigns for legal aid for the poor, medical diagnosis and treatment for mentally ill prisoners, and education as well as work programmes to facilitate rehabilitation.[3]

Fired by an almost sacred indignation at any brutal injustice perpetrated by the state, the libertarian **Ronald Kidd** (1889–1942), founded the **National Council for Civil Liberties** in 1934. Having first witnessed the use of police *agents provocateurs* in 1932 in instigating violence and then arresting some of the hunger marchers, **Kidd** had gone on to publicise and campaign against all police harassment of demonstrators and strikers. He later excoriated police partisanship in tolerating the Mosleyites' violence against East End Jews. Beginning in a tiny, barely accessible room, by 1940 the **NCCL** had become a significant, influential British national organisation with 4,000 members. **Kidd** believed in the indivisibility of freedom for every individual and group, even in war time, and he fought against many of the new emergency 'security laws', including the banning of the ***Daily Worker*** and the BBC's attempt to censor broadcasts. Above all, **Ronald Kidd** campaigned against imprisonment without trial, right up to his own premature death from exhaustion. 'The public side of him ... the side that serves humanity, was superbly developed', wrote **E. M. Forster**, who concluded his funeral eulogy for **Kidd** with the exhortation 'May we continue the fight that is never done!'[4]

The ardent young anti-fascist **Margaret Dorothea Layton** (1911–1962), was the eldest daughter of **Sir Walter Layton**, the editorial director of the ***News Chronicle***. She had worked to help endangered Jews in Austria, even hiding one, the Reuters journalist Albert Greisinger (whom she later married), in the boot of her car as she drove both of them out to safety. The Gestapo condemned her for being a 'follower of the Harand movement'. Irene Harand (1900–1975) was a Catholic human rights activist in Vienna who in 1933 had founded her 'World Movement against Racial Hatred and Human Suffering', later known as the Harand Movement. She took on Hitler himself in 1935, publishing at her own expense *Sein Kampf, an Answer to Hitler from Irene Harand*, which was publicly burned in Salzburg in 1938. A large price was put on her head. Harand escaped first to the United States, where she founded a women's Anti-Nazi League, before starting the Free Austria Movement in London in 1941. She would later be numbered 'one of the Righteous Among the Nations' at Yad Vashem for her fearless stand against anti-Semitism. The nearest that the Gestapo could get to capturing her was to plan to arrest young **Margaret Layton.**

The child of Salvation Army officers, **Leah Manning** (1886–1977) was a reforming activist on many fronts. An ardent Christian Socialist, she had as a young teacher in the 1920s campaigned for free school milk, opened after-school play centres, and headed the first open-air school for undernourished children. A **Fabian** socialist, member of the **ILP** and briefly a left-wing Labour MP, as well as the assistant education officer on the NUT, **Leah Manning** became an outspoken anti-appeasement anti-fascist in the 1930s. In 1934 she supported the communist-backed 'Co-ordinating Committee for Anti-Fascist Activities'. She organised medical supplies for Spain and supported the evacuation of the Basque children to Britain during the Spanish Civil War. As a Labour MP after 1945 she campaigned for women's access to birth control and for their access to analgaesia in childbirth. **Leah Manning** was called '*Politikerin*' by the Gestapo in 1939, but 'her political outlook rested on warm humanitarian commitment rather than a theoretical position'.[5]

It should be noted here that **Eleanor Rathbone**, in addition to being the British MP most committed to refugee rescue, was also Britain's outstanding humanitarian reformer-in-general before 1940. In the 1920s she had campaigned successfully for British women to have equal rights as guardians of their children; she had lobbied for maintenance orders for deserted wives, for divorce law reform and for better widows' pensions – as well as for free milk for the children of the unemployed. In the 1930s she had campaigned against child marriage – with its attendant premature deaths in childbirth – in British India. And for the whole of her national political life she campaigned for a 'Family Allowance' to be paid to the mother, giving all women in the home at least the beginning of economic independence as some acknowledgement of their unpaid daily labour.

Ernest Thurtle (1884–1954) was the Blacklisted author of *Shot at Dawn*, published in 1930, a polemical work on behalf of the three hundred British soldiers executed by firing squad in the First World War. The men had been shot for 'cowardice or desertion', although in fact they had almost certainly been suffering from 'shell shock' or post-traumatic stress. In 1930, as Labour MP for Shoreditch, **Turtle** managed to get the death penalty abolished in the British Army. Presumably the Gestapo did not approve of such a precedent for their *Wehrmacht*, which threatened death for any German soldier who did not obey orders. At least 30,000 German soldiers were sentenced to death in the Second World War.[6]

Finally, the very independent-minded Catholic 'equality feminist', **Monica Whately** (1889–1960), was yet another of those women who felt impelled, after suffrage had been won in Britain, to intervene on behalf of desperate others. She had worked for famine relief through the Save the Children Fund in central and eastern Europe in the 1920s. She then set herself to become an intrepid battler against fascism, using the power both of words and of collective intervention. Indicted as a *Schriftstellerin* (woman writer), by the Gestapo, her impassioned, self-published pamphlet *Women Behind Nazi Bars* (1938), alerted readers to the Nazi practice of imprisoning German women as hostages for their communist or socialist husbands. She directed what was almost a one-woman **British Movement against War and Fascism** from her own home on Endell Street, championing civil liberty, democracy and the **League of Nations Union**, and working with Jewish activists for a boycott of German goods. She stood successfully against Oswald Mosley, winning the London County Council ward of Limehouse – despite the constant disruption of her election meetings by his fascist followers. It is hardly surprising that she won a place on the Gestapo's 'Most Wanted' list. **Whately** would go on to work after 1945 for colonial liberation, including Indian independence, and later for the struggle against apartheid.[7]

What all these Blacklisted humanitarian reformers had in common, whatever their political or religious affiliation or their chosen field of action – medicine, the disabled, the mentally ill, the struggle against war, the rescue of refugees or the needs of the imprisoned – was their 'skin too few'. Each of them felt compelled to act for suffering, friendless others, and they were all judged unfit for a Nazi Britain that would practise '*Haerte*' on principle. The Gestapo were not 'obeying orders' in singling out these British heroes of humanity for immediate arrest in 1940. What motivated them was the urgent need to identify leading, publicly declared British anti-Nazis. That these particular anti-Nazis had, in their turn, been motivated by revulsion against Nazi inhumanity was irrelevant.

PART THREE

GUNNING FOR THE CULTURED

7

Some 'Degenerate Artists'

The compilers of the Great Britain 'Most Wanted' list had a very simple test for the artists to be arrested. What were their politics? Were they opponents of Nazism? Very few British artists were on the Gestapo's radar as individuals. But the compilers of the Black Book *were* aware of the activism of the **Artists' International Association**, (**'*Kuenstlerinternationale, British Sektion*'**) as an allegedly 'communist/ Marxist' group. It was Blacklisted under '*Vereinigungen*' in the *Sonderfahndungsliste GB*; Blacklisted **Aldous Huxley** had written the foreword to the association's catalogue for its 1935 exhibition 'Artists against Fascism and War'. And the Gestapo also Blacklisted the **Artists' Peace Campaign** at 10 Golden Square, and the **International Society for Contemporary [Art]** at 18 Great Marlborough Street. The SS would have raided all these groups' correspondence with British artists in order to glean more political targets for arrest. It has already been seen that in the *Informationsheft* section 'Important Museums', the Gestapo had Blacklisted the **New Burlington Gallery** for their 'anti-German' exhibition of 'degenerate [German] art' in 1938 and had noted with disfavour the **National Gallery**'s inclusion of 'a row of Jews' among their 4,000 portraits.

It would also not have escaped the Gestapo's notice that in June 1937 the Blacklisted **National Joint Committee for Spanish Relief** had mounted a huge 'Grand International' Rally in the Albert Hall, chaired by the **Duchess of Atholl** in aid of Basque refugee children, and that among the listed supporters on the published programme were the British artists Vanessa Bell, **Jacob Epstein**, Duncan Grant, Barbara Hepworth, Henry Moore and Paul Nash – not to mention the cartoonist **David Low**. Nor that in October 1938, the **New Burlington Gallery** had mounted Picasso's 'Guernica' exhibition, the profits going again to the **National Joint Committee for Spanish Relief**. The two exhibitions' organisers included the anti-fascist **Wilfrid Roberts** MP and the **Earl of Listowel**, and their patron supporters also included the Blacklisted **Gerald Barry, J. D. Bernal, Professor P. M. S. Blackett, Fenner Brockway, Lord Robert Cecil, Chalmers Mitchell, E. M. Forster, Victor Gollancz, Professor Julian Huxley, Rose Macaulay, Naomi Mitchison, H. W. Nevinson, Hon. Harold Nicolson, Philip Noel-Baker, Harry Pollitt, D. N. Pritt, Eleanor Rathbone, Stephen Spender, Dame Sybil Thorndike, Professor Trend, H. G. Wells, Rebecca West** and **Virginia Woolf**.[1]

Blacklisted British Artists

Born in New York, the sculptor **Jacob Epstein** (1880–1959) had moved to London in 1905 and became a British citizen in 1910. He was listed by Amt RSHA 11B2, the branch of the Gestapo concerned with 'ideological opponents in general, including Jews, Marxists, Liberals etc.'. **Epstein** was anathema to the Nazis, as a Jew, as a 'primitivist' artist and as an opponent of fascism. His work was subjected to much popular and critical hostility in Britain in the 1920s and 1930s, for its 'ugly', naked explicitness. Deeply influenced by non-European, African and Oceanic sculpture, **Epstein** 'took the brickbats for modern art', according to Henry Moore, and it was only after the Second World War that he would be generally recognised as a great sculptor and a pioneer of modernism. As well as supporting the **Artists' International Association** on behalf of Republican Spain in the late 1930s, **Epstein** also 'acted as spokesperson for the London Group in urging artists to refuse cooperation with a Nazi attempt to organize an exhibition of British art *excluding Jewish artists* in Berlin in 1937'.[2]

The sculptor and journalist **Clare Sheridan** (1883–1970) was listed, surprisingly, as a *Schriftstellerin* or 'writer'. Charismatic, artistically gifted, a free-loving stormy petrel in the 1920s and 1930s,

Sheridan had been battered by the deaths of husband, child and lover in the First World War. Initially enthusiastic about the promise of the Russian Revolution, she travelled to the Soviet Union in 1920 where she sculpted busts of Lenin, Trotsky and Kamenev, becoming briefly the mistress of the latter two political leaders. Her alleged 'communism' and notorious promiscuity led to an MI5 file and to her social ostracism by the British Establishment. Soon disillusioned by events in the Soviet Union and hurt by her isolation in Britain, **Sheridan** left for New York, becoming a roving European reporter for American papers, sending dispatches from the Irish civil war, war-stricken Greece, Ataturk's Turkey and Mussolini's Italy. Her real passion, however, was still for portrait sculpture (influenced by **Epstein**) and for wood-carving (influenced by Native American Indians). Her inclusion in the Black Book may be due less to her early left-wing political and personal involvement with the Soviet Union, than to her being the first cousin of **Winston Churchill** and hence valuable as a hostage.[3]

Refugee Artists

Just how thorough the Gestapo attempted to be is seen in their inclusion in the Black Book of the little-known Jewish watercolour painter of landscapes, harbour scenes and portraits, **Eduard Arnthal** (1893–1950). After studying in Weimar and Munich, Arnthal settled and exhibited in Munich in the 1920s, going into exile after 1933. Twelve of his paintings and drawings were later seized as 'Degenerate Art' and destroyed in Germany.[4]

The Austrian sculptor and left-wing political caricaturist **Siegfried Charoux** (1896–1967), '*Bildhauer [sculptor] Emigrant*', was listed under Amt RSHA IV A1, 111A – the Gestapo section combating communist or Marxist views. His wife **Margarethe Charoux** was also listed, in her case as '*Reisende*' ('traveller'). **Charoux** left Vienna for London on political grounds in 1935. He had completed busts of Lenin and the Italian anti-fascist martyr Mateotti and he had just unveiled his memorial in Vienna's *Judenplatz* to the eighteenth-century writer

Gottfried Lessing, the great proponent of Enlightenment tolerance. The Nazis would duly demolish it and melt it down after 1938. 'England freed him as an artist and as a human being ... without fear of political persecution.'[5] He said his style changed 'completely from his distorted Austrian to a more free and tranquil one'.[6] Nevertheless, **Charoux** was still interned briefly on the Isle of Man as an 'enemy alien' in 1940. He became a British citizen only in 1946 and went on to become an associate of the Royal Academy, contributing a monumental group, 'The Islanders', for the Festival of Britain in 1951. His best-known works are probably his bronze bust of Stafford Cripps; *The Motor Cyclist*, outside the Shell Building in London; and *Civilisation – The Judge* outside the London Law Courts.

A more anguished, haunted figure was **John Heartfield** (1891–1968), who had anglicised his name from Helmut Herzfeld in 1917 as a protest against the anti-British hysteria then rife in Germany. He was labelled '*Karikaturist*' and listed under Amt RSHA V1G1, 111A5, the Gestapo section concerned with 'German cultural life'. After the First World War he had become a Communist and a Dadaist who mocked the bourgeois take on 'reality'. **Heartfield** was the pioneer of a photo-montage art that was even more clearly political than the work of **Charoux**. Already in the 1920s he had produced his first satirical political photo-montages and in 1932 he created 'Adolf the Superman', an X-ray of Hitler's spine made of gold coins below his ranting mouth. In the spring of 1933 **Heartfield** narrowly escaped arrest by the SS and fled to Czechoslovakia where he was promoted to fifth on the Nazis' Czech 'Most Wanted' list. In 1934 he montaged a swastika in the form of four bloody axes, a favourite Nazi method of execution, in order to convey what the Hitler Reich really meant by 'Blood and Iron'. In 1938 he had to leave Nazi-invaded Czechoslovakia and flee to England, where he was given long-term refuge by Diana and **Fred Uhlman** – despite his adherence to the Stalinist Communist Party line – which they did not share. Unfortunately 'there was little appetite or commercial demand for the bitingly witty anti-fascist montages that **Heartfield** had so excelled in producing.'[7] Only Stefan Lorant employed **Heartfield** on a regular basis in ***Picture Post***. On

15 October 1938, **Heartfield** showed what he thought of the prospects for world peace after the Munich Agreement in his photo-montage of elephants sporting wings.[8] Despite his brave, fiercely anti-Nazi art for nearly a quarter of a century, **Heartfield** was interned as an 'enemy alien' by the British in 1940. After the war he settled in the German Democratic Republic. There he needed the support of Bertolt Brecht, who considered him to be one of Europe's most significant artists, against the East German Communist authorities who suspected that his sojourn in Britain might have corrupted him.

The great Expressionist painter and writer **Oscar Kokoschka** (1886–1980) was indicted by the Gestapo for 'being on the committee of the **Free German League of Culture**' in refugee London. Largely self-taught in Vienna, influenced by Van Gogh and Edvard Munch, **Kokoschka**'s artistic interest was in expressing a human being's inner self. His early portraits used swirling colour and agitated, nervous brush strokes to try to portray a sitter's unquiet psyche. Seriously wounded in the First World War and a sufferer from shell shock, **Kokoschka** had soon been disillusioned by the brutal development of the Russian Revolution and in 1920 he wrote his 'Dresden Manifesto' denouncing the callousness of *all* political militancy. An anti-Nazi from the beginning, he had spoken out against its anti-Semitic and anti-humanist approach to culture and education and he had resigned from the Prussian Academy of Arts in protest against the exclusion of Käthe Kollwitz. In 1934 he fled Vienna for Prague where other expatriate and dissident Czech artists gathered round him, calling themselves the *Oskar Kokoschka Bund*.

In 1937 **Kokoschka**'s works had been removed from German museums and eight of his paintings were then displayed in the Nazis' Munich exhibition of '*Entartete Kunst*' ('Degenerate Art') in July–November 1937. His 'Self- Portrait of a Degenerate Artist', 1937, is now held in Edinburgh Art Gallery. Hitler had declared that, in the name of the German people, he forbade these modernists to represent their false observations as reality, let alone as 'Art'.

After the Munich Agreement, helped by the **British Committee for Refugees from Czechoslovakia** who also got out all the members of the *Oskar Kokoschka Bund*, **Kokoschka** fled from Prague to London at the end of 1938. Although famous in central Europe, occupying 'a position in the centre of German painting, even though exiled',[9] **Kokoschka** was almost unknown in Britain. Here too he was initially received with 'critical incomprehension'.[10] **Kokoschka** lived in London and Scotland throughout the war and produced some large anti-war paintings indicting all the powers responsible for the suffering of the Second World War. In 1942 he donated his fee for a portrait of the Soviet ambassador to Britain to the International Red Cross for aid to both the German and the Russian soldiers wounded at Stalingrad. In 1946 he became a naturalised British citizen; he was awarded the CBE in 1959 and was made an honorary doctor of Oxford University in 1963.[11]

The painter and writer **Fred Uhlman** (1901–1985) was Blacklisted by Amt RSHA V1G1, 11B5, which was concerned with 'Ideological opponents, Jews, etc.'. Like **Kokoschka**, he was indicted by the Gestapo for being 'On committee of **Free German League of Culture'**. Formerly a committed Social Democrat lawyer in Stuttgart, **Uhlman** had been warned in March 1933 that he was listed for imminent arrest. He fled to Paris, where, unable to obtain paid work and totally untrained as an artist, he nevertheless became a successful naive 'colourist' painter, selling his work privately. He then moved to Spain to live more cheaply – only to be driven out again in 1936, this time by the outbreak of the Spanish Civil War. He arrived in England, penniless and knowing no English. However, Diana Croft, the rebellious daughter of a Conservative British MP, met **Uhlman** in Spain, and she married him in November 1936 against her parents' wishes. Together they made their Hampstead home a London base for many political and artistic refugees from Nazism, including **Heartfield**.[12] Meanwhile **Uhlman** co-founded the **Free German League of Culture** which 'organised an impressive programme of lectures, exhibitions, concerts, cabaret revues and even theatrical productions.'[13] Like **Kokoschka**, **Uhlman** came to distance himself from the **Free German League**'s uncritically pro-Soviet stance. In June–July 1940, to his deep shock and dismay, he was interned as an 'enemy alien' for six months, during which time he produced grim drawings, later published under the title 'Captivity', as well as a bitter, depressed *Internment Diary*.[14] On his release he continued to paint, achieving national and eventually, post-war, international recognition.

Uhlman had a warm, vital, engaging personality despite suffering from periods of acute depression. After the war he learned that both his parents had been murdered in Theresienstadt and that his sister and her baby had also died in the Holocaust. He published his confessional, self-deprecating memoir, *The Making of an Englishman* (1960) and his poignant novella *Reunion* (1977) – later a successful film, scripted by Harold Pinter – about the loss of homeland, childhood, family and friendship that had been inflicted upon German Jews.[15]

8

Punishing the Publishers

The Nazis had the whole social fabric and culture of Britain in their sights. What they aimed to suppress above all was the dissemination of any ideas hostile to fascism, to war and to Hitler's megalomania. Therefore Britain's many publishing houses were in the front line, and the names and addresses of those thought by the Gestapo to be most hostile to Nazi Germany are scattered within the heterogeneous, alphabetical listing of the many targeted businesses in Part Two of the *Sonderfahndungsliste GB*. The publisher **Methuen**, for instance, is sandwiched between **Marconi** and **Midland Bank**.

The 1930s in Britain may have seemed in retrospect to have been, in Auden's words, 'a low dishonest decade', wilfully deluded about the 'inevitable' triumph of humanistic socialism. Nonetheless, those same years were felt by others to be a time of hugely energetic hope against hope – a period of tremendous, idealistic, collective effort both by middle-class intellectuals and by politically alert working-class men and women, all trying to prevent both the triumph of fascism *and* a Second World War. Few, if any, could bear to realise then that those two aims would prove mutually exclusive.

Not since the 'New Life Socialism' of the 1890s had the British printing presses been so busy. Two events were central to all that publishing activity – the introduction of Allen Lane's Sixpenny **Penguin**s and of **Victor Gollancz's Left Book Club.** The **Penguin**s were born in 1935, the **Left Book Club** in 1936.

But even before that date, almost as soon as Hitler had seized power, there had been a spate of British publications that expressed foreboding. Perhaps overconfident in the political effectiveness of mockery, in 1933 Arthur Barker published the first anti-Hitler comic book, *Hitler The Truffle-Eater* (updating *Struwwelpeter*). In it, Hitler is satirised as 'Adolf Head-in-Air' – a stupid, greedy, ineducably conceited boy. It was written by the distinguished Jewish civil servant Humbert Wolfe and published anonymously.

There were no laughs, however, in Edgar Mowrer's *Germany Puts the Clock Back* from **John Lane** in 1933, or in *The Brown Book of the Hitler Terror and the Burning of the Reichstag* – a searing, anonymous report put together by the 'World Committee for the Victims of German Fascism' (in fact André Simon), also in 1933. Robert Dell's *Germany Unmasked* had come out in 1934, and Dmitrov's own account of *The Reichstag Fire Trial*, published by **Gollancz**, had also appeared in 1934. G. P. Putnam and Sons had brought out the refugee Stefan Lorant's vivid account *I was Hitler's Prisoner – Leaves from a Prison Diary*, which went into four impressions between April and August 1935; it would later be reissued as one of the early Penguin Specials in 1939. (Stefan Lorant would also be the founding editor of the ground-breaking ***Picture Post***, seen by nearly half the adult population between 1939 and 1940, see pp. 154.)

Penguins combined quality, accessibility and, above all, cheapness. For the first time a British reader could buy a book for the price of ten cigarettes and pick it up at the local Boots or Woolworths or even from a slot machine – 'The Penguincubator' – on Charing Cross Road. The sheer speed of the mass production and distribution of the political Penguin Specials was phenomenal. The **Duchess of Atholl**'s *Searchlight on Spain*, for example, came hot off the press in 1938 after her fact-finding visit. And immediately after Munich, Sheila Grant Duff's *Europe and the Czechs* 'was typeset, proofread, corrected, printed and bound within ten days. 50,000 copies were packed and sent out on Friday night and by Monday morning orders were received for another 70,000.'[1]

In 1939, newly commissioned Penguin Specials included Louis Golding's *The Jewish Problem*; J. Rose's *Poland*, *Our Food Problem*, by Clark and Titmuss; Peter Thoene's *Modern German Art*, on the Nazis' destructive attack on modernism in Germany; *Why Britain is at War*, by **Harold Nicolson**; and *Science and War*, by Solly Zuckerman and **J. D. Bernal**. It was estimated that 30 million Penguins had been sold by the start of the Second World War – including popular contemporary fiction and detective novels. By September 1939, Allen Lane, 'the onlie begetter', of **Penguins**, helped by his brothers John and Richard, could fairly be regarded as the people's publisher, the *de facto* single most important figure in twentieth-century British publishing. No wonder the Gestapo and the SS would plan to close **Penguin** down – or take it over?

In parallel with Penguin Specials was the **Left Book Club**, founded in February 1936. **Victor Gollancz** realised that there was an eager market among worried left-wing readers wanting to know how they could play an effective part, as he wrote in his announcement in the ***New Statesman***, 'in the struggle *for* World Peace and *against* Fascism'. Every month a club member (motto 'Knowledge, Unity, Responsibility'),would receive a selected, 'serious' political book for 2/6d (two shillings and sixpence) as well as a free copy of *Left Book News* with announcements of local left-wing meetings and campaigning activities, including radical amateur drama productions. The **Left Book Club** books, always covered in their distinctive plain orange-red, included *World Politics 1918–1935* by **R. Palme Dutt**, *The Private Manufacture of Armaments* by **Philip Noel-Baker,** *Anti-Semitism Historically and Culturally Examined* by **Veit Valentin**, and *The Spirit and Structure of German Fascism* by the American economist Robert A. Brady with a foreword by **Harold Laski**. (In that 1937 foreword, **Laski** warns that 'the inescapable outcome of [Fascism] is war ... It is a grim outlook; and there is little on the horizon to make it less grim.') Very soon, spontaneous **Left Book Club** discussion groups sprung up – so many that one Dr John Lewis and his staff had to be appointed to support and coordinate them nationwide:

> At its height, there were over 1,200 local groups. [In addition] there were specialist groups – librarians, musicians, writers and readers, poets, film workers, teachers, doctors, lawyers, civil servants, journalists, clerical workers, accountants, commercial

> travellers, policemen, London art students, even Paddington railway workers. A distressed areas group studied and published conditions in South Wales, and the Stepney group led tours of the slums of East London.[2]

In addition there were all the pamphlets and leaflets that were distributed in their millions through the local **Left Book Club** groups: over 300,000 copies of **John Strachey**'s *Why You Should Be A Socialist*, May 1938; 2 million copies of a one-page leaflet 'The Hitler Menace', rushed out during the Munich Crisis, September 1938 and 10 million copies of a leaflet on Spain. During the twelve months preceding spring 1939, 2 million books, half a million pamphlets and 15 million leaflets had been distributed through the club. All in all, the **Left Book Club** 'was a broad socialist grassroots movement' influenced but never "owned" by communism ... [And despite] all his weaknesses and failings [**Gollancz**] was absolutely genuine in his concern for humanity'.[3] By September 1939 the **Left Book Club** had a membership of 50,000. The publisher and future broadcasting and television entrepreneur **Norman Collins** (1907–1982), was the dynamic marketing deputy chairman of **Gollancz** in the 1930s in its **Left Book Club** days. He was also then connected with the liberal, anti-fascist ***News Chronicle***. (The best-selling author of *London Belongs to Me* (1946), **Collins** later became a founding father of 'independent', i.e. commercial, television in the 1950s.) It is no wonder that the Gestapo should have targeted **Gollancz** and his committed office staff, including his daughter **Ruth Gollancz**, '*Leiterin des* ***Linksbuch-Clubs***', his secretary Sheila Hodges, and **Collins**, all at the centre of that anti-fascist readership network at **14 Henrietta Street**. What a treasure trove the Gestapo would have found by raiding and seizing the **Left Book Club** membership lists.

But there were many other London publishers whom the Gestapo also targeted, often simply condemning them with the inaccurate but lethal accusation that they were 'Marxist'. Frequently a publisher could be damned in the *Sonderfahndungsliste* for just one anti-Nazi book. Thus Arthur Barker Ltd were proscribed for their *Hitler The Truffle Eater* in 1933. Heading the other unacceptable publishers, in alphabetical order, are **Francis Aldor**, guilty of having published *Dachau the Nazi Hell* by Lawrence Wolfe and **G. R. Kaye** in 1939. (**G. R. Kaye** was also personally on the Black List as a leader of the **Union for Democratic Control of Foreign Policy**.) Next come **Allen and Unwin**, labelled 'Marxist' for publishing G. Warburg's *Six Years of Hitler: the Jews under a Nazi Regime*, also in 1939. **Stanley Unwin** is individually listed as one of the 'Most Wanted' in the Black Book, presumably because he had been instrumental in saving the Jewish art publisher of Phaidon, Bela Horowitz, in Vienna.[4]

Inexplicably, the deeply respectable and conservative **William Blackwood and Sons** are suspect for *Tales from the Tyrol*, while, more understandably, the **Bodley Head**, which had fostered the founding of **Penguin**, is labelled 'Marxist' and its director, **John Lane**, is mentioned by name. **Bonner and Co.** are indicted for having brought out *The True Germany*, while 'The British Non-Sectarian Anti-Nazi Council to Champion Human Rights' is guilty of **Monica Whately's** pamphlet *Women Behind Nazi Bars*. **John and Edward Bumpus Ltd**, **Constable**, **Hamish Hamilton**, **Jarrold Publishers**, **Martin Lawrence** and **Weekend** are all simply damned as 'Marxist'. **Jonathan Cape** is Blacklisted for having brought out Douglas Reed's *Insanity Fair*, which foretold the imminent end of Austria, and **J. M. Dent**, publisher of the great Everyman Series, is damned for having published Ernst Henri's *Hitler over Europe*, already in 1934 prophesying a Second World War.

At this point, surprisingly, **Victor Gollancz** is not mentioned as the publisher of the **Left Book Club** – which is condemned under a later, separate list of 'Associations or Societies'. He himself is only listed for immediate arrest for having published the socialist **John Strachey's** 400-page *What Are We To Do?* in 1938. **Hamish Hamilton** is condemned for having published the American journalist **John Gunther**'s best-selling 1936 report *Inside Europe*, and **William Heinemann** for Mary Dunstan's novel *Banners over Bavaria*, which had tried to be balanced and explain why so many Germans had at first believed it their patriotic duty to back National Socialism. **Hutchinson and Co.** are also guilty for having published Gregory's *Dollfuss and His Times* in 1935 and **Felstead**'s *Germany and Her Spies* in 1940, as well as the Quaker Rennie Smith's *Peace Verboten*. **Long Acre Press** is simply assumed to be left wing because they published *The People*. **Macmillan, Malik Publishing Co.** and **Massie Publishing Co.** are Blacklisted without giving any reason at all, whereas **Methuen** is condemned for the historian **Sidney Roberts'** *The House that Hitler Built* – with its overtone of the rat-ridden 'House that Jack Built' (see p. 250). **Novello Editions** are condemned as a 'Jewish (music) publishing house', as are **Shapiro, Valentine and Co. Pallas Publishing Co.** is condemned for *Europe into the Abyss*, whereas **Peace Book Co., Reuters**, and **Sidgwick and Jackson** are all Blacklisted without any further explanation. Finally, **Penguin** is indicted just for **Leo Amery** and Richard Keane's 1939 colloquium on *Germany, What Next?*; **Rich and Cowan Ltd** for Reginald Garbutt's *Germany, The Truth* (1939); and **Selwyn and Blount** for John Brown's 1935, *I Saw for Myself*.

Walter zu Christian and his Gestapo team had not managed to read quite every book critical of Hitler and Nazism published in Britain between 1933 and March 1939; nevertheless their Gestapo department RSHA IV B4, 'Combating the Opposition', had been impressively thorough. It is clear from the above roll call that neither **Penguin** nor the **Left Book Club** had a monopoly in producing books that were critical of what was happening in Nazi Germany. 'General interest' commercial publishers in Britain were also alert to the increasing concern over politics, including foreign politics, felt by the common reader in Britain after 1933. In order to silence all anti-Nazi writers in Britain, it would only be necessary to close down every such writer's publisher.

Can one be certain about what would have happened to these Blacklisted British publishing firms under Nazi occupation? The analogy with the experience of publishers in occupied France and Vichy France after 1940 is not straightforward. There were differences determined by place and time – there was a more tolerant approach in the Vichy South at first than in Paris, and before as opposed to after 1942. There was German censorship, although French publishers had also to censor themselves prior to publication. Any manifestation of anti-German feeling was banned and any Jewish presence as author or translator eliminated. It was forbidden to publish any author whose work was banned in Germany. However, some French writers, especially poets, believed that they could outwit censorship through ambiguity. And there was a new collaborationist press. A very few French writers refused to publish at all until after the Liberation.[5] The new 'Otto List' in July 1941 in France consisted of more than a thousand banned authors from all over the world, one of whom was **Virginia Woolf**, and included the French writers Aragon, Duhamel and Malraux as well as the French Jews Maurois and Proust. 'The Otto List was enforced by French police officers, who inspected booksellers' premises across the city, seizing and impounding nearly three quarters of a million books and closing down eleven of the seventy or so publishing houses they raided. Other Otto Lists followed.'[6] It is therefore more than probable that all the Blacklisted *British* publishers, with their undeniable track record in the *Sonderfahndungsliste* of having published anti-Nazi books before 1940, would also have been raided and closed down.

9

Targeting Creative Writers

As with painters and sculptors, British-born writers were selected for arrest on purely political grounds. It is possible that the number of writers is so small because the Gestapo reasoned that once they had shut down all anti-Nazi British publishers, there would be no need to hunt out every anti-fascist British writer. It is all the more significant, therefore, to note which writers were singled out for anathema from 1939 to 1940.

First there is the mysterious inclusion of **Professor Lascelles Abercrombie** (1881–1938), 'Georgian' poet and literary critic, about whom little more incriminating can be found than his support for the **Society for Cultural Relations with Russia** and the fact that his younger son Michael, a biologist, had joined the Communist Party. Admittedly, his name did head a list of supporters for the 'Grand International [fundraising] Meeting at the Albert Hall in aid of the Basque Refugee Children' in June 1937, under the auspices of **the British National Committee for Spanish Relief**.

Indeed in compiling their own 'Most Wanted' list, the Gestapo were often greatly helped by the many *British* lists of anti-fascist supporters and activists in the late 1930s. The **Committee for Spanish Relief** had been founded in December 1936 by, among others, **Wilfrid Roberts** MP and the ***Manchester Guardian*** journalist **G. T. Garratt** – in addition to the **Duchess of Atholl** and **Eleanor Rathbone**. Its three areas of concern were the care of refugees, the rescue of civilians from war zones, and medical relief. One may assume that when a name recurred sufficiently often on Spanish relief supporters' lists, the publicly declared British anti-fascist would then become a 'usual suspect' and qualify for the *Sonderfahndungsliste GB*.

The brilliant comic playwright **Noel Coward** (1899–1973) was not given to putting his name on lists, though he had been passionately and explicitly anti-fascist and anti-appeasement within his own private circle throughout the late 1930s. His later public literary commitment to the British war effort would include the plays *This Happy Breed* (1939) and *Blithe Spirit* (1941), which would boost morale by keeping 'Londoners laughing for the rest of the war',[1] and his patriotism would soon be expressed in the film *In Which We Serve* (1942). But in addition, known to almost no one but himself and the Gestapo, **Coward** had been recruited as an official – and significant – British spy, of which, more below.

There can also be no doubt as to why **E. M. Forster** (1879–1970), was anathema in Nazi eyes. In his fifties, the unassuming, hitherto retiring novelist, essayist and broadcaster 'emerged as a public figure representing the liberal conscience'.[2] **Forster**'s holy of holies was each unique, irreplaceable human being – what Alexander Herzen had called 'the irreducible monad of personality'. In the name of that irreplaceable individual, **Forster** came out of his corner fighting, and he grew into a devastating, subversive anti-fascist polemicist with a BBC audience of millions. His exhortation to question powers that be had first been memorably expressed in his 'Roger Fry: an Obituary Note' (1934) published in *Abinger Harvest* in 1936:

> ... Roger Fry rejected authority ... He rejected authority absolutely ... If you said to him, 'This must be right, all the experts say so ... Hitler says so, Marx says so, Christ says so, *The Times* says so,' he would say 'Well. I wonder. Let's see.' ... You would come away realizing that an opinion may be influentially backed and yet be tripe.

Forster had been elected as the first president of the radical **National Council for Civil Liberties** in 1934 and he had also attended the June 1935 International Congress of Writers in Paris. Although he was aware of that Congress's dominant communist, indeed Stalinist, orientation, he still believed it was necessary for writers to participate in an outspoken common front against fascism. His own pulpit, apart from his regular 'Notes for the Way' in the feminist ***Time and Tide***, owned by **Lady Margaret Rhondda (Haig)**, was the BBC microphone. 'The radio talk was a completely new genre, a re-invention of the spoken word [and **Forster**] brought to it a uniquely personal style, a human voice of technology.'[3] **Forster**'s BBC producer Jean Rowntree called him 'a natural broadcaster who combined the rhythms of natural speech with a pattern of thought that made [him] easy to remember'.[4] His mild voice and even tone could not have sounded less like the ranting, hysterical Goebbels or Hitler, and **Forster**, at nearly 60, now 'began to speak for humanity'.[5] The wishy-washy, 'woolly liberal' proved to be a devastating truth-teller. After each broadcast he would ask the talks producer and technicians anxiously 'Was I convincing?'[6]

Forster's belief in the worth of each individual human being, as well as his first-hand experience of Egypt and India, had made him a lifelong anti-imperialist and anti-racist. 'Take the evil of racial prejudice … is there no racial prejudice in the British Empire? Is there no colour question?'[7] For **Forster** 'there was no doubt that [Nazi]anti-Semitism was the worst … of all things … making it impossible for him to be a pacifist'.[8]

> Jew-mania was the one evil which no one foretold at the close of the last war … no prophet, so far as I know, had foreseen this anti-Jew horror, whereas to-day no one can see the end to it … To me, anti-Semitism is now the most shocking of all things … For the moment all that we can do, is to dig in our heels and prevent silliness from sliding into insanity.[9]

Therefore **Forster** had to be an anti-appeaser. He recognised that there would be no alternative to fighting Hitler's war, declaring in his 1939 BBC talk 'Post-Munich', 'if Fascism wins we are done for, and … we must become Fascist to win'. It was a 'hideous dilemma'. As for the totalitarian state, **Forster** was prepared to resist it at whatever personal cost. The Führer principle was no principle at all – on the contrary:

> Love and loyalty can run counter to the claims of the State. When they do – down with the State, say I, which means that the State would down me ... The dictator-hero can grind down his citizens till they are all alike, but he cannot melt them into a single man ... they are obliged to be born separately, and to die separately, and [so] will always be running off the totalitarian rails.'[10]

In September/October 1940, still at the height of the invasion scare, **Forster** gave 'three sombre talks' that fully explain why he was on the Nazi Blacklist:[11]

> 1. 'Culture and Freedom':
> My belief is that if the Nazis won, culture would be destroyed in England and the Empire ... In Hitler's war Germany is not a hostile country, she is a hostile principle. She stands for a new and a bad way of life and, if she won, would be bound to destroy our ways. There is not room in the same world for Nazi Germany and for people who don't think as she does ...
>
> 2. 'What has Germany done to the Germans?'
> It is most important to remember that Germany had to make war on her own people before she could attack Europe ... [During] the past seven years she robbed and tortured and interned and expelled and killed thousands and thousands of her own citizens ... On the surface, the Nazi creed seems not too bad; scratch the surface and you will find intolerance and cruelty ... Think of Einstein, Freud, Mann ... in exile. Think of the burning of the books ... It is all part of a single movement, which has as its aim the fettering of the writer, the scientist, the artist and the general public all over the world.
>
> 3. 'What would Germany do to us?'
> Destruction of national culture is part of their programme of conquest. In Czechoslovakia ... they have barred the operas of Smetana and the plays of Capek. They have revised school

> books, falsified Czech history, forbidden the singing of Czech national songs ... In Poland the fate of culture has been still more tragic, since Poland is a conquered country ... Poland is the model which the Nazis would follow if they got over here ... They would treat Oxford as they treated Cracow.[12]
>
> They are stamping out culture everywhere in Poland as far as they can ... the Poles are [held] naturally inferior to Germans ...

Forster had no illusions about what would be his own fate when, as he then expected to happen very soon, Hitler invaded Britain:

> Those [writers] of any eminence would probably be interned and shot ... [But] what would be disastrous is the intimidation of our younger writers ... [The Nazis] have identified civilisation with the state, and the National Socialist state cannot be secure until no civilisation exists except [its own] ... This being so, I think we have got to go on with this hideous fight. I cannot see how we are to make terms with Hitler, much as I long for peace.

Thus **Forster** found himself having to be an unheroic hero, speaking out at what he knew to be his own personal risk against an apparently invincible totalitarianism. But he also had to fight against what he saw as creeping fascism within his own country, and even within his esteemed BBC. Supporting the **National Council for Civil Liberties**, **Forster** protested against the violation of liberty in the name of 'security' in recent British anti-sedition laws. And when the BBC issued a wartime Blacklist of its own, banning pacifist and communist speakers, **Forster** (like the composer Vaughan Williams) protested. He demanded, even though he himself was neither a pacifist nor a communist, that they cancel the broadcasting of three of his own talks. The BBC gave in.

The author of the genetic engineering dystopia *Brave New World*, and pacifist editor of *An Encyclopaedia of Pacifism* (1937), **Aldous Huxley** (1894–1977), was also Blacklisted as a writer. In his collection of essays *Ends and Means* (1937), **Huxley** 'attempted to relate all social problems, the problems of international politics, of economics and education, to ethics'.[13] It was not an enterprise that would have commended itself to the Gestapo, especially since 'it became a kind of Bible to the Peace Pledge Union'.[14] What the Gestapo did not know was that **Huxley** had left Britain for the United States in 1937 and would not return.[15]

The president of the English section of Blacklisted **PEN International** (1938–1944) was **Storm Jameson** (1891–1986). Although not listed by name in Part One of the Black Book, the novelist and pamphleteer was on 'The Berlin death list'[16] and she would certainly have been one of the 'Most Wanted' at the **PEN**'s (Poets, Essayists, Novelists) Club, 59–61 New Oxford Street, London WC1 (listed in Part Two of the Black Book under suspect '*Vereinigungen*'), since she and **Hermon Ould** and a typist were the only people there each day. Founded in London in 1921, **PEN**'s aims were: '1) To promote intellectual cooperation and understanding among writers; 2) To create a world community of writers that would emphasise the central role of literature in the development of world culture; and 3) To defend literature [and to that end freedom of expression] against the many threats to its survival.'

In 1933 **PEN International** (under the presidency of **H. G. Wells**) had expelled German **PEN** because it had not protested against the Nazi burning of books and had tried to muzzle the German Jewish author Ernst Toller. Between 1933 and 1940, **PEN International** had been active in defence of imprisoned writers and of writers driven into exile.

Both the rise of Nazism in the 1930s and the continuing extreme inequality in capitalist Britain sickened **Jameson**: 'There really was a stench. On one side Dachau, on the other the "distressed areas" with their ashamed workless men and despairing women.'[17] Continually shuttling between Prague, Vienna and Paris in the late 1930s, **Jameson** tried to help endangered writers escape and survive as refugees in Britain. 'We [at **PEN**] answered every letter, we tried to get the visas needed, an effort involving us in hundreds of letters to the Home Office and visits to overworked refugee organisations. For one person we got out, ten, fifty, five hundred sank.'[18] By the end of the

1930s **Storm Jameson** had to renounce her pacifism – the price of surrendering to Nazi barbarism was just too great.

Her colleague, **Hermon Ould** (1886–1951), was a dramatist, a children's writer and a critic as well as being the international secretary of **PEN**. He had translated and adapted for the stage Ernst Toller's *Hoppla We're Alive!* set after the crushing of post-First World War popular uprisings – a work that had been burned by the Nazis – and the novel by Klaus Mann, *Pathetic Symphony* (1938), about the gay composer Tchaikovsky. **Ould** was Blacklisted because of guilt by those political associations and also for his role in aiding persecuted writers through **PEN International**. In 1941 he organised and edited a symposium on writers' freedom.[19]

The novelist and journalist **Rose Macaulay** (1881–1958), a great admirer of the work of **E. M. Forster**, was a fellow supporter of the **NCCL** and of **PEN International**. She became a columnist for *The Spectator* and for ***Time and Tide*** as well as an occasional writer for the ***New Statesman*** in the mid 1930s, and was an outspoken anti anti-Semite and a critic of Mussolini and Oswald Mosley. Mistakenly, she at first regarded Hitler as 'a strident Jack-in-the-box from a beer cellar', who could simply be laughed out of court, and she totally rejected totalitarian dictatorships of whatever hue – 'I don't want a Leader. I like to think I am capable of leading myself.'[20] Appalled by the prospect of a Second World War, she supported the Peace Pledge Union – until Hitler annexed Austria in 1938. Then, aged nearly 60, **Macaulay** joined the Voluntary Ambulance Corps, driving night after night through the London Blitz. Like **Kingsley Martin** and **Leonard** and **Virginia Woolf,** she was prepared to kill herself if Hitler invaded.[21]

The outstanding historical novelist who had written *The Conquered* (1924), a devastating re-creation of what it had been like for the inhabitants of Gaul to have suffered defeat by Julius Caesar's Roman armies, **Naomi Mitchison** (1897–1999), was the sister of the Blacklisted scientist **J. B. S. Haldane** (p. 293) and a fearless, independent-minded, feminist socialist in her own right. In February 1934, representing the **Fabian Society** and commissioned by **Victor Gollancz**, she had gone to 'Red Vienna', recently defeated by the Dollfuss government.

There she interviewed, in prison, the widow of the hanged workers' leader, Koloman Wallisch, and met many of the surviving, despairing Austrian Socialists. She gave them money and messages of solidarity, dodging police searches; finally, she carried papers back secretly to their exiled comrades in Britain. Her vivid report, *Naomi Mitchison's Vienna Diary*, was published in 1934 by **Gollancz**, but its warnings about Nazism and impending war were discounted or ignored. In 1938 she wrote *The Moral Basis of Politics* in which she criticised Stalinism as well as fascism and affirmed the necessity to resist oppression through both individual and collective action. In 1939 her novel, *The Blood of the Martyrs*, on the persecution of Christians under Nero, drew parallels with the persecution of socialists and Jews by Mussolini and Hitler. But it was probably her *Vienna Diary* that put her on the Black List. Eventually **Mitchison** felt forced to renounce her pacifism in the face of what she believed was imminent Nazi invasion. She lived to join the struggles against apartheid and nuclear weapons.[22]

The popular novelist, playwright, social commentator and broadcaster **J. B. Priestley** (1894–1984) OM 1977, was a non-Marxist, non-revolutionary socialist. Although absorbed by his efforts to conquer the London stage between 1932 and 1939, **Priestley** also spent time and energy testifying to his antipathy to fascism. Already on 22 October 1933 he had written in the *Sunday Chronicle:* 'I dislike Fascism because it gives itself military airs, is politically regressive, settles no important problems; and when successful has always shown itself to be the enemy of political and intellectual liberty.'

However, that did not make **Priestley** a communist: 'There is, as Mr **H. G. Wells** has said, "a book-burning Nazi 'oaf'". But there has also been a book-burning Bolshevik 'oaf'. The fact is, of course, that all these brutally intolerant folk are oafs, whether they are wearing red, black or brown shirts … We do not want the "War of the Shirts here."'[23] In December 1936 **Priestley**'s work was banned in Germany, supposedly because he was a socialist and president of **PEN** worldwide, although in fact he was only the president of its London centre. (He was also banned in the Soviet Union.) By April 1939, of course, **Priestley** no longer saw Hitler or his 'oafish' followers as any sort of joke:

It simply will not do to see Hitler and his friends, and all the saluting and screaming youths who obey them, as ordinary men with a few grievances who want to see their country as one of a settled, prosperous order of nations in a peaceful world. They are dragon-slayers with magic swords. They are characters in a fairy-tale, but now it is an evil fairy-tale, turning all Central Europe into a haunted, bloodstained forest…

Every nation has two faces … And the tragedy – not only for Germans but for all of us is that [the] dark face has eclipsed the bright face …

The Jews, with their strong humorous sanity, were a very valuable leaven in German public and cultural life. Perhaps no people really needed the Jews more than the Germans did … It was characteristic of the evil genius that has been at work that the Jews should be the chief victims of oppression.[24]

However, **Priestley** was also bitterly critical of class-bound, unjust Britain:

We are not a democracy but a plutocracy roughly described as an aristocracy. All our government is done by the Right People … You can see the private income outlook at work. It does not by any means necessarily coincide with the best interests of the country … And as four out of five newspapers are owned and directed by the same sort of people, it follows that the weakness of such political gentlemen will not be mentioned and corrected by most of the Press.[25]

Priestley was particularly incensed when any left-wing arguments in Britain were dismissed as subversive propaganda, whereas right-wing opinion passed as innocuous and natural:

Millions of decent folk here sincerely believe that the reason why … we could not stand up to the dictators earlier was because we were not strong enough … because a lot of muddle-headed

> Liberals, Radicals, Socialists ... would not allow Britain to rearm ...
>
> But the real reason why we did not stand up to the dictators long before ... is that the Right Wing, which dictated our foreign policy, did not want to stand up. [They were] making friends all the time with [our] enemies ... People who protest against the present organisation of our society are not wilfully setting their faces against some God-given division of wealth, privilege and power ... What they are saying is 'Try a little red in place of all this blue.'[26]

It was also in July 1939 that **Priestley** urged that **Churchill** *must* be given a place in any future War Cabinet.[27]

Early in the Second World War, **Priestley** 'put the power of his mind – and his voice – at the service of the state, most notably in a series of broadcasts that boosted the morale of Britons but also advanced **Priestley**'s own social agenda for the country.'[28] His Sunday night Home Service broadcasts – *Postscripts* – in his unmistakeable Yorkshire voice, immediately after the nine o'clock news, won an international as well as national audience. They were a deliberate counter 'in voice, upbringing and outlook to the normal BBC voices'[29] – as well as being a counter to the pro-Nazi propaganda talks by 'Lord Haw-Haw'. The first 'test broadcast', on 5 June 1940, was on the evacuation retreat from Dunkirk, with **Priestley** declaring: 'What began as a miserable blunder, ended as an epic of gallantry ... [when the little ships including even the paddle steamers 'Brighton Belles' and 'Brighton Queens'] sailed into the inferno, to defy bombs, shells, magnetic mines, torpedoes, machine-gun fire – to rescue our soldiers.' To him the Nazis were 'a kind of overgrown species of warrior ant' (9 June 1940); '[The] time must come when either we must destroy them or they [will] destroy us' (23 June 1940).

Priestley's weekly *Postscripts* between 5 June 1940 and 20 October 1940 reminded his hearers that the British soldiers returning after the First World War had been rewarded with unemployment and poverty, and he insisted that this should not happen again: 'Either we are fighting to bring a better world into existence or we are merely assisting at the destruction of such civilisation as we possess.' (Preface to *Postscripts*, Heinemann, 1940, p. vii.); 'We're not fighting to restore the past; it was the past that brought us to this heavy hour.' (14 July, 1940); '[We] must stop thinking in terms of property and power and begin thinking in terms of community and creation.' (21 July 1940); '[The] old strictly nationalistic divisions don't quite fit. There are millions of Germans who are praying that Hitler will lose.' (4 August 1940); '[We're] fighting ... to bring into existence an order of society in which nobody will have far too many rooms in a house and nobody have far too few.' (22 September 1940)

'If all this, together with certain obvious elements of social justice and decency seems to you Socialism, Communism or Anarchy, then you are at liberty to call me a Socialist, a Communist or an Anarchist.'

By the time he said these words in the final Postscript in October 1940, **Priestley** had become too left wing for **Churchill** himself and for the Ministry of Information to stomach. Though his broadcasts had won over 14 million listeners and boosted civilian morale during some of the worst months of the Blitz, he was taken off the air. **Priestley** was furious. 'There can be no doubt that when my *Postscripts* were cut short the [Ministry of Information] and your people [the BBC] went against the wishes of the vast majority of the people of this country, thousands and thousands and thousands of whom have written and spoken to me about it, always with suspicion of the government, for they knew this was a most undemocratic move.'[30] **Priestley** lived on to co-found the Campaign for Nuclear Disarmament in 1957.

One of the 1930s' modernist English poets, **Stephen Spender** (1909–1995), was a Gestapo target for racist as well as for ideological reasons, since his mother was half Jewish. In addition, he was briefly a Communist in the 1930s, writing:

> Oh young men oh young comrades
> it is too late now to stay in those houses
> your fathers built where they built you to breed
> money on money ...

It is too late to stay in great houses where the ghosts are prisoned
– those ladies like flies perfect in amber
those financiers like fossils of bones in coal. …

Spender took part in the Spanish Civil War against Franco but was soon disillusioned by the Stalinists there. His *Poems from Spain*, 1939 included 'Two Armies' that stresses the humanity of fascist and anti-fascist fighters alike:

Deep in the winter plain, two armies
Dig their machinery, to destroy each other.
Men freeze and hunger. No one is given leave
On either side, except the dead, and wounded.
These have their leave; …
All have become so nervous and so cold
That each man hates the cause and distant words
Which brought him here, more terribly than bullets.

In the London Blitz, **Spender** served as a fireman.

Unlike **Spender,** the novelist, short-story writer, letter writer and poet, **Sylvia Townsend Warner** (1893–1978), remained an enthusiastic, uncritical communist for several years from 1935. She helped the Red Cross in Barcelona to support anti-Franco forces and in 1937 she was a delegate, like **Forster** and **Spender**, to the International Writers Congress in Madrid. She remained left wing and served on the executive committee of the Association of Writers for Intellectual Liberty, which amalgamated with **For Intellectual Liberty** from February 1936 until 1940. Backed by **Margery Fry**, **Rose Macaulay**, and **E. M. Forster**, **'For Intellectual Liberty'** was 'a rallying point for intellectual workers in active defence of peace, liberty and culture'. Among its concerns were fascism, anti-Semitism, the League of Nations and the Spanish Civil War. The movement's papers are held in Cambridge University Archives, Manuscripts Room.[31]

Even the world-famous pioneer of science fiction and popular scientific educator, **H. G. Wells** (1866–1946), is Blacklisted simply as

'Schriftsteller'. His *Shape of Things to Come*, 1933, had accurately prophesied future war in the air and even the atom bomb. In reaction against that horror, 'He wanted to guide humanity to a better world'[32] – a peaceful one directed by science and not by irrational tribal ideologies. In 1934 he agreed to **Violet Bonham Carter's** suggestion that he should join Romain Rolland, Heinrich Mann, Lion Feuchtwanger and Lucien Levy-Bruehl on the foundation committee of 'The Freedom Library' – the German Library of Banned Books in Paris, in commemoration of the books burned by Goebbels the year before. 'It set out to collect all works that had been burned, banned or silenced in Germany, to put the émigrés' personal libraries at the disposal of all, and to collect documents on the international antifascist struggle … Added later were works written in exile.'[33]

Before 1939, **Wells**, an outspoken anti-fascist founder member of the **NCCL** and the British president of **PEN**, wrote the first draft of a fundamental Declaration of Human Rights. In order to banish fear from human life, **Wells** said in his 1940 publication *The Rights of Man*, there had to be a new international law 'for the common welfare … a code of fundamental human rights'. His initial draft included the right to privacy and rejection of secrecy: 'All registration and records about citizens shall be open to their personal and private inspection. There shall be no secret dossiers in any administrative department.' **Wells** also spelled out the right to nourishment, housing, healthcare and mental care; the right to education, the right to have home and private property protected; the right to work and earn and be free from slavery, the right to move freely about the world; the right to public trial and to detention for a short fixed-term only; freedom from torture and the right to finite terms of imprisonment.[34] It is not surprising that the Gestapo planned to eliminate him.

The feminist novelist and essayist **Rebecca West** (1892–1983), once the lover of **Wells**, married the banker Henry Andrews who later left his German branch of Schroders in 1933 on account of the new regime's anti-Semitism. Thus **West** knew about Nazi Germany from the inside. An implacable anti-totalitarian, her *Black Lamb and Grey Falcon* (1941) highlighted the imminent threat of the eradication of Yugoslav culture(s) by Germany. During the war she supported both Jewish and Yugoslav refugees in her home.[35]

Leonard Woolf (1880–1969) was not only a writer but also a publisher at his Hogarth Press; he was a **Co-operative** and **Fabian** socialist, and a dedicated **Labour Party** advocate of decolonisation. In 1916, **Woolf** had published *International Government*, a blueprint for a new League of Nations; he was joint editor of the *Political Quarterly* from 1931, and in 1935, financed by **Sidney Bernstein**, he brought out Frederick Voigt's pamphlet, *The Persecution of the Jews in Germany*, at the Hogarth Press. An atheist Jew, **Woolf** wrote his own Jeremiad, *Barbarians at the Gate*, in 1939, lamenting that in 'civilised' Europe: 'Large numbers of persons are continually being killed, imprisoned, tortured, or beaten, without any kind of legal trial or process, by European governments ... Freedom of speech, of opinion, of the Press – all the most elementary forms of civil liberty – have been destroyed.' **Woolf** did not care whether the persecuted were bourgeois or *kulaks*, or Jews or 'Reds' – *all* political sadism was incompatible with civilisation. He detested every kind of totalitarianism but he also understood how it had some deep roots in injustice and suffering under the 'economic barbarism of capitalism':

> Hitler's success was able to change Germany from a civilised into a barbarous master-slave society, because after 1921 vast numbers of Germans were economically pathological and socially neurotic. [Hitler] used economics and ideas to convert them to ... a [domestic] policy of violence, lawlessness and persecution, externally [to] a policy of war. (*Barbarians at the Gate*, p. 139)

Nevertheless **Leonard Woolf** refused to believe in the ultimate world victory of fascism:

> The Fascist State ... is a purely temporary phenomenon ... It will destroy itself inevitably ... The insoluble problem which has faced and destroyed every dictatorship – the fact that the dictator must some day die – still remains unsolved in Hitler's

> Germany and Mussolini's Italy … It is practically certain that … a war… will destroy the Fascist dictatorships and their regimes. (*Barbarians at the Gate*, Conclusion)

But before that promised end, as a Nazi invasion threatened Britain, **Woolf** [36] kept a suicide pill on him.

Leonard Woolf's wife, **Virginia Woolf** (1882–1941), the great modernist novelist, was also Blacklisted. A lifelong pacifist, **Virginia Woolf** believed that the roots of war lay in our species' deficient power of imagination: 'The reason why it is easy to kill another person must be that one's imagination is too sluggish to conceive what his life means to him – the infinite possibilities of a succession of days which are furled in him, and have already been spent.' [37] All her experimental, elegiac novels can be seen as attempts to render that succession of 'furled' days through her discovery of the flashback – the 'beautiful caves' of memory in our stream of consciousness. 'I think that gives exactly what I want; humanity, humour, depth.'[38]

Virginia Woolf could feel nothing but contempt for the male supremacist competition that so often culminates in a nationalistic, militaristic dictatorship – and even in international war. Men have been socialised by every society into believing that their virility depends upon their success in dominating – in both the private and the public worlds. It was the warrior male, in whatever uniform, who constitutes the problem and who in every age has shut women out from political decision-making. Woolf cited Hitler's speech to his Nazi Old Guard in August 1935, identifying manliness with readiness to kill: 'In battle we have won the German Reich, and in battle we shall maintain and guard it … He who wishes to disturb our peace will no longer fight against a nation of pacifists but against a nation of men.' But every nation is also a nation of women, and **Virginia Woolf** asked in her pacifist, feminist, anti-fascist polemic *Three Guineas* in 1938: 'Why should I kill women? … As a woman I have no country. As a woman I want no country. As a woman my country is the whole world.'[39]

Sophocles' *Antigone* was **Virginia Woolf**'s foundation text for her resistance to the brutal fascisms of the mid 1930s, and she instanced a contemporary German woman, Frau Pommer of Essen, arrested for refusing to hate Jews, as a contemporary Antigone.[40] In her last published essay, 'Thoughts on Peace in an Air-Raid' (1940), **Virginia Woolf** would declare: 'there is another way of fighting for freedom without arms; we can fight with the mind.' She insisted on the need for *both* sexes to wage mental fight against our seemingly ever-recurrent recourse to competitions in violence. And women also needed to face their willingness to be dominated – 'Hitlers are bred by slaves'.[41]

It is unlikely that the Gestapo actually read the writing of **Virginia Woolf**. But they would have noted her name listed on many anti-fascist campaigning groups and protests. In March 1936 she signed a protest letter with **Aldous Huxley** and **Wells** against the planned British Union of Fascists' meeting in the Albert Hall, and in July 1936 she wrote to her nephew Julian Bell: 'Every day almost I get rung up to be asked to sign this, subscribe to that … but I sign and I protest and so on.' She was on the founding committee with **Margery Fry** of **For Intellectual Liberty** and, unlike Yeats, she backed the campaign to get the imprisoned German pacifist von Ossietzky awarded the Nobel Peace Prize. (Yeats had refused to side with any form of government. 'Communist, facist, nationalist, clerical, anticlerical are all responsible according to the number of their victims … I am not callous, every nerve trembles with horror at what is happening in Europe.' Letter, 1936, quoted in Richard Ellmann, *Yeats, The Man and the Masks*, 1961, p. 282.) In August 1936 **Virginia Woolf** signed a letter urging the government to support the Spanish struggle against Franco; in December 1936 she wrote 'Why Art Today follows Politics' for the ***Daily Worker***; and in June 1937 she attended a meeting in aid of refugee Basque children.[42] And in October 1938 she is listed with **E. M. Forster** and **Naomi Mitchison** as one of the patrons of the exhibition of Picasso's *Guernica* at the New Burlington Galleries.[43] After her death, her work was added to the '*Liste Otto*' of forbidden writings in occupied France in July 1941. 'The *Liste Otto* [named after Abets, Hitler's ambassador to occupied France], banned nearly a thousand writers, including of course all Jewish writers and thinkers and extending its disapproval to Shakespeare and **Virginia Woolf**.' [44]

Refugee Writers in Britain

What could the many writers, poets, artists and intellectuals who had left Germany in 1933 actually do in British exile that could obstruct the Nazis, given that 'Hitler's rise to power was already their defeat? [Their] emigration sustained the very survival of German culture. Yet it could do practically nothing against the dictatorship.'[45] Refugee writers in Britain were, in their own minds, Cassandras doomed to prophesy the truth but never be believed:

> Europe refused to rouse itself from its slumber when the émigrés issued warning after warning [about] Nazi Germany … [Instead they themselves] became the butt of hatred. As Koestler wrote: 'Anti-Nazi refugees who talked about the German concentration camps and Hitler's plans for world-conquest were regarded as fanatics and fomenters of hatred' … It would take a World War for the world to discover what the émigrés had reiterated constantly since 1933, i.e. that the Nazis behave like Nazis.[46]

Nazism had declared war on Germany's writers from the start, not only by the public burnings of their books on 10 May 1933 but also, three days later, when the Prussian Ministry for Science, Art and Popular Education published a list of works whose distribution was 'not recommended'. The proscribed writers were Jews, communists, socialists, Republicans or pacifists, and their work was to be withdrawn from German libraries, and either burned or kept in 'a poison cupboard'.

Once in exile in Britain, the refugee writers did try to play a vigorous part in anti-Nazi intellectual activities in London:

> London in the late Thirties had not only a Free German League of Culture, an Austrian Centre, a Rudolf Fuchs House, a PEN club for German Authors Abroad, later a Club 43 and Kurt Hiller's GUDA (Group of Independent German Authors); throughout the worst of the bombing, poems were being written and remarkably being published in German.[47]

The Austrian and German writers exiled in Britain before 1939 and listed for immediate arrest in the Black Book include the political poet, journalist and author of the utopian novel *Nordpol* (Kurt) **Karl Doberer** (1904–1993), who fled Germany in 1933, eventually reaching Britain via Czechoslovakia. After having been interned as an enemy alien he was freed to work for the German broadcasts of the BBC and represented German **PEN** in exile in London. Then there was **Hans Flesch-Brunningen** (1895–1981), the Jewish Austrian Expressionist writer who had left Germany in 1933 for penniless exile in London. From 1934 to 1963 he was president of the Free German Cultural Association in London, and was head of the Austrian section of the BBC from 1939 until 1958. He wrote, *inter alia*, *Vertriebene, Essays on The Exiled from Ovid to Gorguloff*, 1933, and *Untimely Ulysses*, 1940. **Fritz Gottfurcht** (1901–1973), was another Austrian writer and critic (both literary reviewer and theatre critic), who fled to London in 1935 with his film actress wife Dorothea, in his case without knowing a word of English. He was the author of film screenplays and cabaret reviews for the *Neue Deutsche Kulturbund* in London (1939–40). He worked with Erich Fried, declaring: 'A great responsibility lies with the writers, artists, musicians who have left Nazi Germany. It is given into their hands to keep German culture, the very language of their country, alive.'[48]

Tragic **Max Herrmann-Neisse** (1886–1941), a Jewish writer of prose and poetry, had fled to England in 1933, revolted by the ruthless, power-mad Nazis – 'aggressive, lawless, intolerant' – and had co-founded German **PEN** in exile with Feuchtwanger and Toller. Homesick from the first, he wrote:

> I sat opposite Byron
> On the park bench
> Cars hurtled wildly past
> And my heart was sick for home.

He applied unsuccessfully for British citizenship and died in London, having written '*Litanei der Bitternis*': '*Bitter ist es, das Brot der Fremde zu essen*' ('It is bitter to eat the bread of a foreign land') and the famous

'*Ein deutscher Dichter bin ich einst gewesen*' ('I was once a German poet').[49]

The Jewish Austrian writer, playwright and theatre critic **Felix Langer** (1889–1970), had also left Germany in 1933, but arrived in Britain only in 1939 . He had spent years in Czechoslovakia combating race hatred and anti-Semitism. He eventually took British nationality after writing *Stepping Stones to Peace* (1943).

The Expressionist novelist and lyric poet **Karl Otten** (1889–1963), had been imprisoned in Germany in the First World War for his pacifist, anti-nationalist politics. In March 1933 he had left Germany for Spain and had later fought against Franco; after the defeat in Spain he went into British exile and became a British citizen. His selected poems included '*Heimweh quaelt mich nach einer anderen Welt*' ('Homesickness torments me with longing for another world'). A sociological analyst of Nazism, **Otten** worked for the BBC, writing 120 hard-hitting radio broadcasts in English during the war, including episodes in a series entitled 'Black Gallery' that dealt with the vicious habits of Nazi leaders as well as other episodes imagining future oppression under Nazi rule in an occupied Britain. He also worked on translations until he went blind in 1944. 'He was an admirable man.'[50]

The world-famous Jewish Austrian writer of *Novellen*, **Stefan Zweig** (1881–1942), an internationalist and a Europeanist, had left Vienna for London (1934–9). Appalled by Hitler's triumphant advance and seeing no hope for a humanistic Europe, **Zweig** then left Britain for the United States in 1940 and afterwards for Brazil. He and his young second wife committed suicide in 1942.

It is hardly possible for refugees – of all people – to persuade their host countries what they should think and how they should act. Feeling themselves to be utterly ineffectual, and having to express their prophecies of doom in a language not even their own, it is not surprising that many refugee writers should have despaired. What is perhaps more surprising is that precisely those writers then mocked for being out of touch with contemporary reality, remote and inaccessible in their ivory towers – **E. M. Forster**[51] and **Virginia Woolf** – should have fought against despair and come out from their corners fighting, engaging time and again with the imminent threat from Nazism.

10

Shooting the Messenger – Blacklisted Journalists

> There is a Nazi view regarding books, the stage, films, sport and even women's dress; and the journalist must rigidly support it.
>
> A. J. Cummings, *The Press and a Changing Civilisation*, 1936

Given that the Nazis had been very quick to persecute and outlaw all German and Austrian dissenting journalists, it was predictable that among those who would have been most immediately at risk in September 1940 under a military occupation of Britain would be the journalists who had tried to alert British public opinion to the menace of Nazi Germany. Moreover, the Gestapo suspected, often correctly, that several foreign correspondents of British newspapers were also working as active secret agents. (See **Harrison**, **Kenney**, **Segrue** and **Tiltman,** pp. 140, 141, 145, 148.) Since so many British anti-fascist thinkers and activists were also occasional journalists in the 1930s, I am concentrating here on those who were *principally* employed by newspapers or who, like **Rowland Kenney**, were primarily engaged with the foreign press.

Heading the list of British-born journalists in alphabetical order was **Gerald Barry** (1898–1968) ('Journalist, *Direktor bei* News Chronicle'). **Barry** had left the *Daily Express* in 1930, refusing to back its imperialist line, and had become editor of the new *Weekend Review*, concerned with the formation of a political and economic think-tank to plan policies to counter the Depression. When that *Review* merged with the *New Statesman* in 1934, **Barry** became a director, but he also worked as features editor on the liberal *News Chronicle*, owned by the Quaker Cadbury family. There he succeeded **Walter Layton** (p. 92) who became the paper's chairman. The *News Chronicle* backed the anti-Franco line in the Spanish Civil War and was consistently anti-Nazi, raising funds for refugees from fascism, especially from Czechoslovakia post Munich. After the war, **Barry** became the director in chief of the Festival of Britain in 1951.[1]

Another journalist listed in the Black Book as working for the *News Chronicle* was its diplomatic correspondent, **Vernon Bartlett** (1894–1983). A survivor of horrific experiences in the First World War, **Bartlett** was deeply committed to the prevention of another world war. From 1922 to 1932 he was director of the London office of the League of Nations. Precisely because he wanted to forestall another war, he was a fierce opponent of the appeasement of Hitler and appalled by the Munich Agreement:

> I am firmly convinced that had Chamberlain stood firm at Godesberg, Hitler would either have climbed down or would have begun the war with far less support from his own people than he had a year later ... It was clear to the Czechoslovak representatives ... that the independence of their country had been signed away by statesmen ... whose fear had stifled all sense of honour.[2]

Bartlett had been diplomatic correspondent for the *News Chronicle* during the Spanish Civil War but in 1938, astonishingly, he stood as an Independent 'anti-Chamberlain' parliamentary candidate and actually won a formerly 'safe' Tory seat. In 1939 he urged much closer cooperation with Russia to form a preventative Common Front against Hitler that might yet save the world from war. In 1940 he was the first BBC speaker on its new North American Service and in 1941, as director of British Press Services, he was sent to Russia to arrange closer wartime cooperation and exchange of information between the British Commonwealth and the Soviet Union. A brilliant broadcaster, his 'wise and compassionate' BBC *Postscripts*, succeeding

Priestley, kept up civilian morale. **Bartlett** would become a founder member of the 1941 committee that was planning a radical socialist post-war Britain and a new 'Commonwealth Party'.[3]

A less consistent radical was upper-class **Claud Cockburn** (1904–1981),[4] the British Communist Party's correspondent for the ***Daily Worker*** during the Spanish Civil War. **Cockburn**'s Stalinist reportage, with its deliberate distortion of mere facts, was excoriated by Orwell in *Homage to Catalonia* as intentional, murderous inaccuracy that targeted the anti-Stalinist, anarchist POUM (*Partido Obrero de Unificacion Marxista*).[5]

In contrast to **Cockburn**, **W. P. Crozier** (1879–1944), the editor of the ***Manchester Guardian*** (1932–44), was totally committed to journalism as the exposure of *factual* truths in the interest of achieving social reform. **Crozier** had worked continuously at the ***Manchester Guardian*** under C. P. Scott since he was 24. Once he became editor he had increased the paper's foreign news coverage, placing a network of foreign correspondents in major European cities. Informed about the rising terror perpetrated by the Nazi Party within Germany by these correspondents, **Crozier**, a man of the liberal left as well as a sympathiser with the stateless Jews, made the ***Manchester Guardian*** internationally known for its damning exposure of Nazism at a time when many others in Britain were still taken in – or even attracted by – the movement's apparent dynamism. The ***Manchester Guardian*** had already been banned from sale in Germany at the end of March 1933 – but **Crozier** still managed to get news out from Nazi Germany. From November 1933 he sent his reporter **Charles A. Lambert** to be his official correspondent in Germany while at the same time employing Frederick Voigt to be his secret, anonymous correspondent, working underground. Voigt was nearly assassinated in Paris by Nazis wanting his documents, which would reveal his German sources – 'had these been seized there would have been hundreds of arrests as a result'.[6] Not only did **Crozier** learn of Dachau and other concentration camps from Voigt, he also learned as early as 1937 of Hitler's plans for an initial 'lightning' military offensive, later to be known as *Blitzkrieg*. A non-believer in 'appeasement', **Crozier** would work himself to death in the war.[7]

C. P. Scott's son, **John Russell Scott** (1879–1949), governing director and chairman of the ***Manchester Guardian***, was also in the Black Book. In 1932 he had become sole owner of the controlling ordinary shares in the paper but in 1936 he had permanently divested himself of all beneficial interest in them, transferring them to a trust. His aim was that the paper should keep its independence, never be profit-making for private benefit, and that its control should be in the hands of those who produced it. 'No man cared less for personal prestige or the gratification of the sense of power.'[8] Another, lowlier, Blacklisted journalist working for the ***Manchester Guardian*** was its news editor, **H. W. Nichols** (1904–1959), a science graduate who had made his name as an investigative journalist, writing on the ownership of the chemical industry. (In 1925 the leading German chemical and pharmaceutical concerns, including BASF, Bayer, Hoechst and Agfa had united as I. G. Farben, the largest chemical and pharmaceutical company in the world. I. G. Farben would become a large Nazi Party donor and a major government contractor; it would use slave labour from Auschwitz and supply Zyklon B for the gas chambers.)

Yet another ***Manchester Guardian*** journalist, **Israel Cohen** (1879–1961), was a much more obvious target for the Gestapo. Born to Polish Jewish immigrants in Manchester, educated at the Manchester Jews' School and Jews' College in London as well as at Manchester Grammar School and University College London, as an adolescent **Cohen** had been appalled by reports of the pogroms in Russia and was inspired by Herzl's solution of Zionism. Between 1918 and 1921 **Cohen** had investigated and reported on the surge of anti-Jewish violence in Poland and Hungary and he wrote on Zionism and anti-Semitism for both Jewish and non-Jewish outlets, representing the ***Manchester Guardian*** at every Zionist Congress until 1945.

The ardent Liberal **A. J. Cummings** (1882–1957), was foreign correspondent, deputy editor and later editor of the ***News Chronicle***. He had possibly the largest politically aware readership in Britain in the late 1930s and was saluted even by the communist/socialist **John Strachey** as 'the foremost political commentator of the democratic Press'.[9] **Cummings**' writing on the Reichstag Fire Trial and on the

Moscow Trial of British engineers in 1933 had already demonstrated his hatred of all totalitarianism. A fierce critic of the Conservative Government, he advocated a broad Left anti-appeasement alliance. He is mentioned as one of the speakers at 'a tremendously important conference' on the Spanish Civil War at the Queen's Hall on 23 April 1938.[10]

Cummings had been the only journalist on the same platform as such pro-Republican, Blacklisted politicians as the Labour MPs **A. V. Alexander**, **Ellen Wilkinson, Philip Noel-Baker** and the meeting's organiser, **Stafford Cripps**, not to mention **Harold Nicolson**, the Liberals **Sir Archibald Sinclair**, **Wilfrid Roberts** and **Megan Lloyd George**, the Left Book Club publisher **Victor Gollancz** and the **Duchess of Atholl**. That would not have gone unnoticed. **Cummings**, called 'the liberal conscience of Fleet Street' in the *ODNB*, had an unswerving passion for a free press:

> The secure existence of hostile newspapers ... is vital to the existence of a free community. It is the supreme safeguard of the elementary rights of human beings. Kill or swamp the Press in any country, and at once for millions life ceases to be worth living. And soon or late, whether they want it or not, they will be inveigled into war. If you cannot write or talk against war you cannot write or talk against war-mongers; ...
>
> I do not profess to be a man of courage; but if there is one cause for which I would be prepared to die it is that of helping to preserve my native land from the shame and misery of a Fascist dictatorship towards which the first decisive step would be the State control of 'that endless book' the Press.[11]

More widely known and remembered, largely because of his BBC broadcasting, was **Sefton Delmer** (1904–1979), a German speaker with intimate knowledge of Germany, where he had been brought up until 1917 and where he had returned in 1927. He became German correspondent for the *Daily Express* from 1929, making the most of his Nazi contacts without being seduced. From 1936 he was in Spain covering the civil war and in 1939 he reported on the German army's invasion of Poland. He then worked on the German Service of the BBC, and when in July 1940 Hitler made his Reichstag speech offering Britain peace terms, **Delmer**, without any official authorisation, responded immediately, telling Hitler via the BBC that he could put the 'peace' terms in '[his] lying stinking teeth'. The Germans were shocked, believing that **Churchill** must have dictated **Delmer**'s response. **Churchill**, who had not in fact done so, was delighted. Thereafter, **Delmer**'s secret war work was successful black propaganda to undermine German morale, especially in the armed forces, by means of misleading radio news broadcasts purporting to come from fervent Nazis.[12]

Coming from a totally different background was **Alexander Easterman** (1891–1983), a Scottish Jewish barrister turned journalist. As foreign editor of Beaverbrook's *Daily Express* from 1926 to 1933, he had, unlike **Delmer**, resigned over the paper's sympathetic policy towards Hitler. As chief foreign correspondent for the ***Daily Herald*** in the 1930s, he was eventually based in Paris in 1939. **Easterman** had close contacts with **Benes** and **Masaryk** in Czechoslovakia and he also wrote on Fascism in Romania.[13] As head of the International Affairs Department of the World Jewish Congress in 1941, **Easterman** would represent the World Jewish Congress among the 1943 Allied negotiators' meeting, which indicted the Nazis' attempt to exterminate all European Jews and which warned that every war criminal perpetrating that genocide would be found and prosecuted. He would later represent the WJC at the Nuremberg Trials.[14]

On the conservative side, the Berlin correspondent for *The Times* since 1925, **Norman Ebbutt** (1894–1968), was an ardent democrat who had sympathised with the Weimar Republic and admired Chancellor Bruening. His despatches after 1933 were full and accurate, with especially well-informed accounts of the split within German Protestantism between the dissident 'Confessing Church', *Bekennende Kirche*, and the new 'German Christians' who complied with Nazism (see p. 201). **Ebbutt** felt acutely frustrated by *The Times*' pro-appeasement editorial line, despite all his attempts to send them well-substantiated reports on Hitler's preparations for war. He was expelled from Germany for alleged 'espionage' in August 1937 by Goebbels, who tried in vain to prevent the large public send-off for **Ebbutt** that was then organised by his indignant journalist colleagues in Berlin.[15]

The anti-imperialist, anti-fascist journalist **Geoffrey Theodore Garratt** (1888–1942) was an outspoken supporter of Indian nationalism and also the correspondent from the war in Abyssinia for the ***Manchester Guardian***. He fiercely opposed the British lifting of sanctions against Mussolini. A leading supporter of the National Joint Committee for Spanish Relief, he himself went to Spain in 1937, organising the evacuation of children, and transport into and out of besieged Madrid. Fearlessly outspoken, he criticised the 'foul and fascist' elements within the British government, alleging that the policy of appeasing Hitler was in fact being dictated by 'pro-fascists in high places', including the Foreign Office. He was also frustrated by the Labour Party's unwillingness to participate with communists in a common front against fascism. **Garratt** was killed by the accidental explosion of a bomb during a military training exercise in 1942.[16]

An elderly Liberal critic of Nazi Germany was **J. L. Garvin** (1868–1946), editor of the ***Observer***, which was owned by Viscount Astor. **Garvin**'s first book, *The Economic Foundations of Peace* (1919), had supported an effective League of Nations that should include Germany – despite his own lifelong grief at the killing of his only son in the First World War. Immediately after 1918 he attacked the Treaty of Versailles' punitive peace terms against a Germany that would now be left with 'no real hope except in revenge'. Then, alarmed by the rise of Hitler, **Garvin** backed both rearmament *and* appeasement in order to try to avert a Second World War. Aged 72 in 1940, **Garvin**'s political influence had declined, but he used what he had to back **Churchill** in becoming both prime minister and minister of defence. For this he was sacked by the Astors in February 1942.[17]

The immensely readable, eloquent and popular writer, Roman Catholic **Philip Gibbs** (1877–1962), had been changed utterly by his experience as a war correspondent in the First World War. His dispatches from the British Expeditionary Force in 1914 had been so vividly horrific about the mass killing on both sides that the War Office had denied him permission to remain at the front. **Gibbs** had then refused to leave; he was arrested and sent home. In 1915, however, he was sent out again as an official war correspondent, but this time from the French and Belgian fronts – after he had reluctantly agreed to submit to censorship of his reports. After the war he published *Realities of War* or *Now It Can be Told* (1920), which exposed the devastating truth about what he had witnessed. **Gibbs** became increasingly aghast at the prospect of a Second World War, having put his faith in an effective League of Nations to maintain world peace. In 1934 he published *European Journey*, where he reported uneasily on the new Italy under Mussolini and on Hitler's Germany. In 1935 he edited *England Speaks*, with essays by the pacifist A. A. Milne, the radical **C. E. M. Joad** and the socialist **Harold Laski**. In 1938 in *Across the Frontiers*, **Gibbs** still hoped that the 'flaming hell' of a war between Germany and Britain could be averted. But in a revised 1939 edition, after the invasion of Bohemia, he admitted that Hitler had 'gone beyond the limit of any excuse' and declared that *Kristallnacht* had 'spoilt all the hopes of those who had been working for better relations between Germany and England for the sake of European peace'.[18]

Predictably, the Gestapo's anathema was pronounced on **Ivan Marion Greenberg**, the Zionist editor of ***The Jewish Chronicle*** (1936–46), and on the son of a Chassidic rabbi in the East End – the Yiddish journalist **Arnold Meyer Kaizer** (1895–1967), who published *This Whitechapel of Ours* in 1944, as well as on **Morris Myer**, the Zionist Yiddish journalist in Whitechapel and enthusiast for Yiddish theatre, who founded *Die Zsayt – Yiddish Times*, that lasted till 1950.[19]

A rare woman in this cohort of unacceptable British journalists was the young Jewish writer for the ***Daily Express*** and ***Time and Tide***, **Charlotte Haldane** (1894–1969). She had first met the scientist **J. B. S. Haldane** (p. 293), in 1925. Both were strongly left wing but she was particularly concerned about the emergence of fascism in Italy and Germany. In 1936 both she and her husband joined the **Communist Party of Great Britain** and she was soon involved in raising men and money for the International Brigade in the Spanish Civil

War, organising the vetting and transport of its British volunteers via Paris. In 1937 she joined the Dependents Aid Committee to raise money for the families of the British Battalion within the brigade, and she herself visited Spain, reporting on the civil war for the ***Daily Worker***. In 1938 **Charlotte Haldane** also reported on the Communist International in China for the ***Daily Herald***. But in August 1941, now a war reporter for the *Daily Sketch* and based in the Soviet Union, **Charlotte Haldane** became disillusioned with Stalinism and, unlike her husband, she left the Communist Party, confessing later (unlike **Claude Cockburn**), that her toeing of the party line had infected her earlier journalism, and had actually made her lie for the cause.[20]

An elusive, intriguing figure in 1930s British journalism about central and eastern Europe is **Hubert Deacon Harrison** (1898–1981), who worked for the ***News Chronicle***, the ***Daily Express***, the *New York Times*, the *Gazette*, and above all for ***Reuters Press Agency***. Short, thick-set and with piercing eyes, the son of a postal worker in Walsall, **Harrison** had been a very young second lieutenant in the Second Royal Tank Corps at the end of the First World War before he entered journalism. The year 1936 found him expelled from fascist Italy for a report he had sent out. In December 1937 he was expelled from monarchist Yugoslavia. **Harrison** had written on the Yugoslav censorship of *The Pirates and the Mouse*, a spoof *Prisoner of Zenda* that mocked the Mickey Mouse lookalike King Michael of Yugoslavia. A Liberal MP jumped up in the Commons to ask whether **Mr Eden** would 'do something to instil a little sense of humour in these people?' **Eden** declined to answer. In January 1939 **Harrison** was recruited by the Secret Service, SOE Balkans, and in October was sent to Budapest, ostensibly as correspondent for the ***News Chronicle***, but also as 'handler' of the Polish spy and saboteur Christine Granville.[21] Shuttling between Budapest and Belgrade, **Harrison** was often seen drunk in public (his 'cover'?) and returned to London, possibly under a cloud, in June 1940. In 1941 he published *The Soul of Yugoslavia*. Eventually he was dropped by SOE, but he did receive an OBE and, having for some reason become *persona non grata* in Romania in 1946, **Harrison**, a born survivor, could then be found in Vienna in 1958, as the 60-year-old vice president of Reuters' foreign press agency, receiving an award. He finally settled safely in Canada, living to the age of 83.

Similarly, the socialist **Rowland Kenney** (1882–1961), indicted by the Gestapo for being a 'British propagandist, secret agent' led a triple life as journalist, servant of the Foreign Office, and secret agent, although in a quite different part of Europe from that of **Harrison** – Norway. **Kenney** had been born into grim poverty, one of nine children, two of his sisters being the famous militant suffragette leaders Annie and Jessie Kenney. His vivid account of unemployment and brutal working conditions around 1900 in the West Midlands in *Westering* (1939) is one of the great underrated classics of British social reportage. **Kenney** eventually surfaced from destitution to become manager and then editor of the young Labour Party's new, struggling ***Daily Herald*** under **George Lansbury**. When based in Norway (with a Norwegian wife and child) in the First World War, **Kenney** became attached to the Foreign Office and was responsible for masterminding British propaganda in the Norwegian press (as well as for sending secret reports back to the Foreign Office about Norway and, later, about Poland). In the interwar years **Kenney** was employed at the Foreign Office and was instrumental in the establishment of the British Council. After September 1939 he was again posted to Norway as British press attaché in Oslo, where, in February 1940, he reported that he had just turned the whole of the Norwegian press against Germany – only to be whisked out of Norway in April 1940 when the Germans invaded.[22]

Totally different again was **Victor Gordon-Lennox** (1897–1968), 'Korrespondent ***Daily Telegraph***'. Born into a conservative aristocratic family, he had served as a young captain in the Grenadier Guards in the First World War where he was wounded. From 1934 to 1942, **Gordon-Lennox** was diplomatic editor for the ***Telegraph***, reporting from every capital in Europe as well as from the League of Nations in Geneva, but often writing against the policy of the current British foreign minister. In fact **Gordon-Lennox** became so committed to opposing the appeasement of Hitler that he secretly reported to **Vansittart**'s personal network in the Foreign Office[23] (and privately printed his own *Whitehall Letter*, criticising Baldwin and **Chamberlain** – for which he himself was 'monitored' by MI5).[24]

Apparently from the other end of the political spectrum, but in fact agreeing with **Gordon-Lennox** over Hitler, was **Kingsley Martin** (1897–1964).[25] The friend of **Harold Laski** and **Leonard Woolf**, **Kingsley Martin** was the eloquent, fierily indignant editor of the left-wing weekly the ***New Statesman and Nation*** from 1930 onwards. 'One of the outstanding journalists of his time – despite some spectacularly wrong-headed political judgements',[26] **Martin** was, and saw himself as, the eternal dissenter, born to keep his own, Labour, side on the right (i.e. left) path. Like so many of his radical contemporaries after 1933, he veered between advocating pacifism on the one hand and collective security on the other, between the cause of human rights and the need to have Stalin's Russia as an ally against Nazism. Week after week the indefatigable **Martin** would declare what ought to take place in Britain and the world – but of course never did.[27]

Another Blacklisted left-wing journalist and, like **Martin,** the son of a Unitarian minister, **William Mellor** (1888–1942), was combative and intense. He had already joined the ***Daily Herald*** in 1913 and was soon campaigning against Britain's participation in the First World War, which he opposed on international socialist grounds. Imprisoned as a conscientious objector against conscription after 1916, **Mellor** then returned on his release to the anti-capitalist ***Daily Herald*** as its industrial correspondent. In 1920 he became a founding member of the **Communist Party of Great Britain** but left it in 1924. In 1926 he became editor of the ***Daily Herald***, increasing its coverage of football and cricket and thereby increasing its sales, but after Odhams Press bought a majority share **Mellor** was sacked from the Odhams Board in 1931. He continued to work on the left of the Labour Party, joining various groups such as the Socialist League to try to persuade a future Labour government to implement socialist policies. After 1933 he was convinced of the necessity for a united front against fascism, consisting of the Labour Party banding together with the British Communist Party and the **ILP**. The TUC disagreed and **Mellor** was sacked from editing the ***Daily Herald***. He then established

The Town and County Councillor, a journal for Labour supporters in local government. In 1937 he was appointed editor of Sir Stafford Cripps' new radical weekly, *Tribune*, but was sacked in 1939 for not renouncing his campaign for a united left-wing common front in Britain. Ironically, at the same time that the Gestapo was Blacklisting him, **Mellor** was also being Blacklisted by the Labour Party as a candidate for parliamentary election. He was, however, later selected for their safe seat of Stockport – only for the general election to be cancelled in 1940 – by which time he had been taken back on the ***Daily Herald***. He died in 1942.[28]

It is hard to credit, but the Gestapo even had an 84-year-old in their sights. **Henry (H. W.) Nevinson** (1856–1941), the veteran radical investigative journalist, had told the world about African slavery in Portuguese Sao Tome in 1905, and had reported every international conflict from 1890 to the First World War, until he himself was wounded at Gallipoli at the age of 60 – after having co-founded the Friends' Ambulance Unit in 1914. In the mid 1930s **Nevinson** succeeded **E. M. Forster** as president of the **National Council of Civil Liberties (NCCL)**, and he also succeeded **J. B. Priestley** as president of the Blacklisted international writers' organisation **PEN**. At the age of 80 **Nevinson** supported the Spanish Republicans, writing in a letter in August 1936: 'I boil with rage day and night about Spain.' And 'I detest the cruel systems of persecution and suppressions now existing under Hitler in Germany, Mussolini in Italy and Stalin in Russia.'[29] After *Kristallnacht* he asked in the ***Manchester Guardian***: 'How can we refrain from rage?' For that and for his *Hitler the Man*[30] he incurred the Nazis' vengefulness. In 1970, almost thirty years after his death, **Storm Jameson** would ask: 'Are there left men such as **Nevinson** was – passionate Quixotes who feel injustice anywhere in the world as a nail driven into their own flesh?'[31]

A much more mysterious inclusion in the Black Book is **George Ward Price** (1886–1961), since he had once been Hitler's favourite British journalist. **Ward Price** had worked for the Nazi-supporting Lord Rothermere, owner of the *Daily Mail*, and was himself an intimate friend of Oswald Mosley and a member of the British Union of

Fascists. To **Ward Price**, the anti-Mosleyites in the East End were just 'Red Hooligans' who deserved all they got. And Hitler's brutal suppression of his own German opponents was merely like 'a jockey [lashing] his horse in a hard finish'. The *Daily Mail*, rooted in Rothermere's violent anti-communism, 'supported Hitler more strongly and more constantly than any other newspaper outside Germany ... It was the only major British daily to take a consistently pro-Nazi line'.[32] **Ward Price**, as special correspondent for the *Daily Mail*, consistently portrayed Hitler as 'a human, pleasant personality, [his] fondness for children and dogs [being] evidence of good nature'.[33] What happened to the cosy relationship between **Ward Price** and Hitler that resulted in the former's eventual inclusion in the Black Book? After the invasion of Czechoslovakia in March 1939, both the *Daily Mail* and **Ward Price** had to change their policy in order to sell their paper; they immediately became anti-Hitler British patriots backing a future British war effort, thus becoming 'traitors to the Führer' in Gestapo eyes. In his *Year of Reckoning* (1939), **Ward Price** finally declared that 'the possibility of cordial relations has now passed away'. However, even after the declaration of war he continued to publish shameless anti-Jewish smears, writing in the *Daily Mail* on 10 October 1939: 'Many enemy agents came here as refugees [and many of them] are Jews ... Many of the German Jews, often themselves immigrants from Eastern Europe, were the worst of their kind ... in Germany, the Jewish aliens formed a class conscious, self- interested community, and the misdeeds of some brought down reprisals on the rest.'

The other maverick journalist was **Douglas Reed** (1895–1976), sub-editor of *The Times* from 1925 and its chief Central European correspondent until 1938. On the one hand a right-wing, imperialist anti-appeaser, **Reed** was the author of the best-seller *Insanity Fair*, highlighting Hitler's megalomania and the coming war, a book which was banned in Germany. Confusingly, however, **Reed** was also an increasingly anti-Zionist anti-Semite who would become the first of the Holocaust deniers – 'there could not possibly have been 6 million Jewish dead'. He actually believed in a worldwide Zionist conspiracy to enslave all humanity. Already in 1943 Orwell had noted that **Reed**'s

Lest We Regret dismissed the Nazis' persecution of German Jews as 'just propaganda', and declared **Reed** to be 'a persuasive writer who could do a lot of harm'. In 1948 Reed settled in apartheid South Africa.[34]

Very different again was **Margaret Haig Mackworth, Viscountess, Lady Rhondda** (1883–1958), the wealthy daughter of a coal magnate and herself the director of twenty-six business companies. So passionate was her youthful feminism that she had addressed heckling crowds, had gone to prison for arson, and had been on hunger strike as a militant suffragette. In 1920 she had founded, subsidised and edited the Equality Feminist weekly journal ***Time and Tide*** whose contributors included the outspoken anti-fascist (and Blacklisted) British women feminists **Vera Brittain**, **Margery Corbett Ashby**, **Charlotte Haldane**, **Rose Macaulay**, **Eileen Power**, **Eleanor Rathbone**, **Rebecca West**, **Ellen Wilkinson** and **Virginia Woolf**. These women were the British counterparts of the German anti-militarist, anti-Nazi feminists whom the Nazis had branded 'pacifist hyenas' (p. 61)[35] It was hardly surprising that **Lady Rhondda**'s ***Time and Tide*** should have been one of the proscribed papers under *Zeitungen* in the *Sonderfahndungsliste GB* and that she, 'arguably Britain's leading feminist'[36] should have stood firmly against a Hitler who believed that it was only natural to confine German women to their homes as they reared 'a strong male sex'.[37]

One journalist – and possible martyr – about whom much more needs to be discovered, was the small, shy but enormously brave Roman Catholic, **John Chrysostom Segrue** (1884(?)–1942), '*Korrespondent **News Chronicle**, frueher Wien*, thought to be in England' according to the Gestapo. In 1918, **Segrue** wrote indignantly criticising the Allied blockade of Germany, his headlines: 'Food Shortage in Germany is now a tragedy/ Hunger kills children/ Spirit of unrest is spreading.' Then, in July 1933, as correspondent from Berlin for the ***News Chronicle***, he reported that Nazi persecution of German Jews was having disastrous economic consequences – and he himself gave whatever financial and personal aid that he could to help the Jews. Later in 1933, now based in Vienna, he asked his schoolboy son to accompany an elderly Jewish journalist to the train taking him out of Austria, making sure that he spoke English loudly to the old man in order to try to afford him protection. In August 1935 **Segrue** all too hopefully reported that there was increasing German unrest threatening the Nazi regime. He was expelled from Germany. In April 1938, after the *Anschluss*, Segrue went into a Jewish district of Vienna where the SS were publicly humiliating local Jews; he had a rag put in his hand by an SS officer and was ordered to help 'his fellow Jewish swine' in washing the street. Having helped an old woman, **Segrue** returned the rag and declared that he was a British subject who now knew that the reports of Nazi brutality were true. He was expelled from Austria. April 1941 found him in Belgrade, where he deliberately missed the last transport out to safety. He was arrested by the German invaders and died in mysterious circumstances in Krakow (conceivably in the POW camp section of Auschwitz) in Nazi-ruled Poland on 11 September 1942. Forty years later the Guild of Jewish Journalists planted fifty trees in Israel 'in honour of the courageous journalist who helped Jews in Germany, Austria and Hungary.'[38]

Two veteran journalists, the Liberal **J. A. Spender** (1862–1942), and the right-wing **Wickham Steed** (1871–1956), were both Blacklisted, although they took up quite different positions on appeasement. **Spender**, uncle of the left-wing poet **Stephen Spender**, was regarded as an appeaser because he was constantly reminding his readers of Britain's military unpreparedness in the late 1930s; **Steed** was an anti-appeaser, constantly reminding his readers of Hitler's determination to have a Second World War. He wrote *Hitler, Whence and Whither* (1934), *The Meaning of Hitlerism* (1934) and *Our War Aims* (1939). **Steed**'s position was complicated by his (like **Vansittart**'s) long-standing hatred of *all* Germans, a hatred that also branched out into a hatred of German Jews – whom he saw as having been both culturally and financially dominant in pre-1914 Vienna and Berlin. **Steed**'s 'solution' was to support the establishment of a nationalist, Zionist state for all Jews, well away from Europe.[39]

The much younger front-line reporter **Philip Pembroke Stephens** (1903–1937) has been described as 'a genuine hero of twentieth-century reporting'.[40] **Stephens** did not report from the safety of an office but always tried to see for himself what was happening on the ground. At the end of 1933 the ***Daily Express*** sent him to Berlin to replace **Sefton Delmer**, but unlike **Delmer**, **Stephens** did not concentrate on proximity to Nazi high-ups, reporting instead on the impact of Nazism on ordinary Germans, and especially on Jewish Germans. He was arrested twice before being finally expelled in June 1934. Thereafter he joined the ***Daily Telegraph*** who sent him to report on the second Italian-Abyssinian war and on the Spanish Civil War. He was one of the first reporters to enter shattered Guernica and privately told the British ambassador that the town had *not* been destroyed by the retreating Republicans but by pro-Franco German and Italian aerial bombardment. Next he was dispatched to cover China where he reported the atrocities committed by the invading Japanese. In November 1937, the last days of the Chinese defence of Shanghai, **Stephens** was allegedly mistaken for a sniper and was shot dead. Despite having been dead for nearly three years, he was still on the Gestapo's 'Most Wanted' list.[41]

In contrast to the deeply serious **Stephens**, **Hannen Swaffer** (1879–1962), '*Schriftleiter* [leader-writer] *fuer* ***Daily Herald***', was a long-lived poseur, though possibly, like the Scarlet Pimpernel, he merely posed as a poseur. A drama critic banned from many theatres because of his vituperative reviews, he liked the company of actors more than seeing them act. Originally a right-wing employee of Lord Northcliffe, **Swaffer** had been converted to socialism, like so many others (for instance **Rowland Kenney**), by Robert Blatchford's *Merrie England*. After 1931 'the cantankerously brilliant' **Swaffer** joined the ***Daily Herald***, becoming its star columnist and a consistent voice for the excluded, the strikers, the refugees. He came to be called the 'Pope of Fleet Street'.[42] In August 1933 he was reported as writing almost daily in support of persecuted German Jews and criticising Anglo-Jewish leaders who did not back the anti-German boycott. He became an outspoken defender of civil liberty for the **NCCL** and an opponent of the death penalty. As a supporter of the popular front forces in the Spanish Civil War, **Swaffer** later visited Madrid, with **Manny Shinwell**, **Ellen Wilkinson**, Aneurin Bevan, **George Strauss** and **Sydney Silverman**, and proved to be the most popular speaker of them all.[43]

Two other journalists with dangerous assignments in the Far East were **Hugh Hessell Tiltman** (1898–1976), and **H. H. Timperley** (1898–1954). **Tiltman** was a reporter for the *Daily News*, and the ***Manchester Guardian***. He had written for the Ukraine Bureau in the early 1930s in response to Pilsudski's mistreatment of Poland's Ukrainian minority. In 1932 he had already published his prescient *Terror in Europe*, alerting readers to the totalitarian ruthlessness of both Stalin and Mussolini. He was then sent to Manchuria – not an easy billet.[44] **Tiltman** was arrested by the Japanese secret police, the *Kempeitai*, and mysteriously charged with 'taking a photograph without a camera'. He had been working with the secret agent Colonel Etherton, with whom he collaborated on three books: *The Pacific – a Forecast*; *Manchuria: The Cockpit of Asia;* and *Japan: Mistress of the Pacific*. Recalled to Europe, **Tiltman** reached Spain just in time to be expelled by the victorious Francoists. Then, in Bucharest, he was sent to witness the first transport of Jews from Austria to the port of Galatz whence they were to be transferred like 'two-legged cattle' to some ocean-going vessel and dumped in Liberia. In June 1939, **Tiltman** was helped to safety away from Berlin, just in time, to New York. He himself best summed up his uncompromising opposition to all totalitarianisms, whether left or right; he had seen Nanking, he had seen Danzig – among all too many other shattered cities:

> The world in the thirties of the twentieth century [has] faced not four wars, but one war on four fronts … Manchuria, Ethiopia, Spain, China, Austria, Czechoslovakia, Albania – each in turn [has] proved that aggression pays; that there [is], in Hitler's words, 'no right but might'. A tragic generation [has] paid the price of that atavistic philosophy in blood and terror … From the North Sea to the Nankow Pass the Great Aggression must be halted, and the nightmares which afflict men's hearts must end.[45]

The Australian journalist **H. J. Timperley** (1898–1954) also reported from China on Japan's brutal invasion for the ***Manchester Guardian***.

Back in London from 1938, he edited the influential *What War Means: The Japanese Terror in China – Eyewitness Accounts* for the Left Book Club. During the Second World War **Timperley** worked for the information office of the United Nations and afterwards for UNRRA in Shanghai. At the end of his life he became a Quaker and, in 1954, co-founded 'War on Want'.

City editor of the ***Daily Herald*** (1930–36), and then its editor (1937–42), **Francis, 'Frank' Williams** (1903–1970), had been converted to socialism by the poverty of Liverpool. He worked as editor at Odhams Press under the reign of **Lord Southwood** (Blacklisted by the Gestapo for being Jewish), who had a 51 per cent majority share of ownership of the ***Daily Herald*** as against the 49 per cent held by the TUC. **Southwood** was for appeasement, **Williams** against, so steering an editorial 'line' was not easy. As city editor, **Williams** had analysed the German economy, especially the figures for twenty-five key raw materials, and so knew that Hitler was preparing to wage war. In the spring of 1939, **Williams** dared to call for **Chamberlain**'s resignation as prime minister and in January 1940 he himself resigned from the ***Daily Herald*** on its suppression of an article he wrote on Finland's resistance to Stalin.

The last Blacklisted British-born journalist in alphabetical order was **G. Gordon Young** (1908–1963), who worked for **Reuters** between 1930 and 1942, having been their Berlin correspondent from 1934 to 1937. In 1938 he was in Bad Godesberg to report on the negotiations between Hitler and **Chamberlain** over Czechoslovakia, and on 12 November 1938 he interviewed Goebbels immediately after *Kristallnacht* on 'the Jewish Question'. He was in Finland when the Soviet Union invaded and then wrote from the Netherlands, only to have to flee yet again, immediately after the Germans invaded Holland in 1940. Young was the first British journalist to enter Germany after its defeat and the first to interview its rocket scientist Werner von Braun in June 1945. His grim awareness of the eternal realpolitik of the armaments industry is seen in his title *The Fall and Rise of Alfred Krupp* (1960).[46]

Can one generalise about this plethora of English journalists during the 1930s who were in the Gestapo's Black Book in 1940? One is struck by two things. First, there is an immense diversity both in their backgrounds and in their opinions. Although they all – except **Ward Price** – detested Hitler, whether they were old, young, Conservative, Liberal, Labour or Communist, some so loathed Nazism that they were too lenient towards Stalin; and some just hated all Germans, including Jewish Germans. Others, like **Tiltman**, saw the brutality of every totalitarian dictatorship. But very few of them were in agreement about what should or could be done to counter the horror, given that most believed that war was the greatest horror of all. Secondly, one is struck by the extreme danger of their work. Being a British foreign correspondent in the 1930s was hardly a sinecure. Sacked by the proprietor of their newspaper, expelled from country after country, constantly risking assassination, arrested, wounded or even killed in foreign wars – those were the risks they constantly ran as they insisted on testifying, however unpalatably, to the truth of what they had witnessed, typing up their reports as the tanks rolled in.

*

For the refugee journalists the situation was quite different: their life-threatening experiences had already been endured and survived before they reached the asylum of Britain. What they then had to face was the struggle to get work in a foreign language against a backdrop of homesickness, exile and a gnawing anxiety for their family members left behind. The left-wing Catholic **Franz Aenderl** (1883–1951), for example, first a Communist and then a Social Democrat member of the Bavarian regional parliament until 1931, had been taken into 'protective custody' in 1933 and incarcerated in Bamberg prison. On his release, he had been placed under *Schreibverbot* and had fled first to Czechoslovakia, then Poland, then Denmark and had finally found refuge in Britain where he worked as a journalist. In May 1940 he was stripped of his German citizenship. From 1942 to 1943 **Aerndel** was employed by the BBC as announcer in Catholic broadcasts from London to Germany and he founded a circle for

Bavarians in exile. He returned to Bavaria in 1946 and became editor of a mid Bavarian newspaper.[47]

The German Czech Jew, **Fritz Beer** (1911–2006), had first been a youthful enthusiast for Zionism and later an enthusiast for the Czech Communist Party, for which he had worked as organiser and journalist – until disillusioned by Stalinism and the Nazi-Soviet pact. He had then fled the Nazis as they overran Czechoslovakia and Poland, finding refuge in London where he joined other literary exiles. 'He volunteered for the exiled Czech Army, saw active service [in the tank corps] in 1939 and 1940 and joined the Allied Forces entering France and Germany after D-Day.'[48] He only learned in 1945 that his elderly father had been murdered in the Holocaust. Always feeling that he never fully belonged anywhere, Fritz Beer eventually wrote a moving *Kaddish for My Father* (2002).

The Jewish Austrian **Willi Frischauer** (1906–1978) had been a successful journalist in Vienna and then a Vienna correspondent in Berlin reporting on the Reichstag fire – the work of Hitler's armed followers. Returning to Austria in 1933, he became the editor of two Vienna newspapers but emigrated to Britain in 1935 where he worked on the ***Daily Herald***. In 1940 he wrote *The Nazis at War*, published by **Gollancz**, warning his fellow Jews of the war aims of the genocidal Otto Strasser. After the war **Frischauer** would force himself to enter the Nazi mindset, writing on the rise and fall of Goering (1950) and on Himmler, *The Evil Genius of the Third Reich* (1953). Both his own elderly parents, he learned in 1945, had been murdered in Theresienstadt.

Formerly a journalist for the conservative *Frankfurter Allgemeine*, **Hans Lothar** (1929–1967), left Germany in 1936 and then helped found the publishers Secker and Warburg. In 1941, with British government support, he founded *Die Zeitung* for German exiles in Britain, intending that it should also be dropped over Germany.[49] **Johannes Maier-Hultschin** (1901–1950) had edited a Catholic German anti-Nazi paper in Poland – and was therefore inevitably condemned by the Gestapo. He just managed to flee to London via Yugoslavia and France in 1940. During the war he, too, broadcast from the BBC, in his case addressing himself to German anti-Nazi Catholics. He returned to West Germany to die.

More extraordinary, and eventually much more 'British' than any of those last-mentioned refugee journalists, was the trajectory of **Siegfried 'Siegi' Moos** (1904–1988). He had been an ardent young Communist in Berlin in the late 1920s and early 1930s, prominent in some of its less well-known offbeat factions such as the 'Berlin Proletarian Freethinkers', who campaigned for divorce and for women's right to have an abortion. By 1930 Moos was the editor and chief theorist of the magazine *Arbeiterbuehne und-Film* ('Workers' Theatres and Cinema'), the publication of the several hundred contemporary German agitprop theatre groups, of which there were then thirty in Berlin alone. He also wrote lyrics for the Communist magazine *Red Sport* and for the musical *Red Start*, which was performed to an audience of thousands in Berlin in February 1932:

The sportsmen call: do not be silent!
Attention now: No need to wait!
Stop kowtowing …
Hone your muscles! Focus your eyes!
Sharpen your brains! Work your lungs! …

Red sportsmen don't believe that
Sport alone can liberate.
Then join the red fighting front
To be soldiers of the class struggle …
Hone your muscles! Focus your eyes! …

Moos left Germany for Britain in 1934, briefly becoming one of the leaders of the German Communist Party in exile in London. However, disillusioned by party infighting and by Stalinism, he then exiled himself from all political activism for the next thirty years. But believing him still to be a Communist, the Gestapo Blacklisted him in 1939. **Moos** became a British academic and eventually an (economics) adviser to Harold Wilson's first Labour Government in 1964.[50]

The legally trained journalist, the Austrian socialist **Oscar Pollak** (1893–1963), had joined the Socialist Workers' Party immediately after the First World War. Between 1923 and 1926 he had written for its paper from London where he was part of the secretariat of the Socialist International. But in 1926 **Pollak** returned to Vienna and became first foreign editor and then chief editor for the *Workers' Paper*. After the civil strife in Vienna, he became a co-founder of the Revolutionary Socialists in February 1934 – but Vienna got too hot to hold him and his wife. They fled first to Brussels in 1936, then to Paris, always working for the Socialist International. Finally, they reached London just in time in 1940 and **Pollak** built up the London Bureau of Austrian Socialists in Exile. There he wrote *Farewell France* (1941), *Underground Europe Calling* (1942), and *It All Started in Vienna* (1944), before he and his wife could return to Vienna in 1945 to re-establish once more the *Workers' Newspaper*.

A still more prominent left-wing journalist was the German **Victor Schiff** (1895–1953), who at the young age of 24, a war veteran and a member of the SPD, had been part of the German delegation at the Treaty of Versailles. He later wrote his eyewitness account *The Germans at Versailles 1919* (1930). Between 1920 and 1933 **Schiff** wrote for the Social Democrat daily *Vorwaerts*, where in 1931 he had strongly supported Chancellor Bruening as the bulwark of German parliamentarianism against the threat of a dictatorship. After 1933 he was arrested twice and imprisoned; he fled as soon as he could, first to Britain and then to France. In Paris he became foreign correspondent for the ***Daily Herald*** as well as writing for various German papers in exile. From 1935 he supported a common front with German communists in exile. In the first two years of the Spanish Civil War, **Schiff** reported on the war for the ***Daily Herald*** until eventually he had to flee mainland Europe for London in 1940. In the *Informationsheft GB* of July 1940, **Schiff** is singled out by the Gestapo as 'one of the most active of agitators against Germany [*Einer der aergsten Hetzger gegen Deutschland*] in the Labour Party'. His address is given as 12 Wilson Street, London EC2. Nevertheless, despite his allegedly 'anti-German' politics, **Schiff** wrote *against* the Allies' insistance on unconditional surrender and a totally 'dictated peace' that would impose one-sided disarmament upon a defeated Germany. After the war he became foreign correspondent for the ***Daily Herald*** in Rome, where he died.

There was one rare woman among the refugee journalists, **Gabriele Tergit** (1894–1982). She had established a reputation before 1933 both as a novelist satirising the late Weimar Republic in *Kaesebier Conquers Berlin* (1931), and as the reporter of court cases for the *Berliner Tageblatt*, believing as she did that criminal trials always reveal the society of their time. So lively was her language and acute her social criticism that **Tergit**'s legal reportage became a new literary genre of its own. She also published in the militantly anti-fascist periodical *Weltbuehne* ('World Stage'). **Tergit** had witnessed and reported on the first case against Hitler and Goebbels for criminal misuse of the press and she drew attention to the dangerous populism of their new Nazi Party. Not surprisingly, therefore, she, a Jewish German, was placed high on the list of opponents of Nazism and on 5 March 1933 at 3 o'clock in the morning the SA tried to break into her home and seize her. **Tergit** managed to escape and she lived the rest of her life in exile – first in Prague and in Palestine but then, from 1938 on, in London; from 1957 until 1981 she was the dedicated secretary of the **PEN** section for German authors abroad.[51]

But by far the most influential refugee journalist in Britain after October 1938 was Stefan Lorant, a Hungarian Jew, who had escaped Nazi Germany after several months' imprisonment in 1933. He was not even on the Black List,[52] but I must include him because he was the founder and first editor of the enormously popular, innovative picture magazine, ***Picture Post***, which was Blacklisted, among other banned newspapers in the *Sonderfahndungsliste GB*. From the start its editorial policy had been anti-fascist and in favour of radical social reform.[53] Its first number, 1 October 1938, carried an article by the owner, Edward Hulton, excoriating the 'Pure Race Theory': 'Science declares that there is not, and can never be, such a thing as a pure race in the world ... The reason the race myth persists in the Europe of today is simply that certain rulers desire to supply a reason for extreme Nationalism.'

Its third number, 15 October 1938, came out at the same time as the Munich Agreement and in it, instead of pigs flying, **John Heartfield** created a photo-montage of 'Happy Elephants' flying, in order to puncture the optimism of British pro-appeasers. And Hulton asked: 'Does Hitler want World Empire?' After *Kristallnacht*, 10/11 November 1938, Lorant's deputy editor Tom Hopkinson remembered an enraged Stefan Lorant exclaiming: 'This bloody Hitler! These bloody pogroms! ... What do the readers want me to do? How am I going to hit back?' On 26 November 1938, ***Picture Post***'s article 'Back to the Middle Ages' showed large, devastating pictures of Goering, Streicher, Hitler and Goebbels – 'the four guardians of German culture today', in full rant – as well as the burning synagogues and anti-Jewish signs all over Germany with, finally, a large photograph of elderly Jews being forced to scrub a Viennese street in front of smiling onlookers: 'Humanity at its Lowest: The Jew-baiter at Work'. Hopkinson commented:

> 'Back to the Middle Ages' remains for me the finest example of the use of photographs for political effect ... they make their point more effectively than thousands of words – a savage and well-earned kick into the vitals of an enemy. [They] sought ... to warn [readers] never to trust to men or a party which could act like this ... [Such] a warning was still desperately needed.[54]

On 17 December 1938 ***Picture Post*** featured very sympathetic images of *Kindertransport* refugee children, in 'Their First Day in England'. The print order for ***Picture Post*** was then a million and soon doubled. By 1940 it was reckoned that half the adult British population had seen a copy and were being educated in the nature of Nazism. No wonder that it was a prime political target for the Gestapo. Lorant himself, however, was not granted English citizenship before the Second World War and left for the United States by the last boat in July 1940. It is now alleged that he was pressured to leave Britain.[55]

Like their English counterparts, the refugee journalists were an unpredictable, heterogeneous assortment. The more left wing they were, the more vulnerable they were to disillusionment over

Stalinism or else to defending the indefensible. And having to write in English instead of in their native German was yet another strain, as they reported back from what appeared to be an ever retreating front line. That these refugee journalists should have survived physically or emotionally at all was a tribute to their inner strength, at a time when, like so many of their fellows, they were suffering from despair at the loss of their homelands and terrible anxiety about every person for whom they cared.

PART FOUR

TARGETING THE BRITISH ESTABLISHMENT

11

The Secret Service

Who spied for Britain – and who was believed? Many of Britain's secret agents were no secret at all to the Gestapo who knew much more about them by 1940 than did the British people, naturally kept in the dark by the Official Secrets Act. When **Thomas Kendrick,** Passport Control Officer (and spy) in Vienna, was arrested by the Gestapo in August 1938, he was appalled – and terrified – to discover just how much the Gestapo had already learned about the British 'secret' service.[1] Clearly there had been more than a few double agents employed by MI6 who were *also* reporting back to the Reich.

Above all there had been the 'Venlo incident' on 9 November 1939, masterminded by the same Walter Schellenberg who was overseeing the final compilation of the *Sonderfahndungsliste GB* and the *Informationsheft GB*. Schellenberg's SD (the Nazi *Sicherheit's Dienst*) remit included counter-intelligence. He set up a 'sting' in the Dutch city of Venlo to catch **Sigismund Payne Best**, a veteran British spy working under the cover of a Dutch import-export business, and his superior, **Major Richard Stevens**, Passport Control Officer in the Hague. These were the two main British agents operating from neutral Holland. They were conned into believing that they were about to meet with anti-Nazi German generals who wanted to end the war with Britain by getting rid of Hitler. The two Englishmen were ambushed, kidnapped, arrested and interrogated by the Gestapo before being sent to Berlin and then on to Sachsenhausen concentration camp.

Max Hastings declared in 2015 that it 'is hard to overestimate the significance of the Venlo Incident – British espionage activities on the Continent suffered a devastating blow'.[2] And Ernest Volkman called it 'the greatest disaster ever to befall British Intelligence'.[3] **Best** and **Stevens** had operated from the Hague, the major transmission centre for all MI6 operations in Europe. By means of a Dutch 'mole', the Nazis had already uncovered the identities of many of the station's agents and informants, but in the five days after the Englishmen's arrest, possibly in an attempt to protect their wives who were also Blacklisted by the Gestapo, **Best** and **Stevens** revealed the identities of still more agents and informers and 'the entire MI6 structure in Europe was destroyed'.[4] Keith Jeffery admits that the damage from the affair was very great[5] and that the *Informationsheft* itself cited **Stevens** and **Best** as its authorities in its convincing résumé about the structure of the British Secret Service. It was even more significant that the disaster of Venlo meant that subsequently the British High Command, including both MI5 and MI6, would refuse to respond to feelers from genuine anti-Nazi opposition elements in Germany for the rest of the war, demanding total unconditional surrender instead.

Of all the names in Part One of the Black Book, at least 600 are alleged either to be secret agents, informants, or, in the case of 333 names, connected with some spy ring or a suspected group of activist resisters (*Taeterkreis*). Among the latter were forty Dutch anti-Nazis linked to the **Stevens/Best** operation in The Hague, who, if they did not manage to escape to Britain in time, were to be arrested by the Nazis immediately upon the German invasion of Holland in May 1940. Among those who did get out to Britain in time was **Lionel Louis Loewe** (1892–1989), a British Jew who had worked for the Secret Intelligence Service, SIS, in Holland.

Walter Schellenberg and Wolfgang zu Christian were naturally eager to impress their superiors with the thoroughness and the reach of their counter-espionage. However, many if not most of the hundreds of their suspect agents are so vaguely itemised, often without even a full name or date or place of birth, let alone a full current address – merely 'thought to be in England' – that they would have been very hard to track down, even if they had been in England in 1940, and are impossible to trace now. Who, for example, was **Alaeddin Jusuf**, British agent last in Ankara, 'thought to be in England'? Or

'British agents' **Bharu**, **Birnbaum, Blaazer** and **Brandt**, all 'thought to be in England' and all classified RSHA IV E4 (i.e. spying on the German army and its military strength) – just like almost every other Blacklisted alleged agent. This chapter will of necessity therefore concentrate on those most important British secret agents in the Black Book of whom something reliable is known.

If the porous MI6 intelligence network had been almost destroyed by the end of 1939, what took its place? On the one hand there was a new chief of MI6, Sir Stewart Menzies, 'C', who, helped by the codebreakers of Bletchley Park from early summer 1941, 'worked very hard to repair some of the damage'.[6] On the other hand there was also 63-year-old **Colonel Claude Dansey** or 'Z' (1876–1947), Sir Stewart Menzies' assistant chief, formerly based in the British embassy in Rome as a 'passport officer' in the 1930s (and already in fact known to the Gestapo as a full-time MI6 operative). Foreseeing a Venlo-type disaster, **Dansey** was the mastermind behind MI6's parallel, rather more secret, Secret Intelligence Service called 'Z'.

Dansey was a deeply damaged personality from an unstable upper-class family, being the eldest son of a violently abusive ex-army officer and gambler and his clinically depressed wife. He was one of nine children, all bullied and beaten and all at war with one another – trust was not an option. Nevertheless it was largely **Dansey** ('a ruthless shit' according to Hugh Trevor-Roper),[7] who did much to rescue British intelligence as a system. But it was alleged that he did not attempt to rescue its agents, such as the Resistance fighters under SOE in France, once they were caught. His own 'Z' agents were not, for the most part, politically motivated volunteers, let alone old public school Foreign Office men – both of them types that **Dansey** despised. He also loathed all university graduates or indeed anyone with intellectual pretensions. Instead, he relied on American industrialists, British bankers, businessmen and journalists stationed abroad such as **Hubert Harrison**, **John Segrue** and **Hugh Hessell Tiltman**, who never took anything down in writing for him but who would use their eyes and report back orally – especially their findings from economic espionage. One such informant was the banker and aviator **Leonard St Clair Ingrams** (*c.*1890–1953), whose wife was connected to the wealthy Barings and whose son Richard would later found *Private Eye*. **Ingrams** senior would work during the war, together with **Bruce Lockhart**, **Richard Crossman**, and **Brendan Bracken**, for the covert branch of the Foreign Office, the Political Warfare Executive, which pretended to be interested in peace negotiations with Himmler. Another banker recruit of **Dansey**'s was **Siegmund George Warburg** (1902–1982), who reported very usefully from Switzerland on his regular meetings with the most powerful German financial expert, Hjalmar Schacht, president of the German Reichsbank. **Warburg**, a Jewish German, had had to flee to Britain in 1934 and later co-founded S. G. Warburg and Co. He was naturalised in 1939. An outstanding merchant banker, although considered an upstart newcomer, **Warburg**, a strong Europeanist, created the Eurobond market.

Another of **Dansey**'s most important secret recruits in the 1930s had been the passionately anglophile Hungarian Jewish film-maker **Alexander Korda** (1893–1951), whose London film company **Dansey** funded clandestinely with money from the Secret Service. For who could have a better 'cover' than a film director, travelling all over Europe in search of film locations and needing to talk to local bigwigs and financiers? (**Korda** would produce *The Scarlet Pimpernel*, *Sanders of the River* – with **Paul Robeson** – and *South Riding* in the 1930s.) One way that **Korda** used his film company was by shooting a deliberately unfinished film, e.g. *King Pausole*, in which he recorded details of the North African coastline in preparation for what **Dansey** knew would soon be an important battle area.[8] **Korda** recruited **Noel Coward** who, constrained by the Official Secrets Act, treated his inclusion in the Black Book, once it was revealed in the ***Manchester Guardian*** in September 1945, as just a hilarious joke. But it had been no joke – as Gestapo counter-intelligence was aware. A committed anti-fascist, **Coward** had originally been part of **Vansittart**'s personal intelligence network, visiting Warsaw, Moscow and Helsinki to gauge Nazi influence in high places and make useful contacts. His perfect disguise was his 'reputation as a bit of an idiot … I was the perfect silly ass

... [people] would say all kinds of things that I'd pass along'.[9] Two of the 'people' were the Duke and Duchess of Windsor, hoping to be set up as king and queen in a Nazified Britain. **Coward** later worked in Paris and then in the United States (both Washington and Hollywood), singing his funny songs – but really there to report back on pro- and anti-British feeling in the war.

Dansey would soon become the most important figure in British intelligence. The defeated governments of almost all Nazi-occupied Europe were in exile in London by September 1940. Their intelligence organisations only functioned with permission from the British, which largely meant **Dansey**, on whom they now had to rely for money, transport and any communication with their homelands. As assistant chief to Menzies, he thus had extensive power over the Secret Services, not just of Britain but of Belgium, Holland, Norway, Poland, Czechoslovakia and, later, the Free French. But it was only with the Czechs that the choleric **Dansey** had much patience. He despised and distrusted the Special Operations Executive (SOE) as amateurs with a penchant for martyrdom, whose chief, Major-General Gubbins, he saw as a rival whom he tried to undermine.[10] As his last great intelligence feat in the Second World War, **Dansey** would be responsible for the transmission to the Soviet Union of vital 'Ultra' intelligence gained from the Bletchley decoders, without the Russians ever discovering – and therefore mistrusting – its British provenance. It is quite possible that this meant the difference between victory and defeat on the Eastern Front, especially at the battle of Kursk.[11] In 1947 **Dansey** died, without a pension, unregretted by his colleagues and apparently almost unmourned, with **Noel Coward** among the few at his funeral.

One of the old guard MI6 officers for whom **Dansey** did have some respect was **Norman Dewhurst** (1887–*c.*1968), whom he himself had recruited for 'Z'. He had **Dewhurst** trained for espionage in Nazi Germany under cover of being a writer in Bavaria. 'He reported on military activities, including the construction of military airfields and even information from an SS corporal on what was happening inside the Dachau concentration camp.'[12] In mid 1938 **Dewhurst** was despatched to Latvia for 'Z', under cover of being a ship's chandler. Unfortunately several of the secret agents whom he had trusted to get him information on German tank manufacture were in fact double agents working for the *Abwehr*; they fed him false intelligence – as well as blowing his cover.

Very different from **Dansey** and from **Dewhurst** was the redoubtable **Frank Foley**, who has already featured in this book as the outstanding rescuer of thousands of hounded Jews in Berlin. But **Foley** was also, simultaneously, an outstanding British secret agent and was a Gestapo suspect as such – 'former leader of Passport Control, Berlin, RSHA IV E4'. One of the Jews whom **Foley** had enabled to escape to Britain was the wife of a young Austrian physicist, Paul Rosbaud, scientific adviser to the Springer Verlag in Berlin. Rosbaud became **Foley**'s vital informant when Rosbaud's close friend, the physicist Otto Hahn, confided in him that he had found a way to split the atom by bombarding uranium atoms with slow-speed neutrons. Hitler then of course ordered German nuclear physicists to start work on creating an atom bomb. A strict ban was imposed on any public discussion of the experiments, but Rosbaud, through his relationship to Hahn, remained in the loop, and throughout the war was able to keep British Secret Services, in the person of **Foley**, updated concerning the deliberate lack of progress made by the German atomic weapons programme.[13]

Foley was forced to leave Berlin in late August 1939, having issued hundreds of Jews, if not a thousand, with less than legal passports and visas for Britain and Palestine up to the very last minute. He was next based in neutral Norway where he smuggled in a secret wireless transmitter, against the orders of the British defence minister Sir Cecil Dormer. Unfortunately, all **Foley**'s intelligence that the Nazis were preparing to invade Norway was disbelieved in London, and when that invasion began on 1 May 1940, he and his staff had to evacuate. He was sent on to France and put in charge of the only secure cipher/wireless link with London, merely to be disbelieved once again, both at home and in the field. After the fall of France, however, MI6 did always make sure to send special liaison units into battle *with* wireless transmitters in order to pass on the results of the code-breakers' work to the commanders.[14] **Foley** continued to make important contributions to the British war effort, notably in heading the 'Double Cross' project to mislead the German High Command about the location of D-Day landings[15] and in 'Operation Crossbow' to counter the V1 rockets (early cruise missiles) from June to October 1944, by giving Germany false information about their trajectory and place of impact.[16]

An Oxford graduate who had won the Military Cross in the First World War, **David Footman** (1895–1983), was a British diplomat in Yugoslavia, Alexandria and Port Said after the First World War. He later became a businessman in Vienna and a banker in Belgrade. In 1935 he joined SIS, later MI6, as leader of Section 1 on political intelligence. The Gestapo gives his London address but does not add details.

The transparent 'cover' of **Thomas Kendrick** (1895–1979), like that of **Foley**, had been as a Passport Control Officer, in **Kendrick**'s case operating from Vienna, where, again like **Foley**, he was instrumental in saving many hundreds, if not thousands of Jews, very often bending the Foreign Office rules, and despite increasing pressure from London to limit Jewish emigration. He was most probably betrayed by a double agent before himself being arrested by the Gestapo, interrogated and deported from Austria in the summer of 1938. During his time in Vienna **Kendrick** had spied on Mussolini's naval movements as well as on Nazi Germany, and, by issuing his not necessarily authorised visas for Britain or Palestine, he saved possibly two hundred Austrian Jews a day. Between 1940 and 1947, once Britain began to hold German prisoners of war, **Kendrick** re-emerged as MI6's secret spymaster-in-chief against Nazi Germany, soon heading a top-secret unit that bugged the conversations of around 10,000 German POWs, including *Luftwaffe* pilots, U-boat crews – and eventually fifty-nine Nazi generals after 1942.[17] From these, of course, it was possible to learn what was being or what had been planned by Hitler even before his orders were transmitted by Enigma.[18]

Just how difficult it could be, both for the Germans and the British, to distinguish between diplomacy and spying is exemplified by **Walter Charles Rudolph Aue** (1891–1977), who had been British vice-consul in Hanover since 1926. When, in 1935, he reported the building of new army barracks and an airport, it made the Gestapo HQ in Berlin accuse him of espionage and the gathering and reporting of military information – thus overstepping his consular brief. The consulate in Hannover was shut down and **Aue** was deported as *persona non grata*. He was moved to Antwerp as British consul-general but then had to flee to Britain in 1940 when Germany overran Belgium. Back in London, **Aue** worked for the Foreign Office and his photograph is one of those inserted at the back of the Gestapo's *Informationsheft* in July 1940 for immediate arrest. There were many men in the Passport Control and Diplomatic Service stationed in Germany and Austria before September 1939 whom the Gestapo knew or suspected, rightly or wrongly, to be secret agents.[19]

An unsavoury example of British espionage was Britain's spy-catcher in Britain, **Lieutenant Colonel Edward Hinchley-Cooke** (1894–1955). Born in Dresden to a German mother and an English father, at the outbreak of the First World War **Hinchley-Cooke** had been expelled from his clerk's position in the British legation in Dresden and deported to Britain. Given his fluent German, spoken with a Saxon accent, **Hinchley-Cooke** was immediately recruited for MI5 in August 1914, liaising between Scotland Yard and the Security Service and decoding letters from suspected enemy agents. He was also 'planted', dressed in a German soldier's uniform, as a stool pigeon in German POW camps. In the interwar years, **Hinchley-Cook**, now a major, and ostensibly part of the Territorial Army, was almost certainly still working for MI5, involved in arresting and interrogating suspected spies. This work intensified after September 1939, and in June 1941 it was he, now a lieutenant colonel, who procured an incriminating sworn statement from the would-be spy, Josef Jakobs, who had been parachuted into Britain but who had broken his ankle on landing and could therefore do no spying. **Hinchley-Cooke** ruled that Jakobs must be tried by a court-martial, which, after ten minutes' deliberation, as **Hinchley-Cooke** had anticipated, ordered his execution by firing squad in the Tower of London. Jakobs was the last person to be executed there; his farewell letter to his family was not sent. Why had he not been treated as a prisoner of war?[20]

A veteran of counter-intelligence in German-occupied Belgium in the First World War, **Theodore Felstead** was a would-be spy-catcher. He published his memoir of that time in *German Spies at Bay in Britain 1914–18* in 1920 and made frequent approaches in the mid 1930s to the Foreign Office to be employed in counter-espionage again. However, he seems to have been treated with some suspicion and it is not clear whether he ever gained RAF clearance in the Second World War. In 1945 he wrote to **Hinchley-Cooke** asking to be commissioned to write an account of the department's activities from 1939 to 1945 but he was turned down.

Two of the most dashing and improbable of all the Blacklisted British secret agents were the Scottish adventurer, **Robert Hamilton Bruce Lockhart** (1887–1970) and the cosmopolitan Irish aristocrat **Conrad Fulke Thomond O'Brien-ffrench, Marquis of Castlemond. Lockhart**, a compulsive womaniser, had engaged in sexual entanglements from the very start of his career, first when he had had an adulterous affair with a Malayan princess while he was a young rubber-planter, and promptly had to leave the country, and next, in 1916–17, when he had had another scandalous affair, this time with a Jewish Frenchwoman in Moscow, where he, a fluent Russian speaker, was then acting as British consul. His superiors in the British embassy judged his behaviour so compromising that he was despatched home to London – only to be sent back to Petrograd in January 1918 with an impossible brief. He was to maintain close links with the new Bolshevik revolutionary leaders, trying to keep them in the war against Germany, but without any *official* support from Britain. He then became romantically involved with an Estonian/Russian aristocrat, Countess Moura von Benckendorff, herself a suspected socialist secret agent (see **Moura Budberg**, p. 175). **Lockhart** then participated in a top secret Allied, principally British, conspiracy to overthrow Russia's new communist regime, using armed intervention, landing from the port of Archangel – and even possibly involving the attempted assassination of Lenin.[21] Betrayed by double-agent Latvian *agents provocateurs* working for Cheka (Soviet Secret Police), **Lockhart** was arrested and imprisoned in the Lubyanka prison, befriended only by **Budberg** (then Moura von Benckendorff), at great risk to herself. He very narrowly escaped execution in Russia by being exchanged in 1919 for Maxim Litvinov, the future Soviet Foreign Secretary, who was at that time in prison in London.

Thereafter **Lockhart** officially left the Foreign Service but kept up his contacts with eastern Europe, especially in Czechoslovakia under **Masaryk**. His *Memoirs of a British Agent* (1932) became a best seller and a film, followed by his books *Retreat from Glory* (1934), and *Guns or Butter: War countries and Peace countries of Europe Revisited* (1938). In 1939 he rejoined the Foreign Office and became British liaison with the provisional Czech government when it was in exile in London. The Gestapo were on his trail in the Black Book because of his secret ties with eastern Europe.[22] He was made deputy under secretary of state, in charge of the clandestine Political Warfare Executive, which masterminded black and white propaganda against the Axis powers and was part of the 'Secret State' between 1941 and 1945.

Conrad O'Brien-ffrench (1893–1980), or 'Z3', was even more of a compulsive adventurer than **Lockhart** – his whole life reads like an improbable fiction. In 1910, at 17, he left his landed family and shipped for Canada to join the 'Mounties' – the Royal Northwest Mounted Police – in Saskatchewan and the wild frontier, but he returned to Britain to be by his dying mother in 1912. In 1913 **O'Brien-ffrench** went back to live at his Irish ancestral home where he joined the Tipperary Militia, and then, promoted to captain, fought with the Royal Irish Regiment at Mons, only to be wounded and taken prisoner in August 1914 on the first day of battle. In between his many thwarted subsequent escape attempts in the First World War, he communicated by invisible ink with MI5, transmitting information from fellow prisoners about German troop movements – and he also managed to teach himself fluent Russian.

After the war **O'Brien-ffrench** was immediately recruited into MI6 and posted to Stockholm as 'ST36' to get information about

Bolshevik Russia from Russian émigrés. Then, after a brief stay in India in 1921–2, where, climbing at over 20,000 feet, he explored some of the Himalayas, **O'Brien-ffrench** returned to Europe and decided to train as a serious painter in London and Paris. By 1930 he had become a successful portraitist of the beau monde, but by the end of that decade he also returned to working as a secret agent, this time as 'Z3' for **Dansey**'s network. His cover was that of a businessman running a travel agency, 'Tyrolese Tours' in Kitzbuehl, Austria, where, in the intervals between mountain climbing and skiing, he established a spy network reaching from Austria to Southern Germany, providing intelligence on the Nazi build-up to the Second World War. It was **O'Brien-ffrench** who transmitted by phone to London the first news of the German advance into Austria. This broke his cover and he had to retire from spying. In the *Sonderfahndungsliste* he is noted as formerly head of his own spy network in Kitzbuehl, but was now 'thought to be in England'. In fact he sat the war out in Trinidad before going on to settle on a ranch in Canada. No wonder Ian Fleming thought of his friend **O'Brien-ffrench** when he came to create James Bond.[23]

Many of the Blacklisted top British secret agents were considerably more hostile to communism than they were to fascism during the interwar years. The Old Etonian **Major Desmond Morton** (1891–1971) was one example. He had joined the Royal Artillery in 1911 and served with distinction in the First World War, ending as a friend of **Winston Churchill** and aide-de-camp to Field Marshal Sir Douglas Haig. He was seconded to the Foreign Office in 1919 and was head of SIS, Section V, concentrating on counter-Bolshevism in the mid 1920s. **Morton** himself secretly ran his own informer inside the British Communist Party, and at the end of 1924 he both disseminated and vouched for the authenticity of the notorious (and fraudulent) 'Zinoviev Letter' that purported to reveal a Comintern plan for the British Communist Party to subvert Britain for armed revolution. It was a media scoop for the *Daily Mail* that successfully destroyed Labour's chances in the next general election. 'Since [**Morton**] … detested the Bolsheviks and disliked the Labour Government, he welcomed the chance to throw a spanner in the works of Anglo-Soviet *rapprochement.*'[24] During the 1930s **Morton** headed economic and industrial intelligence, and during **Churchill**'s 'wilderness years' it was **Morton** who passed to his friend 'details of German rearmament which empowered the unheeded prophet to cry forth warnings to the world'.[25] In 1939 **Morton** became principal assistant secretary at the Ministry of Warfare and was a personal assistant to **Churchill** in 1940, eventually opposing British support for Tito and his partisans in Yugoslavia.

Another ultra right-wing, anti-communist influence on **Churchill** was **John Baker White** (1902–1988). **White** was connected to Special Branch through his stepfather, but his most important influence was his mother, a great friend of the conspiracy theorist to end all conspiracy theorists, Nesta Webster. Webster believed that world domination was continuously being planned by the Jews, aided by satanists, occultists, **Freemasons** and communist revolutionaries. She wrote *World Revolution: The Plot against Civilisation* (1921–2), *Secret Societies and Subversive Movements* (1924), and *The Need for Fascism in Britain* (1926). She joined the British Union of Fascists, wrote for the anti-Semitic periodical *The Patriot* and praised Hitler. She expressed no contrition after 1945 at the revelation of the hecatombs of murdered Jews, including at least a million children, not to mention the Nazis' killing of 3 million Poles and 20 million Russians.[26]

White followed Nesta Webster and his mother's lead. 'I saw Bolshevism as a manifestation of the anti-Christ and from that followed dedication.'[27] He joined a private intelligence agency 'The Industrial Intelligence Bureau', IIB, run by a Sir George McGill, that investigated all forms of 'subversion' in Britain, including communism. '[It was] financed by the Federation of British Industries and the Coal Owners' and Ship-owners' Associations, to acquire intelligence on industrial unrest arising from the activities of Communists, Anarchists, … the IRA and other "subversive" organisations.'[28] **White** infiltrated communist circles in London and Cambridge and soon cooperated with the 'Economic League' of big business, including the Mining Association, in breaking the miners' strike of 1926. The Economic League then employed **White** as its director from 1926 to 1939. A dossier of socialist and 'subversive' organisations was compiled – 'a permanent clearing house of information in connection with alien organisations and individuals'.[29] Files were collected on young British communists and trade union activists, sometimes with the help of the police, and were then disseminated to employers who wanted to vet all their job applicants politically in order to weed out potential 'troublemakers'. Thus at the very time when **White** was on the Gestapo Blacklist as a secret agent ('**John White-Baker**, *N. Offizier*') he himself was responsible for compiling a secret blacklist of the left-wing 'enemy within', in order to help those British employers who funded his work. In the 1920s and 1930s the Economic League organised thousands of public meetings and distributed millions of leaflets annually, and began collecting centralised records on communist trade union organisers (some obtained from police files).[30]

White's inclusion on the Gestapo's Blacklist was all the more ironic since **White**, although very wary of the 'socialism' in National Socialism, was himself an anti-Semite and a great admirer of Hitler. In his *Dover-Nuremberg Return* (1937) he wrote:

> [Hitler] looks, speaks and behaves like a national leader ... he has natural dignity ... In a little over four years he has brought a great nation out of the depths and given it back its soul ... Hitler could never have created the present regime and maintained it ... without ... very great ability, courage and perseverance ... He is without question a very great man.[31]

No one on the Gestapo Black List was more adulatory of the Führer, unless it was the *Daily Mail* journalist **George Ward Price.** In 1937 **White** was invited to the Nuremberg Rally and also to the German embassy in London – only to be crossed off their standing guest list and transferred to the Black Book when, at the very last, his Economic League grew critical of Hitler's intentions towards Britain – in July 1939. **White** spent the war doing black propaganda for the Political Warfare Executive and after 1945 became a Conservative MP, while continuing to support the secret Economic League. The

Economic League was at last exposed in 1990 and formally closed down in 1993.[32]

Refugee Spies

Unsurprisingly, those secret agents who had fled to Britain after experiencing the sharp end of Nazism themselves tended to be consistently anti-fascist in their politics. Some of them were lifelong communists, including the most spectacular spy of them all, 'Sonia', i.e. Ursula Kuczynski, who was apparently just a quiet British housewife in Oxfordshire, but who recruited and 'managed' Klaus Fuchs, and her brother Juergen – a double agent in the Second World War working for both the USA and the Soviet Union. They were the children of the refugee statistician **Professor Robert René Kuczynski** at Oxford (p. 235) and both of them, ironically, remained undetected either by MI5 or by the Gestapo. Similarly, the refugee photographer Edith Tudor-Hart, née Suchitzky, who worked secretly for the Communist Party and helped recruit the Cambridge spy ring,[33] remained undetected by either the Gestapo or MI5.

Foreign-born secret agents who *were* on the Black List included **Hermann Peveling** (1904–1976/7), a refugee from Prague, where he had escaped from prison, turning into 'Eric Singer' and working for British intelligence in London before becoming an authority on the analysis of handwriting.[34] Many Czech refugees were socialists or communists and hence regarded with suspicion by Conservative MI5 and MI6, even though the Soviet Union was still Britain's vital ally against Hitler.[35] The Czech refugees included **Emil Strankmueller** (1902–1988), an army major Czech agent working for the British, based in London throughout the war, as were **Oldrich Tichy** (1898–1992), later a general, and their leader, **Colonel Moravec. Strankmueller's** life vividly exemplifies the roller coaster of mid-twentieth-century central European history. Born in Austria, resettled in Prague, trained as an army officer, he became head of Czech military intelligence. He flew to England just before the Nazi invasion of Czechoslovakia, was employed by MI6 on dangerous intelligence work in Yugoslavia,

Holland and France before they fell to the Nazis, and was then stationed in London for MI6. Immediately after the war was over he returned to Czechoslovakia, only to find himself imprisoned for three years by a Stalinist government suspicious of his ties to Britain. On release he worked as a dustman and janitor, was partially rehabilitated in the 1960s, and in 1992, after being dead for four years, he was posthumously made a major general.

The most elusive chameleon, the most wily, brilliant secret agent of them all in this period, however, must, I think, have been **Jona Ustinov – 'Klop'** i.e. 'bedbug' (1892–1962), the father of Peter Ustinov.[36] Born in Jaffa, Palestine, to a Russian aristocrat father who was in exile for defying the Tsar, and a half-German, half-Ethiopian mother, **Klop** had Russian, Polish Jewish and African grandparents and had been brought up in Palestine, France and Germany. He was understandably anti-nationalistic; nevertheless he opted to become a German citizen in 1914 and then found himself having to fight for Germany throughout the First World War. After having been awarded the Iron Cross, **Klop** worked as a journalist for the Wolff Foreign News Agency in Berlin in 1918 but he was then also recruited by the Weimar Government's Foreign Office to be a spy in Bolshevik Russia. He told the suspicious Cheka that he was a Dutch greengrocer, but he was also secretly dealing in the black market in art while trying to get exit permits for himself and his new wife Nadia, a Russian artist and an aristocrat who needed to flee the deterioriating political scene.

The end of 1920 found them in London. **Klop** was still a secret German Foreign Office agent, reporting daily to the German embassy in London under the 'cover' of being a Wolff News Agency journalist.[37] He possessed outstanding social skills as a warm, charming host, witty raconteur, knowledgeable cosmopolitan – and flirt. Soon he had good friends in the British Foreign Office; he gave talks about Germany on the BBC, and the **Klop**s' London flat became a social and artistic salon. After the Nazis came to power, **Klop** still managed to hang on to his anti-Nazi contacts – as well as to his Secret Service contract in the German embassy in London – until 1935, when he was told to reveal his 'racial' origins and give documentary evidence of his 'Aryan' forebears. **Klop** replied that he would do so if Herr Dr Goebbels did the same about his – and was promptly sacked. Prudently, **Klop** had already made plans to apply for British citizenship and on 21 November 1935 he stopped being German and became both a British citizen *and* an agent for MI5, under cover of being an art dealer.

Klop kept an eye on the White Russian exiles for MI5, especially on any who were so anti-communist that they favoured Hitler. Similarly he made friends with and reported on the left-wing Czech and anti-Nazi German exiles, using the opportunity to write anodyne reports that reassured MI5 and the Foreign Office adviser **Lord Vansittart** that these particular exiles posed absolutely no security threat to Britain.[38] Simultaneously, while working for MI6 he reported to **Vansittart**'s private intelligence network in the Foreign Office on Nazi spies in Britain as well as on Edward VIII's and Wallis Simpson's dubious attraction to the Third Reich. **Klop** was judged by Dick White of MI5, not surprisingly, 'the best and most ingenious operator I had the honour to deal with'.[39]

The greatest weapon in **Klop**'s secret armoury was his friend, the anti-Nazi **Wolfgang Gans Edler, Herr zu Putlitz** (1899–1975), who also happened to be first secretary and head of the consular department at the Nazis' German embassy in London and 'possibly the most important human-source intelligence Britain received in the pre-war period.'[40] **Von Putlitz** had always been left-wing despite his aristocratic birth. He had been persuaded by **Klop** to join the Nazi Party in order to fight it from within, passing on vital intelligence and thereby trying to thwart Hitler's plans. The most crucial year was 1938 when **von Putlitz** warned the British Foreign Office via **Klop** about Hitler's aggressive intentions towards the whole of Czechoslovakia, over six months *before* Munich. **Klop** went still further, secretly hosting German generals incognito in his own London flat, when they tried to get the message across that they would mount a military putsch against Hitler if the British made it clear at Munich that the invasion of Czechoslovakia would mean a Second World War. The British government, unsure whether or not the promise of such a putsch was genuine, then of course did the opposite, appeasing Hitler by ceding the Sudetenland.[41] Both **Klop** and **von Putlitz** were in despair. In May 1938 **von Putlitz** was sent to Holland to become first secretary of the German embassy at the Hague. He told **Klop** that Holland was now the first port of call for Nazi military intelligence against Britain and he supplied Britain with lists of Dutch collaborators. The stealing of those lists was betrayed by a Gestapo 'mole' and **Klop** had to get **von Putlitz** – plus his male lover – out of Holland within twenty-four hours. They were flown out by a Dutch air ace to Shoreham airport on 15 September. Now that an enraged Hitler had learned that **von Putlitz** had always been working against Nazism, the latter's cover was blown and he left for the USA. He returned to Britain in 1944 to give evidence at the Nuremberg War Crimes Trials, and later at trials in the GDR. But **von Putlitz** could never be at home in either Germany – he loathed the return of Nazis to positions of respectability in West Germany, where the right wing regarded him as a traitor; he detested the Stalinist totalitarianism in East Germany which saw him, a gay, as contaminated by the 'decadent' West. As for **Klop**, he continued to work for MI5 and MI6, perhaps most notably as the chief interrogator of Walter Schellenberg, who had had **Klop** twice on his *Sonderfahndungsliste*, as both **Ustinov**, 'Journalist', and under his cover name, **Middleton-Peddelton.**[42]

The widowed divorcee, **Countess Moura Budberg** (1893–1974), is still to this day one of **Klop**'s most controversial intimate friends and informers. She was the Estonian-Russian literary translator of Maxim Gorky, as well as a multi-lingual literary agent and a wartime worker for the French Resistance periodical *France Libre*. Warm and charming, as well as highly intelligent and well read, she had been the lover of Kerensky, of **Bruce Lockhart**, of Maxim Gorky, among several others – and was now the partner of **H. G. Wells**. Whose side was she really on – other than her own and her children's need to survive? Clearly the Gestapo found her suspect as an Estonian Russian, as a left-winger and as the lover of the Blacklisted **Wells**. On the other side, the Soviet Union never forgot that she had been closely implicated with **Bruce Lockhart** when he was arrested for allegedly plotting to kill Lenin, and that she had then chosen twice to leave the Soviet Union. They certainly exacted a price for her intimacy with Maxim Gorky, who had been in unpatriotic exile in Italy and Germany in the 1920s. As for MI5, they could never decide whether **Budberg** was a spy for the Nazis or for the Kremlin. Right-wingers in MI5 believed the latter. 'She was considered too great a security risk to be allowed near the BBC' – although the BBC in fact did continue to use her deep politico-cultural knowledge of Russia.[43]

Klop was instructed by MI5 to inform on **Budberg** and he used the opportunity to vouch for her anti-Nazism, for her anti-Stalinism *and* for her loyalty to her adopted country Britain. **Colonel Edward Hinchley-Cook**, 'the seasoned MI5 interrogator, spy and bloodhound'[44] was very suspicious of **Budberg**'s friendship with the wife of Ivan Maisky, the Soviet ambassador to Britain in the 1940s, but MI5 never dared to try to have her arrested and interned – she was simply far too well connected. She applied successfully to become a British subject in 1947. **Budberg** and **Klop** would become something of a double act at her countless very entertaining alcohol-fuelled parties, attended in the late 1930s by **Bertrand Russell**, Kerensky, **Harold Nicolson**, **Freud**, **Duff Cooper** and **Anthony Eden**; in the 1940s by **General Sikorski** and Sir Leonard Woolley; and in the 1950s by **Julian Huxley**, **Kingsley Martin**, **Rose Macaulay** and Carol Reed – among many brilliant others from the arts and politics. Her huge circle had naturally also included Guy Burgess and his friends. In 1950 she tried to tip **Klop** off about James MacGibbon and she also told him that Anthony Blunt was a secret communist who still sent reports back to the Soviet Union. Did he believe her? Certainly the Foreign Office did not. At her funeral in 1974 the Russian Orthodox Church in Kensington was packed.

Each of these Blacklisted secret agents was unlike any other, whether British-born or refugee. They differed in class background, occupation, educational level and politics, as well as in nationality, sexuality and gender. What they did have in common was their impotence in averting international disaster. For however accurate the information they provided, notably about Hitler and his intention, ever since 1933, to have a world war, their warnings were not acted upon. The one great exception to this was **Dansey**'s success in convincing Stalin that the vital 'Ultra'/ Bletchley information about German plans before the battle of Kursk came from a Soviet and not from a suspect British intelligence source.

Ever since 1917, 'the threat of Soviet subversion remained the greatest concern' within the British Establishment – much greater than the rise of fascism.[45] Even after Mussolini's' dictatorship was established, Italy was still regarded by the Tory government as a British ally. And when, in the mid and late 1930s, Paul Rosbaud via **Frank Foley** supplied the latest accurate information about Hitler's secret weapons and advanced military planning, and the SIS supplied correct information about rising German aircraft production, Stanley Baldwin knew that the British electorate was still not ready to contemplate a Second World War, either to prevent it or to prepare for it. So nothing was done.

As for influencing or even informing the formulation of foreign and defence policy, or bringing important industrial developments in potential enemy countries to the attention of British policy-makers, the impact of **Desmond Morton**'s Industrial Intelligence Centre (IIC) was negligible.[46] All that **Morton** could do was supply the leading anti-appeaser **Churchill** with information with which he then tried, in vain, to convince the Conservative Party and parliament. And when **von Putlitz**, the secret agent within the German embassy in London, told **Klop** who told **Vansittart** who told **Neville Chamberlain** more than six months ahead precisely what Hitler was going to do in the Sudetenland and Czechoslovakia, **Chamberlain** refused to believe what he could not bear to hear. Appeasement – and the Second World War – went ahead.

There is one last question raised by this general disbelief among those in power in the West concerning the intelligence that they were being given. Had **Foley**'s scientific information from Paul Rosbaud about the Nazis' continued *non*-success in acquiring an atomic bomb been disseminated among the scientific community in Britain and the United States, might there have been no American atomic bomb in 1945?[47]

12
The Army

Easy rifle shot. I could pick the bastard off from here as easy as winking.

Colonel Noel Mason-MacFarlane, military attaché in Berlin

There are many British military officers listed to be arrested immediately in September 1940, but with too few details for accurate identification. Who were **Major R. A. Adams**, 'assistant to the Air attaché', or **Major Burton**, 'presumed to be in England', or **Captain Butcher**, 'last in Riga, now England' or **Captain Featherton**, **Major Harold Gibson**, **Captain Leslie Remvik Grant**, **Major Mac Harper**, **Colonel Haywood**, **Captain J. Heyward** (or **Heywards**?), **Captain Stanley Howard** and **Major Humphrey** – among a great many others? Often without any details about their dates or place of birth, their address, respective regiment or recent posting, it will require more searches by experts in British military history 1939–40 to succeed in tracing many more of these officers. Not to mention whether or not, as alleged, they were all secretly working for military intelligence – if that can now be divulged. Why the Gestapo should have selected certain professional soldiers rather than thousands of other British officers is not always clear. Certainly, in many cases the cause lay in their historic – or suspected current – dual role as spies.

For instance the Chief Scout and founder of the worldwide Boy Scouts movement, **Lord Baden-Powell**, born in 1857 and now 82 years old, had specialised in reconnaissance and military intelligence in the field during both the Boer War and the First World War. He was also a lieutenant general and was, the Gestapo believed, ultimately responsible for training the world's Scouts to be anti-German British spies – like the Boy Scouts in Austria, according to the *Informationsheft* (p. 32).

Similarly, **Colonel Julius Guthlac Birch** (1884–1971), who had been part of the British post-Second World War administration in the Rhineland, was now Blacklisted as an intelligence officer – as was 73-year-old **Brigadier General Sir George Kynaston Cockerill** (1867–1957), once an explorer in the Hindu Kush, who had been deputy director of intelligence in the First World War. And **Major Thomas Denis Daly** (1892–1956), of the Royal Welch Fusiliers, had been a military attaché in Berlin from June to September 1939, his brief having been to acquire intelligence on the German army's strength and strategy. More vaguely, **Captain R. C. Feilding**, DSO, of the Coldstream Guards, twice mentioned in dispatches in the First World War, is cited in the *Sonderfahndungsliste* as part of the *Julius Petschek Taeterkreis* under the auspices of the Gestapo's Dept 111 that reported on 'Spheres of German Life'. Like **Feilding, Lord Angus Graham** (1907–1992), 'Lt. in the Royal Navy', is listed as another member of the *Julius Petschek Taeterkreis*, but in his case more improbably, for **Graham** was a white supremacist settler farmer in Southern Rhodesia with alleged Nazi sympathies. He reported in September 1939 to the Royal Naval Volunteer Reserve and served on destroyers in the Second World War.

One very distinguished veteran on the Black List was 70-year-old **Admiral Sir Reginald Hall** (1870–1943), who had been director of naval intelligence in the First World War, specialising in decryptions and radio intercepts. He had been involved with the arrest in Britain of **Franz von Rintelen** (1878–1949), the ace German spy operating from the United States from 1914 to 1916 as a secret naval intelligence officer sabotaging Allied shipping in the Atlantic from his cover as a Swiss businessman. **Admiral Hall** had successfully interrogated **Rintelen**, extracted his confession and had him extradited for trial and conviction in the US. During the 1920s, **Hall** became a right-wing Tory associated with the Economic League that spied on left-wingers in British trade unions.

The outstanding soldier associated with military intelligence who was targeted in the *Sonderfahndungsliste GB* was **Colonel Frank Noel Mason-Macfarlane** or 'Mac' (1889–1953), who had been awarded the Military Cross in the First World War for his conspicuous gallantry and was appointed military attaché in Berlin from 1938 to 1939. An exceptional linguist and an inspiring leader, '"**Mac**" was a very fine fighting soldier, with an acute brain, a realistic understanding of people and events, and a gift of lucid exposition.'[1] It was **Mason-Macfarlane** who had famously contemplated shooting Hitler from his house in the Charlottenburger Chaussee – 'Easy rifle shot. I could pick the bastard off from here as easy as winking' – but his superiors forbade him to try. He became director of intelligence with the British Expeditionary Force in France from 1939 to 1940 and a commander during the retreat to Dunkirk. He was then head of the Joint Intelligence Centre operating from Gibraltar, before going to Moscow from 1941 to 1942 as head of the British Military Mission.

Another outstanding officer with a complex role to play was **Major General Sir Edward Louis Spears** (formerly Spiers) (1886–1974), who was bilingual in French and English and of part Jewish descent. He had been at the French War Office in August 1914, liaising with British agents in Belgium when, as liaison officer with General Lanzerac of the French Fifth Army, on 23 August 1914 he had alerted Sir John French, commander of the British Expeditionary Force, to Lanrezac's retreat, 'thus saving the isolated British from almost certain annihilation'.[2] After having been wounded four times and awarded the Military Cross, **Spears** was made head of the British military mission to the French War Office. Encouraged by his friend **Churchill** after the First World War, he became first a National Liberal and then a Conservative MP. **Spears** was a passionate Francophile and a Churchillian protestor in parliament against the appeasement of Hitler after 1933. In the Second World War he detested Vichy and admired and supported **de Gaulle** – whom he had personally airlifted out of France in June 1940 in order to lead the Free French from London. They would later fall out, however, over independence for Syria and the Lebanon, opposed by **de Gaulle** but supported by **Spears**.

Other suspected secret agents were **Captain Kenneth Killey** (1889–?), possibly a submarine commander, who was listed as a secret agent based in Copenhagen in 1939, and South African-born **Colonel John Montresor** (1912–1992), '*engl. Offizier, Taeterkreis Davidi Peter, Stapo Innsbruck*'. **Christopher Rhodes** (1914–1964), '*Brit. Offizier d. Pass Control*', won the Croix de guerre in the Second World War, becoming a lieutenant colonel; thereafter he had a successful career as an actor in upper-class and military officer roles.

One last example of a Blacklisted professional soldier who did also work for British military intelligence was **K. W. D. Strong** (1900–1982), labelled, mistakenly, a corvette captain by the Gestapo. He was in fact an intelligence officer in Germany and later an assistant military attaché in Berlin from 1938 to 1939. He was general staff officer in the British War Office German Section from 1939 to 1940, eventually becoming a brigadier general and soon major general staff (intelligence) at Allied HQ. As Eisenhower's chief of intelligence, **Strong** participated in the decision to invade Normandy on 6 June 1944 and he would later receive General Jodl's unconditional surrender by Nazi Germany on 8 May 1945.[3]

Whom did the Gestapo target in the navy? Captain **Victor Hilary Danckwerts** (1890–1940), was not a secret agent but was, presumably, singled out for his important naval role as director of plans for the Admiralty. Ironically, he would himself be sacked in 1940 by **Churchill** for having too vigorously opposed the latter's scheme for a naval confrontation with Germany in the Baltic.[4] Lieutenant Commander **Reginald Fletcher** (1885–1961) had also been a naval officer in the First World War but had since become a Labour MP, very vocally anti-appeasement – which explains his inclusion in the Black Book.[5] In the Second World War he served in the London docks 'supervising the fitting of guns to merchant ships';[6] he later worked at Grimsby on east-coast convoys. **Leonard Kirkpatrick** (1890–1939,) a retired naval captain, was allegedly in the '*Taeterkreis George Campbel*' (sic); he later commanded an armed merchant cruiser in 1942. **Captain Richard Shelley** (1892–1968) was captain of the fleet (Mediterranean Fleet) in 1940 and **H. N. Stoddart** was an Admiralty naval assistant who became Second Sea Lord in the Second World War. The Gestapo's reference to 'Prague' when listing 'Commandeur' **Frederick Victor Stopford** (1900–1982), who later became a rear admiral, suggests that they may have confused him with *Robert* Stopford, the Treasury official sent out to Prague in 1938 with emergency visas for would-be refugees, including Jews.[7]

Among the Blacklisted airmen, **Glyn Hearson** (1902–?), named as a naval commander based in Shanghai, may have been implicated in the Venlo incident or, very possibly, the Gestapo had confused him with **John Glanville Hearson** (1883–1964), a squadron and wing commander in the Royal Flying Corps in the First World War and the RAF's first director of training in 1918. As Air Officer Commanding the No. 1 (Air Defence) Group he had retired from the RAF in 1927 but then returned ten years later as air commodore, in order to establish and command Britain's barrage balloon organisation in the event of war. Another outstanding pilot in the First World War, **Captain Oscar Philip Jones** (1898–1980), became the leading pilot captain for Imperial Airways and BOAC, pioneering both survey flights and long-haul civil aviation routes to Africa, Canada, the Middle East and Russia. In the Second World War **Jones** was flight captain for UK landplanes as well as a senior pilot training officer; and by his retirement in 1953 he would have flown over 21,600 hours on 118 different types of aircraft.[8]

A squadron commander and a wing commander in the Royal Flying Corps in the First World War, **Sir John Maitland Salmond** (1881–1968), had been a trainer of pilots in military aviation at flying schools. By the end of the First World War he was General Officer Commanding the RAF on the Western Front. Appointed Chief of Air Staff in 1930 and marshall of the Royal Air Force in 1933, **Salmond** was vehemently against aerial disarmament at the disarmament talks in Geneva, 1933. When Hitler withdrew from the talks in 1934, all mention of British aerial disarmament ceased. In 1938 he returned to the RAF as chairman, Air Defence Cadet Corps, and in 1939 he was appointed director of armament production at the Ministry of Aircraft Production under **Beaverbrook** – with whom he fell out. In 1940

Salmond chaired a committee to enquire into the failure of British fighter defences to cope with German night bombing, leading to the dismissal of Hugh Dowding from Fighter Command. In August 1941 he became '[Director]-general of flying control and air/sea rescue ... [causing] many lives to be saved'.[9]

The so-called 'Father of the RAF', **Hugh Montagu Lord Trenchard** (1873–1956), was older than **John Salmond**, but a much less experienced and skilled pilot. Granted a pilot's licence after only two weeks' tuition, including just sixty-four minutes in the air, in 1912 **Trenchard** became a trainer of pilots for the Royal Flying Corps. By November 1914 he was operational commander for the corps and soon served admiringly under General Haig who shared his aggressive instincts. **Trenchard** supported the prohibition throughout the First World War against equipping British planes with parachutes lest that diminish the pilots' commitment to waging incessant attack – even after their machines were on fire. 'The understanding that pilots were difficult to train and far more valuable than aircraft didn't sink in.'[10] Finally, after the war was over, and in part goaded by the fact that Germany had issued its own airmen with parachutes in 1918, parachutes in British planes were allowed.

During the 1920s **Trenchard** was Chief of Air Staff of the new RAF and responsible for establishing the dogma that heavy 'stra tegic' bombing – as would be perpetrated by his disciple 'Bomber' Harris (1942–5) – would win a war. **Trenchard** chose not to prioritise the building up of an effective *defence* air force in order to protect British civilians who would be at the receiving end of such 'strategic' bombing themselves. The 68-year-old **Trenchard** 'composed a memorandum in May 1941 which completely misjudged the German character ... [saying] the German nation is peculiarly susceptible to air bombing',[11] while British morale, he believed, would be secure under bombardment. In fact both peoples would stoically endure the horror of indiscriminate mass destruction from the air – which has since been judged, in theory at least, to be a war crime. In 1946, after Hiroshima and Nagasaki, **Trenchard** still insisted in a paper published by the Air Ministry 'that the bomber remained the central instrument of air power, and a strategic air offensive the only proper function of that instrument'.[12]

A notable military man in the *Sonderfahndungsliste* – and one who stands somewhat alone because of his aristocratic background and royal connections – is **George Lascelles, Earl of Harewood** (1882–1947), son-in-law of King George V. He had served in a battalion of the Grenadier Guards in the First World War, been wounded three times and gassed. Thereafter his interest was in the Territorial Army. But **Lascelles** was probably Blacklisted less for his military record and role than for his eminence as a Freemason, being Provincial Grand Master in West Yorkshire. 'The King and his family are the strongest connection between Britain and the member states of the Empire by being simultaneously the Empire's political and Masonic leadership.'[13]

It is clear from the above discussion of Blacklisted army personnel just how peculiar and arbitrary were the criteria for inclusion. One may conclude therefore, since the Gestapo's main area of interest and expertise was *counter*-intelligence, that their chief ambition, in their hurried, very incomplete listing of British military officers in September 1939, was to try to seize all those whom they either knew to be, or else suspected of being, secret spymasters or spies.

13.

Business and Industry – Friend or Foe to Nazi Germany?

Under occupation, the British economy would, of course, have been taken under Nazi control. Which industrial and commercial concerns did the Gestapo consider the most important? Were the Nazis planning to expropriate and take them all over from their British owners and directors – or were they hoping that many in British big business would be willing to collaborate with their new German masters? And what would be the policy towards those businessmen, industrialists and financiers who were British Jews?

Of supreme economic importance was the oil industry, which the invaders planned to requisition at the outset. And so we find listed **Anglo-Iranian Oil, Anglo-Saxon Petroleum Ltd, Shell Transport and Trading** and **Warsop Petrol Drill and Tools**. But other giants such as **ICI** – (leader of its technical section, **John Paterson**) and 'producer of gas weapons' ('*Kampfgas*'), as well as several car factories – **Rover**, **Standard Motor Company**, **Wolseley** and the **Federation of British Industry** itself are also Blacklisted under '*Firmen*'. Heavy industry targets included **Atlas Steel and Iron Works**, **Sheffield Iron and Steel Works**, **Workington Steelworks**, **the British Aluminium Co.** ('*Leader* **Freeman-Horn**'), **British Metal Co. (Corporation)** ('*Leader* **Oliver Lyttelton**') and **Industrial Mining Development Ltd**, as well as several engineering factories such as **Birmingham Small Arms Company**, **Dacre Engineering Co.** and **Loewy Engineering Co.** Presumably they would all have been taken over and their products sent to Germany. The banks singled out in the Black Book, without explanation, are **Barclays** and the **Midland**.

The many individual leaders of British industry and big business in whom the Gestapo took a strong interest, whether as potential collaborators or as useful hostages, are for the most part connected with the above enterprises. The most important of all were the 'oil men', and pre-eminent among them was the 'rugged Scot' **Sir Andrew Agnew**, CBE (1882–1955). Far from having been born with a silver spoon in his mouth, **Agnew** was the son of a Scottish grocer and had never gone to university. He was clearly of outstanding intelligence, however, and had worked his way up as a young man in the Straits Settlements and Singapore, marketing Shell. On his return to Britain in 1919, before he was 40, he was appointed manager of Anglo-Saxon Petroleum, a subsidiary of Shell, and by 1935 he was managing director of **Shell's Transport and Trading**. Crucially, in the late 1930s **Andrew Agnew**, knighted in 1938, 'took on' the despotic chairman of Royal Dutch Shell, Sir Henri Deterding (1866–1939), known as the 'Napoleon of oil', and allegedly the most powerful man in the world. Deterding's infatuated support for Hitler after 1933 threatened oil supplies to Britain in the event of a war; in 1935 he was already planning to 'sell' Nazi Germany a year's oil reserves on credit. Alarmed by this intelligence, **Agnew** asked the British government to have the British embassy in Berlin investigate, in order that he 'could take suitable action with his colleagues on the Board [of Shell] … in good time'.[1] **Agnew** then joined – or led – his fellow Shell directors in forcing Deterding, now 70, to retire as general manager of Shell at the end of 1936. But Deterding was still a force to contend with. Even after he died, in February 1939 (and granted a Nazi state funeral in Germany which had to be attended by **Agnew**), Deterding's estate included 'preference shares' which were deposited in London – although coveted by Germany – and which could contribute to control of Royal Dutch Shell. **Agnew** travelled to Holland in April 1939 to make it clear to his fellow directors that the British government would never allow the shares out of Britain and hence her oil supply from Shell was not endangered – at least for as long as Holland was not occupied. Almost certainly the Gestapo was cognisant that

Agnew was no 'friend to Germany', unlike Deterding, and put him on the *Sonderfahndungsliste GB*.

In the Second World War **Agnew** was unanimously nominated by British oil companies to chair Britain's Petroleum Board or 'POOL' of Shell-Mex, BP, Anglo-American and Benzole; they suspended their competition with one another for the duration and ran every part of Britain's network for the import, storage and distribution of oil. POOL's success 'was due largely to **Agnew**'s extensive knowledge of the oil industry and the respect that he commanded within it'.[2] It was possibly the most important merger in history and, not surprisingly, **Agnew** was an *ex-officio* member of the War Cabinet.[3] If eventual Allied victory was dependent on oil, the British supply of oil had ultimately depended on **Sir Andrew Agnew**. But who has heard of him?

Agnew's friend and ally, **Frederick Godber** (1888–1976), managing director of Royal Dutch Shell Group, was the son of a carpenter. He chaired the overseas supply committee of the Petroleum Board in the Second World War, coordinating oil supplies to all the war fronts as well as for Britain's domestic needs. After the war he chaired the Help Holland Fund, raising money for the liberated but starving Dutch.[4]

The director of the Midland Bank and Prudential Insurance between 1941 and 1953, **Sir George Barstow**, CH (1874–1966), was also on the Black List. Unlike **Agnew** and **Godber**, he was one of the Establishment since birth; he had been educated at public school and Cambridge, and had then risen to be a senior civil servant in the Treasury. **Barstow** was appointed governing director of **Anglo-Persian Oil** (or **Anglo-Iranian**) until 1946.[5] But the man who was really behind **Anglo-Iranian** was its chairman from 1927 until his death in 1941, the brilliant polymath **John Cadman**, later **Lord Cadman of Silverdale** (Blacklisted under '**Silverdale**') (1877–1941), the son of a mining engineer. **Cadman** had begun as a Staffordshire mining engineer, conspicuously brave in colliery rescue work. He had then developed his interest in geology and petroleum technology to become 'the leading British authority on oil' by 1914 and was the first 'professor scientist to become a chairman of a British industrial company with a capital of tens of millions of pounds',[6] having established the first academic study of petroleum mining in Britain, at Birmingham University. In 1923 **Cadman** was appointed managing director of the **Anglo-Persian Oil Company**, in 1927 he became its chairman and in 1933 he successfully negotiated with the Shah of Iran to save 25 per cent of the concession area of **Anglo-Iranian Oil** for Britain.[7] **Cadman** then set up the Iraq Petroleum Company, also becoming its chairman, and devising a pipeline to bring Iraqi oil to the Mediterranean. He was a director of the Suez Canal Company and of the Great Western Railway, as well as chairman of the Committee of Enquiry into the Post Office. He was also technical adviser to the government of Nigeria. Not satisfied with all those vital enterprises, **Cadman** did pioneering work after 1935 on developing television, and then, after 1937, on the future of international aviation. He died prematurely of exhaustion under the pressure of war work in 1941. But it was as an 'oil man' that **Cadman** made 'probably the greatest contribution to oil ever achieved by an individual Briton'[8] and there was no way in which the Gestapo could have taken over the Blacklisted **Anglo-Iranian Oil Company** without first disposing of **Cadman**.

The world's first multinational company – and the largest non-manufacturing company then in Britain – was the Anglo-Dutch giant soap and food firm **Unilever**. Its directors' report in July 1940 announced net profits and a carry-over balance totalling £8,232,435 gained from a sales turnover of £97,500,000. The goods it dealt in included soap and toiletries, chemical cleansers, margarine and edible fats, palm oil, whale blubber, fish and canned fish, processed meats, canned and dried fruit, and ice cream. The Gestapo made very sure of controlling **Unilever** and they Blacklisted its directors, including its governor, **William Hulme Lever**, **Second Viscount Leverhulme** (1888–1949), and its chairman **Francis D'Arcy Cooper** (1882–1949). (**Cooper** was also chairman of the Niger Company Ltd, and of MacFisheries Ltd as well as a director of Prudential Assurance.) The vice-chairmen **Albert van den Bergh** and **H. R. Greenhaigh**, and the directors **C. W. Barnish**, **Clive John van den Bergh**, and **Sidney van den Bergh** ('Jude') (1898–1977), were all also on the Black List.[9]

Some among the Gestapo-targeted, Blacklisted businessmen, such as the Bank and Railway director **Lord David Davies** (1880–1944) and the chair of Lloyds, **Neville Dixey** (1881–1947), were anti-fascist Liberals who had supported the League of Nations and were therefore, of course, politically unacceptable to the Gestapo. **David Davies'** ideas would later be important to the UN doctrine on sanctions and to the formation of an international UN policing force. The brilliant lawyer and Liberal politician **Clement Davies**, KC, MP (1884–1962) (another director of **Unilever**), had stood out in the late 1930s as the backbench MP responsible for a landmark inquiry into tuberculosis in Wales. His anti-appeasement intervention in the anti-Chamberlain action group in May 1940 played an important role in the formation of the War Coalition under **Churchill.**

There were several other outstanding individual 'captains of industry' targeted in the *Sonderfahndungsliste GB*, such as **Richard Rapier Stokes** (1897–1957), chairman and managing director of Ransomes and Rapier Ltd, an engineering firm that produced munitions including shells, mortars, guns and tank turrets in the First World War. (For **Stokes**'s contested political views, see p. 351). Then there was 'Cunard Royden', the ship-owner **Sir Thomas Royden**, CH (1871–1950), who was a one-man, Figaro-like general factotum in the world of big business. Not only was he director of the Cunard Steamship Company and of Cunard White Star, but he was also chairman of the Liverpool Ship-Owners' Company and president of the Chamber of Shipping of the United Kingdom. In addition, **Royden** was chairman of the Imperial Continental Gas Association, a director of the Suez Canal, of the **Midland Bank** and the London Midland and Scottish Railway, not to mention of **Shell Transport and Trading.** Hitler liked to refer to Britain as a 'plutocracy'. It is a piquant fact that not only was **Royden** Blacklisted by the Gestapo as a leading conservative player in British economic life, but his younger sister **Maude Royden** was also Blacklisted, in her case for her radical politics and pacifist activism – a pacifism that she would finally renounce in order to combat Hitler's genocidal policy against the Jews. Which **Royden** was more of a political embarrassment to the other we can only speculate. Nevertheless, they remained devoted to each other all their lives; Maude was proud of her brother as a model employer, while he backed her highly unusual vocation as a woman minister and preacher at the Guildhouse, London.[10]

The chairman of Baldwins Iron and Steel Company Ltd, **Sir W. Charles Wright** (1876–1950), had been controller of iron and steel production for the Ministry of Munitions of War, from 1917 to 1919. Between 1937 and 1938 he was president of the British Iron and Steel Federation and thus obviously of great strategic importance, deserving to be Blacklisted. Finally, there was the other big player named in the British metal industry, the managing director of the **British Metal Corporation, Oliver Lyttelton** (1893–1972). He was of particular interest since the **British Metal Corporation** had been 'established at the instigation of the British government with the long-term strategic objective of undermining Germany's domination of the metal trade'.[11] **Lyttelton** soon became, in addition to heading the **British Metal Corporation**, chairman of the **London Tin Corporation.** Cultured and witty, he was a cunning operator, actually managing to join the board of Germany's rival firm IG Metall, and, as the Gestapo noted, thereby becoming an important member of the '*Personenkreis* **Merton**' (Merton circle). Thus he became one of the few men who, 'through their multiple interlocking directorships effectively controlled the global metal trade,' claiming 'L'etain [tin], c'est moi!'[12] In September 1939, **Lyttelton** was appointed controller of non-ferrous metals, securing vital supplies of metals in wartime, before being made a member of the Coalition War Cabinet in 1941.

Lyttelton's close friend and international colleague, the refugee tycoon **Richard Israel Merton** (1881–1960) (the '**Israel**' imposed by Nazi law), is especially significant as a German industrialist case study under the Nazis. A lifelong German patriot, born into an assimilated Christian (Protestant) family, with one Jewish grandmother, and having no links at all with the observant Jewish community in his home city of Frankfurt, **Merton** was a brilliantly successful industrial administrator with a family tradition of public service, financing much of the culture and philanthropy of Frankfurt from the profits of

IG Metall. In 1930 he had married a widowed German princess, Elisabeth zu Sayn-Wittgenstein-Berleburg, through whom he had four princely stepsons. The 1919 Treaty of Versailles had been a personal trauma for the ex-German army officer **Merton**, who had attended the Paris deliberations which were, as he always maintained, a crime against defeated Germany. Hitler's comparable righteous indignation had at first blinded **Merton** concerning the dictator's brand of nationalism and **Merton** began by hoping that Nazism would revitalise Germany's economy. He even tried to ingratiate IG Metall with the new Nazi government by commissioning a portrait of the Führer, presented by the firm to Hitler 'as a lasting memorial to the historic time in which we live'. That was in 1934. From 1936 on, however, **Merton** was himself, step by step, the target of predatory Nazism, forced out of his position at IG Metall, according to the useful Nuremberg 'Laws of Aryanisation'. His family firm was expropriated and his remaining wealth seized by the state without compensation. Then, on 11 November 1938, there was *Kristallnacht*. **Merton** tried to go into hiding but was arrested by the Gestapo and taken in a roofless lorry to Buchenwald. He was released three weeks later on condition that he leave Germany at once – but then, mysteriously, could not obtain an exit visa – or not without bribing the Gestapo. **Lyttelton** paid.

There followed seven years' exile in wartime Britain where **Merton** was supported as a consultant for the British Metal Corporation, and by **Lyttelton**. Unlike his doomed personal assistant, **Lina Wertheimer**, many of **Merton**'s former Jewish colleagues were by then safely in Britain, but now Blacklisted for Gestapo arrest as '*mitarbeiter Merton*' – e.g. **Karl Baer**, **Helene Berendson**, **Artur** and **Walter Ellinger**, **Richard Erlanger** and **Julius Sommer**. Many more former employees also appealed to the exiled **Merton** for assistance as late as 1939. He tried to procure visas for them all but failed. One Merton stepson would be murdered by the Gestapo, another was killed in the German invasion of the Soviet Union. In 1948, **Merton** returned to rebuild Frankfurt and West Germany, both economically and socially. His looted assets were reissued to him by the Bundesrepublik and he became once more a great cultural and philanthropic benefactor. All his life **Merton** believed in the decent majority of 'good Germans', as opposed to a minority who were thugs and dupes, beyond the pale in their unspeakable brutality and anti-Semitism. So profoundly did he need to see himself as 'a good German' that he refused to be defined as a Jew and therefore as unfit to be a German. He later declared that he never read *Mein Kampf* in the early 1930s. It might have been better had he done so.[13]

Where the *Informationsheft GB* differs from the earlier *Sonderfahndungsliste* is in its overview of prominent *British*-born Jews with powerful roles in politics, finance, banking, business and the media. Predictably, there is no section of the *Informationsheft* (other than that on the **Freemasons**) that is more clearly imbued with Nazi paranoia. In the section 'Judaism's Current Situation', under 'Politics', we find: ' … one of the most senior officials in the Home Office was the Jew ***Sir Cecil Kisch*** (1884–1961), who established the Reserve Bank [of India] whose counsel in turn were the Jews ***Sir Henry Strakosch*** (1871–1943), and ***T. E. Gregory-Gugenheim*** [sic]. In the current **Churchill** Cabinet … **Eden, Cooper** and **Churchill** himself have to be seen as representatives of Jewish interests.'[14]

As for the Jews in parliament: '[The] best-known among them are ***Thomas Levy*** (1874–1953), leader of the Textile Committee in the Commons, **L. Silkin** … leader of an important committee of London's local government; the Jew ***Sir Isidore Salomon*** [sic] (1876–1941), is chairman of the very important Select Committee on Estimates.'[15]

British Jews were alleged to be particularly influential in London: '***Sir Percy Simmons*** (1875–1939), has been chairman of the London County Council, the Fire Brigade, the Committee for Theatre and Music Halls, of the Improvement Committee, etc. ***Sir Samuel Joseph*** (1888–1948), was … a Sheriff of London for a considerable time.'

The last mentioned, ***Sir Samuel Joseph***, born into the wealthy Gluckstein cousinage, had used his gift for organisation to build up the major Bovis Construction Company. A Lloyds underwriter and Alderman of the City of London, he was elected Lord Mayor of London in 1942, the first Jew to hold that office for forty years. He was the father of Margaret Thatcher's future Cabinet minister, Sir Keith

Joseph. Nothing is said of the competence or otherwise of any of the above public figures, the only thing thought to be significant – and sufficiently damning – was that they were all Jews.

It was the same in the world of finance. 'The influential Jews' ***C. J. Hambro*** (1897–1963), and ***Lord Goschen*** (1866–1952) (governor of Madras, 1924–9) were directors of the Bank of England, and 'also hold leading positions in the so-called "big five" banks'. (***Hambro*** was later to do outstanding work for SOE in Norway, preventing German nuclear scientists from acquiring 'heavy water' vital to the making of an atom bomb.)[16] **Lord Bearstead** (i.e. Colonel Walter Horace Samuel), together with two other Jews, ***F. D.*** and ***P. M. Samuel***, 'is a director of the most significant bank, Samuel and Co. Its capital of £2,000,000 does not begin to reflect the huge influence this company exercises in international finance.'[17] In many cases a bank's capital is quoted as though it constituted the personal assets of the directors. The same is true for the companies Samuel Montagu and Co., with Jewish directors **E. L. Franklin**, **L. S. Montagu**, **Lord Swaythling** and **C. M. Franklin**. 'Japhet and Co has the Jew ***Sammy [Saemy] Japhet***[18] as chairman and "the Jews" ***Paul Lindenberg***, ***Max Frontheim*** and ***Gottfried Loewenstein*** as directors. The Jewish company Erlangers Ltd has ***Emile d'Erlanger*** as chairman[19] with ***Frederic d'Erlanger*** (composer as well as banker) and ***Leo d'Erlanger*** as his representatives. ***Sir Albert Stern*** (1878–1966),[20] is important at the ***Westminster Bank*** and at ***Stern Bros***, as well as being director of seven other financial companies.'[21] Finally, **Sir Osmond Elim d'Avigdor-Goldsmid MP** is named as chairman or director of at least seven different trading companies. Almost all of these men are here 'outed' in the *Informationsheft* as Jews for the first time by the Gestapo – the **Rothschilds** and other Jewish financiers having already appeared in the earlier *Sonderfahndungsliste GB*.

Under 'The Economy', the director of **Imperial Chemical Industries** and Nickel Company, **Henry Mond** 2nd Baron **Melchett** (1898–1949) was also a director of Barclays Bank, is listed. The family motto on its coat of arms was 'Make Yourself Necessary'. ***Peter Montefiore-Samuel***, and **Sir Robert Waley** (i.e. **Waley Cohen**)[22] are mentioned as 'the two directors of Shell'. 'Other significant Jews in the oil industry are **B. Maisel** and ***Johanna Maisel***, the directors of Petroleum Trust and Orient Oil and Finance Co. Ltd.' It is then alleged: 'To a large extent the British food industry is … in Jewish hands. ***Sir George Schuster*** is chairman of big conglomerates: Home and Colonial Stores Ltd, Lipton Ltd, Maypole Dairy Co. Ltd and Allied Suppliers. These companies have branches all over England and more or less hold a monopoly position.' (The massive network of the Cooperative Stores throughout Britain is overlooked.) Instead, ***Sir Isidore Salmon***, chairman of Lyons (share capital £10,000,000), is named as the owner of huge food distribution and catering interests. The founders of J. Lyons, **Louis Halle Gluckstein** and **Sir Samuel Gluckstein**, are not named in the *Informationsheft* but had appeared in the earlier *Sonderfahndungsliste*. Their catering empire included Corner House restaurants and the Trocadero, Strand Palace, Regent Palace and Cumberland Hotels.[23]

Listed in the insurance business are **Sir Lionel de Rothschild**,[24] chairman, and **Lord Bearstead** and **Lord Roseberry**,[25] directors of Alliance Insurance, while 'the Jews **Sir George Schuster** and ***Sir Charles Seligman*** are directors of Commercial Union which runs twelve other companies'. As for the gold and diamond business, it is alleged to be almost exclusively Jewish, with ***Sir George Albo*** (sic)(i.e **Albu**) being chairman of the General Mining and Finance Corporation, ***Geoffrey Joel*** the director of ***De Beers***, and ***Sir Ernest Oppenheimer*** chairman of twenty-four branches of the gold and diamond industry in South Africa. Finally, we have the banker and financier **Sir Henry Strakosch,** who had been naturalised British in 1907, and was chairman from 1924 to 1943 of some of the richest gold mines on the South African Rand, as well as having a financial interest in copper. A world authority on currency and international finance, he was influential in the economy of India and in many European states in the 1920s and 1930s, in addition to being a member of the channel tunnel committee and chairman of *The Economist*.[26]

The clear message therefore for the German occupation forces from their Handbook, the *Informationsheft*, was that almost the whole of Britain was really controlled by very rich, assimilated British Jews, many of whom had not hitherto been named by the Gestapo as essential targets. The section on 'Judaism's Current Situation' in the *Informationsheft* (translated as *Invasion 1940*, pp. 83–5 and 100–104: see Appendices 1 and 2) ends with listing all the British Jewish, including many Zionist, organisations – together with their addresses and chief office holders, from **Lord Melchett**, **Lord Rothschild**, **Chaim Weizmann** and **Ben Gurion** to the **Marchioness of Reading** and **Viscountess Samuel.**

In the media – press, radio and film – British Jews are also said to have a great and perniciously 'anti- German' influence, above all ***Ivor Montagu*** (1904–1974), and ***Sidney Bernstein*** (1899–1993). ***Ivor Montagu*** had rebelled against his plutocratic, Orthodox Jewish background as the son of the banker **Samuel Montagu**, **Lord Swaythling**; he had been a convert to socialism since his youth and had joined the **Communist Party of Great Britain**. An enthusiast for the art of film and the early achievements of Soviet cinema, he was the first film critic on the ***Observer***, the ***Daily Worker*** and the ***New Statesman***. As a film producer himself he had made the documentary *Free Thaelmann* in 1935 and later several anti-Franco films on the Spanish Civil War, including *In Defence of Madrid* and *Behind the Spanish Lines* in 1938. His bitter film on **Chamberlain**'s Conservative Party record on social welfare in Britain, sarcastically titled *Peace and Plenty* (1939), showed rat-ridden slums, and working-class children with rickets and rotting teeth. He also attacked the Tories' appeasement of Hitler in that film, which was made for the British Communist Party. Ironically, ***Ivor Montagu*** was also under the scrutiny of MI5.[27]

Sidney Bernstein was, with ***Montagu***, the man whom the Gestapo held to be chiefly responsible for the production of recent '*deutschfeindlich*' films and for acting as unofficial 'film censors' – although in fact they both attacked film censorship and were themselves censored by the British authorities. In 1933 ***Bernstein*** wrote that 'the British Board of Film Censors have … stated they will not pass any film … showing the Nazis in a bad light'.[28] ***Bernstein***, a member of the Labour Party and the **Left Book Club**, was also under the scrutiny of MI5 as a (wrongly) suspected communist. He owned scores of cinemas and theatres and himself became a film producer, sometimes with the young Alfred Hitchcock. An ardent, practical anti-Nazi, ***Bernstein*** helped many German Jewish and other German anti-Nazis in the film industry to flee Germany and to find work in Britain. In addition, according to his biographer Caroline Moorehead, 'he wrote letters, signed petitions, effected introductions ... sent donations'.[29] Despite the Hitler-appeasing censorship imposed on the British film industry by directives from the Home Office and the Foreign Office, between 1939 and 1941 ***Bernstein*** did produce several anti-Nazi films, including *London Can Take It*, and *In Which We Serve*, to try to persuade the Americans to join Britain in fighting the war. In 1945 he went to Belsen and, with Hitchcock, he there supervised the work of Allied cameramen documenting the liberated camps for a feature-length documentary that was subsequently halted on the orders of the Foreign Office as being too 'incendiary'. It was concealed in the Imperial War Museum and only shown by the BBC in 1984 as *Memory of the Camps*.[30]

This Gestapo section on Jews in the media ends with ***Isidore Ostrer*** and his brothers ***Mark*** and ***Maurice Ostrer*** being named in the *Informationsheft* as owners of many film businesses. 'The largest and most important [of the] ... numerous Jewish-owned film companies is owned by the brothers ***Ostrer***, who also own several hundred cinemas and music-halls'. It was the textile mill owner and banker ***Isidore Ostrer*** (1889–1975) who had begun building up the Gaumont British Cinema Corporation in 1927, at the time of the first 'talkies'. He owned 350 cinemas by the mid 1930s, and in 1934 at the Gaumont studio at Lime Grove he produced the film of Feuchtwanger's *Jew Suess* – to be distinguished from the 1940 Nazi version *Jud Suess*. The Gaumont chain was sold in 1941 to J. Arthur Rank.[31]

Oscar Deutsch (1893–1941) had opened his first Odeon cinema in Birmingham in 1930 followed by a chain of Odeons, first in the south-east and, by 1939, all over Britain; he was 'the entertainer of the nation'. According to the *Informationsheft*, 'a great part of the British film industry, as well as 500 Gaumont-British and Odeon cinemas being welded into one, are now under the control and ownership of *dieser Jude*, **Oscar Deutsch**' – but he, too, sold his holdings to J. Arthur Rank in 1941. An observant, Orthodox Jew, **Deutsch** 'was a strong supporter of rearmament in the late 1930s [and helped] significant numbers of German Jews to escape the Nazi threat'.[32]

What was planned to be done with all 'these Jews' who were British? If the experience of wealthy Jewish Germans after 1933 is at all indicative, all British Jewish bankers and big businessmen would have been summarily expropriated, had their possessions sequestrated and themselves been taken into 'protective custody', i.e. concentration camps. There were also other outstanding refugee Jewish businessmen/financiers/industrialists such as the **Petschek** family, the Czech bankers and coal owners, suspected by the Gestapo of controlling a network of secret agents and activists ('*Taeterkreis Petschek*') whom we find targeted more than once in the *Sonderfahndungsliste* and who would certainly have been shown little mercy.

But what of the *non*-Jewish British businessmen? Were they also to be taken into custody, whether as hostages, or as punishment for non-cooperation – or would they have been willingly recruited to serve the Reich with all their international contacts and expertise? That fundamental question is complicated by the fact that a significant sector of British banking, business and industry had already had a close, even cordial, socio-commercial relationship with Nazi Germany between late 1935 and 1939 – as is evidenced by the Anglo-German Fellowship in those years. That fellowship had been established to succeed the original Anglo-German Association, which had had distinguished Jewish members, including its president, **Lord Reading**. The new Fellowship, in contrast, had *no* Jewish members and was blatantly sympathetic to Nazi Germany – while claiming to be non-political. This Anglo-German Fellowship was the counterpart to the established *Deutsch-Englische Gesellschaft* in Berlin and was promoted by von Ribbentrop, soon to be German ambassador to Britain. Members of the elitist Fellowship included such influential peers as Lord Nuffield, Lord Lothian, Lord Londonderry, Lord Redesdale and the Duke of Wellington, more than a dozen Conservative MPs on the far right, the governor of the Bank of England, Montague Norman, and the merchant banker E. W. D. Tennant, a financial backer of the Fellowship. Other backers were Geoffrey Dawson, the editor of *The*

Times, and the directors of Tate and Lyle, ICI and Distillers, members of the 'Cliveden Set' and **Frank Cyril Tiarks**, who visited Germany to give a friendly lecture in Cologne as late as March 1939. Its 'corporate members' included Price Waterhouse, **Unilever**, Dunlop Rubber, Firth-Vickers, Stainless Steel and several banks.

> Exchanges were organised with the Hitler Youth, the British Legion, German ex-servicemen and … *the Deutsch-Englische Gesellschaft* … in Berlin. Members also organised [English] country-house parties where they potted game with delighted visiting Nazis, discreetly raised the swastika among the rhododendrons, dressed up in jackboots, and drank toasts to the Führer. Such activities appealed to a clutch of society hostesses, including Lady Emerald Cunard, Lady Sybil Colefax, Lady Londonderry and [anti-Semitic] **Nancy Astor MP** who happily entertained von Ribbentrop and helped to make Nazism fashionable.[33]

Nancy Astor's intimate friend Philip Kerr, Marquess of Lothian, believed in Hitler's peaceable intentions right up to the invasion of Czechoslovakia in March 1939.

The ostensible purpose of the Anglo-German Fellowship was to build social, sporting, commercial and cultural ties with Nazi Germany in the interests of economic advantage and European peace. Off the record, however, was the hope (which had also often been voiced by Sir Henri Deterding, director of Shell), that there should be an alliance with Germany that would, sooner rather than later, make triumphant war against 'Bolshevik' Russia.[34] 'Hitler himself entertained representatives of the Anglo-German Fellowship along with Lord Rothermere and **Lord Beaverbrook**.'[35] Ironically, therefore, the very people who were disseminating the threat of a non-existent world conspiracy of Bolsheviks, Jewish financiers and **Freemasons**, were themselves conspirators. Most of those eminent members of the Anglo-German Fellowship are conspicuously absent from the *Sonderfahndungsliste GB.* A few others, such as **Frank Cyril Tiarks**, a former supporter of Oswald Mosley, *are* Blacklisted, perhaps because they had resigned from leadership positions in the Fellowship, either, like Lord Mount Temple, after *Kristallnacht* or else, even later in the day, after Hitler's invasion of Czechoslovakia in March 1939. The maverick **Nancy Astor** cooled towards von Ribbentrop as the Second World War approached and she, therefore, was placed on the Black List just at the last minute as someone who was no longer 'a friend to Germany' – like **Ward Price**, and **John Baker White** – to her eventual great relief. The Anglo-German Fellowship itself was only disbanded on 4 September 1939.

More research is needed before one can do more than speculate, let alone generalise, about what would have been the Nazi occupiers' relationship with British big business and the degree of collaboration or resistance that would have operated after a German invasion. It is hard to envisage either **Sir Andrew Agnew** or **Frederick Godber** ever collaborating (or being invited to collaborate) with the Nazi occupiers. But in an analogy with Vichy France, there would almost certainly have been contrasting instances of collaboration and of resistance in industrial Britain. Given the *Wehrmacht*'s stated policy of the expropriation of British raw materials and the planned deportation of the forced labour of British males aged from 17 to 50 to work in Germany, it is very possible that some leading industrialists, as in wartime France, might have started by collaborating in order to protect their own workforce from deportation, and they might then have turned to secret resistance and even sabotage. But other individual business leaders, much more sympathetic to Nazism than to communism, would most probably have believed that the future, including their own and their shareholders' futures, now lay with the all-conquering Nazis. The recent opening of MI5 files has revealed that 'Probably hundreds of Rightwing extremists joined [purported Nazi] networks [including the British branch of Siemens] during World War Two, unaware that they were run by British intelligence, seeking to identify Nazi sympathisers in Britain.'[36]

14

The Church

> Jesus Christ is the only Lord …There should be no other authority.
>
> Barmen Declaration, May 1934

It is perhaps surprising, given the fundamental opposition between the Nazis' rejection of compassion and Christ's command to love our neighbour, forgiving others seventy times seven, that the Gestapo should have selected so few British religious leaders in their *Sonderfahndungsliste* for immediate arrest. Just how different the Nazis' version of 'Christianity' was from that based on the Sermon on the Mount was officially articulated by the Nazi Party itself. In February 1937, Hanns Kerrl (1897–1941), the Nazi minister of church affairs who had been a member of the Nazi Party since 1923, declared:

> National Socialism is the doing of God's will … God's will reveals itself in German blood … Count Galen tried to make clear to me that Christianity consists in faith in Christ as the son of God. That makes me laugh … No, Christianity is not dependent upon the Apostles' Creed … True Christianity is represented by the party and the German people are now called by the party and especially the Führer to a real Christianity … the Führer is the herald of a new revelation.[1]

In 1939 Goebbels declared that there was an insoluble opposition between the Christian and a heroic-German world view. In his private diary, April 1941, he wrote 'It is certain that Jesus was not a Jew.'

Somehow the Galileans had managed to be 'Aryan'. As early as 6 June 1932, Kerrl had been quoted in *Time* magazine claiming that Hitler was Jesus Christ. In other words, the Nazis had their own new religion now, and Christians in Germany would be well advised not to make trouble but to work alongside or even to join its ranks. Soon it would not be the Bible but *Mein Kampf* that lay on Protestant 'German Christian' church altars, together with a sword; the Bible itself would be published without the Jewish Old Testament and the swastika would replace the cross. That Hitler was now the *de facto* God of the 'German Christians' was made clear in an article in ***Picture Post*** in July 1939, 'Inside a Nazi School', where the leader of the Nazi Teachers' Union, Hans Schwemm, is quoted: 'Lord God has sent Adolf Hitler to us … he has allowed us the grace to become a people again. We will, Adolf Hitler, so train the German Youth that they will grow up in your world of ideas, in your purposes and in the direction set by your will.'

However, a large minority of Lutheran pastors in Germany, led by Niemoeller, Karl Barth and the future martyr Dietrich Bonhoeffer, had dared to oppose Hitler's attempt to unify all Protestant churches in this new pro-Nazi 'German Reich Church'. Already in 1933 Niemoeller had rallied more than a third of all Lutheran pastors to unite against the official anti-Semitism; he was forced to retire in November 1933 and would be sent to Sachsenhaussen concentration camp in 1937 and later to Dachau. In May 1934 the 'Theological Declaration of Barmen', largely drafted by Karl Barth (later in exile in the USA) declared six theses:

1. The source of revelation is only the Word of God – Jesus Christ. Any other possible sources (earthly powers, for example) will not be accepted.
2. Jesus Christ is the only Lord of all aspects of personal life. There should be no other authority.
3. The message and order of the church should not be influenced by the current political convictions [e.g. anti-Semitism].
4. The church should not be ruled by a leader ('Führer'). There is no hierarchy in the church.

5. The state should not fulfil the task of the church and vice versa. State and church are both limited to their own business.
6. Therefore, the Barmen Declaration rejects (i) the subordination of the Church to the state… and (ii) the subordination of the Word and Spirit to the Church.

These and the subsequent theses became the chief document of the dissident, Confessional (or *Bekennende Kirche)* church in Germany which would be outlawed in 1937 and have to go underground. Seven hundred of their pastors had already been arrested in 1936 after Martin Niemoeller had denounced the government's anti-Semitism and, once the 'Aryan Paragraph' was adopted ('non-Aryan', i.e. Jewish) Lutheran pastors of part-Jewish descent or else married to Jewish wives, were all defrocked. Several of the most prominent refugee Lutheran pastors connected with the dissident *Bekennende Kirche* in Germany who had fled to Britain were tracked down by the Gestapo and listed in the *Sonderfahndungsliste* as 'Most Wanted'. Seven dissident German Lutheran pastors were named.

Those seven included **Pastor Amsling**, a vicar in London – '*Emigrant, evgl. Geistlicher (Vikar) (Taeterkreis* [resistance ring] **Hildebrand** [sic] – **Boeckheler – Rieger – Freudenberg**), Gestapo Amt RSHA 11b – ideological opposition and Amt RSHA VIH3 – ideological opposition abroad'. **Pastor Franz Hildebrandt** (1909–1985), an associate of Niemoeller, had been arrested in Germany, but fled into exile; he was listed by the Gestapo as '*Bekennende Kirche*' and even as an '*illegaler ND*' – a secret agent. He lived and worked with **Julius Rieger** and conducted Anglo-German church services in Cambridge after September 1939. It was the ***Bishop of Chichester***, ***George Bell***, a staunch friend of the future martyr Dietrich Bonhoeffer,[2] who intervened time and again to try to get entry permits and support for the dismissed German pastors of the *Bekennende Kirche* who were particularly at risk in the late 1930s.[3] **Hildebrandt** was close to ***Bishop Bell*** but himself later became a Methodist minister rather than an Anglican priest. In May 1940 he and his German congregation were interned, but were released in October. He edited *And Other Pastors of thy Flock: German Ministers' Tribute to Bishop Bell* (1942). Eventually **Hildebrandt** became a Presbyterian and worked as a minister and hospital chaplain in Edinburgh until he died. **Pastor Martin Boeckheler** (labelled 'Protestant Minister' with his full London address in the *Sonderfahndungsliste GB*) had been the Lutheran pastor for the German community in Hull after 1933 and was then successor to Bonhoeffer in Sydenham, London. Ironically, despite his long residence in Britain and anti-Nazi witness, he was interned as an 'enemy alien' by the British government from 1940 to 1945 and served as a pastor in internment camps in both Britain and Canada.[4]

The pastor of the German Lutheran St George's Church, in Aldgate, now Tower Hamlets, **Dr Julius Rieger** (1901–1984), had worked there since 1931. He himself had a Jewish mother and the Aldgate church was known by some London Germans as 'the Jewish church'. He had been converted to the *Bekennende Kirche* by Bonhoeffer and was in close contact with ***Bishop Bell*** in giving shelter to persecuted Christian Jews from Germany. He supported Bonhoeffer in his anti-Nazi resistance and was himself the most significant British link keeping people in Britain informed of the fate of the *Bekennende Kirche* in Germany. He lived in Britain between 1931 and 1953 and was interned in 1940 on the Isle of Man. After the war he worked as a pastor in British camps for German POWs.[5] **Dr Adolf Freudenberg** (1894–1977), a former diplomatic official in the German embassy until 1934, who was later ordained, had been driven to emigrate to England in March 1939 because of his marriage to a 'non-Aryan' – **Frau Freudenberg**, '*Juedin*', also in the Black Book. He had become a minister of the *Bekennende Kirche* in 1938 and joined **Julius Rieger**'s church in London. After April 1939 he organised refugee work for the World Council of Churches, provisionally in London,[6] which from 1940 on he then carried out as director of the Committee for Ecumenical Aid to Refugees at the council's office in Geneva. **Freudenberg** was the strongest ally and the most crucial source of funding for the rescue activities in Vichy France of Pastor Pierre Trouville, chief chaplain of Protestant refugees and camp internees in France.[7] In Geneva, **Freudenberg** managed to give Bonhoeffer a refuge on several occasions in the Second World War, enabling him to contact fellow anti-Hitler resisters. He himself returned to West Germany in 1947.

Another Blacklisted Lutheran refugee was **Pastor Herbert Friedrich Friess** (1909–1997). Ordained in 1934 and anti-Nazi from the start, he had suffered deprivation and persecution and was finally expelled from Germany in 1939. ***Bishop Bell*** personally invited him to come to England under the auspices of the Church of England Committee for Refugees. **Friess** served first as travelling secretary of the Anglo-German Christian Fellowship in Wartime and then worked, together with his wife **Hildegard Friess**, in an industrial mission in Sheffield. Eventually he lived and died in Ireland, as dean of Killala. 'Few could have met Herbert without recognition of his ability, his inner calm, and his sense of good humour ... He left his mark among the people whom he served.'[8]

The last Blacklisted refugee pastor was **Carl Gunther Schweitzer** (1889–1965), the former Protestant superintendent in Wustermark, Germany, who, after enduring house searches and interrogations and enforced early retirement in Germany, sought refuge in 1939 in Britain, again helped by ***Bell***. The Gestapo accused him of being in the '*illegaler Nachrichtendienst der Bekenntnisfront*' ('illegal secret service of the Confessing Front'). He had Christian Jewish parents. He was interned on the Isle of Man but ***Bell*** got him out and **Schweitzer** then taught young German émigrés at the Training Centre for Post-War Christian Service in Leicester. According to ***Bishop Bell*** '... our attitude to the refugees is a test of our attitude to God, as well as of our attitude to man ... To despair of our being able to do anything, is to be guilty of infidelity, just as to be the cause of men becoming refugees is to sin against the Almighty.'[9]

It was not only anti-Nazi Lutheran pastors, however, but also 'Non-Aryan', i.e. Jewish, German Christians, whom ***Bell*** rescued. 'Unwearyingly he worked to bring out those who were vulnerable or to reunite families divided by exile ... Hundreds of them looked upon him as their friend and protector ... He never failed them.'[10] Indefatigable, but unsuccessful in his efforts to energise the British government and the Church of England to realise the racist persecution that was then being suffered by German Christian Jews, and to intervene on their behalf, ***Bell*** took personal responsibility, together with sympathisers in his own diocese, for coming to their aid.[11]

The Gestapo had not at first anticipated much serious resistance from religious leaders of any persuasion in Britain. One must assume that their experience in Germany between 1933 and 1939, including their Concordat with the Vatican, and the recent establishment among the Lutherans of a dominating majority of pro-Nazi Protestants called 'German Christians', had reassured the Gestapo until September 1939 that the great majority of British religious observers, so long as their religious practices were not interfered with, would also be compliant, if not actually complicit, with a Nazi occupation. But whereas the *Sonderfahndungsliste* had named very few religious leaders of any persuasion, the later *Informationsheft GB* of July 1940, with invasion now imminent, decided that it was important to anticipate religious resistance and therefore to scrutinise the various churches in Britain, especially, of course, the established Church of England, because of their 'unchristian hostility to Germany'.

Thus the *Informationsheft* highlights the British **Ministry of Information**'s special 'Religious Division' and states that it kindled anti-German feeling throughout the neutral nations by identifying the British government's war policy as a *Christian* matter and hence a religious task. The Ministry's papers were to be seized immediately. The Gestapo was especially interested in the phenomenon of Buchman's evangelical Moral Re-Armament movement. They noted its support by ***Lord Salisbury***, ***Lord Addington*** and ***Lord Halifax*** *inter alia*, and suspected it of being strongly represented among English diplomats and 'readily accepting anti-German propaganda'. The Gestapo did not like any of the Church of England's international – and above all its *internationalist* – contacts, for instance with the ***Church Esperantist League*** (***Rev. A. J. Ashley***, Brighouse, Yorkshire), which aimed to make Esperanto a world language and had global pacifist connections.

The Gestapo, as supporters of the Nazi state control of religion, were also suspicious of the ***Archbiship's Commission on Relations of***

Church and State, supported by ***Lord Robert Cecil***, and by ***Sir Philip Baker-Wilbraham***, secretary of the National Assembly of the Church of England, as well as by the medieval historian ***Professor E. F. Jacob*** and the ***Marquess of Hastington***, given that ***Commission***'s sharp criticism of Nazism and of Germany as a totalitarian state. They were wary of the Church of England's ***Council of Empire Settlement*** that tried to strengthen England's influence in the Dominions. And they particularly suspected the Church of England's ***Council on Foreign Relations with the Eastern Churches***, which allegedly contained the fiercest anti-German ('*die groessten Deutschenhetzer*') Anglican clerics, whose correspondence and records demanded immediate 'safe-keeping' – ('*Sicherstellung*'). They especially targeted ***Bishop Harold Jocelyn Buxton*** (1880–1976) with his remit for Gibraltar and for Anglican congregations in Spain, Portugal, Greece, Rumania, Bulgaria and Yugoslavia. ***Buxton*** had published *Substitution of Law for War* in 1925 and he had been a prominent supporter of the Mayor's Armenian Fund, from 1918 to 1926. 'Who remembers the Armenians?' Hitler had famously asked, taking that as a green light for genocide against the Jews.

The Gestapo did not like the sound of the ***Church Socialist League*** (***Rev. Paul Stacy***, Coventry), or the ***Modern Churchmen's Union for the Advancement of Liberal Religious Thought*** (***Rev. E. Schomberg***, Trafalgar Square), and least of all the ***British Christian Council for International Friendship***, ***Life and Work*** and the **League of Nations Union** (***Bishop of Chichester***, ***George Bell*** and ***Dean of Chichester***, ***Arthur Stuart Duncan-Jones***).

Bishop Bell (1883–1958) had an 'essentially humane quality of … intelligence'.[12] His two great commitments were the ecumenical movement and the church's role in fighting for peace and social justice. After 1933, as we have seen, he worked intensely to support those Germans who he knew were resisting Nazism; but he also campaigned vigorously to support other refugees from Germany, both in his own diocese and right across Britain. His reward in Nazi Germany was to be 'greatly hated', and his very name was anathema to the Nazi government.[13] Once the Second World War started, ***Bell*** never forgave the British government for refusing explicit support for resistance groups in Germany; he met Bonhoeffer for the last time in June 1942 in neutral Sweden where he was told of the plan to assassinate Hitler. In August 1940 ***Bell***'s had been almost the only voice in the House of Lords to deplore the internment of 'enemy aliens' with its waste of the creative gifts possessed by committed anti-Nazis. He went out of his way to support refugee Jewish German artists, venerating as he did the artist's unique gifts and vision.[14] He testified that he had visited the Merseyside internment camp of Huyton where 'I saw crowds of men, useful men, distinguished-looking men, walking aimlessly about, with absolutely nothing to do'.[15] ***Bell*** was the only bishop to criticise the policy of indiscriminate arrest and internment of 'enemy aliens' and actually to visit the internment camps and listen to the prisoners, declaring afterwards in the House of Lords, 6 August 1940: 'I have been an active and public opponent of Hitler in his attacks on the Churches and on the Jews since 1933. I desire the defeat of Hitlerism as strongly as anyone in this country. But the refugees are not Hitlerism; they are the enemies of Hitlerism.'[16]

Bell also attacked the British government for waging 'total war' against the people of Germany, causing **Anthony Eden** to call him 'this pestilent priest'. Already in 1941 he had written to *The Times*, describing the British bombing of unarmed women and children in Germany as 'barbarian'. On 14 February 1943 he spoke in the House of Lords against 'Bomber' Harris's policy of the 'area bombing' of cities, as being worthy of the Nazis' 'Might is Right' world view; he declared that it actually called into question the humane values for which Britain had gone to war. And in June 1944 he again urged the House of Lords to vote against the British fire-bombing of German cities as a disproportionate and illegal 'policy of annihilation' – a crime against humanity. But ***Bell***'s protest was unsupported in the House of Lords, and earned the hostility of **Churchill**, of **Vansittart** and of Brigadier General 'Bomber' Harris, not to mention a cartoon in the *Daily Mail* showing a bishop carrying a placard saying '*Let's* not to be nasty to the Germans'. After the war, ***Bell*** protested against the mass expulsion of ethnic Germans from central and eastern Europe. His two books, *Christianity and World Order* (1940) and *The Church and*

Humanity (1946) best express his urgent moral prophecy.[17] His ***Dean of Chichester, Arthur Stuart Duncan-Jones*** (1879–1955), another anti-fascist, had published *The Struggle for Religious Freedom in Germany* in 1938.

The only other outstanding Anglican leaders who were individually named in the *Sonderfahndungsliste* were **Canon Raven** and **Maude Royden**. They were seen by the Gestapo not as religious figures at all, but as dangerous political leaders on account of their constant explicit anti-Nazism and pacifism, and their large public followings. In the *Informationsheft*, ***The British Christian Council for International Friendship***'s liaison committee with the **League of Nations Union**, the Gestapo alleged, 'holds the most valuable material on the political activity of the Anglican church'. The Gestapo also Blacklisted the ***Church Lads' Brigade*** (general secretary, ***H. F. Peerless***) and the ***Church Army***. The latter's founder and general secretary, the outdoor preacher ***Rev. Wilson Carlile***, CH, DD (1847–1941), was, at 93, the oldest 'Most Wanted' person of all in the Black Book. The Gestapo thought, mistakenly, that his so-called ***Church Army***, founded in 1882 to bring active Christianity and relief to the slums in Westminster, was operating within the actual British Army.

The other major Protestant denominations and organisations in England that the Gestapo had their eyes on were: the ***Methodists***, numbering 1.5 million; the *Congregationalists*, 500,000; the *Baptists*, 400,000; and the *Salvation Army*, 260,000. **William Lansdell Wardle**, DD, MA (1870–1947), was singled out as '***President of the Methodist Conference***'. Dean of the faculty of theology at Manchester University, **Wardle** would not have endeared himself to the Gestapo by having published a scholarly *History of the Religion of Israel* (Oxford, 1936), given that the Nazi edition of the Bible omitted the Old Testament altogether. Moreover, the Gestapo also accused the ***Methodists***, in particular, of championing the ecumenical movement, allegedly influenced by what the Nazis considered to be the **Freemasons**' idea of a World Council of Christian Churches. The international ***YMCA*** (General Secretary ***F. J. Chamberlain***) was also accused by the Gestapo of being 'completely in the hands of the **Freemasons**'.

The Student Christian Movement (general secretary ***Canon Tissington Tatlow*** and secretary ***Rev. R. D. Mackie***) was especially suspect in the *Informationsheft* for taking a leading role in the ***World Union of Christian Students.***

> ***The World Union*** is an international association of democratic pacifist character and it pretends to work for the spread of Christianity among students. But from the past few world conferences it has become clear that the ***World Union*** under English leadership has strong political tendencies and at different times members have sharply criticised Germany. It was owing to the ecumenicist and internationalist 'Apostle of the student world', Canon ***Tissington Tatlow***, DD (1876–1957), 'more than to any other one man that the [Student Christian Movement] came to exercise its great influence over the life of the church'.[18]

Not only the champion of Christian students and teachers the world over, ***Tatlow*** was also earmarked for being chairman of the Blacklisted British universities' **International Student Service**, which supported Jewish refugee students in Britain in the 1930s and in the Second World War.

The 20,000 **Quakers** in Britain had received especially hostile attention from the Gestapo already in the *Sonderfahndungsliste* for being pacifists as well as very active rescuers of German, Austrian and Czech Jews.

The **Roman Catholics** were seen by the Gestapo as a distinct cultural and educational sector, estimated to have about 3 million adherents in Britain including Scotland and Northern Ireland. They were said to be of predominantly Irish background, with their own press outlets and disproportionate representation in the Diplomatic Service, the Foreign Office and the Privy Council. In Germany's current struggle against its aggressors ('*seinen Angreifern*'), the Catholic Archbishop of Westminster, ***Cardinal Hinsley*** (1865–1943), seemed to the Gestapo to have sided with the best-known Anglican 'anti-Germans'. For unlike the Italian cardinals, ***Hinsley*** had opposed Mussolini's aggression in Abyssinia and had consistently criticised Hitler – although he had supported Franco. The *Informationsheft* accuses him of founding a parachute regiment called 'Sword of the Spirit'; in reality, 'Sword of the Spirit' was a *religious* ecumenical movement that reached out to non-Catholic clergy in the Second World War, inviting them to join British Catholics in opposing totalitarianism.

Observant British Jews of course constituted a special religious category. The few rabbis in the *Sonderfahndungsliste GB* are representative of three different versions of Judaism. They include the Hebrew scholar, and supporter of the World Jewish Congress and the Zionist movement, **Rev. Dr Abraham Cohen** (1887–1957), with his address in Edgbaston, Birmingham; and **Rabbi Joseph Hertz**, CH (1872–1946). **Hertz** was a Hungarian-born Hebrew scholar who, after having studied, and having worked in New York and South Africa, was Chief Rabbi in Britain from 1913 to 1946. Not Orthodox enough for some recent Jewish immigrants from eastern Europe, **Hertz** was, on the other hand, also opposed to Reform and Liberal Judaism. The father-in-law of Rabbi Schoenfeld, he agreed with Schoenfeld in opposing the *Kindertransport* rescue if it meant that Jewish refugee children could be allocated to gentile homes in Britain. Better a dead than a living but non-observant Jewish child. A keen religious Zionist in the 1920s and 1930s and a powerful critic of fascist persecution of Jews, in 1942 **Hertz** founded, with Archbishop William Temple, 'The Council of Christians and Jews' to combat anti-Jewish bigotry.[19]

The third Blacklisted rabbi, **Rabbi Israel Mattuck** (1883–1954), was the founding leader of liberal Judaism in Britain along with Lily Montagu and Claude Montefiore. Socially radical and an eloquent orator, **Mattuck** chaired the 'London Society of Jews and Christians', the oldest interfaith organisation in the UK, founded in 1927. Its aims were to increase religious understanding and mutual respect for the differences of faith and practice and to combat religious intolerance. He published the *Liberal Jewish Prayer Book* (1926), *What are the Jews?* (1937), *Jewish Ethics* (1947), *The Essentials of Liberal Judaism* (1953), and, posthumously, *Aspects of Progressive Jewish Thought* (1955).

Once the Nazi occupation of Britain seemed suddenly imminent, by

July 1940, the *Informationsheft GB* turned its attention to practising Jews in general in Britain. First they attempted to list all 'émigré' organisations in Britain supportive of Jewish refugees, irrespective of whether or not those particular Jews were believers, Orthodox or liberal, or even agnostics or atheists. (See Appendix 1) But there follows a much fuller four-page list of 'Jewish Organisations' which covers *all* the leading Jewish organisations and chief administrators with their London addresses. We find Orthodox **Agudas Israel**, and the **Sephardic World Union**, as well as **B'nai B'rith** – Children of the Covenant – the oldest world Jewish service organisation. The recently founded **World Jewish Congress**, which tried to counter Nazism's anti-Semitism and lobbied for the founding of a Jewish state, is listed, as well, of course, as all the main institutions of Anglo-Jewry such as ***The Anglo-Jewish Association*** and ***The Board of Deputies of British Jews***. The **Jewish Colonisation Association**, which focused on supporting Jewish resettlement in the USA, Canada and South America is on the list, as is **The Freeland League for Jewish Territorial Colonisation**, which focused on Australia. Far more Jews are named in relation to Zionism, both left-wing and right-wing – the ***Jewish Agency for Palestine (Zionist)***, the fundraising ***Keren Hayesod Committee***, the religious Orthodox **World Mizrachi Organisation**, the ***Zionist Federation of Great Britain*** and the ***Women's International Zionist Organisation (WIZO)*** with all their leading activists, both men and women. (See Appendix 2 for the complete list.)

At first the Gestapo selected only the most influential Jews in Britain for arrest. One can only think that under Nazi occupation, and sooner rather than later, all synagogues in Britain would have been shut down or destroyed and their congregations 'dealt with'.

It is clear from their choice of religious leaders that the Gestapo did come to anticipate some political resistance, not only from a handful of Jewish rabbis and from the more numerous Jewish campaigners for a national home, but also from some dogged British churchmen. There would have been more than a few pestilent priests who would have rejected the Nazis' rewriting of Christianity and congregations who would have refused to acknowledge Hitler as the world's new Redeemer. They too would have had to 'disappear'.

PART FIVE

ELIMINATING BRILLIANT MINDS IN THE HUMANITIES

1. *(top left)* Dr (later Lord), Christopher Addison, the most distinguished medical man ever to sit in Parliament; Labour Peer and initiator of British council housing in the Addison Act, 1920.

2. *(top right)* Dr (later Dame) Janet Vaughan, haematologist, researcher on pernicious anaemia in pregnant women, organiser of blood transfusion service in the Blitz and later campaigner against (carcinogenic) nuclear weapons testing.

3. *(left)* Dame Sybil Thorndike, actress and tireless activist in humanitarian causes. In the Thirties she championed Welsh miners, Indians campaigning for Independence, refugees and the (lost) cause of peace.

4. Dr Hilda Clark, indomitable Quaker medical and relief organiser, first with maternity patients trapped near the front line in France in the First World War and then, with her life partner Edith Pye, in post-war starving Poland, Vienna and Greece.

5. Doreen Warriner, economist and refugee rescuer in Czechoslovakia after the betrayal of Munich. She only left Prague when warned that she was next on the list to be arrested by the Nazi occupiers.

6. The 'Red' Duchess of Atholl, so called because of her astonishing interventions on behalf of the victims of fascism. Her implacable anti-appeasement stance eventually lost her the Tory whip.

7. Margery Fry, penal reformer, co-founder of the Howard League and campaigner (in vain) for the abolition of capital punishment the world over.

8. Victor Gollancz, publisher and founder of the Left Book Club. He hoped both to fight fascism and to avert the Second World War but the two aims were mutually exclusive.

9. J. B. Priestley, successful playwright, novelist and broadcaster. He proved too left wing for the Establishment and his immensely popular BBC *Postscript* talks were dropped.

10. Eleanor Rathbone, Independent MP for the Northern Universities. She was an 'Army of One' in her two campaigns – for financial independence for mothers via adequate Family Allowances and for Jewish refugees' right to be freed from British internment as 'enemy aliens'.

11. Frank Foley, British Passport Officer, a 'doer of the word' as he bent the rules to issue thousands of visas to imperilled Jews queuing outside his Berlin office.

12. Bishop George Bell, unpopular, lone champion of Christian Jewish refugees and even more unpopular and alone in his later opposition to the fire-bombing of Germany.

13. Maude Royden, spellbinding preacher and pacifist leader who finally renounced pacifism because 'Hitler was worse than war'.

14. Fritz Saxl, art historian who brought the cultural riches of Hamburg's Warburg Institute to safety in London and then succoured other art historians fleeing Nazism.

15. Klaus Wachsmann, musicologist and pioneer of World Music, recording traditional African musicians in Uganda *c.* 1940.

16. *Picture Post*, 15 October 1938, after Chamberlain's Munich 'Peace in our Time' deal with Hitler – John Heartfield's 'The Happy Elephants' i.e. 'If pigs could fly …'

17. *Picture Post*, 26 November 1938, (anon.), photo after*Kristallnacht*, 'Back to the Middle Ages' – Jews made to scrub Vienna streets with their hands.

18. *Picture Post*, 1 July 1939, 'A typical classroom in the Germany of 1939': 'History' has become reading the Nazi press.

19. David Daube, polymath, master of ancient languages including Aramaic; world authority on Roman Law.

20. Gabriele Tergit, incisive writer of socially critical reportage on criminal trials in Berlin; initiator of a new literary genre.

21. Virginia Woolf, modernist, feminist, novelist, targeted by the Gestapo for her public resistance to Fascism.

22. F. L. Lucas, Cambridge English literature don, tireless anti-Nazi polemicist and a leading code-breaker at Bletchley.

23. Marie Jahoda, socialist refugee from Vienna; co-founder of the discipline of Social Psychology and writer on the psychological impact of long-term unemployment.

24. Ernst Chain, biochemist who would share the Nobel prize in 1946 with Fleming and Florey for the discovery of therapeutic penicillin.

25. Hugh Blaschko, pharmacologist whose research tackled many diverse diseases, including high blood pressure, clinical depression, schizophrenia and Parkinson's.

26. Patrick Blackett and 27. Max Born – two Nobel prize-winning physicists; both opponents of nuclear weapons research and dedicated to the prevention of nuclear war.

28. The physicist Leo Szilard drafting Einstein's (fatal?) letter to Roosevelt, urging the necessity for atomic research to acquire the bomb before Hitler did.

29. Jos Wedgwood, Labour MP, champion of granting asylum to German socialists and Jews from the moment of Hitler's assumption of power; devastating opponent of Conservative prime minister Chamberlain's appeasement policy.

30. John Strachey, the most widely-read socialist writer in Thirties' Britain; his world-view grew ever darker – 'The history of every great nation is tragic' (*The Strangled Cry*).

31. Lady Violet Bonham Carter, leading Liberal and humane campaigner, including for the abolition of the death penalty in Britain. '[In] all her causes she would never compromise or give up …'

32. Rudolf Olden, anti-Nazi lawyer and journalist in pre 1933 Berlin; a refugee in Britain, he was refused 'naturalisation' and drowned with his wife on the torpedoed ship taking him to work in the US.

15

Art Historians and Musicologists

The brilliant intellectuals on the Gestapo's 'Most Wanted' list are so numerous that it is necessary for clarity's sake to classify them under various branches of the humanities and the sciences. It was not by happenstance that so many of the academic refugees – almost all of whom applied for and received British nationality – were brilliant. Indeed some had already achieved such international eminence in their various fields that they were cherry-picked by British universities for their outstanding gifts and invited to join home-grown leading intellectuals, some of whom had also been secretly earmarked for arrest by the Gestapo. For example the Oxford professor of physics, then called 'experimental philosophy', George Lindemann, wanted to raise the quality of his Clarendon Laboratory to rival the Cavendish Laboratory at Cambridge and he 'quickly seized the opportunity to import scientific talent from Germany' as early as May 1933.[1]

Most of the refugee academics, however, were identified and supported, not on self-serving but on altruistic grounds, by British intellectuals outraged that the Nazis, in their racist mania, had begun dismissing and expelling all Jewish intellectuals from Germany. Spearheaded by Sir William Beveridge, director of the London School of Economics, on 22 May 1933, forty-one prominent academics, including Maynard Keynes, **Gilbert Murray**, George Trevelyan and seven Nobel laureates in science and medicine (among them Ernest Rutherford) wrote to *The Times* announcing the foundation of the **Academic Assistance Council**. The council would 'raise a fund … providing maintenance for displaced teachers and investigators, and finding them work in universities and scientific institutions …

The society's income from its formation to the outbreak of war was nearly £100,000, equivalent to about £8 million today, *most of it from private individuals*'(my emphasis).[2]

By May 1945, 2,541 refugee scholars, most of them Germans and Austrians, had been registered with the council (soon renamed the ***Society for the Protection of Science and Learning***) – which had also been registered secretly by the Gestapo, together with its London HQ addresses, in the *Informationsheft* as well as in Part Two of the Black Book, '*Vereine*' ('Associations') as the **Academic Assistance Council** – '*Notgemeinschaft deutscher Wissenschaftler im Ausland*' ('Emergency association for German scholars abroad'). Not even the Gestapo, however, could identify and Blacklist every single one of the 2,541 refugee scholars, let alone all the British-born academics who opposed Nazism. Given the sheer numbers of those hundreds, if not thousands, of academics who *were* wanted for arrest on the invasion of Britain, it would need many volumes to do full justice to all their achievements. Therefore I shall highlight here just the outstanding Blacklisted intellectuals who were pioneering ground-breakers in their disciplines, or who founded whole new fields of study, beginning with art history and musicology.

'In December 1933, two little steamers brought the whole contents of [Hamburg's] *Kulturwissenschaftliches Bibliothek* [Cultural Studies Library] *Warburg* [including] fifty-five thousand books, thousands of slides, photographs, letters and heavy furniture, to London.'[3] From a Nazi perspective, of course, that move was an act of treason, depriving the Reich of valuable materials connected with German cultural history. German Jews were meant to get out but *not* to take their treasure with them. The Warburg librarians and researchers, whose visas had been granted after consultation with Anthony Blunt and Kenneth Clark, spanned and connected the world's history of ideas with the world of images from prehistory to the present, emphasising the continuous influence of antiquity. And in order to let readers make ever new connections and discoveries, the British public would be granted open access to the library stacks in order to browse. Hitherto in Britain, 'art history' had largely comprised biography, connoisseurship and technical appreciation. But with the arrival of the Blacklisted Jewish staff of the Warburg, the world's treasure trove of images now began to be studied in its cultural context as well as being given meticulous, scholarly documentation. For example the interdisciplinary and historical aspect of the Warburg Institute

> informed projects like the very successful photographic exhibition *English Art and the Mediterranean*, held in 1941 ... By demonstrating the manifold interactions between British art and the Continent, the attempt was to highlight, at the height of the war, the integrity of European culture, surviving all the atrocities of war and the corruption of culture under Nazism.[4]

The director of the Warburg Institute from 1933 to 1948, **Dr Fritz Saxl** (1890–1948),[5] became a British citizen in 1940, and was the person primarily responsible for establishing and maintaining the institute in Britain, both in body and spirit. His task included helping – by sponsoring and employing – as many as he could of the great number of German and Austrian, mostly Jewish, art historians in the 1930s who were driven out of their lectureships and homeland and who turned to the institute as their first port of call in the storm. And for their part, the entire staff of the Warburg in London had already volunteered in September 1938 to, in Dorothea McEwan's words, 'give their services to the British Community in case of war.'

Saxl was aided in his task of finding sponsorship for other refugee art historians by his partner, **Dr Gertrud Bing** (1892–1964), an authority on German philosophy and the art criticism of Gotthold Lessing. She had been the founding librarian of the original Warburg in Hamburg, and served as deputy director of the Warburg in London from 1933 to 1955, and as director from 1955 to 1959.[6] Hugely energetic and warm, **Bing** was a good listener and a tireless letter writer on others' behalf. At the beginning of the Second World War she became an auxiliary ambulance driver in the Blitz – despite being officially still an 'enemy alien'. Ernst Gombrich, author of the seminal *The Story of Art* (1950), was her devoted younger colleague and protégé.

Other Blacklisted Warburg luminaries included **Dr Paul Jacobsthal** (1880–1957), an authority on Greek vase painting and on Celtic art who became a lecturer at Christ Church, Oxford, and the Hungarian **Dr Frederick Antal** (1887–1954), who fled Berlin and became a lecturer in art history at the Courtauld Institute. The author of *Florentine Painting and its Social Background* (1947), he soon became the leading, pioneering exemplar of Marxist social history of art in Britain. He published an important study of Hogarth, and was a formative influence on the young Anthony Blunt.[7] The Viennese-born **Dr Otto Kurz** FBA (1908–1975), librarian of the Warburg Institute in 1944, became professor of art history at the University of London in 1965 and then Slade professor of fine art at Oxford in 1971. **Dr Richard Salomon** (1884–1966), who had converted to Protestantism when he was 18, was a polymath who specialised in European medievalism. In spite of the fact that he was now a Christian, he was still nevertheless labelled 'undesirable' as a Jew in Germany in March 1934. He then taught at the Warburg and later moved to the USA.

The authority on Tuscan architecture and on Michelangelo, as well as on Flemish-influenced medieval tapestries, **Dr Martin Weinberger** (1893–1965) became professor at the Institute of Fine Art, New York University. He donated his collection of photographs of French Romanesque and Italian Renaissance sculpture and architecture to the National Gallery, London. Versed in six languages, **Dr Edgar Wind** (1900–1971) was an interdisciplinary specialist in Renaissance iconology and author of the famous *Pagan Mysteries of the Renaissance – An Exploration of the Philosophical and Mystical Sources of Iconography* (1958), which is still highly prized by readers today. **Wind** helped found the *Journal of the Warburg and Courtauld Institutes* in 1937 and, after fifteen years in the United States as professor of philosophy and art, he became Oxford's first professor of art history in 1955. A brilliant lecturer, he was said to be equally at home in art, literature, history and philosophy; his approach to art was that of the cultural historian.[8] Finally, **Dr Rudolf Wittkower** (1901–1971), who was a British citizen all his life although born in Germany, taught at the Warburg Institute from 1934 until 1956. His most important, though now controversial, book, *Architectural Principles in the Age of Humanism,* an analysis of the architecture of Palladio, was published in 1949.[9]

On the fringes of the Warburg was **Dr Alfred Scharf** (1900–1965), a wealthy independent researcher at the Institute on Renaissance Knowledge of Classical Sculpture. His several research specialities included fifteenth-century Italian painting, seventeenth-century Dutch and Flemish painting, and European drawing from the fifteenth to the eighteenth centuries. He lectured at the Courtauld and was a consultant for the National Art Collection; he donated notable drawings to the Ashmolean Museum in Oxford and wrote on Rembrandt's drawing of hands.[10] Although he had arrived in Britain already in 1933, he was only 'naturalised' in 1946. Recently, on 11 September 2017, he was featured in the BBC TV programme, *Fake or Fortune*, where his judgement was vindicated concerning the authenticity of a charcoal and pencil drawing by Gauguin that he had once owned and later bequeathed to a grandson.

Largely independent of the Warburg, although influenced by its approach, was the prolific and ground-breaking art historian **Dr Helen Rosenau** (1900–1984). She had arrived in Britain in the autumn of 1933, having been expelled from university teaching and research as a German Jew. The British Federation of University Women then supported her as she renewed her studies, this time at the Courtauld. She published *Design and Mediaeval Architecture* (including that of cathedrals) in 1934, and 'The Synagogue and Protestant Church Architecture', in the *Journal of the Warburg and Courtauld Institutes* in 1940. Greatly interested in the sociology of art, **Rosenau** worked with the sociologist **Karl Mannheim** at the LSE from 1941. Her pioneering work on *Woman in Art: from Type to Personality* was published in 1944 and is the foundation text for all later feminist art history. A tutor in adult education in the 1940s, **Rosenau** became a British citizen in 1945 and later a senior lecturer at the universities of Manchester and London.[11]

The most famous of all refugee art historians in Britain, and the one most lastingly identified with England, was of course **Nikolaus Pevsner**, CBE, FBA (1902–1983), who was born into a Russian Jewish family in Leipzig. Ironically, he had started out a conservative German nationalist who happened to have an academic interest in English art and architecture. He had worked first at the Dresden Gallery and then, until 1933, at the University of Goettingen. Although he had converted to Lutheranism in his youth, he was still rejected by Nazi Germany. Forced into exile in Britain in 1933, he at first lived precariously on a temporary research fellowship, on publishers' advances, and as a buyer of modern textiles, glass and ceramics for a London furniture showroom. But **Pevsner** soon set himself to wrestle for England's aesthetic and historical soul. In 1936 he completed his *Pioneers of the Modern Movement: from William Morris to Walter Gropius*. In 1937 he published a critical view of British design standards, *An Enquiry into Industrial Art in England*, and gradually he came to see his mission as opening English eyes to their own architecture and championing early modernism. He became a frequent contributor to the *Architectural Review*.

Interned as an 'enemy alien' in 1940, **Pevsner** was released after three months and worked for a considerable time in London helping to clear the bomb debris of the Blitz. He wrote reviews and art criticism for *Die Zeitung* – an anti-Nazi publication for Germans living in England, financed by the British Ministry of Information. His *Outline of European Architecture* (1943), sketched out during his internment, was a great success. Eventually, in 1942, he was appointed to a secure post as a part-time lecturer at Birkbeck College, University of London, where he remained until 1969, and he also lectured at Cambridge. By the time he was 'naturalised' in 1946, **Pevsner** had already started out on his marathon enterprise of travelling the length and breadth of the country to produce his great forty-six volume county by county survey, *The Buildings of England* (1951–74) for **Allen Lane** at **Penguin**, of which he was the sole author of thirty-two volumes, *Cornwall* being the first. 'What distinguished the exile's work from his British antiquarian predecessors was the sheer scale and professionalism of the endeavour.'[12] **Pevsner**'s love of England and its buildings shines through, never more movingly than in his photograph of the Buckinghamshire village of Fingest, with its haystacks and church tower in the evening sun. By 1955 he would feel authoritative enough to lecture the English on 'The Englishness of English Art' for the BBC Reith lectures.

There was only one British-born architect listed in the Black Book – **Dr Frederick Francis Charles Curtis**, FRIBA (1903–1975), who had been a lecturer at the Technical University of Darmstadt until he left Germany for political reasons in 1933. He lectured at the Liverpool School of Architecture from 1936 to 1946, was appointed architect to the Great Western Railway in 1947, and in 1948 became the first chief architect of British Railways. **Pevsner** praised his modernist designs in Surrey, Middlesex and Derby.

There were of course many more German and Austrians refugee art historians in Britain in the 1930s other than those I have instanced because they were listed in the Black Book. Why were all the others not listed? Gestapo ignorance is the simplest explanation. What the Gestapo did do was to concentrate on one famous, Jewish-funded and Jewish-founded institution, the Warburg, and in so doing they netted an extraordinarily gifted and learned group of original thinkers who changed the very nature of the discipline of art history in Britain. Honouring one of their most distinguished disciples, Ernst Gombrich, the sculptor Anthony Gormley has recently acknowledged the huge debt that Britain owes to these particular immigrants in the 1930s: 'British cultural life has never quite been the same since they arrived.'[13]

Three Blacklisted refugee musicologists

If art history seems an absurd intellectual discipline for the Gestapo to have targeted, the historical study of music is even more unexpected. **Dr Mosco Carner** (born **Mosco Cohen**) (1904–1985), for example, wrote his doctoral dissertation in Vienna on the apolitical, technical subject of sonata form in the work of Schumann. After becoming a conductor in Czechoslovakia and then in the still free city of Danzig, **Cohen** was prescient enough to enter Britain on a tourist visa in 1933. He changed his name from **Cohen** to **Carner** and established himself in the 1930s as a very successful guest conductor of the Royal Philharmonic, the BBC Symphony Orchestra and the London Symphony Orchestra – as well as being a music critic. Nevertheless he was still interned as an 'enemy alien' in 1939. He became a 'naturalised' British citizen in 1940. **Carner** was a masterly writer in English, bringing out works on Dvorak's church music and an essay collection, *Of Men and Music*, in 1944. He published *Hugo Wolf Songs* in 1983 and, above all, two authoritative critical biographies of the very different composers Puccini (1958) and Alban Berg (1975).[14]

A less straightforward professional trajectory was that of the composer and authority on seventeenth-century English chamber music, **Dr Ernst Hermann Meyer** (1905–1988), the son of a Jewish doctor and a painter in Berlin, both of whom were murdered in Auschwitz. A musical prodigy, **Meyer** started composing when he was 11; later he wrote his doctorate on seventeenth-century north German composers and, at the end of the 1920s in Weimar Berlin, he became a composition pupil of Hanns Eisler, the friend and collaborator of Brecht. Eisler converted **Meyer** to communism in 1930, at the time of the Great Depression. The composer of the first protest song against anti-abortion laws, Eisler was included in the Nazis' *Entartete Musik* ('Degenerate Music') exhibition held in Düsseldorf in May 1938. As a Jew and the composer of militant protest songs himself, **Meyer** fled Nazi Germany for Britain in 1933, where he was soon befriended by the communist composer and lecturer at the Royal Academy of Music, Alan Bush, who was in contact with the exiled Kurt Weill and Hanns Eisler. **Meyer** studied seventeenth-century English chamber music at the Royal Academy and lectured both for the Workers' Educational Association and at Bedford College, London. He also composed music for British documentaries before, during and after the Second World War. In 1946 he published his authoritative *Early English Chamber Music: The History of a Great Tradition from the Middle Ages to Purcell*. Despite having been awarded a guest professorship at King's College Cambridge in 1945, **Ernst Meyer**, like other communist exiles in Britain, experienced difficulty in obtaining an exit visa (*Ausreisepass*). In 1948 he settled in East Germany. There he remained a loyal Communist Party member, committed to Marxist-Leninism, but also, as professor at the Humboldt University, he was devoted to his scholarly field of seventeenth- to eighteenth-century music and sociology. As president of the Georg Friedrich Handel Society of Halle from 1967 to 1988, **Meyer** co-founded the great annual Handel Festival there, which still flourishes today. He is buried in the Friedrichsfelder Central Cemetery, Berlin, in a plot that also commemorates his eight family members who were murdered in concentration camps.

The scholarly field of the ethnomusicologist **Dr Klaus Wachsmann** (1907–1984), could not have been more different. He was a pioneer in the study of African traditional music and, funded by the British government from 1949 to 1957, he compiled the first important, extensive collection of African field recordings and photographs ever made, now held in the British Library. **Wachsmann** had been prevented on racist grounds from completing his university studies on pre-Gregorian chant in Germany in 1933 and he had been forbidden to marry his 'Aryan' fiancée Eva, a concert singer. In 1936 they migrated to Britain where, funded by the ***Society for the Protection of Science and Learning***, he studied two African languages, Luganda and Kiswahili, at London's School of Oriental and African Studies. The Church Missionary Society then enabled them to go to Uganda in 1937 and work for the Protestant Mission there. (**Wachsmann** had been brought up a Lutheran by his non-practising Jewish parents but eventually became an Episcopalian, while still always cherishing his Jewish heritage.) He soon dedicated himself to researching traditional African musical culture – a culture that Nazi ideology denied could possibly exist among '*Neger*'. The Gestapo had no idea that **Wachsmann** was in Africa, and hence included him as one of their 'Most Wanted' in Britain in 1940. From 1944 to 1947 he was educational director of the Ugandan Protestant Mission, and in 1948, having co-founded the International Folk (later World) Music Council, he became the founding curator of Kampala's Uganda Museum with its great collection of East African musical instruments. Many of his photographic records went to the library archive at Makerere University, Kampala. In 1958 **Wachsmann** received the Royal African Society's

Bronze Medal for his 'Devoted Service to Africa' and in 1971 he published his *Essays on Music and History in Africa.*[15]

Musicology was not of itself a suspect branch of learning. Only **Ernst Meyer's** activities as an open communist from 1930 to 1940 were politically anathema to the Nazis. Otherwise all that concerned the compilers of the *Sonderfahnungsliste* was that each one of these scholars, no matter if a convert to Protestantism or an avowed agnostic, was a distinguished Jew.

16

Attacking Ancient Classicists

It might seem baffling that the Gestapo should have bothered to include on their 'Most Wanted' list a 74-year-old translator of Ancient Greek, famous for such lyrically evocative lines in a Euripidean chorus as, 'The apple trees, the singing and the gold', but **Gilbert Murray** (1866–1957) (OM 1941), was in fact the very incarnation of the Western liberal humanism that Nazi Germany sought to extirpate. Not himself a pacifist, **Murray** had nevertheless championed the conscientious objectors of the First World War and stood by his internationalism, however unpopular, throughout his life. He had supported the League of Nations from its very inception as an idea in 1916, and served as the influential vice-president and later president of the League of Nations Society, later Union – a citizens' support association for international peace. The British section of the international **League of Nations Union** was of course Blacklisted by the Gestapo. In 1933 **Murray** had contributed to *The Intelligent Man's Way to Prevent War*; in 1937–8 his lectures on 'Liberality and Civilization' were published and in 1941 he translated Sophocles' *Antigone* – the foundation text for all non-violent resistance to tyranny – a work that was also central to the thinking of **Virginia Woolf** in the late 1930s. He made a sustained but unsuccessful effort to save the German refugee lawyer, writer and teacher **Rudolf Olden**, to whom he gave asylum in his own home. After the war **Murray** became one of the founders of Oxfam and, persevering in hope to the end, in 1948 he published *From the League to the UN*. In his mid eighties he served as president of the United Nations Association in Britain.

Another Oxford classicist, **E. R. Dodds** (1895–1978), the Irish nationalist and socialist successor to **Murray** as Oxford professor of Greek, and author of the seminal *The Greeks and the Irrational*, was an outspoken anti-fascist. 'Hitler stood for the systematic denial of all that I most valued – my right to form my own judgement and speak my own mind.'[1] Feeling increasingly isolated as an anti-appeaser in Oxford, he continues, 'I was increasingly convinced that appeasement [far from preventing war] only made the Day of Wrath more certain.' **Dodds** became a Labour activist and joined the Blacklisted left-wing political organisation **For Intellectual Liberty (FIL)**, co-founded by **Margery Fry**, which pledged to resist fascism and any attack upon democratic freedom. He had a lasting influence on the young 1930s poets Louis MacNeice and **Stephen Spender**. **Dodds** backed a united anti-fascist front between British Communists and Labour, even after the latter had banned it; and the only time as an adult that he could 'remember actually weeping was after Dunkirk, when a remnant of Britain's defeated army marched silently down [Oxford] High Street under my windows'.[2] His outspokenness did not go unnoticed. He guessed correctly that he had signed enough letters to *The Times* to win a place on Hitler's Black List. **Dodds** would play a significant role in the post-war de-Nazification of the German education system, agreeing with Heinz Koeppler of Wilton Park that 'the most we could do was to help the Germans to re-educate themselves'.[3]

In Weimar Germany **Eduard Fraenkel** (1888–1970), was already generally acknowledged as one of the very greatest classical scholars of the twentieth century, eminent in both Greek and Latin, writing in German and being translated into English. Yet again Germany's loss was England's gain when **Fraenkel**, professor at Freiburg, co-founder of the periodical *Gnomon* and author of a famous book on Plautus' adaptations of Greek plays, was forbidden to teach as a 'non-Aryan' in Germany and was invited by the English poet and classicist A. E. Housman to become professor of Latin at Corpus Christi College, Oxford, where he remained from 1934 to 1951. He became a British citizen in 1939 and a member of the British Academy in 1941. As well as writing on the comedies of Plautus, **Fraenkel** published on Virgil and Horace, on Aristophanes and Euripides and, above all, his monumental edition (and sometimes idiosyncratic interpretation) of Aeschylus' *Agamemnon*. As a tutor **Fraenkel** could be intimidating, especially to his women students, although Dame Mary Warnock, née Wilson, found that his extraordinary learning and teaching outweighed his personal defects. Towards the end of his life, **Fraenkel**, who never forgot or forgave the wicked cruelty and stupidity of the Nazi period, became increasingly concerned with Sophocles' depiction of doomed heroic natures in tragic conflict with their hostile world. In the words of Sophocles' Electra: 'With evil all around me, there is nothing I can do that is not evil.' After the death of his wife of fifty-two years, **Fraenkel** took his own life. '[He] personified the urge to learn from and enjoy the achievements of the ancient world and he has left a gap that nobody can fill.'[4]

All German scholars in the humanities were so well grounded in Ancient Greek and Latin that several refugee academics such as **David Daube** went on to apply that knowledge to other disciplines, such as comparative literature or comparative law, or the history of economics. For example, the classicist **Fritz Heichelheim** (1901–1968), a specialist in economic history from Ancient Egypt to the Roman Empire, began his life as an academic refugee at Cambridge by cataloguing the Greek coins in the Fitzwilliam Museum in the late 1930s. He was 'naturalised' as a British citizen at the end of the Second World War, having tried to volunteer for the British Army but been rejected on the grounds of his age. Appointed lecturer at the University of Nottingham in 1942, **Heichelheim** directed the excavation of a Roman site at Cross Hill before moving to the University of Toronto, where he wrote his authoritative *History of the Roman People*.

Of all the brilliant intellectuals in this section, none was more brilliant – or more erudite – than the polymath and greatest twentieth-century authority on ancient law, **David Daube** (1909–1999). Indeed it is difficult to know where to place him, for as well as being a great law professor, **Daube** was also a great linguist, a radical religious thinker, an expert in comparative law, an historian of ideas, a literary critic and the world authority on Roman law. But no sooner had he graduated as doctor of law from the universities of Freiburg and Goettingen in 1932 than the Nazis came to power; his doctoral thesis on Old Testament law could not be published, and he fled to Cambridge, becoming a fellow in Roman law at Gonville and Caius College, Cambridge from 1938 to 1946 and then a university lecturer from 1941 to 1949. Assisted by Cambridge faculty and students, **Daube** also risked returning to Europe several times throughout the later 1930s in order to rescue relatives, friends and even just acquaintances. '**Daube**'s English, rudimentary when he first arrived in England, [soon] became witty and idiomatic.'[5] Deeply versed in Greek, Latin, Hebrew, Aramaic and Christian literature, not to mention the German, English and French literary classics, **Daube** used his familiarity with the religious and legal teaching of the Ancient World to transform the study of Roman law.[6] Even more radically, **Daube** began an intellectual revolution, the fruit of his work with the Cambridge New Testament scholar and professor of divinity, C. H. Dodd, through his concept of 'New Testament Judaism', which reinterpreted the New Testament in the light of the Talmud, and argued that the teaching of Jesus needs to be read as the last book of the Old Testament. **Daube**'s most important book was *The New Testament and Rabbinic Judaism* (1956). He believed, perhaps too hopefully, that a realisation of the true continuity between Judaism and Christianity would bring Jews and Christians closer to mutual understanding.[7]

During the war, after a brief period of internment, **Daube** worked in London, helping with school and hospital evacuation, and he was granted British citizenship in 1951. He became a Fellow of All Souls and was Regius Professor of Civil Law at Oxford from 1955 to 1976, while also teaching in California and Germany. His later lively and politically relevant essay collections include: *Collaboration with Tyranny in Rabbinic Law* (1965), *Civil Disobedience in Antiquity* (1972), *Johann Ben Baroqua and Women's Rights* (1982), and *Appeasement and Resistance* (1987). His last papers, published in 1994 and 1995, were a reappraisal of Judas. Born into Orthodox Judaism, **Daube** became a questioner: ' … despite a cover of playfulness, he was both deeply serious and unsure of ultimate truth. Even the pope had doubts, he said: he knew, because he had asked him.'[8] Venerated and honoured throughout the

Western academic world for his contributions to the study of Talmudic and Roman law as well as to the New Testament, **Daube** died leaving just a few hundred pounds.

Another brilliant polymath and historian of ideas was **Hermann Kantorowicz** (1877–1940). Legal historian, medievalist, legal theorist, legal philosopher, comparative-international lawyer, classical philologist, social scientist, political theorist and political activist – **Kantorowicz** was every one of these at some point in his career. He was more interested in the philosophy behind all law than merely in the history of law, which he defined as 'a body of rules prescribing external conduct and considered judiciable' (*Definition of Law* 1938, 1958). 'Judges should apply pre-existing legal rules as individual cases require and should declare new law derived from custom and social usage.'[9] His introduction of social usage brought sociology into law to complement a priori values-based jurisprudence. A specialist in criminal law, as a university teacher in pre-Nazi Germany, **Kantorowicz** had published the *Case against Capital Punishment* (1912), the *Case for the League of Nations* (1924), *Pacifism and Fascism* (1925), and *Verfolgungseifer, The Drive to Persecute* (1928/9). These works were all profoundly anti-fascist and he was dismissed from his post at the University of Kiel on both racist *and* political grounds in 1933. He then taught in the USA, and, after 1934, in Britain – at the LSE, Oxford and Cambridge. In 1935 he published his work on *Dictatorships* and in 1938 he completed his most important work *The Definition of Law* (published posthumously by Cambridge University Press in 1958). He became assistant director of research in law at Cambridge from 1937 to 1940; but by the time the Gestapo had planned to arrest him towards the end of 1940, **Kantorowicz** had died in Cambridge. His son Tom Carter joined the British Army and wrote a memoir of his father. **Kantorowicz**'s scholarship and his humane, radical, intellectual curiosity have ensured that his influence as a jurist has lasted into the twenty-first century;[10] the most recent international conference on his thought was held in Helsinki in 2018.

But the Western study of antiquity reached farther back than the Greeks and Romans. For example, Blacklisted **Dr Elise Baumgaertel**

(1892–1975) was a distinguished Egyptologist who pioneered the study of the archaeology of pre-dynastic Egypt. She had participated in German excavations at Wadi Sheik before being forced out of Nazi Germany in 1934 for being a Jew. In Britain she was supported by the academic communities of archaeology and Egyptology and she eventually helped to catalogue the Flinders Petrie collection at University College, London. During the war she was hosted by Somerville College, Oxford, where she worked on her book *The Cultures of Prehistoric Egypt*, the first volume of which was published in 1947. She resisted more recent findings based on the new technique of radiocarbon dating that disputed her claim that Egyptian civilisation was founded in the upper, not the lower, delta of the Nile,[11] which somewhat detracted from her reputation in later years.

One of the most tragic figures among the cultural historians was **Dr Leonie Zuntz** (1908–1944), an expert on the ancient Hittites. Despite her grandfather's conversion to Christianity she was still classified as a Jew by the Nazis; and in 1935 she fled to Oxford where, like **Baumgaertel**, she was given a place to live at Somerville College under the principal Helen Darbishire. She was only able to undertake language teaching and unpaid work at Jesus College as a Hittite scholar – as well as proofreading for the Oxford University Press. She died in Oxford in 1944. It is thought that she committed suicide.

Despite her grounding in classical philology, the field of the distinguished Indologist, comparative philosopher and philologist, **Professor Dr Betty Heimann** (1888–1961), was the history of Hindu philosophy. A rare, enthusiastic and lively teacher of ancient Sanskrit, **Heimann** was dismissed on racist grounds from her chair in Germany, despite having been the first German woman ever to receive a doctorate in ancient Indian literature and thought, as well as the first to qualify as a German university teacher of Sanskrit and Indian philosophy. Awarded an American-funded research year in India from 1933 to 1934, she was granted first a post and then a professorial chair at the School of Oriental and African Studies, University of London, on her return to Europe. She was supported – and helped to survive – by the British Federation of University Women. In addition to her commentaries on the Upanishads of the Veda before 600 BC and the birth of Buddhism, one of her major works was her study, *Indian and Western Philosophy, A Study in Contrasts* (1937). 'India forces us to give up our own modes of thought if we wish to get near her' (from the preface). For whereas Western philosophy puts man in the centre of the discussion, in Indian thought humans are treated as equalled by nature and other living creatures. Having been granted British citizenship in 1939, **Heimann** was appointed to teach Indian philosophy at Oxford, and after the war she took up a chair at the University of Colombo in Ceylon, the first woman to be a professor there.

Finally, yet another historian of ideas, **Erich Langstadt** (1910–1989), was a specialist in a very different, religious field – in his case the work of the early Christian theologian (later ascetic and millenarian Montanist) Tertullian, AD *c.*160–*c.*220. **Langstadt** published on Tertullian's writings on 'Sin', and after his forced emigration to Britain, he became librarian at the University of Leeds.[12]

It would seem that what the Gestapo focused on in selecting British-born classicists for immediate arrest was their high-profile liberal or left-wing politics. In the case of Jewish classicists, however, with the exception of **Kantorowicz**, it was not their anti-fascism which damned them in Gestapo eyes but their sheer intellectual brilliance. It did not fit the Nazi stereotype of the 'parasitic Jew' that these particular men and women should have achieved such international veneration. Therefore they, rather than the hundreds of less famous, younger Jewish 'emigrant' intellectuals, would have to be the first to 'disappear'.

17

Economists of All Kinds – but not All Economists

Economists may object to being classified under the humanities rather than the sciences. However, their field of enquiry is indisputably focused on an aspect of human interaction and its effects on humans. And the refugee economists were especially notable for their recognition of this fact, notwithstanding their expertise in statistics, mathematical formulae, graphs and modelling.

Only two of the Gestapo's Blacklisted economists were not refugees. A British-born economics graduate from the new London School of Economics, **Sir Theodor Emanuel Gugenheim Gregory** (1890–1970) was professor of economics at the University of London from 1927 to 1937 as well as professor of social economics at the University of Manchester, from 1930 to 1932, and author of *Gold, Unemployment and Capitalism* (1933). A member of the Reform Club, the traditional 'home' of progressive liberals, he was indicted as 'Jew' in the Gestapo's *Informationsheft* and that was enough.

The Liberal Party activist **Sir George Paish** (1867–1957), 73 in 1940, was also a member of the Reform Club and a socially reforming liberal in his economic thinking. A pioneering statistician, his books had included *Saving and Social Welfare* (1911); *The Economics of Reparation* (1921); *World Economic Suicide* (1929); *The World Danger* (1939), and *The Defeat of Chaos* (1941). **Paish** would not have endeared himself to Nazi ideologues when he became chairman of the Blacklisted **Abyssinia Association** founded in April 1936 'to render all possible aid to Ethiopia during the war [against Mussolini]; to assist the Emperor Haile

Selassie ... at Geneva [i.e at the League of Nations] and to endeavour to safeguard the interests of Ethiopian refugees'. In June 1936 the **Abyssinia Association** urged Prime Minister Stanley Baldwin to refuse to recognise fascist Italy's annexation of Ethiopia and also urged, in vain, that economic sanctions be imposed on Mussolini. In January 1939 the association had announced a public protest meeting, 'Abyssinia Betrayed,' in central London.[1] Among **Sir George Paish**'s fellow supporters on the **Abyssinia Association** council were those familiar anti-Nazi bêtes noires of the Gestapo, **Sir Norman Angell**, **Vyvyan Adams** MP, **Geoffrey Mander** MP and **Eleanor Rathbone** MP – as well as **Sylvia Pankhurst.**

F .M. Scherer's article 'The Emigration of German-speaking Economists after 1933',[2] and Harald Hagemann's article 'Dismissal, Expulsion, and Emigration of German-speaking Economists after 1933'[3] survey over one hundred uprooted academic economists in Britain, but they do not focus on those on the Black List. The Gestapo-targeted economists include **Moritz Julius Bonn**, **Fritz Burchardt**, **Adolf Loewe**, **Jacob Marschak**, **H. C. Hillmann**, **Robert René Kuczynski**, the **Liepmann** brothers, **Hermann Levy**, **Marie Dessauer-Meinhardt**, **Eduard Rosenbaum**, **Charlotte Leubuscher**, **Kurt Mandelbaum** and **Hans Singer**. (The monetarist **Paul Einzig**, 'Redakteur', editor of the *Financial News* and controversial, prolific expert on currency turbulence in the 1920s and 1930s, was *not* one of the refugee economists who arrived after 1933 but a Romanian/Hungarian Jew who had lived in Britain since 1919 and was naturalised in 1929. He was an implacable anti-Nazi.)

The internationally famous economic theorist in crisis-ridden Weimar Germany, **Mauritz Julius Bonn** (1873–1965), had been part of the League of Nations' investigation into the shortage of gold currency and the problem of capital flight due to the uncertain political and economic conditions during the Great Depression of the early 1930s. His dismissal on 'racial' grounds by the Nazis from his post as rector of the Trade Institute in Berlin was almost as notorious throughout the world as was the exiling of **Einstein**. From 1933 until 1938 **Bonn** taught at the LSE and participated in Liberal summer schools in Oxford and Cambridge, becoming a well-known member of the Reform Club. During the Second World War he was a visiting professor in the United States where he worked unofficially for the British government, endeavouring to enlist America as an ally against Nazi Germany. Forced to become 'a wandering scholar', he died in London in 1965.[4]

The liberal Social Democrat, statistician and co-founder of the economic theory of cyclical growth in industrial economies,[5] **Fritz** [later **Frank**] **Burchardt** (1902–1958), was dismissed from his German university post in 1933. He managed at first to remain in Germany on the editorial staff of the *Frankfurter Zeitung*, but in 1935 he accepted a research position at All Souls to join the new Oxford Economists' Research Group and later the Oxford Institute of Statistics, at first as its librarian and deputy director before eventually becoming its influential director until his death. In 1940, **Burchardt** experienced the traumatic hiatus in his life and career of being interned behind barbed wire as an 'enemy alien' on the Isle of Man – until an indignant Maynard Keynes successfully interceded for him in November 1940. In 1944 **Burchardt** edited *The Economics of Full Employment,* focusing on the Keynesian insistence on the necessary role of public investment, especially in hard times. He would become a Fellow of Magdalen College and of Nufffield College, Oxford, as well as a reader in economics and social statistics and 'did more than anyone to establish Oxford as a leading centre of applied economics'.[6]

The convinced Weimar Social Democrat, **Adolph Lowe**, born **Loewe** (1893–1995), had taught **Frank Burchardt** at the Kiel Institute for Global Economics, and like him had emigrated to Britain. He was awarded a Rockefeller scholarship and then taught at the University of Manchester. Forbidden as 'an enemy alien' from enlisting in the British war effort, despite having received British citizenship, **Lowe** moved to America in 1940 – at the same time as he was included in the Black Book. He became a pioneer in his field of combining economics with sociology and taught in New York until his mid eighties.

From a contrasting national and political background, the 'Father of Econometrics', **Jacob Marschak** (1898–1977), was a young Soviet

Menshevik in the Ukraine at the time of the Russian Revolution, who had then emigrated to (revolutionary) Germany in 1919. In 1933 he had to leave his university post at Kiel and he moved to Oxford, later joined by **Burchardt**, to teach at the Oxford Institute of Statistics – of which he became the founding director in 1935. Between 1938 and 1940 **Marschak** published a series of articles (with Helen Makower and H. W. Robinson) that showed differences in unemployment rates as the decisive determinant in regional mobility of labour in the UK. Because of the institute's financial connection with the Rockefeller Foundation, **Marschak** was enabled to leave Britain and move to the United States, becoming a distinguished economist at Chicago and Yale.[7]

A younger left-winger was **Hermann Christian Hillmann** (1910–1990), not Jewish but dismissed from his work as a research statistician because his supervisor was Jewish and, more important, because he himself had been president of the Social Democrat Students' Organisation in Germany before 1933. **Hillmann** emigrated to Scotland and eventually found work as 'economic investigator' at the University of Dundee's School of Economics and later at the University of Manchester. He became a British citizen in 1940 and worked under the British historian Arnold Toynbee's planning strategy for solutions to the economic problems of a future Germany under Allied occupation after the war.

The doyen of economic statistics, however, especially demography and its economic implications, was **Robert René Kuczynski** (1876–1947), now regarded as one of the founders of modern vital statistics and demography. The son of a very wealthy banker, **Kuczynski** had been an early convert to left-wing politics and solidarity with the exploited working class. He had calculated in 1929 that there were 600,000 people living five to a room in Berlin. He left Germany in 1933 with his family and 20,000 books and became a lecturer at the LSE and later Oxford. His best-known work in the 1930s was on the demography of the slave trade between Africa and the Americas, estimating that *c.*15 million slaves had been trafficked by Europeans over 300 years, but he also published work on the methodology of measuring population growth, on colonial populations, and on 'Living-space and Population Problems'. Three of his children became Soviet spies, including Juergen Kuczynski and Ursula, nee Kuczynski, code-name 'Sonia', who, while living an apparently ordinary life as an Oxfordshire housewife, helped to recruit the nuclear scientist Klaus Fuchs to share Western atomic secrets with Russia after the Second World War.[8]

The rocky and often obstructed academic path for refugee economists is well illustrated by the **Liepmann** brothers, sons of a German banker. **Leo Liepmann** (1900–*c*.1954) had had a distinguished academic career in Germany before being forced to flee to Britain in 1935. There he became principal researcher for William Beveridge at the LSE, enabling the publication of the ambitious survey *Prices and Wages in England from the 12th to the 19th Centuries* (1939). However he was then interned on the Isle of Man as an enemy alien and his academic career never recovered. **Leo Liepmann** worked as a fire-fighter in the Blitz from 1940 to 1941 and later as an interpreter for the British occupation in West Germany between 1947 and 1953, eventually returning to Britain to become an extra-mural tutor in Oxford. His death date is unknown. His brother **Heinrich Liepmann** (1904–1983) was a doctoral student and then a research assistant of Max Weber. After fleeing to Britain in 1936, **Heinrich Liepmann** managed to publish an English translation, in 1938, of his magisterial work on *Tariff Policy, Export Movements and the Economic Integration of Europe, 1913–1931*, but that was the end of his academic career. Interned in Britain from May 1940 until February 1941, he was unable to take up a scholarship he had been offered in Canada. He worked as a translator for the Royal Institute of International Affairs at Chatham House during the war, and then became a German teacher at a grammar school.

Another academic economist, **Hermann Levy** (1881–1949), although he belonged to a fully assimilated Jewish family in Berlin and had himself been baptised as a Protestant, and despite his having been a nationalistic, militaristic publicist for Germany in the First World War, was nonetheless sacked by the Nazis from his chair in economics in Berlin and driven into exile in 1933. His works on industrial Germany, the shops of Britain, monopoly and competition, national health insurance, economic liberalism, and his book *Large and Small Holdings: A Study of English Agricultural Economics*, are still in print today. He died in London.

The radical social thinker Richard Titmuss befriended and helped the gifted economist **Dr Marie Dessauer**, later **Dessauer-Meinhardt** (1901–1986), with her eventual naturalisation as a British citizen. An unusually highly qualified woman economist from an eminent Jewish family, which was related to the international Wassermann banking dynasty, she obtained her Ph.D. in Germany in 1933 for her seminal work on the English banking system, *The Big Five*. Forced to flee Frankfurt on racist grounds, she began working for William Beveridge at the LSE in 1934, assisting him with his history of prices and wages. From 1937 until 1941 she became senior research assistant at the LSE's economic research division headed by the classical liberal, anti-Keynesian monetarist Friedrich Hayek. **Dessauer-Meinhardt** (her married name) turned away from Hayek's individualist politics, however, to assist the very different, socially committed Richard Titmuss in 1941, who became famous for his book *The Gift Relationship*, which affirmed the practice of voluntary, unpaid blood donation in Britain as a symbol of the social obligation fundamental to a morally decent society. Together, Titmuss and **Dessauer-Meinhardt** worked during the Second World War for the British Ministry of Economic Warfare, publicising the truth about levels of rickets, dysentery, tuberculosis and typhus in Nazi Germany, aimed at undermining German morale. They then collaborated on developing a new discipline of 'social medicine', mapping the correlations between social class and different diseases, thereby documenting for the first time the impact of inequality upon health. '**Meinhardt**'s expertise with statistics, and all kinds of quantitative analysis, was invaluable to … [this] new discipline.'[9] As a person she was remembered as being 'very clever, very loyal and hugely undervalued'.[10] Richard Titmuss had supported **Dessauer-Meinhardt** at the most vulnerable time of her life, when not only was she herself stateless and struggling to survive, but she had also found out that both her parents had been murdered in Theresienstadt in 1942. After her own death, she in turn bequeathed a generous legacy to the Titmuss Memorial Fund, which to this day supports both students in need and social policy and health research.

A more prominent figure at the LSE at that same time was **Eduard Rosenbaum** (1887–1979), who had served on the Hamburg Chamber of Commerce, directed its library of commerce, and published an analysis attacking the economic consequences for Germany of the Versailles Treaty of 1921. He was nevertheless forced by the Nazis into early retirement in 1933 because he was a Jew. Helped by Keynes, **Rosenbaum** resettled with his family in Britain and obtained a temporary position in the LSE library. In 1940 Keynes had to intervene again on his behalf in order to get him released from internment on the Isle of Man. Eventually **Rosenbaum** became the head librarian at LSE, determining the direction of its collections, a position he retained until retirement in 1952. Despite the deaths of two of his brothers and sisters in Nazi concentration camps, **Rosenbaum** returned periodically to fire-bombed Hamburg after the war in order to contribute to its resurrection, including the rebuilding of its library of commerce; and he also worked till the end of his life for the reconciliation of Britons and Germans.

One of the most positive branches of the otherwise 'gloomy science' of 'political economy' in the twentieth century has been development economics. And this field, 'which evolved predominantly in Great Britain and in the United States at the United Nations … is among those areas where the contributions made by German-speaking émigré economists are most significant'.[11] Its trail-blazer was a woman, **Dr Charlotte Leubuscher** (1888–1961), who had been a pioneer woman student of economics, history, philosophy and law at Cambridge, Munich and Berlin before the First World War. Her first publication was a study of the struggle for employment of British railway workers in 1911; in 1921 she brought out *Socialism and Socialization in England*, and in 1927, *Liberalism and Protectionism in English Economic Policy since the War*. **Leubuscher** then started to look at the economic foundations of the British Empire, writing 'The South African Native as Industrial Worker and City Dweller' in 1931 and 'Tanganyika – A Lesson in Economic Policy under Mandate' in

1944. A rare woman professor at Goettingen and then Berlin, she was no longer allowed to teach in Germany after 1933 because she was half-Jewish. In England she taught at Cambridge, at Manchester and at the LSE, while continuing her pioneering research into colonial, under-developed economies. She wrote on the unfair lack of trading balance in *The West African Shipping Trade 1909–1959*, and on *Bulk Buying from the Colonies*, published posthumously in 1966. The former work was a study of the vicissitudes of a shipping monopoly. The fact of monopoly troubled **Leubuscher**, as did the secrecy of the shipping conferences' deliberations.[12]

Kurt Mandelbaum, later **Kurt Martin** (1904–1995), a Jewish refugee from the left-wing Frankfurt School for Social Research, approached the problem of development economics not in the British Empire but in south-east Europe in his seminal *The Industrialization of Backward Areas* (1945). After his British war work with Allied intelligence, he too had joined the Oxford Institute of Statistics, eventually moving to the University of Manchester where he helped establish its economics department as a major centre for development economics research and teaching.

But the most renowned and influential of all the development economists who had come to Britain as German Jewish refugees in the 1930s was **Professor Sir Hans Singer** (1910–2006). **Singer** was one of Maynard Keynes' first Ph.D. students in 1933 at Cambridge, receiving his doctorate in 1936. He published two papers on unemployment in Britain before finding himself interned on the Isle of Man in 1940. Once again, an incandescent, enraged Keynes acted swiftly and got the prisoner released. 'If there are any Nazi sympathisers at large in this country, look for them in the War Office and our Secret Service, not in the internment camps.'[13] A former economics student of **Singer** at the University of Manchester can still remember him as he was then – short, round, almost bald – and very nervous after his internment and facing the continued threat of a possible Nazi invasion of Britain. He taught his students conscientiously, but much, much too fast, according to the students, about local government finance and statistics. There was no sign as yet of his eventual, heroic role in trying to reform the whole world system of international trade.[14] For after teaching at the University of Manchester, **Singer** became a founding economist at the United Nations where he remained for the next twenty years. He was best known after the 1950s for the Prebisch-**Singer** thesis, which states that the terms of international trade *always* move against producers of primary products and so reinforce world poverty. He became a passionate advocate for increased foreign aid and low interest UN loans to the Third World – always blocked by the US and the UK. He was called 'one of the wild men of the UN' by the president of the World Bank and attacked by Senator Joseph McCarthy for his work for the Special United Nations Fund for Economic Development. A David against the Goliath of multinational corporate capitalism, **Singer** was the founding inspiration for the international movement for Fair Trade, and in 2001 the UN World Food Program awarded him the Food for Life Award for his contribution to the battle against world hunger.[15]

Can one generalise about why the Gestapo singled out these economists for immediate arrest and not the scores of other German/Austrian refugee economists in Britain? Ignorance on the part of the Gestapo is one explanation – they could only focus on those they had heard of and most of their targets had already achieved a name for themselves so were fish worth catching. Moreover, many of these economists had already earned a left-wing political record of some sort in Germany, the exceptions being **Hermann Levy** and **Eduard Rosenbaum**. For these last, perhaps there is no rational explanation.

18

Down with Humane Educationists

The son of a Presbyterian minister and of Anna Lindsay, an activist in the cause of oppressed women, **A. D. Lindsay**, CBE (1879–1952) was the famous Master of Balliol who became a lifelong, idealistic campaigner for social – and especially educational – reform. His outstanding achievement was his support for that Cinderella of causes, part-time adult education.[1] Like R. H. Tawney, **Lindsay** cared deeply about access to higher learning for working people. He involved himself both with WEA summer schools and university extension courses and, when a professor in Glasgow, he lectured to the ('Red') Clydesiders and co-founded the Scottish Institute of Adult Education. **Lindsay** was regarded frostily as 'unconventional' at Oxford for being on the left in politics, for advocating conciliation rather than confrontation during the General Strike, and for becoming an adviser to the Labour Party and the Trades Union Congress on education. The Gestapo labelled him a *Volksfrontanhaenger* – supporter of the people's front – no doubt referring to his stance on Spain as well as to his advocacy of a united front in British politics, Labour and communist, against the fascist-sympathising right. He had stood as the independent, but unsuccessful, parliamentary candidate for Oxford City, opposing appeasement in October 1938. Aged 61 in 1940, he was still considered to be a dangerous opponent of the Reich. His writing and teaching always focused on the demands of genuine democracy – see his *The Modern Democratic State* (1943) – and 'as a public intellectual he had few peers'.[2] **Lindsay** would survive until 1952, becoming the first principal of the new, pioneering University College of Keele in the Potteries.

Further education in general in Britain was specifically targeted by the Gestapo. For example the *Sonderfahndungsliste*'s section on 'Associations' Blacklisted **The National Adult Schools Union**, which had long been associated with one of the Gestapo's bêtes noires, the Quakers, and had been strongest in the North,[3] as well as the allegedly 'Marxist' educational propaganda of the **Fabian Society**, and of the **League of Nations Union**. But above all it targeted the secular and often left-wing **WEA – Workers' Educational Association** – inspired by Albert Mansbridge and the great socialist historian and egalitarian, R. H. Tawney.[4] Often in partnership with the universities' outreach in local adult education, the **WEA** had, by the mid 1930s, become a valued, liberal, questioning, mind-expanding, largely voluntary British institution. In 1939 its dynamic national network comprised 2,172 branches offering one-year courses as well as shorter courses in the social sciences, philosophy, psychology and the arts, with 39,844 students in all – most often taught by left-wing academics.[5] Closing down the **WEA** under German occupation would have had an incalculably deadening effect.

An historian and philosopher of education who had specialised in the neglected history of the education of German women was **Dr Professor Elisabeth Blochmann** (1892–1972). She had studied at Jena, Strasburg, Marburg and Goettingen after nursing German wounded in the First World War. She received her Ph.D. in history at the age of 31, lectured at the (humanistic) Pestalozzi-Froebel House from 1926 to 1930, and then became professor of social and theoretical pedagogy at the Academy of Education in Halle, only to be dismissed on racist grounds in 1933. Very unusually for a refugee, **Blochmann** almost immediately received a post at an Oxford women's college, Lady Margaret Hall. She became a British citizen in 1947, having already been appointed university lecturer in education at Oxford in 1945. After much hesitation, in 1952 at the age of 60, **Blochmann** decided to return to Germany, accepting a call to build up a new department, The Blochmann School of Philosophy of Education.[6]

That the Gestapo could be absolutely correct and even prescient in their identification of the most dangerous anti-Nazis is nowhere more clear than in their inclusion of the adult educationists **Friedrich, 'Fritz', Borinski** and **Herbert Sulzbach** in their *Sonderfahndungsliste GB*. **Borinski** (1903–1988), the son of Protestant converts from Judaism, originally followed his father by studying law, becoming a doctor of Jura in 1927. He did not, however, practise law but instead, as an idealistic Social Democrat, worked in adult education for young workers in Leipzig and near Chemnitz during the 1920s and early 1930s. Dismissed in July 1933 because of his politics and because of his Jewish grandparents, **Borinski** fled to England, supporting himself by giving German lessons while he studied sociology at the LSE, where he came under the influence of **Karl Mannheim**. His association with **Otto Strasser**'s deviant alternative socialism to that of the Nazis, the *Schwarze Front*, had made **Borinski** especially *persona non grata* in Nazi Germany and he was stripped both of his German citizenship and of his doctorate. In 1940 he was interned by the British as an 'enemy alien' and actually deported to Australia, where, promptly and characteristically, he set up a camp school for his fellow internees.

He returned to Britain in 1941. From 1943 to 1946 **Fritz Borinski's** work had two sides. He co-founded the German Educational Reconstruction Committee (GER) in London, together with the exiled German Jewish literary historian Werner Milch and the exiled German socialist progressive educationist Minna Specht, in order to help the British government plan a new educational philosophy and education system for its section of a post-war occupied Germany. At the same time **Borinski** was working at Wilton Park in Buckinghamshire on the political re-education of German prisoners of war in Britain, many, of course, if not all of whom were convinced young Nazis. Wilton Park was dedicated to reconciling and re-educating former rivals and enemies; it was the brainchild of **Winston Churchill** who had already written a circular in 1943 asking for ideas about working for and with a democratic Germany after the war. He noted the proposals of a German Jewish refugee, Heinz Koeppler, lecturer in history at Magdalen College, Oxford, who became the first warden of Wilton Park. It was founded on 12 January 1945 as a forum of open debate which would help to educate Germans in the re-establishment of multi-party democracy on their release home. Its library contained both *Mein Kampf* and the writings of **Churchill**; the fundamental principle there was freedom of speech. **Borinski** set up a special section staffed by refugees, named *Aufbau* (reconstruction), and became a leading tutor in the political education in citizenship of thousands of German POWs at Wilton Park.[7] Lecturers on the nature of democracy included Jennie Lee MP, **Victor Gollancz**, **Bertrand Russell**, Lord Beveridge, **Lady Violet Bonham Carter** and **Lady Astor**. Several of **Fritz Borinski**'s first principles were put into practice in the British sector of West Germany where he, an active Social Democrat once more, concentrated on re-establishing adult education in West Germany – the *Volkshochschule* – until 1965. He was director of the adult education college in Goehrde in the easternmost corner of the Federal Republic. For him, genuine citizenship *had* to involve political literacy – which demanded the individual's lifelong, responsible participation in the maintenance of a democratic society rooted in humane values.[8]

Borinski's kindred spirit was **Herbert Sulzbach**, 'Schriftsteller' (1894–1985). At first sight **Sulzbach's** inclusion in the Black Book seems baffling. Had he not recently published his uncritically patriotic First World War diary, *Zwei lebende Mauern* (1935), recounting his four years with the German artillery – a book that had been enthusiastically received in Nazi Germany and translated into English the same year as *With the German Guns*? Had he not been awarded the Iron Cross *twice*? The explanation of course is crudely simple – **Sulzbach** was a Jew – and the Gestapo were not mistaken in identifying him as a profoundly anti-Nazi German.

In 1938 he left Germany for Britain with his wife and sister-in-law, only for them all to be interned on the Isle of Man early in 1940. On his release he volunteered to enlist, aged 45, as a private in the Pioneer Corps – then the only military unit in which 'enemy aliens' could serve. His light engineering tasks in the corps consisted of building defensive walls and ditches to slow or halt a German invasion that never happened, and in 1944 he got himself transferred as a translator/interpreter to the new British prison camps for German POWs. There he discovered his vocation.

Herbert Sulzbach became an inspired, even visionary, adult educationist; he succeeded in de-Nazifying thousands of Nazis. How did he achieve that? First, he believed that it could be done – that the great majority of Nazis did not have to remain irredeemably brainwashed all their lives long, despite the fanatical Nazi atmosphere at first in the POW camps. As Anthony Grenville wrote, **Sulzbach** 'had the courage to confront evil without hatred, rejecting with due severity those who remained wedded to Nazism while being willing to embrace the good in those who wished to change'.[9] Quiet, slightly built, **Sulzbach** addressed the prisoners simply as fellow human beings who now had huge problems. He set himself, patient but totally dedicated, to wean them from racist, militarist, nationalistic totalitarianism, and win them over to humanism and democracy. He showed them pictures of Belsen. There was free, open political discussion and no censorship of letters or of reading matter. It helped, of course, in communicating with those German ex-soldiers that **Sulzbach** himself had been a long-serving soldier in two world wars and perhaps he was such a successful fisher of men because he realised that he himself had changed; he no longer confused nationalism with patriotism.

Nothing was too good for the 'further education' of 'his' people now. In addition to sport and cultural offerings and self-organised educational and technical courses, **Sulzbach**, like **Borinski** and Koeppler, enlisted some outstanding, idealistic, visiting speakers. The professor of international law, **Norman Bentwich**, the violinist Yehudi Menuhin, the publisher **Victor Gollancz**, the pastor – and ex concentration camp prisoner – Martin Niemoeller, the military historian and army reformer Basil Liddell Hart (who had opposed 'total war' against Germany), the diplomat and writer **Harold Nicolson**, and the historian Hugh Trevor-Roper, not to mention the composer Benjamin Britten, all came to 'his' prison camps to talk. On 11 November 1945 **Sulzbach** managed to persuade almost every one of his 4,000 German prisoners to stand alongside him and pledge themselves to take part in the reconciliation of all people and the maintenance of peace, renouncing national hatred. From 1946 to 1948 he worked as chief interpreter at Featherstone Park Camp for former SS officers. In 1947 **Sulzbach** became a British citizen and co-founded the transnational town-twinning initiative, itself a further education project, and one that might help repair damaged relationships between France, Germany and the UK. 'Find towns that had suffered during the world wars and pair them. Then encourage people from the areas to meet, mix and get along.'[10] **Sulzbach** worked for Anglo-German reconciliation, as a cultural attaché to the German embassy in London, from 1951 until his death in 1985 aged 91.

One other Blacklisted Jewish educationist, **Dr Hans Weil** (1898–1972), a socialist pioneer of anti-authoritarian pedagogy, had been dismissed from his academic position as lecturer in education at Frankfurt University in 1933 and fled to Italy. He then in 1938 had to leave his small experimental boarding school,[11] 'Recco' on the Mediterranean, where he taught German refugee children 'social humanity' and several different languages including German, and fled to Britain. But he could not find work in Britain, and, in 1940, perhaps fearing imminent internment or else a Nazi invasion, he fled via Ireland to rejoin his family in the United States. The Gestapo believed him to be still in Newcastle-upon-Tyne and planned to arrest him there.

19

Erasing Historians

> There will always be those who seek to impose a particular view of history.
>
> Final Report of Historical Working Party, April 1990, discussed in W. Lamont, ed., *Historical controversies and historians*, UCL, 1998

No subject is more fiercely contested than history. It is not surprising, therefore, that what all the British-born historians in this chapter had in common was their published, anti-Nazi view of events. The former lecturer at the University of Glasgow, **H. N. Brailsford** (1873–1958), for example, who later taught part time at the LSE and wrote on radical Enlightenment and Romantic thinkers, was also the outstanding and most prolific socialist journalist of his day in Britain, attacking both fascism and Stalinism. He was one of the few supporters of the **Left Book Club** and the ***New Statesman*** who criticised the Soviet show trials: '[Stalin's] Russia is a totalitarian state, like another, as brutal towards the rights of others, as careless of its plighted word … In this land the absolute power has wrought its customary effects of corruption.'[1] Among his most important books in the 1930s, written when he was in his sixties, were the case for Indian independence, *Rebel India* (1931), as well as *Spain's Challenge to Labour* (1936) and *Democracy for India* (1939).[2]

Similarly, the socio-economic historian **G. D. H. Cole** (1889–1959), as well as being reader in economics at the University of Oxford, was a committed socialist thinker and leading light among the **Fabians**. His Socialist League tried to influence the British Labour Party to stick by its left-wing principles in the 1930s. **Cole**'s greatest contributions to British social history were *The Condition of Britain* (1937), written with his wife Margaret, *The People's Front* (1937), for the **Left Book Club**, and *The Common People* (1938), written with Raymond Postgate.[3]

The senior research fellow of Corpus Christi College, Oxford, from 1937 to 1946, was **R. C. K. Ensor** (1877–1958), whose name appears in the Gestapo's *Informationsheft GB* in two places:

> 1. '*Universitaeten und gegnerische Kulturinstitute – Oxford Universitaet*' ('Universities and opposition cultural institutions – Oxford'), from the beginning of the present war since spring 1939, began to work on a new series of 'Oxford–Pamphlets' against Germany … [the first] was **Ensor, R. C. K**: '*Mein Kampf*' …
> 2. Under 'English specialists on Eastern and Central Europe', we have, after ***C. A. Macartney*** and ***Dr B. Manilowski***, '***R. C. K. Ensor***, vice-president Corpus Christi College. One of the sharpest opponents of National Socialism in England, who has addressed himself thoroughly to the Führer's foreign policy in Europe.'[4]

The fact that **Ensor** is singled out in this way in the *Informationsheft*, but had not been listed at all in the *Sonderfahndungsliste*, confirms that the latter, which also includes several people who were either dead or had already left Britain, had gone to press before the former had been completed. **Ensor** himself had been an opponent of the Boer War, a Labour councillor in the East End and a journalist before going to Oxford in 1932 as deputy to the Gladstone professor of political theory and institutions. His authoritative historical magnum opus, *England, 1870–1914*, was published in 1936. His pamphlet 'Herr Hitler's Self-disclosure in *Mein Kampf*' (July 1939), talks of Viennese Hitler's youthful hatreds: '[He hated] the Hapsburgs, the Czechs, the Jews, the socialists and parliamentary institutions … [Hitler based] principle and practice … upon the gullibility of humanity … his policy must be one of annexation by force … From first to last [*Mein Kampf*] is a plea for remorselessly exploiting power.' **Ensor** concluded that there was no alternative for Britain in 1939, therefore, but to fight Hitler.

Ironically, the distinguished diplomatic historian, **G. P. Gooch**, CH (1873–1968), as well as being a Liberal dedicated to the promotion of international peace, had devoted years of his life as a pioneer revisionist on the subject of responsibility for the First World War. His thirteen-volume diplomatic history indicted not just Germany – as had been the orthodoxy behind the Treaty of Versailles – but also Britain and her Allies, especially Tsarist Russia in July 1914. But the Gestapo probably never read him, so **Gooch**'s even-handedness did not weigh enough in Nazi eyes to exonerate him for his consistent anti-militarism and his encouragement of refugees like **Otto Lehmann-Russbueldt** (p. 59) to contribute to the *Contemporary Review*, which **Gooch** edited.[5] Similarly, the economic historian **J. A. Hobson** (1858–1940), the famous octogenarian critic of British imperialism, was suspect simply for his socialist diagnosis and prescriptions.[6] Presumably **Sir Bernard Pares** (1867–1949), professor at the University of London where he directed the School of Slavonic and East European Studies from 1922 to 1939, and who published an authoritative work on the history of Russia, was suspect for his excessive concern and respect for Slav '*Untermenschen*' ('sub-humans').[7]

The brilliant medievalist and economic historian, **Professor Eileen Power** (1889–1940), who pioneered the historical study of medieval women, was the radical academic who was most closely associated at LSE with William Beveridge in the establishment of the **Academic Assistance Council** to rescue persecuted German Jewish scholars. The Gestapo would also have noted her membership of the **Union for Democratic Control of Foreign Policy**, which advocated an anti-militarist, anti-imperialist, internationalist approach to foreign policy – anathema to Nazism.[8]

R. W. Seton-Watson (1879–1951), another specialist in East European history at the University of London, was earmarked by the Gestapo as a supporter of the new Slav nations, Yugoslavia and Czechoslovakia, after 1918. It was also noted against him that he was a member of the Czech committee of the International Peace Campaign – '*Friedensfeldzug*'. A fierce anti-appeaser, **Seton-Watson** was a friend of **Jan Masaryk** and **Eduard Benes**, who in 1940 headed the Czech government in exile in London. **Dr Cecil Roth** (1899–1970), Fellow of the Royal Historical Society and reader in post-biblical Jewish studies at Oxford from 1939, was Blacklisted for his magisterial historical accounts not of Slav '*Untermenschen*' but of '*Unmenschen*', '*Non-humans*' as he, a Jew, evidenced not only the persecution but also the great cultural contribution of the Jewish diaspora in western Europe ever since the Middle Ages. He had published throughout the 1930s on the history of the Jews in Spain, England and Italy, culminating in his tragically timed *The Jewish Contribution to Civilization* (NY, 1941).[9]

Two final examples of the *political* selection of British historians for immediate arrest in September 1940 are **Professor Stephen Roberts** (1901–1971), and **Donna Torr. Roberts** had studied as an Australian postgraduate at the LSE under **Harold Laski** (p. 264). As history professor at the University of Sydney, **Roberts** had published on French colonial policy and on Australian domestic and foreign policy in the 1930s, but at the same time he had become an international analyst, notorious in Nazi eyes for his best-known book, *The House that Hitler Built* (1937), which was translated into several languages. **Roberts**, who had interviewed Nazi leaders and attended Nazi rallies, not only exposed the menace of the Reich and its brutality towards Jewish Germans even before *Kristallnacht*, but he also concluded that Germany was set on having a Second World War. *The House that Hitler Built* went into several editions. **Roberts** then included a supplementary chapter to update his analysis in June 1938, warning explicitly that 'The whole tenor of Nazi teaching and practice leads only in the direction of Pan-Germanism; to be achieved if necessary by war.' The Gestapo did not realise that by 1940 **Roberts** was safely in Australia.

The Marxist historian **Donna Torr** (1887–1975), daughter of an Anglican cleric, had been converted by the Russian Revolution from Labour Party activism to co-founding the **Communist Party of Great Britain** in 1920. An independent scholar and a Germanist, she had vividly translated and edited the *Marx–Engels Selected Correspondence* in 1934, re-edited Marx's *Capital*, vol. 1, in 1938, and translated Engels' *The Origins of the Family* in 1940. She had also published a brief biography of ***Tom Mann***, the veteran dockers' leader and champion of the 'common people', whom she herself had known. After the Second World War **Torr** would mentor the seminal and productive Communist Party Historians' Group in Britain, including Christopher Hill, Eric Hobsbawm and E. P. Thompson.[10]

In the case of refugee historians, their political views were less significant in Gestapo eyes than was their eminence and, of course, their Jewishness – though hardly one of them would seem to have been religiously observant. (The outstanding historians of the ancient world, **Professors David Daube, Betty Heimann, Erich Langstadt** and **Hermann Kantorowicz** have already been discussed in chapter 16, above, 'Attacking Ancient Classicists'.) In contrast to these classicists, the 60-year-old socio-economic historian **Dr Moritz Elsas** (1881–1952), was a specialist in contemporary social history. He had had to leave his position as eminent German researcher for the Rockefeller-funded International Committee on the History of Prices and Wages, and had fled to London in 1933. There, supported by Keynes, he became a lecturer at LSE where he researched the history of workers' incomes and outgoings in Britain in the twentieth century. Between 1936 and 1940 he also published his two-volume *Survey*, in German, of *The History of Prices and Wages in Germany since the Middle Ages*. **Elsas**'s immense treasure trove of research data for that work was believed lost, only to be rediscovered in 1963 in a basement at LSE and transferred to the University of Goettingen and then to Leipzig; it has since proved a priceless historical resource. **Elsas**'s important, influential publications on British socio-economic history include *Housing before the War and After* (1942) and *Housing and the Family* (1947).

Another contemporary historian was **Otto Kahn-Freund** (1900–1979), whose speciality was contemporary labour law – of which he would became the doyen as well as its founder as an academic study. **Kahn-Freund** had been a judge of the Berlin Labour Court since 1929, already alert to the Weimar regime's hostility to trade unions. When he ruled, in 1933, that radio workers had been unfairly dismissed on the false accusation that they were communists, he himself was dismissed from his position as judge. He fled to Britain and enrolled at the LSE, where by 1936 he became an assistant lecturer in law. He also became a barrister at the Middle Temple in 1936 and a British citizen in 1940. **Kahn-Freund** believed that the state should allow collective labour to negotiate freely with capital. As the senior lawyer on the 1965 Donovan Commission, his thinking would influence both the British Industrial Relations Act 1971 and the Trade Unions and Labour Relations Act 1974. He became a QC in 1972 and was knighted in 1976.

Professor Dr Gustav Mayer (1871–1948), on the other hand, was too old at 66 to be employed in British universities after his arrival in Britain in 1936. Nevertheless, he was still clearly a target for the Gestapo not only because he was a Jew but because of his work as the pioneer historian of the German Labour Movement. His two-volume biography of Engels had been pulped in Germany in 1933.

The specialist in the history of twentieth-century international law, **Georg Schwarzenberger** (1908–1991), was increasingly concerned to move away from the theory of rules for the world as it should be, to a realistic appraisal of international relations as they in fact *are* – always driven by power politics. He had arrived in Britain as a young postgraduate dismissed from his German university as a Jew, but one who was also under threat of concentration camp because of his Social Democrat activism from 1932 to 1933. His first study had been of the League of Nations Mandate for Palestine; his second was on the Constitution of the Spanish Republic in 1933. **Schwarzenberger** became a lecturer in international law at the University of London from 1938 to 1945, when he also became a British citizen – Germany having stripped him of citizenship as well as of his doctorate. In 1941 he published *Power Politics: A Study in World Society.* After the war he learned that his entire Jewish German family, his parents, his brother and sister and their children, with the exception of one young niece, had all been murdered by the Nazis.

The historian of political thought, **Dr Reinhold Aris** (1904–*c.*1964), had left Germany, where he had taught at the University of Jena, and already in 1933 had become a researcher at the University of London and then at Cambridge before becoming senior lecturer at Bristol. His book *History of Political Thought in Germany 1789–1815* (1936) had a preface by **G. P. Gooch.**

It is especially interesting to revisit the innovative, indeed revisionist, historical work of **Dr Veit Valentin** (1885–1947), who was presumably singled out for the Black Book on account of his heretical historical interpretations of German nationalism and nationhood. A professor of history at the University of Freiburg, **Valentin** had dared to criticise Bismarck's anti-British foreign policy, and the idea of a 'right' to German conquest under the banner of Pan-Germanism. Under immense political pressure, he agreed not to publish his work on German foreign policy in 1917 (it was only published after the war in 1921) and forfeited his chance of a continued professorial career at any German university. **Valentin** belonged both to the German League for Human Rights – democratic, secular, pacifist, internationalist and anti-racist, and to the left-wing, socially liberal German Democratic Party, founded in November 1918. The latter was committed to democracy and republicanism and consisted largely of middle-class civil servants, teachers and entrepreneurs; it was called 'the party of Jews and professors'. A supporter of the Weimar Republic from 1921 to 1931, **Veit Valentin** then tried to integrate the histories of German radicalism, German liberalism and German pacifism since the 1848 Revolution – on which he was the acknowledged authority – into the narrative of Germany's movement for national unification. His was a nuanced, 'enlightened' perspective like that of **Rudolf Olden** (p. 366) which did not appeal to Prussian traditionalist historians, let alone to the new Nazis.

Dismissed from his position in the National Archives in Potsdam in 1933, **Valentin** went to London where he lectured at University College and mixed with the 'Bavarian Circle' of German émigrés, including **Franz Xaver Aenderl**, who was himself Blacklisted as an alleged American secret agent. On being stripped of his German citizenship in 1939, **Veit Valentin** re-emigrated to America, where he continued to publish monumental work on the history of Germany as a society rather than as a nationalistic state, and where he finished his third volume of the *Historia Universal, Weltgeschichte* ('Villages, Men, Ideas') in 1939. In 1944 he published an essay 'A New World Citizenship' in the *Contemporary Review*, and in 1946, his last work, *The*

German People: Their History and Civilization from the Holy Roman Empire to the Third Reich. **Veit Valentin** has been judged an '*Aussenseiter*' ('outsider') by German historiography because of his insistence on trying to combine social history, individual biography and the history of ideas. But perhaps it is time for such historian-outsiders to be allowed in from the cold.[11]

Another intellectual 'outsider' was **Raymond Klibansky** (1905–2005), a brilliant polymath and historian of ideas. The Nazis were not interested in his views on the influence of Plato through the centuries, nor in his connection of Renaissance art history with philosophy, but simply Blacklisted him as an 'Emigrant', having forbidden him, a Jew, to teach philosophy at Heidelberg in 1933. (He had refused to alter his teaching according to Nazi anti-Semitic ideology and had been threatened with death.) Having been instrumental in the successful transport of the **Warburg Insitute**'s library from Hamburg to London, and after teaching from 1934 at King's College London and Liverpool University, from 1936 to 1946 **Klibansky** was a lecturer at Oriel College, Oxford. He was granted British citizenship in 1938 and published *The Continuity of the Platonic Tradition during the Middle Ages* in 1939. A man of action, in the Second World War **Klibansky** was attached to the Political Warfare Executive and is credited with intelligence information on the Allied campaign in Italy and with successfully preventing an Allied bombing attack on the hospital at Kues which held many priceless historical documents. After the war he would take part in the de-Nazification of Western Germany. He lived to be 100, thinking and writing almost to the end.

So disparate are these targeted refugee historians in 1940 that nothing unites them other than their forebears' Judaism.

20

Masters of the Word – Some Linguists and Literary Critics

Words mattered to the Nazis. Mastery of demagoguery was essential to both Hitler and Goebbels, as is made clear in J. P. Stern's *Hitler: The Führer and the People*, especially his chapters on the terrible potency of 'The Language of Sacrifice', 'The Language of Nature' and 'The Language of Prophecy'.[1] But when they disliked words, the Nazis had a simple solution: they burned them. The Nazi book burnings, orchestrated by the Nazi German Student Union in May 1933, tried to purge Germany of the words of 'traitors', 'emigrants', Marxists, pacifists, liberals, 'decadents' – and Jews. They declared that they were thereby cleansing Germany of all 'Un-German Spirits' and making way for a 'pure' national language as they burned tens of thousands of volumes from 4,000 proscribed titles on the night of 10 May, cheered on by torch-lit processions and fired up by bystanders in their thousands. The literary critic **F. L. Lucas** commented bitterly: 'First they burnt their own books; then Warsaw and Rotterdam. It is interesting that savages should have more respect for the power of literature than most of the literary.'[2]

Six years later, as they anticipated their imminent occupation of Great Britain, the Gestapo turned their attention to some masters of language and literature who might reinforce anti-Nazi ways of thinking. Therefore, in addition to their lists of proscribed British publishers and creative writers, they believed that they must also weed out suspect scholars in Britain who were translators and literary critics, some of whom suffered precisely because they were polyglots.

For example, the Russianist **Leo Loewenson** (1885–1968), had been born in Moscow and had studied in Russia, but when he was living in Berlin in 1914 he was conscripted into the German Army against Russia because his father had German nationality as a German Jew. He served both as a medical orderly and as a Russian interpreter until he was taken prisoner as a German by the Romanian Army. On his release he settled in Germany, helping to establish the very important library of Russian culture in the Friedrich-Wilhelm University in Berlin – only to be forced out from Germany as a Jew in 1933, after which he resettled in Britain. The British later imprisoned him in an internment camp for being a German. However, the School of Slavonic and East European Studies (SSEES) at University College London, which had already employed **Loewenson** as a Russianist, appealed successfully for his release and he worked there as a librarian, as well as a tutor in Russian and Soviet studies, from 1940 until 1956.[3]

The Germanist and conservative anti-fascist, **Emily Overend Lorimer** (1881–1949), who had studied at Somerville College, Oxford, was 'Most Wanted' by the Gestapo, not because of her editorial activities in Cairo and Basra in the First World War, nor because of her philological assistance to her husband on the North-West Frontier of India. The Nazis targeted **Lorimer** because of her November 1933 article on 'Hitler's Germany' in *John O'London's Weekly*; her 1934 abridged translation of one of the key texts of Nazi ideology, Moeller van den Bruck's *Das Dritte Reich*; her translation of **Willi Frischauer**'s *Twilight in Vienna* in 1938; and her detailed attack, in April 1939, in the liberal feminist ***Time and Tide***, on the latest translation of *Mein Kampf* by an Irish employee of Goebbels, a 'translation' which **Lorimer** declared was a dangerous travesty since it avoided every hint of the original's brutality and megalomania. Finally, the Gestapo wanted her silenced for her book, *What Hitler Wants,* a Sixpenny *Penguin* Special published in 1939.

Lorimer was convinced that the British did not take Hitler's aggressive intentions in Europe sufficiently seriously in the 1930s because they could not read German. They had not read the whole of *Mein Kampf* and they had not been able to read the whole because it had not been fully or adequately translated, although she had welcomed the **Duchess of Atholl**'s attempt to set the record straight. What **Lorimer** did in *What Hitler Wants* was simply to ventriloquise Hitler's own account of his heroic climb from trench soldier to destined Führer, his assertion of Germany's innocent martyrdom in the First World War, of the 'stab in the back' by Jews and pacifists, of the self-evident need for German *Lebensraum* throughout Eastern Europe, his brazen lies about working for peace with France and the West, his call for German total obedience, his racist appeal to the sanctity of 'Nordic' blood, and his insistence on the *right* to be merciless. **Lorimer** then strengthened that self-exposure of Nazism with her translation of Alfred Rosenberg's *The Mythus of the Twentieth Century*, which asserted, in its Nazi publisher's words: 'the only correct path into the future [is] the Myth of the Blood, which under the Sign of the Swastika … awakens the Soul of the Race'. **Lorimer** ended *What Hitler Wants* with a grim summary of Nazism in action, practising terror at home while country after country abroad was overrun. She had the courage to insist that Hitler and his followers meant exactly what they said about German supremacism – even though the majority of her British contemporaries, including her own government, preferred not to see it but trusted that appeasing Hitler would give them peace.[4]

In total contrast to the Nazis' aggressive nationalism, the 'quiet internationalist', Professor **J. B. Trend** (1887–1958), wrote in 1921 that 'Intellectual activity should be guided by the supreme art of life, that of doing good to other people rather than being great oneself.'[5] **Trend** was the first professor of Spanish at Cambridge in 1933. As well as writing *The Origins of Modern Spain* in 1934, his wide cultural interests led **Trend** to study Spanish musicology and he became a world authority on the contemporary composer Manuel de Falla. His many travels to Spain and his wide contacts there in the 1920s and early 1930s led him to invite contemporary Spanish poets and distinguished thinkers such as Miguel Unamuno to Cambridge. Once the Spanish Civil War began, **Trend** was quietly a key figure in the rescue and reception of refugee Spanish intellectuals – as the Gestapo duly noted.

The orientalist **Professor Erwin Rosenthal** (1904–1991) gained his D.Phil. in Germany in 1932 with a dissertation on the political thought of the fourteenth-century Arab, Ibn Khalud, sociologist, historian, philosopher and statesman. In 1933 **Rosenthal** was driven out of Germany for being Jewish and became a lecturer in Hebrew and Semitic languages at the University of London. He was then appointed lecturer in Semitic languages at the University of Manchester from 1937 to 1948 and reader in oriental studies at Cambridge from 1948 to 1967. His publications included *Political Thought in Mediaeval Islam* (1958), *Judaism and Islam* (1961), and, after extensive travel in the Muslim world, *Islam in the Modern National State* (1965).

The distinguished Germanist **Dr Richard Samuel** (1900–1983), despite being a Protestant, was persecuted as a Jew and fled Germany for England in 1934. He became a lecturer at Cambridge on completing a second doctorate. He was briefly interned as an 'enemy alien' but then served with the British Pioneer Corps and wartime political intelligence. In 1947 he emigrated to Australia and became distinguished professor of German and founder of the Australian Goethe Institute. A world authority on the writing of Novalis and Kleist, **Samuel** ended his life honoured as a great Germanist both in Australia and in West Germany.[6]

After he had been dismissed on 'racial' grounds from his 'extraordinary chair' in Berlin in 1933, the sinologist **Professor Walter Simon**, later CBE, FBA (1893–1981), taught Chinese (Mandarin) at the School of Oriental and African Studies, University of London, between 1934 and 1960. He was interned briefly on the Isle of Man. In 1947 he became a professor in London. **Simon** made a valuable contribution to understanding and speaking the new Chinese national language as transcribed into Latin script in the early 1940s. His other work focused on the more esoteric subject of Tibetan linguistics and phonetics. The Gestapo could not have been less interested in **Simon**'s extraordinary linguistic knowledge, least of all his classical Tibetan; it was enough that **Walter Simon** should have been an eminent Jew.[7]

It is not surprising that **Joseph Leftwich** (1892–1983) should have been a target on the *Sonderfahndungsliste*, given his consistent celebration of Jewish cultural identity. The son of a Polish cobbler, he had emigrated to the East End of London with his family when he was 5 years old. One of the 'Whitechapel Boys' with the war poet Isaac Rosenberg and the painter Mark Gertler, **Leftwich** was editor of the London bureau of the Jewish telegraphic agency and, although not himself a Zionist, he issued daily reports on the movement's development between 1920 and 1936. The leading translator and literary critic of Yiddish literature in English, **Leftwich** published *What will Happen to the Jews?* in 1936 and an anthology of Yiddish poetry, translated into English, *The Golden Peacock*, in 1939.

Very different from the East End working class **Leftwich** was the headmaster's son and Cambridge don, the humanist literary critic of comparative literature, **F. L. Lucas** (1894–1967). He was ostensibly placed on the Black List for his connection with the '*Emigrantenzeitschrift, Die Zukunft*' ('the émigré paper, *The Future*'). In fact, **Lucas** was one of the most tireless and outspoken of all the British opponents of Nazism and appeasement, certainly the most vehement university opponent, ever since he had read *Mein Kampf* in the original in 1933 and had recognised, as had **Emily Lorimer**, that Hitler meant exactly what he said. Having been badly wounded by shrapnel in the lung during the Battle of the Somme, gassed in the Ancre offensive of 1917, and left partially deaf for life, **Lucas** was hardly an enthusiast for war. Appalled by the triumphalism of the victors, he later judged that 'We were too ready to go on fighting without offering terms' after 1917 (*Journey under the Terror, 1938* (1939)). Nevertheless he still considered that world conquest by Hitler would be even worse than another world war. From 1933 to 1939 he published over forty letters in the press, mostly in the ***Manchester Guardian***, once the pro-appeasement *The Times* refused to publish him after 1935. **Lucas** warned about the rearmament of Nazi Germany; he condemned Italy's aggression in Abyssinia; he excoriated Blackshirt marches in Britain; he protested against the Conservative Government's policy of non-intervention in Spain; and he wrote letter after letter supporting political and Jewish refugees and was profoundly shocked and shamed by **Chamberlain**'s abandonment of Czechoslovakia in October 1938. In addition to those letters, his anti-Nazi campaign included satires, articles and books, especially *The Delights of Dictatorship* (1938), and his *Journal under the Terror, 1938* (1939). He spoke frequently at public meetings, organised petitions to parliament and met many refugees from Nazism.[8] 'I cannot grow used to "the surge in totalitarianism" nor to the courtship lavished on this new barbarism ... How can honourable "leaders" of a free society fraternize with the gang-drivers of a servile state...?' was **Lucas**'s impassioned question. He went on to warn that: 'The men who betrayed Abyssinia are still in power, busy preparing, some of them, to betray Czechoslovakia and even France. And, in the city, Dives ... remains quite capable tomorrow of making fresh loans to save despotism in German, Italy, or Japan ... '[9]

The Times obituary on **Lucas**, headed 'Writer with love of liberty', 2 June 1967, declared: '[his] passionate love of liberty made him an early and eloquent denouncer of Fascism and Nazism ... By 1938 he could think of little else.'

The Nazis took note and Goebbels himself actually replied to **Lucas** in August 1939, 'advising' him to heed British public opinion in favour of appeasement. What **Lucas** dreaded most was an accommodation between Hitler and right-wing British conservatism between 1938 and 1939, and he was fearless in naming what he called the fifth column within the British Establishment – aristocrats like Lord Londonderry and press barons like Lords **Beaverbrook** and Rothermere. In September 1939 **Lucas**, a brilliant linguist, was one of the first academics recruited as a code-breaker at Bletchley to work on 'Enigma' as translator, intelligence-analyst and head of research in Hut 3 on the 4 p.m. to 2 a.m. shift. He accurately deduced German convoy routes to North Africa in 1941, contributing to the first Allied victory in the Second World War. No English literary critic did more to 'connect' art and life – as **E. M. Forster** had advocated in *Howards End* – for **Lucas** believed in the value of literature for *life's* sake. For him, as for the Oxford classicist **E. R. Dodds**, the *Iliad*, and the plays of Euripides, Sophocles, Aeschylus, Shakespeare, Ibsen and Chekhov were not just of literary or historical interest. They made him play a committed role in the real-life tragedy of his own time.

If it was hard to stand by one's station as an English anti-Nazi literary scholar in pro-appeasement Britain, it was still harder for a refugee to do so. To be a literary critic who has to operate in a foreign language is almost impossibly difficult, given the exceptional sensitivity to linguistic nuance that literary criticism requires. The witty, brilliant but intimidating Jewish theatre critic **Alfred Kerr** (1880–1948), known as the *Kulturpapst* ('Culture Pope'), fearing the confiscation of his passport on Hitler's seizure of power, immediately fled to Zurich. He was deprived of German nationality, his books were publicly burned in May 1933, and a reward was announced for his capture, dead or alive. The family moved to Paris and then, with the financial assistance of **Alexander Korda**, arrived at last in England in March 1936. Far from being a 'Culture Pope', all that **Kerr** could do in his late sixties in exile was continue to work in German among his fellow-refugees, co-founding the **Free German League of Culture** in 1938, and serving the exiled German branch of **PEN.**[10] **Kerr** was officially registered by the British police as a 'friendly enemy alien' and in 1947 he was 'naturalised', having been sponsored by George Bernard Shaw. In October 1948 **Kerr** was asked by the British Control Commission to visit Hamburg where the theatre audience gave him a standing ovation; but that same night he suffered a stroke and decided to end his life.[11]

The mother of the literary publisher **Kurt Maschler** (1898–1986) was murdered in Theresienstadt; his sister survived Bergen-Belsen. He himself obtained Austrian citizenship in 1933 and founded a publishing company in Switzerland in 1935 in order to be able to publish the banned (and burned) books of Erich Kaestner of *Emil and the Detectives* fame. In 1937 **Maschler** fled first to Vienna and then, after the *Anschluss* in 1938, to Amsterdam; finally, in 1939 he reached England where he became a well-known publisher for Atrium and Faber & Faber and brought out the poetry of Erich Fried. The annual **Kurt Maschler** Award in Britain goes to an outstanding children's writer and illustrator. His son, Tom Maschler, would become a well-known publisher and also initiate the Booker Prize.

Another Jewish German literary critic, **Albert Malte Wagner** (1886–1962), a distinguished writer on Hebbel, Lessing, Goethe and

Kleist, as well as a university lecturer and newspaper editor, fled to Britain in 1934. He founded, with Ernst Toller, the 'Society of the Friends of the Burned Books' or 'Freedom Library', originally in Paris, then in London (see **H. G. Wells**). **Wagner** became an examiner of the Civil Service commissioners and also a professor of German at Bedford College, University of London. In 1949 he went to East Germany to take up a chair in German language and literature as well as in the history and sociology of European literatures, at the University of Jena. But on his retirement in 1955 he chose to live his last years in Britain.

The anti-Nazi linguists and literary critics, like the educationists **Borinski** and **Schulbach,** refused to emulate their enemy by banning or burning Nazi texts – although that would be the policy of the American occupation in 1946 in relation to the arts.[12] Instead, all that the Blacklisted linguists and literary critics had at their disposal were their own words and the words of other anti-Nazi writers. Implicitly, they believed in Milton's credo in his *Areopagitica* in favour of unlicensed printing in 1644: 'Let her [Truth] and Falsehood grapple. Who ever knew Truth put to the worse in a free and open encounter?'

21

Philosophers and Socio-Political Theorists

The Gestapo were not concerned about possible opposition from Britain's leading philosophers in 1940. There are no logical positivists in the Black Book, no writers on ethics or aesthetics from Oxford or Cambridge, and no Wittgenstein. **Bertrand Russell**, who had written *Which Way to Peace?* in 1936 and *Power: A New Social Analysis* in 1938, was Blacklisted but he had in fact left Britain in 1939 to teach in the United States.

Professor Ernest Barker (1874–1960), however, was, at 66 years old, both on the Black List and still living in Britain. He had started life as a Manchester scholarship boy from a poor home and had become an eminent academic, connecting his deep understanding of Greek thinkers, especially Aristotle, with his own approach to the new field of political science. A lifelong liberal like **E. M. Forster** and **F. L. Lucas,** he championed the individual against the state and voluntary, inclusive social groups against the claims of 'the nation'. Immediately, in 1933, **Barker** exposed the evils of Nazi propaganda by publishing an annotated English version of a Nazi history textbook for 1914–33, in the Oxford series '**Friends of Europe**' pamphlets. An exemplary 'citizen scholar' even in old age, **Barker** also attracted Gestapo attention by acting as treasurer to the **ISSO (International Student Service Organisation)**, the proscribed British university society that supported impoverished non-British students, which in 1940, given that contact with Nazi-occupied Europe was impossible, meant displaced young Jews then at British universities.[1]

The husband of the fervent pacifist writer **Vera Brittain** and father of the future Labour and SDP politician Shirley Williams, **George**

Catlin (1896–1979), although labelled '*Politiker*' by the Gestapo, was not a politician but a political thinker. He wrote on Hobbes and on Mary Wollstonecraft; he edited *New Trends in Socialism* (1935), co-edited *Studies in War and Democracy* (1937), and edited *The Story of the Political Philosophers* (1937). He was a **Fabian** socialist and supported Gandhi's movement for Indian independence.

The self-taught atheist reader of Plato, Spinoza and Hume, **Chapman Cohen** (1868–1954), was an activist as well as a thinker. He was an indefatigable lecturer and militant organiser as well as writer on the subjects of determinism, freethinking and secularism.[2] He was still editing *The Freethinker* in 1951 when he was 83, and he was also a militant socialist – but too much of an anti-authoritarian ever to be a card-carrying Marxist. Almost certainly he was on the Gestapo 'Most Wanted' list simply because, like **Freud**, he was a well-known Jew.

Similarly, the permanent *enfant terrible* of British philosophy, **C. E. M. Joad** (1891–1953), was an incurable anti-authoritarian. Influenced by **Fabian Socialism**, by George Bernard Shaw and by **H. G. Wells**, **Joad** was a brilliant populariser of philosophical ideas and argument. During the 1930s he was bitterly opposed to Nazism while still supporting pacifism. He backed the popular front government in Spain during the civil war and joined **Rebecca West**, **Sybil Thorndike** and **Fenner Brockway** to found the 'Committee to Aid Homeless Spanish Women and Children'. In 1938 he published his *Guide to the Philosophy of Morals and Politics,* and in 1939 the Penguin *Why War?* By 1940 he had become such a national figure on the BBC Brains Trust that he was considered by the general British public to be the greatest philosopher of the day. He was certainly the best known and he would have had to be silenced.

Another unacceptable thinker was the political theorist **Harold Laski** (1893–1950), professor of political science at the London School of Economics, regarded as the most influential intellectual on the left wing of the Labour Party in the 1930s. A non-believer in traditional Judaism, **Laski** still 'earned' Nazi opprobrium by having come from a Jewish background. By 1930 he was a Marxist who still had hope for Stalin's Russia, but he could never resolve the conflict within himself – and within society at large – between the claims of liberty and equality, between personal fulfilment and social justice. On the executive of the **Fabian Society** from 1922 to 1936 and a co-founder of the **Left Book Club** with **Gollancz** since 1936, **Laski**'s vision was of a future co-operative socialist world commonwealth – but he increasingly doubted whether the overthrow of global capitalism could in fact be achieved without force. His gifts were as a writer and brilliant lecturer but the much more conservative Labour Party came to find him counter-productive at election times when his Conservative opponents would demonise him as an apologist for violent class revolution. However, 'few people have devoted such energy to a sincere attempt to combine liberty, equality and internationalism in theoretical terms'.[3]

Aged 82 at the time of her inclusion in the Black Book, **Beatrice Webb** (1858–1943), '*Ehrenpraesidentin*' ('Honorary President') of the **Fabian Society**, had neither attended nor taught at any university. Although born an heiress, she became a socialist and, self-taught, she was influenced by studying the history of the co-operative movement and by the philosophy of Herbert Spencer. An active **Fabian,** she had published *Industrial Democracy* in 1897 as well as co-authoring books on socialism and the cooperative movement. In 1909 **Beatrice Webb** had co-founded, with other **Fabians**, the London School of Economics, which would become a hugely influential centre for radical university teaching and learning in the social sciences during the 1930s as well as an intellectual home for many political refugees. She herself, in 1909, had been the leading author of the Minority Report to the Royal Commission on the Poor Law. In that report she had sketched out a future Welfare State in Britain which would 'secure a national minimum of civilised life … open to all alike, of both sexes and all classes … [including] sufficient nourishment and training when young, a living wage when able-bodied, treatment when sick, and modest but secure livelihood when disabled or aged'. In 1935 **Beatrice Webb** co-published the derided *Soviet Communism: A New Civilization*, mostly authored by her husband **Sidney Webb, Lord Passfield**. Its account of the real achievements in Soviet Russia by

1932 was vitiated by its uncritical Stalinism. The **Webbs** did write that they hoped the world would copy Soviet central planning via non-violent reform and *not* by a revolution, but they omitted any critical reference to the famine in the Ukraine, to the Purges, or to the Gulag. This was not out of naivete or ignorance. **Beatrice Webb**'s posthumously published diaries reveal her awareness and disquiet, but she kept silent out of a patrician certainty concerning what was good for others to know and believe – or not to know. And perhaps in her advanced old age, faced with the choice between Soviet Russia and Nazi Germany, it was simply unbearable to testify in public to doubts about Stalin's version of communism.[4]

The political and religious philosopher **Dr Edward Conze** (1904–1979), was a British national by birth and therefore could settle in Britain after 1933, where he did some university and evening class teaching, although he was considered ineligible for a permanent university post. In 1936 he wrote *Spain To-day: Revolution and Counter-Revolution*. His thinking then moved away, after 1939, from dialectical materialism to a preoccupation with reading and translating Buddhist texts, and to attempting meditation himself. (It may have been his collaboration in political writing with **Ellen Wilkinson** MP in the 1930s, that caused him to be Blacklisted.)

The philosopher of the new field of sociology, **Morris Ginsberg** (1889–1970), would be classified in Britain today as a 'migrant' rather than as a 'refugee'. Born in a small rural East European ghetto and speaking only Yiddish, **Ginsberg** left Tsarist-Russian Lithuania and came to join his father in Liverpool in 1904 when he was 15. He had hungered to learn something of the western European secular knowledge about which he had heard but from which he had been excluded in his closed, unquestioning Orthodox Jewish community, where he had been able to study nothing but the Talmud and the Torah in Hebrew. Once in Britain, where his father had a tobacco factory, **Ginsberg** worked all day, but his acquisition in his spare time, not merely of English but also of French, German, biology, chemistry and physics, as well as history and philosophy, was quite phenomenal. In 1910 he won a scholarship in sociology to University

College London where he graduated in 1912 with first-class honours in philosophy and sociology.

Ginsberg was soon lecturing at the LSE on sociology, ethics and the history of political ideas.[5] The LSE asked for his enlistment in the army after 1916 to be postponed, since he was standing in as lecturer for the now serving officers Sergeant R. H. Tawney and Major **Clement Attlee** – and was irreplaceable. In 1921 **Ginsberg** published *The Psychology of Society*; in 1923 he was appointed full lecturer at LSE, in 1924 he became reader, and, in 1929, professor. He edited *The Sociological Review*, and his book *Sociology*, written for the Home University Library in 1934, became a classic. He wrestled all his life with the problem of how societies may evolve morally, publishing *Moral Progress* in 1944 and *Reason and Unreason in Society* in 1947. Ginsberg's understanding of the diversity of morals in societies, groups and individuals never made him a cultural relativist. On the contrary, he held that it is possible to find common ground in establishing humane, even universal, moral values, but that socially conditioned behaviour, whether of individuals or societies, is never finally fixed or stable and may regress as well as improve. Ethical principles are not situational but human behaviour is.

He opposed every kind of totalitarianism, affirming instead the individual's capacity to question and to reflect. '[The] liberal mind is characterised by an abhorrence of fanaticism, a … readiness to count the cost in terms of human happiness and human lives, a [profound] awareness of the effects of violence both on those who employ it and those who suffer it.' It was **Ginsberg**'s bitter fate to live at a time of terrible moral regress and infectious irrationality. As A. H. Halsey wrote: '**Ginsberg** was seldom exuberant, often sad, and sometimes despairing.'[6] Whether or not he had been a Jew, **Morris Ginsberg** would still have been on the Black List, given his total commitment to anti-fascism.

The co-founder of the new academic subject of social psychology was the Austrian refugee ***Marie Jahoda*** (1907–2001). Born into a family of upper-class, secular, Social Democrat Viennese Jews, she became an active Social Democrat, though never a communist, in her teens.

She qualified as a teacher in 1928 and gained her D.Phil. in 1933, having co-authored what would become a classic study of the socio-psychological impact of long-term unemployment. Many copies of that book, *Die Arbeitslosen von Marienthal* (*The Unemployed of Marientahal*) (1932), were actually burned because of its socialist content and its Jewish authorship. In late 1936 she was arrested by the Schuschnigg dictatorship for allegedly working for the Social Democrat Party, which had recently had to go 'underground'. Imprisoned for nine months in 1937, ***Jahoda*** was only released through the intervention of the French Socialist prime minister Léon Blum, and on condition that she leave Austria at once, which meant separating from her 7-year-old daughter, her friends and her work, having had her Austrian citizenship revoked. Devastated, she had to leave for Britain even before the *Anschluss*, and would not see her daughter, re-settled in the US with her divorced father, for seven years. The *Informationsheft GB* included 'die Juedin ***Marie Jahoda***' for special attention.

Once in Britain, ***Jahoda*** continued her socio-psychological field research with unemployed miners and then worked for the Foreign Office on evaluating enemy and domestic civilian morale in the Second World War. She also broadcast for the secret BBC radio programme, *Rotes Wien*, run by **Richard Crossman** for the Ministry of Information. In 1945, ***Jahoda*** went to the US to be reunited with her daughter and established herself as a radical writer and researcher in her books *Prejudice* (1952) and *The Authoritarian Personality* (1954), both dealing with racism, anti-Semitism and emotional disorder. During the McCarthy period she was almost certainly under secret surveillance by the FBI. On returning to Britain in 1958, ***Jahoda*** continued to make a significant contribution to the new field of social psychology as a professor at Brunel and Sussex universities as well as at the Social Sciences Research Council. She was listed in the Black Book both because of her Jewish antecedents and because of her left-wing political activism and writing. In the *Sonderfahndungsliste* she is named as **Lazarsfeld-Jahoda, Marie, Dr**, '*Schriftstellerin, Juedin, Taeterkreis SPD Auslandszweigstelle*' ('writer, Jewess, foreign branch of the SPD's activist ring') together with her London address.[7]

The Hungarian-born founder of the sociology of knowledge, **Professor Karl Mannheim** (1893–1947), was largely educated in Germany where he lived during the Weimar years, teaching sociology at Heidelberg before being given a chair at Frankfurt. On his forced migration to Britain after 1933, he lectured in sociology at the LSE. During the 1930s **Mannheim** became increasingly concerned to find a middle way between totalitarian socialism and the uncontrolled laissez-faire individualism favoured by Hayek. He eventually arrived at the paradox of 'planning for freedom'. During the Second World War he taught at the London Institute of Education as well as at LSE, with his focus being always on the nature of how to educate in order to produce democrats. As the founding editor of *The International Library of Sociology and Social Reconstruction* in 1942, which 'dealt from a scientific point of view with urgent problems of economic and social planning', **Mannheim** was 'one of the most influential of Britain's sociologists'.[8] He wrote *Man and Society in our Time*, advocating anti-authoritarianism in both family and school in order to help form a socially educated personality. He was thought to have influenced Britain's 1944 Education Act. The compilers of the Black Book were probably aware of **Mannheim**'s 'record' of having associated with Marxists during Hungary's short revolution before 1919 and therefore found him very suspect.

Confusingly, there was another Blacklisted Jewish refugee sociologist also called Mannheim; **Hermann Mannheim** (1889–1974), in his case working in criminology, on the borderlines between sociology and law. Naturalised in 1940, he had switched from criminal law, of which he had been a distinguished professor in Germany as well as a judge, to become a pioneer of criminology and penal reform at the LSE in Britain from 1935. Among his most thought-provoking and original books are *The Dilemma of Penal Reform* (1939), *Crime in England Between the Wars* (1940), *War and Crime* (1941), and *Criminal Justice and Social Reconstruction* (1946). **Hermann Mannheim** helped to advance the study and treatment of juvenile delinquency in Britain; he was the founding editor of the *British Journal of Delinquency*, later *British Journal of Criminology*, and he was closely associated with the Howard League for Penal Reform.[9]

The other Blacklisted refugee philosopher of sociology was a tragic figure, **Dr Georg Rusche** (1900–1950), famous for co-authoring, with Otto Kirchheimer, one book, *Punishment and Social Structure*, in 1939. That book had developed from an earlier work by **Rusche**, *Labour Market and Penal Sanction: Thoughts on the Sociology of Criminal Justice* (1939). **Rusche** and Kirchheimer held that punishment through the ages has been a species of class domination. Already in 1933, **Rusche** had pointed out that 'the criminal law and the daily work of the criminal courts are directed almost exclusively against those people whose class background, poverty, neglected education, or demoralisation drove them to crime'. (A point also made by his contemporary Simone Weil, who could not bear the sight of an upper-class judge passing learned sentence on an inarticulate defendant.) **Rusche**'s Marxist analysis would prove a seminal classic, influencing later theorists of criminology and social control like Michel Foucault, *Discipline and Punish* (1977), D. Garland, *Punishment and Modern Society* (1990), and Loic Wacquant, *Punishing the Poor* (2009). For his own part, **Rusche** led an erratic, itinerant life, fleeing Nazi Germany after 1933 for England, then going to Palestine and finally back to England where he was interned in 1940. In 1950 he committed suicide in London.[10]

What all the refugee philosophers of sociology had in common, as well as their Jewish origins, was their humane insistence on distinguishing the environmental determinants of crime from a mere primitive recourse to alleged 'bad blood'. Together, they made a formidable contribution to British thinking about society, including British society itself.

PART SIX

ELIMINATING BRILLIANT MINDS IN THE SCIENCES

22

Some Mathematicians

The scientists in the Black Book are particularly difficult to classify because they often changed from one field to another or else managed to combine different specialities. I shall focus on their work up until 1940 but also pay attention to the applications of their work during and after the Second World War, especially in regard to its value to medicine. The most vivid book in English about the outstanding German-speaking Jewish refugee scientists who found asylum in Britain is *Hitler's Gift: The True Story of the Scientists Expelled by the Nazi Regime* by Jean Medawar and David Pyke (Arcade Publishing, New York, 2012). The authors point out that in April 1933 the British Cabinet had already

> resolved to try and secure for this country prominent Jews who were being expelled from Germany and who had achieved distinction whether in pure science, applied science, such as medicine or technical industry, music or art. [This would] not only obtain for this country the advantage of their knowledge and experience but would also create a very favourable impression in the world.

The German collective biography by Ruerip and Schuering on expelled Jewish scientists from the Kaiser Wilhelm Institute, Berlin, *Schicksale und Karriere* (Wallstein, 2008), is also indispensable.

The subject of mathematics may be seen as a bridge between the arts and the sciences since it is grounded in the philosophical area of logic, as attested by **Bertrand Russell**'s work in *Principia*

Mathematica and his *Introduction to Mathematical Philosophy* (1919). As a non-mathematician, I shall focus only on those aspects of the mathematicians' lives relevant to their inclusion in the Black Book. There are just three Gestapo-listed mathematicians who grew up as children in Britain.

Professor Selig Brodetsky (1888–1954) would now be classified as a child migrant rather than a refugee, even though he had experienced the trauma of witnessing his uncle's murder during a pogrom near Odessa when he was 5 years old. In 1894, when he was 6, he migrated with his mother and three siblings to join his father in the East End of London. There, the second of thirteen children of an Orthodox Jewish family, he lived in extreme poverty, but his brilliance at the Jews' Free School in Whitechapel won him a scholarship to the Central Foundation Boys' School of London, and in 1905 he won another scholarship to Trinity College, Cambridge. In 1908 he was Senior Wrangler, the top mathematician of his year, a triumph that did not altogether please the anti-immigrant, right-wing British press, although some editorials did note 'that if the Aliens Act [1905] restricting immigration had been passed earlier the **Brodetsky** family would have been barred'.[1] **Selig Brodetsky**'s first academic post was in applied mathematics at the University of Bristol; during the First World War he worked on optical instruments such as submarine periscopes and mathematical aeronautics. In 1920 he became reader in mathematics at the University of Leeds and then professor from 1924 to 1948, much of his work being on aeronautics. His pioneering book, *Mathematical Principles of the Aeroplane*, was published in 1921.[2] Simultaneously **Brodetsky** was devoting himself to serve the Association of University Teachers, of which he was president from 1935 to 1936, the **League of Nations Union** and the **Zionist Movement** in Britain. He was obviously a prime Jewish target for the Gestapo in 1940. In 1940 he was elected head of British Jewry as president of the ***Board of Deputies of British Jews*** until 1949 – the first East European immigrant ever to hold that position, which he did until 1949. Then, after a short, unhappy, crisis-ridden period as president of the Hebrew University of Jerusalem from 1949 to 1950, his health broke down and **Brodetsky**

returned to Britain where he wrote his *Memoirs from Ghetto to Israel* (published posthumously in 1960). He was a Fellow of the Royal Astronomical Society and of the Institute of Physics.

Another mathematician specialising in aeronautics, **Professor Hyman Levy** (1889–1975), had been born to a large working-class, socialist, Zionist family in Edinburgh. His father was a struggling picture-frame maker and dealer and **Levy** never forgot the misery caused by the poverty around him that he witnessed in his youth. As a student at Edinburgh University he co-founded a branch of the **Fabian Society** and became a convinced Marxist. His left-wing views actually made him refuse a postgraduate scholarship to Cambridge in 1912, on the grounds that Cambridge University was too much a part of Britain's unequal class society. During the First World War **Levy** volunteered to serve in Air Command, and, when flying in an open-top plane, he developed the theory behind bomb sights. After the war he became a specialist in differential equations and on mathematical applications to aeronautics, working at Imperial College, London, as professor from 1923 until 1954. Like **Julian Huxley**, **J. D. Bernal** and **J. B. S. Haldane**, **Levy** was committed to the social liberation of humanity through scientific rationalism; he was a proselytising rationalist despite being married to a Christian, and in 1940 he published *Science, Curse or Blessing?* He moved from Labour Party activism in the 1920s to communism in the 1930s and beyond. In July 1934 he agreed to support the communist-inspired 'Co-ordinating Committee for Anti-Fascist Activities' in Britain led by **John Strachey**. He was a well-known public speaker, both in person and on the radio, and his academic standing in Britain did not suffer from his politics. However, although obviously well qualified to work on decoding 'Enigma' at Bletchley in the Second World War, **Levy** was rejected from that top secret work on political grounds.[3] Ironically, he was expelled both from the Labour Party as a 'Left extremist' and later from the **Communist Party of Great Britain** on account of his public denunciation of Stalin's atrocities, including the persecution of Soviet Jews, after publishing *Jews and the National Question* in 1958. The Gestapo, for its part, marked **Levy** down in the 1930s both as a Jew and as an outspoken, committed socialist and anti-appeaser – *'Einkreisungsfront Anhaenger, Jude'* ('supporter of the encirclement of Germany, Jew').

The only other British-raised mathematician, the outspoken anti-Nazi **Sir Sidney John Chapman**, is discussed as a geo-physicist (p. 309). Among the refugees, **Dr Hans Arnold Heilbronn**, FRS (1908–1975), when still in his twenties, was called 'one of the most promising German mathematicians'.[4] Even with that, and despite his patronage by the distinguished Edmund Landau, he still had to flee Germany for Britain in November 1933. In 1934 he was working at the University of Bristol on number theory. From 1935 to 1940 he was a visiting fellow at Trinity College, Cambridge, while also managing to get his parents and his sister out of Germany in time. In 1940 he was interned by the British as an 'enemy alien' and on his release joined the army's Pioneer Corps and later the Intelligence Corps. From 1946 until 1962 **Heilbronn** was first reader and then professor of mathematics at Bristol. However, convinced that the government's plans for university expansion, endorsed by the Robbins Report in 1963, would mean a fall in academic standards, **Heilbronn** then left Britain for North America, where from 1963 to 1974 he became professor of mathematics at the University of Toronto.[5]

Closely associated with **Heilbronn** at Cambridge was the geometer **Richard Rado**, FRS (1906–1989), who was one of those 'cherry-picked' by Lindemann in Germany after he had completed a brilliant D.Phil. thesis at the University of Berlin in 1933. Enabled to get out of Germany in early 1933 by Lindemann's recommendation for a scholarship funded by **Sir Richard Mond**, **Rado** completed a second Ph.D. in 1935; he was a temporary lecturer at Cambridge until 1936 when he moved to the University of Sheffield. After the war **Rado** became reader in mathematics at King's College London and then professor at Reading until his retirement in 1971. The 'kindest and gentlest of men ... fascinated by mathematical beauty',[6] **Rado** had very wide mathematical interests and was also a highly gifted musician, like his wife, the singer Luise Zadek. He was elected a Fellow of the Royal Society in 1978.

The algebraist **Dr Bernhard Neumann**, FRS (1909–2002), who was also at Cambridge in the 1930s, was a leading thinker in group theory. Awarded his doctorate by the University of Berlin in 1932, he remained there as an unpaid assistant in the experimental physics laboratory at the Kaiser Wilhelm Institute. He also become secretly engaged to his fellow-student in Berlin, the mathematician and group theorist Hanna von Caemmerer. On Hitler's accession to power, **Neumann** left Germany for Cambridge where he registered for a second Ph.D., awarded in 1935, in which he introduced a new major area into group theory research. Despite his brilliance, **Neumann** was then unemployed for two years until appointed as a temporary assistant lecturer in Cardiff in 1937 where Hanna later joined him and they finally married. Interned as an 'enemy alien', **Neumann** was released in 1940, although he could have been released earlier had he had help from the University of Cardiff. He then served the British Army for the rest of the war in the Pioneer Corps, the Royal Artillery and the Intelligence Corps, finally volunteering to be part of that corps in post-war Germany in order to track down Hanna's family in the British Sector.

In 1946 **Neumann** refused the offer of a post at Cardiff University, which had failed to support him in 1940, and took up a post as a lecturer in Hull instead. In 1948 he was appointed to the University of Manchester, commuting from Hull until Hanna was appointed to Manchester also, ten years and a Ph.D. later. While at Manchester, **Neumann**, now a Fellow of the Royal Society, became interested in the history of mathematics, and in particular in the Ada Lovelace papers, eventually writing on her and on her mathematics tutors Auguste De Morgan and Charles Babbage. In 1962 the **Neumanns**, who by then had five nearly grown-up children, moved to two posts at the Institute of Advanced Studies, Australian National University, Canberra, where **Bernhard Neumann** lived until his death almost forty years later.[7]

Another group theory algebraist was **Dr Kurt Hirsch** (1906–1986), whose Berlin Ph.D. was on the philosophy of mathematics. Of part Jewish descent, though brought up a Christian, he had rejoined the

Jewish faith in 1928 in order to marry Else Bruehl. To support his wife and young family, **Hirsch** had become a populariser of science for the liberal paper *Die Vossische Zeitung*, which was closed down in 1934 by the Nazis. A former fellow student of **Neumann**'s, **Hirsch** was met by him when he arrived in London as a refugee from Nazism in 1934 and followed him to Cambridge, where he lived close by and completed a second doctoral thesis in 1937. **Hirsch** became a lecturer in mathematics at the University of Leicester in 1938 but was interned on the Isle of Man in 1940 where he worked as a cook. Released through pressure from the vice-chancellor of Leicester – in contrast to **Neumann**'s treatment by Cardiff – **Hirsch** returned to his Leicester University post, which was made permanent in 1944. Meanwhile he combined teaching with chess and became county chess champion. In 1947 he and his wife were granted British citizenship and in 1948 **Hirsch** moved to King's College, Newcastle, working under Rogsinki in pure mathematics and beginning his long sequence of translations of Russian mathematicians. His final post was as professor at Queen Mary College, London, where he built up a strong algebra school.[8]

The Gestapo's inclusion of **Hirsch** on the Black List may be explained by his association with the liberal *Vossische Zeitung*, but the grounds for selection of the other mathematicians seems mysterious, unless it be explained by their sheer brilliance and fame. **Albert Einstein** himself was on the Black List as '**Dr Alfred Einstein**, Emigrant', possibly damned by his internationalist pacifism as well as by his world eminence – and his Jewishness – but he, of course, had already left for the United States in 1933 and by 1940 had become an American citizen.

23

Jewish Inventors in the Material Sciences

When it came to engineering, the Gestapo were astute in identifying some of the most gifted and beneficial refugees for immediate arrest, and although they may not be household names, all made indispensable contributions to modern life as we now know it. For example, 'aeroplanes, burglar alarms, computers, dishwashers, escalators ... products manufactured anywhere in the industrialised world have at least one type of component in common: printed circuits'.[1]

Who invented the printed circuit board? The Austrian **Paul Eisler** (1907–1992), 'a quiet, gentle loner',[2] was the outstanding pioneer of electronic technology who invented the foil method of producing printed circuits. He had been prevented from working in engineering in Austria in the 1930s by anti-Semitic pressure in high places, so he had had to work as a printer instead – and was employed by the socialist paper *Vorwaerts* before it was closed down. It was experience that would be crucial to his later invention. **Eisler** moved to Britain in 1936, without work or work permit, but failed to interest financiers in backing his idea. In 1940 he was interned briefly as an 'enemy alien'. On his release in 1941 he joined the army's Pioneer Corps for a short time but then managed to get a lithography company to invest in his printed circuit board – giving him just a nominal fee of £1 for the patent. Although **Eisler** demonstrated the first radio set incorporating printed circuits to hundreds of enthusiastic British and American engineers and military personnel, it was not the British Ministry of Supply but the United States military that recognised its vital potential. They developed a proximity fuse fitted with electronic circuits which was used in anti-aircraft shells at Antwerp in 1944–5 as well as in helping to defend

London against the V1 rockets. '**Eisler**'s invention played a major role in bringing down some 4,000 of German's flying bombs, the "doodlebugs" launched against Britain towards the end of the war.'[3]

Another vital invention for twentieth-century electronic communication, not to mention culture, was the cathode tube used in televisions. A Telefunken radio engineer, the electrical engineer **Hans Gerhardt Lubzynski** (1910–1997), a refugee who escaped to Britain in 1934, was responsible for important improvements to that invention. The United States Patent Office granted him, when at EMI Ltd, Hayes, Middlesex, patents for an electronic discharge device, an improved cathode-ray tube, a light-sensitive electrode, and an electron multiplying electrode in 1941. He was 'naturalised' in 1946. In 1964 he published a report, 'Television Technology and Application' in *Nature* on the International Television Conference held in London in 1962.

A research engineer specialising in coal-dust-based heating technology, **Professor Paul Rosin** (1890–1967), when driven from his distinguished post in Freiburg and seeking asylum in London at Imperial College, took his enforced transplantation as an opportunity to make his research internationally known. His equation estimating the distribution of particles is still used today. What Rosin did specifically for Britain and her war effort was not only to work in the petroleum war effort department but also to develop the mechanism that would enable aircraft to land in fog. In 1945 he published his 'Total, recoverable and returnable heat in combustion gases', a pioneer study in renewable energy.[4]

Finally, the electrical engineer **Dr Adolf Schallamach** (1905–1997) had been forced to leave Breslau in 1934 just before the point of completing his doctorate. He found a post at the Davy Faraday Laboratory of the Royal Institution from 1934 to 1943, and was a pioneer researcher there in the mechanism of rubber friction essential for understanding the wear on tyres. He became a Fellow of the Institute of Physics in 1942. In 1943 **Schallamach** joined the British Rubber Producers' Research Association and as a research physicist he investigated the friction and abrasion properties of rubber.[5] Ever since, countless drivers the world over owe their safety to him.

24

Biochemists and Other Medical Researchers

What **Fritz Saxl**'s Warburg Institute was for refugee historians of art, and what the LSE was for refugee economists, Sir Frederick Gowland Hopkins' Dunn Institute in Cambridge was for refugee biochemists. The Nobel prizewinner, Hopkins, aged nearly 73 in 1933, was an internationalist and a politically conscious man who had co-founded the **Academic Assistance Council** with William Beveridge and A. V. Hill. He actively recruited persecuted Jewish scientists in his field:

> The Dunn Institute under Hopkins had … an unusual feature for the time: Hopkins did not discriminate against hiring Jewish scientists, unlike the large majority of American, British and German universities and medical schools. This may have helped Hopkins assemble such a strong group of researchers.[1]

As the Nobel prizewinning biochemist **Hans Krebs** fondly remembered:

> Hopkins was the central figure, beloved and respected as a natural leader … His concern ranged far beyond biochemistry, Cambridge University and the Royal Society. What struck me in particular contrast to the German scene, was the strong social conscience of Hopkins and his school. Between 1933 and 1935 the laboratory sheltered six refugees from central Europe: **Friedmann**, Lemberg, **Chain**, **Weil-Malherbe**, **Bach** and myself.[2]

Dr Stefan (later **Stephen**) **Bach** (1897–1973) completed his Ph.D. in biochemistry at the Dunn Institute between 1935 and 1937. His special interest was in cancer research and enzymology. He was briefly interned in 1940 as an 'enemy alien', until vouched for by Hopkins himself, and he received British citizenship in 1946. He went on to be reader in chemical physiology at the University of Bristol from 1951 to 1963, publishing his research on the retardation of tumour growth in the *British Journal of Cancer* in 1965.[3]

The distinguished professor of physiology **Ernst Joseph Friedmann** (1877–1956), who, at the age of 57, had been expelled from his personal chair in Berlin, was twenty years older than **Bach.** He went to work at the Dunn Institute in Cambridge from 1934 until his death over two decades later. His speciality was sterols and related compounds.[4] Another Blacklisted researcher on cancer was **Dr Hans Weil-Malherbe** (1905–2004), a doctor and researcher who found refuge at the institute from 1933 to 1935. From 1935 to 1947 he was employed in research by the British Empire Cancer Campaign and from 1947 to 1958 he was director of research at Runwell Mental Hospital in Essex. He then moved to America where he worked from 1958 to 1978 as head of neuro-chemical research at the National Institute of Mental Health in Washington. He died at the age of 98.[5]

Ernst Chain (1906–1979), who would become famous before he was 40, had fled Berlin for Britain in April 1933 with the equivalent of £10 in his pocket and was then helped by **J. B. S. Haldane**, who said later that his assistance to **Chain** to an initial position at University College Hospital 'might be seen as the best and most important action of my life'. **Chain** then moved to the Dunn Institute to do a Ph.D. under Gowland Hopkins between 1934 and 1935. It was Hopkins who recommended him to Oxford's School of Pathology where he researched snake's venom, tumour metabolism, lysozymes, and biochemistry techniques. **Chain** became a British citizen in 1939 and began work with Howard Florey on natural anti-microbial substances, one of which was *Penicillium notatum.* At first neither man dreamt of a possible practical medical application for their research but a year later, in 1940, they discovered the therapeutic impact of penicillin on mice. It would take four more years of work before they could purify and synthesise concentrated penicillin for human application, but by D-Day, 6 June 1944, hospitals and pathologists were ready with the antibiotic to treat the expected huge number of casualties. In 1946 **Chain** shared the 'Nobel Prize for Physiology or Medicine' with Alexander Fleming and Florey, and became world-famous. He was made a Fellow of the Royal Society in 1948 and was knighted in 1969.[6]

The last refugee member of Hopkins' Dunn Institute was **Sir Hans Krebs** (1900–1981), son of a Jewish German ear, nose and throat surgeon. **Krebs** was a qualified physician as well as a medical researcher, trained in both chemistry and biochemistry. Before the triumph of the Nazis, **Krebs** was studying how the waste product urea is made in the liver from the breakdown of proteins. He discovered an endless cyclical process fundamental to the body's chemistry. Thirty years later, the medical significance of **Krebs**' discovery would be revealed when no fewer than five diseases were discovered to depend on the failure of the enzymes which build urea in the liver. Gowland Hopkins had already recognised the significance of **Krebs**' fundamental research in Germany and the moment that Freiburg University dismissed him on racist grounds in April 1933, Hopkins invited **Krebs** to come and work with him in Cambridge. He arrived, together with his equipment and research samples, in July of that year. In 1935 **Krebs** was offered a lectureship in pathology at the University of Sheffield where he worked for the next nineteen years, becoming naturalised in 1939. He was made professor of the new department of biochemistry in 1946, as well as head of the Medical Research Council's Unit for Cell Metabolism. It was in Sheffield that **Krebs** discovered the '**Krebs** citric acid cycle', building on his earlier research into how carbohydrates, proteins and fats are oxidised to provide the energy needed for every activity in the body. During the war **Krebs** worked for the Medical Research Council investigating the importance of vitamins A and C. In 1947 he was made a Fellow of the Royal Society, in 1953 he was awarded the Nobel Prize in 'Physiology or Medicine', and in 1958 he was knighted. After 'retiring' to Oxford, **Krebs** published more than a hundred research papers before his death in 1981.

The son of a distinguished Jewish professor of dermatology

and pioneer of social medicine in Berlin, the medical graduate **Dr Hermann** (later **Hugh**) **Blaschko** (1900–1993), was a lifelong friend of **Hans Krebs**, who had treated him for tuberculosis in Germany before Hitler came to power. **Blaschko** was a research assistant in physiology at the Kaiser Wilhelm Biology Institute in Berlin in 1925 and then at Jena, Heidelberg, and later, very productively, at University College London. However, his research was interrupted by recurrent periods of pulmonary tuberculosis and he was recuperating in a sanatorium when the Nazis took over. Realising that he must leave Germany at once, **Blaschko** left with only the equivalent of £20, and a few weeks after his own arrival, he went to meet and welcome his equally impecunious friend **Krebs** at Victoria Station. **Blaschko** first rejoined his mentor, Professor A. V. Hill, at his laboratory in the pathology department of the Medical School of the University of London. He then became a temporary assistant in the physiological laboratory in Cambridge and was simply labelled 'Assistent, Cambridge (Emigrant)' in the Black Book, with no allusion to his real crime of having been born a Jewish German. It was 1944, eleven years after his arrival in Britain, before **Blaschko** was at last offered a permanent university post, at Oxford. His work on the application of biochemical methods for solving pharmacological problems was to prove indispensable, for example in connection with the enzyme's transformative role in the absorption of adrenalin:

> **Blaschko** found out how adrenalin and other monoamine compounds [are] made, stored and broken down in the body and what their effects [are] … He discovered the monamine oxidate inhibitors which [have come] to play a very large part in the treatment of depression and were the first real advance in the drug treatment of the disorder.[7]

Blaschko's research was also to prove crucial to the development of the first drugs to control high blood pressure. He 'should be more famous than he is' as Medawar and Pyke point out. The warm tribute to him in the *ODNB* makes it clear that he was not only a very great scientist but also a marvellous human being. *The Times* obituarist on 28 April 1993 wrote: 'In the world of medicine few have made more pioneering contributions than **Hugh Blaschko**.' And his eminent scientific colleagues, many of them Fellows of the Royal Society, attested to his 'extraordinary achievement [in improving] the outlook in diseases as diverse as hypertension, depression, schizophrenia and Parkinson's Disease'.[8]

Yet another pioneer was the radio-biochemist **Dr Walter Max Dale** (originally **Deutsch**) (1894–1969). **Dale**'s research background in Germany enabled him to develop a radio-biochemistry laboratory at the Christie Cancer Hospital in Manchester and then at the Holt Radium Institute. He became a world authority on the effects of X-rays on enzymes and on the protective effect of additional solutes. He also founded and edited the *International Journal of Radiation Biology*.[9]

A last brilliant biochemist was **Albert Neuberger** (1908–1996). He was a lifelong friend of **Ernst Chain**, and began as a distinguished graduate in medicine in Germany before being forced to flee. He gained a Ph.D. at the University of London in 1936 with a thesis on amino acids and proteins. He went on to carry out research at the Dunn Institute in Cambridge, and at the start of the war, together with his outstanding doctoral student Fred Sanger, he published important work on the protein value of potatoes, thus providing essential research findings relevant to British nutrition in wartime. His other contribution to the war effort was to go out to India to be a medical consultant on nutrition for the army. **Neuberger**'s original work on glycol-proteins and their blood-clotting factors proved to be vital for treating dialysis patients with kidney failure and his later work on porphyrins helped in the understanding of acute porphyria. As professor of chemical pathology at St Mary's Hospital Medical School, London, until 1973, **Neuberger** relished the opportunity to combine his scientific research with its medical application.[10]

Whereas many of these biochemists carried out fundamental research without knowing whether or not their findings could or would have medical applications, other refugee scientists hoped from the outset to contribute to medicine. For example, **Professor Dr Philipp Ellinger** (1887–1952), like **Dr Franz Bergel** and **Dr**

Ernst Brieger (see p. 57), was a brilliant pharmacologist. He had been awarded not just one but two doctorates in medicine and had become professor at Düsseldorf University's Medical School by 1932, only to be dismissed on racist grounds. In a famous letter of May 1933, expressing moral revulsion at the unjust dismissal of all Jewish German academics, the *non*-Jewish cardiovascular pharmacologist, **Dr Otto Krayer**, had then (uniquely) refused to take over **Ellinger**'s professorial chair. For that he himself was dismissed and forbidden to use any German state libraries or scientific institutions. **Krayer** thereupon also left as a refugee for Britain, needing the support of the British **Academic Assistance Council**. He worked at University College London, and was included on the *Sonderfahndungsliste* before he eventually left for research posts at the American University of Beirut and later Harvard. **Dr Philipp Ellinger**, also supported by the **Academic Assistance Council**, had found work at the Lister Institute for preventive medicine in London. In 1937 and 1938 he was sent by the British Medical Council to research pellagra in Egypt and in 1939 he became a British citizen. **Ellinger** did fundamental research on microscopy of the diseased liver, on the role of nicotinamid deficiency in causing pellagra, and on the group of vitamins known as Riboflavins.[11]

The medical researcher in embryology, cancer and radiation treatment, **Dr Alfred Glucksmann** (1905–1985), was dismissed from Germany in 1933 and went to Strangeways research laboratory in Cambridge. His best-known contributions were a histological analysis of human tumours before and after radiation treatment and a study of hormonal factors in the malignant process. The pathologist **Dr Fritz Jacoby** (1902–1991) was a pioneer refugee medical researcher at an exciting period of research, first at Strangeways and then in the mid 1930s working on tissue cultures with **Hugo Blaschko** and others in the histology unit of the department of physiology. He moved to the University of Birmingham and worked as part-time scientific consultant for the British Empire Cancer Campaign. During the war **Jacoby** collaborated on a research study reporting to the Medical Research Council War Wounds Committee on the anti-bacterial treatment of war wounds through sulphonamide drugs, and he investigated the very earliest batches of penicillin supplied by **Chain**. From 1947 until 1969 **Fritz Jacoby**, co-founder of the British Tissue Culture Association, pursued his research into the growth of malignant cancer cells, including ovarian cancer, at the University of Cardiff.[12]

Even though he was a Jewish German **Dr Hans Laser** (1899–1980) had at first been granted exceptional protection from dismissal from his work on cell culture at the Kaiser Wilhelm Institute, Berlin, because of his heroic record in the First World War. **Laser** had actually injected himself with smallpox in the *Seuchen Lazarett* (plague hospital) of his military hospital in order to better understand the disease. However, he was finally dismissed from Berlin on 1 January 1934 and fled to Britain where he was helped by the **Academic Assistance Council** to a research post at the Molteno Institute of Biology and Parasitology in Cambridge. He worked there until his death, having gained not only a doctorate in medicine but also a doctorate in philosophy and a doctorate in science. In 1939 in Germany the state stripped him of his German doctorate. After the war he learned that both his mother and brother had perished in concentration camps. In Britain, **Laser** became a permanent member of the scientific staff of the Medical Research Council, his special fields being malaria and radiation/radiotherapy research. He was refused compensation from West Germany after the war, on the grounds that it could not be *certain* that he would have become a professor had he not been forced into exile.

A man esteemed to be 'of immense erudition and wisdom, ever helpful, ever courteous, his laboratory staff idolised him',[13] was **Dr Hans Loewenthal** (1899–1986). He had worked in Berlin at the Koch Institute for Infectious Diseases, later to be notorious under Nazi direction during the war for deliberately infecting prisoners in Buchenwald with lethal doses of typhus in 1941. As a refugee in Britain, Loewenthal first worked at the London Hospital Medical College, researching streptococcal infections. After 1945 he was appointed pathologist in charge at the Chase Farm Hospital, Enfield, and he was a member of the Medical Research Council's committee on trials of streptomycin.

The physiologist **Dr Hans Schlossmann** (1894–1956), a pharmacologist who had specialised in the treatment of diphtheria and pneumonia in children, had been dismissed from his German post in 1933, despite his First World War record, and after going to Holland and South Africa, found a post in the Cambridge University physiology department from 1935. Yet again Germany's loss was Britain's gain.

Finally, this roll call of Blacklisted medical researchers includes **Dr Kurt Eisenberg-Merlin** (1905–?), who was a specialist in the preventive medical aspects of health and safety in buildings. He became a researcher at the Bland Sutton Institute of Pathology, Middlesex Hospital, investigating questions of bacteriology, hygiene, toxic dust, ventilation, heat and noise in the built environment. His counterpart was **Guenter Nagelschmidt** (1906–1980), who applied his expertise in mineralogy to the problems of health and safety in coal mining. **Nagelschmidt** worked at the Safety in Mines Research Establishment and was a member of the Medical Research Council's Health Commission, investigating pneumoconiosis in South Wales' coal miners and coal-trimmers between 1940 and 1943. He 'brought the techniques of X-ray diffraction analysis and electron microscopy into [the] assessment of airborne dust, coal-mine strata and dust in lungs at necropsy'.[14] **Nagelschmidt** concluded that most dust in coal mines was a hazard and his findings influenced legislation in Britain for the improved protection of miners.

Perhaps no academic subject in British universities besides art history, sociology, biochemistry and medical research was quite so revolutionised and enriched by refugees after 1933 as was psychiatry. During the mid 1920s and early 1930s, the re-founded Maudsley Hospital had already established its position as the outstanding research and treatment centre in Britain for mental illness and mental handicap and had the status of a clinical section of the University of London. The Maudsley's pioneering director, Edward Mapother, was a man suspicious of system-building philosophies, and he promoted an eclectic therapeutic. He attacked psychoanalysts as 'therapeutic chanticleers', but nevertheless he tolerated all forms of attempted therapy at the Maudsley Hospital, ranging 'from hormone treatment to Jungian analysis'. Alert to the scientific approach to psychiatric research in Germany, for example at the universities of Munich and Heidelberg, and acutely aware of the disgraceful Nazi treatment of Jewish academics, Mapother urged the Rockefeller Foundation to fund scholarships for distinguished researchers in psychiatric illness to enable them to come to the Maudsley after 1933, to the enormous benefit of his institution.

For example, **Dr Erich Guttmann** (1896–1946) arrived in 1934 from Munich where he had already taught in the clinical research department. His research in London included experiments on himself, and he reported the effects of mescalin and benzedrine in the *Journal of Mental Science* (1936) and the *British Medical Journal* (1937). (For his work on art therapy and schizophrenia, see p. 56.)

An even more distinguished refugee researcher and teacher at the Maudsley was **Dr (Med.) Willy Mayer-Gross**, FRCP, FRS (1889–1961), later regarded as the real co-founder of British psychiatry, who had held an 'extraordinary chair' in phenomenological psychiatry at the University of Heidelberg from 1929 and had edited the neuropsychiatric journal, *Der Nervenarzt* from 1928 to 1934. That did not protect him from having his home seized by the Nazi Party without notice. Awarded a research fellowship at the Maudsley by the Rockefeller Foundation in 1933, **Dr Willy Mayer-Gross** was soon recognised as the outstanding personality there. He too had no patience with psychoanalysis, regarding it as contemporary quackery, and devoted himself to the transformation of psychiatry into a science. 'Naturalised' in 1939, he spent the war years doing two jobs – travelling to and from Dumfries, and in Birmingham, doubling up as a distinguished researcher and consultant in both. Eventually he would be acknowledged for taking British psychiatry so far forward that it would come to play a leading international role in the world of mental health diagnosis and treatment.

As a world figure **Mayer-Gross** would serve the World Health Organization in the 1950s, going out to India to help establish its first psychiatric centre for teaching and research at Bangalore. He wrote on depersonalisation disorder, on the diagnosis and treatment of schizophrenia and Alzheimers, on the therapeutic uses of insulin and mescalin and on the clinical examination of patients with cerebral diseases. He was the first to report that an excessive use of tranquillisers could convert one psychosis into another, and was principal author of the classic textbook *Clinical Psychiatry* (1954). He had been made a Fellow of the Royal Society in 1951. West Germany offered him back his old home in Heidelberg in 1960, but **Mayer-Gross** was still unsure whether or not to accept it when he died suddenly in Birmingham in 1961. His obituary in the *British Journal of Developmental Disabilities, (BJDD)*, called him 'a born teacher' and 'a truly great man'.[15]

The last member of the refugee psychiatric team at the Maudsley in the 1930s was the neuropathologist **Dr (Med.) Alfred Meyer** (1895–1990). **Meyer**'s most significant work was on the anatomical aspects of frontal leucotomy and the structural abnormalities in the brain associated with temporal lobe epilepsy. While he was professor of neuropathology at the Institute of Psychiatry in London, **Meyer** also did pioneering work on the pathology of epilepsy.[16]

Very different was **Dr Erich Wittkower** (1899–1983), who founded not just one but two new branches of psychiatry – psychosomatic medicine and interdisciplinary transcultural psychiatry. **Wittkower** tried to make connections between very disparate theories and world views, 'between psychiatric and social theory, [between] Pavlovian reflexology and Freudian psychoanalysis, [he was a Kleinian] and … between voodoo and psychotherapy'.[17] **Wittkower** had pioneered the field of psychosomatic medicine in Weimar Germany and had published extensively on the emotional factors in asthma, cardiac pain, skin diseases, colitis and tuberculosis. His *The Influence of the Emotions on the Gall Bladder* had been published in Germany in 1929 and his other early publications had included studies of the influence of the emotions on cholesterol levels, hypertension and gastric secretion. After moving to Britain in 1933 (and working at the Maudsley), **Wittkower**'s research projects on the influence of emotional states on various organs were published in the *Journal of Mental Science*. During the Second World War **Wittkower** served in the British Royal Army

Medical Corps, developing its officer selection programme. In 1950 **Wittkower** left London for McGill University, Montreal, where he began his new work, founding interdisciplinary transcultural psychiatry in collaboration with the department of anthropology.[18]

Listed simply as a doctor in the Black Book, both **Dr Paula Heimann** (1899–1982) and her husband, also a physician trained in Heidelberg and Berlin, had belonged to the radical International Society of Doctors Against War in Germany. Between 1924 and 1927 she had trained in psychiatry and from 1929 she had also begun psychoanalytic training under Theodor Reik. In 1933 **Paula Heimann** emigrated to London, becoming secretary to Melanie Klein while also retaking her medical qualifications and working with Klein, who had no medical qualifications, in analysis. In 1938 she became a member of the British Psychoanalytical Society. However, after the war **Heimann** broke with Klein over the subject of the analyst and 'counter-transference', seeing the therapist's emotional response to the patient (and vice versa) not as a taboo but rather as a factor that could contribute positively both to psychological understanding and to therapy.

*

A summary of the areas of medical research in Britain made by Blacklisted refugee scientists after 1933:

Alzheimers: **Willy Mayer-Gross**
Antibiotics: **Ernst Chain**
Asthma: **Erich Wittkower** and **Willy Mayer-Gross**
Blood pressure: **Hugh Blaschko**
Cancer: **Stefan Bach**; **Hans Weil-Malherbe**; **Walter Max Dale**, formerly **Deutsch**; **Franz Bergel**; **Alfred Glucksmann**; **Fritz Jacoby**; **Hans Laser**, **Joseph Weiss**; **Karl Weissenberg**
Cardiac disease: **Erich Wittkower**; **Otto Krayer**
Circulatory disease: **Karl Weissenberg**
Depression: **Hugh Blaschko**

Diptheria: **Hans Schlossmann**
Epilepsy: **Alfred Meyer; Erich Wittkower**
Gall bladder: **Erich Wittkower**
Genetics: **Hans Grueneberg; Ursula Philipp**
Kidney disease: **Albert Neuberger**
Leprosy: **Ernst Brieger**
Liver disease: **Hans Krebs; Philipp Ellinger**
Malaria: **Hans Laser**
Nutrition deficiency: **Gottfried Fraenkel; Albert Neuberger**
Parkinson's disease: **Hugh Blaschko**
Pellagra: **Philipp Ellinger**
Pneumoconiosis: **Guenter Nagelschmidt; Emmy Klieneberger**
Porphyria: **Alfred Neuberger**
Schizophrenia: **Hugh Blaschko; Willy Mayer-Gross**
Tuberculosis: **Erich Wittkower; Ernst Brieger**
Vitamin deficiency: **Hans Krebs; Franz Bergel**
War wounds: **Fritz Jacoby**

25

Biologists – including Physiologists, Geneticists and Zoologists

The polymath **J. B. S. Haldane** (1892–1964), brother of **Naomi Mitchison**, brother-in law of **Dick Mitchison** MP and husband of **Charlotte Haldane**, made many important contributions to evolutionary biology, physiology and genetics as well as to mathematics and the popularisation of science. In 1938 he published *ARP Air Raid Precautions* connecting his physiological research with his personal experience of the impact of stress on the body during air raids in the Spanish Civil War and predicting what the effects would be of air raids on Britain in a future Second World War. Before 1940 **Haldane** had already hypothetised the chemical origin of life, pioneered the new branch of science called 'population genetics', and constructed some of the first human gene 'maps'. These 'genetic maps' were relevant to haemophilia and malaria. None of that either awed or disturbed the Nazis, who were concerned by nothing but **Haldane**'s high-profile Marxism. By 1940, **Haldane** was chairman of the British Communist Party's ***Daily Worker*** and that alone made him a prime target. Despite his allegiance to Lenin and even to Stalin at times, **Haldane** was in many ways anti-authoritarian and would not have been allowed to survive in any totalitarian state. Had he been silenced and/or executed in 1940, we would not have had his *Science and Everyday Life* (1940), his *New Paths in Genetics* (1941) or his *The Biochemistry of Genetics* (1954).[1]

Haldane's friend **Sir Julian Huxley** (FRS 1938) (1887–1975), brother of the writer **Aldous Huxley**, was also a Darwinian evolutionary biologist, stressing the importance of natural selection and believing that the progressive evolution of humane ethics was possible. Secretary of the London Zoological Society from 1935, he had been a national figure on the BBC Brains Trust since 1939 and was a brilliant populariser of science. Originally pro-Soviet, **Julian Huxley** became hostile to Marxist-Leninism as a dogmatic, persecuting alternative religion. In 1940 he was one of the eminent British despatched to the US to try to persuade America, i.e. Roosevelt, to join Britain against Hitler. His views on 'race' were not those of the Nazis, since he pointed out that Jews were not a 'race' any more than were Catholics and he abominated any assumption that one race was superior to another. In 1942 he published his important *Evolution: the Modern Synthesis.* A secular humanist and lifelong internationalist, **Huxley** became the first director general of UNESCO in 1948. 'The unity of mankind … is the main thing.' He also co-founded the Ecological Society, the Society for the Study of Animal Behaviour, the Society for the Study of Evolution and the World Wildlife Fund.[2]

Huxley's predecessor at the London Zoo, **Sir Peter Chalmers Mitchell** CBE (1864–1945), was already famous in 1940 for having planned and established Britain's first open-air zoo, Whipsnade, where animals lived in large enclosures, not in cages. He was in the Black Book presumably because of his identification with Spain, where he had lived since 1936, writing *Counter-attack in Spain* (1937) and reporting on his experience in Malaga as the city fell to the Francoists, in 1938. 'He was popularly regarded as a communist but had no affiliation to any political body.'[3]

Yet another specialist involved with the well-being of animals in zoos was the superintendent of the Zoological Society of London, the parasitologist, **Dr (Med.) G. M. Vevers** (1890–1970), who introduced general principles of hygiene to wild animals in captivity and improvements in diet and housing. What the Gestapo was suspicious of was **Vevers**' honorary office as deputy chairman of the Society for Cultural Relations with Russia and his history of frequent journeys to the Soviet Union in the 1930s collecting rare specimens of animals for British zoos. Moreover, on 11 February 1939, **Vevers** had been one of the signatories to a letter in the *British Medical Journal*, with **Haldane**, **Huxley** and **Marrack**, pleading for London support for the children's food ship and the convoy about to leave for devastated Spain after the civil war.

As for all the distinguished refugee biologists, geneticists, physiologists, zoologists and botanists listed in the Black Book, they were included by the Gestapo simply on racist grounds, unlike their British-born counterparts above, who were seen as being *politically* dangerous to a Nazi occupation. For example the polymath **Gottfried Fraenkel** (1901–1984), a pioneering entomologist who was also an endocrinologist and nutritionist, had undertaken non-political doctoral work on the physiology of marine invertebrates. He had gone on to research insects and above all locusts in Palestine, working in the desert on how to achieve locust control. Driven from his post in the University of Frankfurt's zoology department in 1933, he was awarded a post via the **Academic Assistance Council** as a research associate of **Haldane** at University College London. **Gottfried Fraenkel** only worked in Britain from 1933 to 1948, but during that time he discovered the blood-borne, insect-moulting hormone in the house fly, and the basics of insect behaviour that he published, with D. L. Gunn in 1940, as *The Orientation of Animals*. In the Second World War **Fraenkel** went on to help the British war effort in two ways – he worked at the Pest Infestation Laboratory in Slough, trying to understand stored-grain pests as the way to achieve pest control, and he also used his knowledge of nutrition to help design the (unloved) British National Loaf (a bread made from wholemeal flour with added calcium and vitamins introduced in the Second World War in 1942 as white bread became unavailable). He reported for the **Fabian Society** on future problems of British agriculture after the war and he wrote the chapter on Britain's nutrient requirements. Britain then lost him to the United States where he would be elected to the National Academy of Sciences in 1968. The full implications of **Fraenkel**'s very varied discoveries would not be understood for decades.[4]

It seems fitting to juxtapose **Fraenkel** with the marine biologist **Dr Fabius Gross** (1906–1950). **Gross**'s pioneering work in the Second

World War was to demonstrate how 'semi-enclosed bodies of water can be enriched by the application of agriculture fertilisers', especially nitrogen. He and his co-workers raised the basic fertility of two Scottish semi-lochs, producing impressive increases in the abundance of plankton and benthos, followed by an equally remarkable acceleration in the growth rate of transplanted and resident fish stocks. In other words, between them **Fraenkel** and **Gross** achieved the miracle of loaves and fishes for the food-rationed British in wartime. **Gross**'s work would go on to be of great relevance to the future of fish-farming in Britain. Gross himself was made professor of marine biology at Bangor University in 1948, only to die of leukaemia in 1950.

Dr (Med.) Hans Grueneberg, FRS (1907–1982), a physiologist and geneticist, was a world authority on mouse genetics and specialist on the mouse skeleton. He had fled to Britain in 1933 and, invited by **Haldane**, become honorary research assistant at University College London, working for his D.Sc. He became a British citizen and served as a captain in the Royal Army Medical Corps from 1942 to 1946. After the war **Grueneberg** was reader in genetics, University College London, and honorary director of the Medical Research Council's Experimental Genetics Unit from 1955 to 1972. His *Animal Genetics and Medicine* was published in 1947 and *The Pathology of Development: A Study of Inherited Skeletal Disorders in Animals* in 1963.[5]

A much more tragic – and unnaturally curtailed – scientific life story was that of the pioneering animal psychologist and sensory physiologist **Mathilde Hertz** (1891–1975). Sixteen years older than **Grueneberg**, **Mathilde Hertz**, daughter of the world-famous physicist Heinrich Hertz, the discoverer of electromagnetic waves, had achieved a distinguished scientific career in Germany before 1933. Originally a researcher on the unpolitical subject of primitive mammalian teeth, she had become noted for her study of shape perception and memory in birds and in a variety of animals, as well as on contour and colour recognition in bees. Her emphasis was on learned rather than on instinctive behaviour and would become unfashionable; it would be over fifty years before her work on optical perception in bees would be rediscovered.

Although three of **Mathilde Hertz**'s four grandparents were not Jews, and although she had been brought up a Protestant, she was still classified as a 'non-Aryan' in June 1933 and dismissed from her distinguished scientific post in Berlin. Max Planck tried to come to her rescue by interceding urgently on the grounds of her world-famous scientist father, her own proven outstanding intellectual achievements in the field of mammalian psychology, and the fact that all eight of her great-grandparents had been christened. Nevertheless the Ministry of the Interior remained adamant about her dismissal on racist grounds – '*Rasseforschung*' – according to the new law of 7 April 1933 on the dismissal of 'non-Aryan' professional state employees. Max Planck tried to intervene yet again, asking in November 1933 for **Hertz** to be made an exception, given that she was working in a branch of pioneering scientific research unique in Germany. Surprisingly, she was thereupon permitted to go on teaching. However, the worsening political atmosphere and policies of Nazi Germany put her under ever-increasing stress and it was reported by A. V. Hill to the **Academic Assistance Council** in October 1935 that 'she will not be able to bear the situation much longer'.

Supported by the council, she decided to flee and in January 1936 began research work in zoology in Cambridge, having brought out her elderly mother and her older sister, a physician, to safety. Her mother died, her sister became mentally ill, and **Hertz** found it less and less possible to concentrate on science, once her homeland and her adoptive land were at war with each other. Partly blind, she became an almost destitute, depressed recluse until, after 1957, the Bundesrepublik paid her the compensatory professorial pension that she would have received under normal circumstances. However, she would always feel herself to be an 'abnormality', truly at home nowhere despite hardly leaving Cambridge, where she would die.[6]

Dr (Med.) Hans Honigmann (1891–1943), like **Hans Grueneberg** and **Chalmers Mitchell** and **G. M. Vevers**, combined his concern for non-human animals with concern for humans. Badly wounded in the First World War and with an underlying heart condition, **Honigmann** had at first felt unfit to take on the post-war responsibility of directing the Posen Zoo. He re-trained and practised as a doctor until becoming director of the zoo in Breslau from 1929 to 1935 – before being dismissed on racist grounds. **Julian Huxley** thereupon invited him to emigrate to undertake research in London. In 1937 **Honigmann** became scientific consultant to the newly established Dudley Zoo. He was interned briefly but released and invited to undertake research in the zoological department at the University of Glasgow, where he died in 1944 after suffering several heart attacks.[7]

The biologist wife of the anti-Zionist philosopher Simon Rawidowicz, **Dr Esther Klee-Rawidowicz** (1900–1980), had been a distinguished researcher on cancer in Germany before being forced to leave for Britain. She did not publish again. The outstanding microbiologist **Dr Emmy Klieneberger-Nobel** (1892–1985), made a last dangerous visit to Nazi Germany in 1938 in a desperate failed effort to rescue her mother and sister but they, together with her older brother, were both murdered. Despite that horror, she survived to work productively all the rest of her life at the Lister Institute of Preventive Medicine in London, pioneering the study of mycoplasmas as the agent of primary atypical pneumonia in humans. She was 'never so content as when working at her microscope on some new revelation of bacterial form or structure'.[8]

Honigmann's obituarist, **Dr Otto Loewenstein** (1901–1999), was also in the Black Book and had been a researcher in the zoology department of Birmingham University since 1934; his specialities were comparative sense, nerve physiology and ecology. His Munich doctorate had been on the labyrinth of the minnow, the labyrinth being the organ that controls balance and which in structure is very like the human inner ear. During his time at Glasgow from 1938 to 1952, and at the Marine Biology Laboratory, Plymouth, **Loewenstein** extended his research to the labyrinth of the skate – pioneering work for which he was made an FRS in 1955 and because of which he would be consulted by NASA after his retirement when astronauts were discovered to suffer from space sickness caused by 'abnormal input to the labyrinth'.[9]

The geneticist **Dr Ursula Philipp** (1908–*c*.1977) had almost completed all the demands of her doctoral degree on the genetics of the

Y chromosome in the house fly *Drosophila melanogaster* in Berlin in 1933 when she too had been forced to flee not because of her politics but because she was Jewish. Helped financially by the **Academic Assistance Council** she went to undertake research under **J. B. S. Haldane** in his new department of zoology, at the University of London. **Haldane** was very impressed by her, writing in 1939: 'I find **Dr Philipp** an invaluable assistant. I should like nothing better than to have her permanently attached to me as demonstrator.' She worked there from 1934 to 1947, becoming a British citizen in 1946. From 1947 until her retirement in 1973 she would work as a distinguished geneticist in the zoology department of the University of Newcastle-upon-Tyne, publishing her findings in *Nature* and in the *Eugenics Review*, and in 1977 she was made a Fellow of the British Eugenics Society.[10]

Two other distinguished entomologists were the specialist in diptera (flies) and coloptera (beetles) at the Imperial Institute of Entomology, **Fritz Van Emden** (1896–1958), and **F. E. Zeuner** (1905–1963), who specialised in the hardly political subject of prehistoric entomology and zoology, geological archaeology and palaeontology. He would publish *Dating the Past* in 1947 and *A History of Domesticated Animals* in 1963. Similarly unpolitical was the work of the botanist **Professor Ida Levisohn** (1901–*c.*1979), who found a place immediately in 1933 as a researcher at Bedford College for Women, part of the University of London. Her speciality was forestry and fungi, and she and her director, Dr M. C. Rayner, worked closely with the pioneer of the organic soil movement, Sir Albert Howard. In 1937–8 they had together corroborated his findings in India and Ceylon regarding the exhaustion of the soil there through the use of artificial fertiliser on tea plants, and the far better health of the roots of those tea plants treated with organic compost. **Ida Levisohn**'s speciality was mycorhiza and mycology (the study of ferns) and she researched fungal infection versus growth stimulation in the roots of pine and spruce, as well as hardwoods, for the British Forestry Commission, as well as researching root material and already fixed roots from abroad, publishing her findings in *Nature*, the *Empire Forestry Review* and the *New Scientist*. After her retirement she moved to Israel.

26

Chemists

Dr Jacob Joseph Bikerman(n) (1898–2005) was a great survivor – a fact he put down to chance; he was, he later wrote, a 'favourite of fate'. Born in Odessa to a Jewish, anti-Tsarist, political journalist father, **Bikermann** had experienced his first anti-Jewish pogrom at the age of 7, after which his family had resettled in St Petersburg. There his father had been arrested and imprisoned for short periods before the Bolshevik Revolution. That revolution and its chaotic, violent, hungry aftermath had coincided with **Bikermann**'s student years. He had managed, nevertheless, to concentrate on physical chemistry and to undertake experimental research despite the extreme shortage of fuel, electricity, water and scientific supplies. He had completed his studies by 1921 but could not receive a university degree because at that time degrees had been abolished by the revolution. In 1922 the family decided to try to emigrate by using false papers pretending that they were repatriated Polish refugees. Once in Poland they then got more forged papers, now passing themselves off as German Jews, in order to enter Germany. **Bikermann** became a writer in German on developments in chemical research while he also undertook post-graduate research at the University of Berlin.

With the Nazis becoming ever more vociferous and finally gaining supreme power in Germany, however, it was time to migrate once again, and the still stateless **Jacob Bikermann** moved to research fellowships, first in Manchester under Professor **Polanyi** and then, not happily, in Cambridge, where he had differences with his academic colleagues and was frustrated by the British government's unwillingness to recognise that there was an imminent Nazi threat to world peace. Between 1939 and 1945 **Bikermann** worked in wartime British industry as director of research into glass fibres and metals as well as for the Printing and Allied Trades Research Association. In 1945 he made his final emigration – to the USA. **Bikermann**'s chief scientific interest was in the puzzle of friction and adhesion – he became a member of the Faraday Society and the British Society of Rheology. He and his brother would publish their joint biography as *The Two Bikermans* in 1975.[1]

In contrast, **Dr Hans Leo Lehmann** (1907–*c.*1993) could not have led a more stable, apparently untroubled, life after his initial uprooting from Germany in 1933. He was born and remained an observant Orthodox Jew. His parents survived through the twentieth century by having emigrated to Palestine in the 1930s, while he himself settled in Golders Green, the heart of Jewish London, and became a researcher at University College. **Lehmann** had a good understanding of English, French and Italian as well as German. His first specialist fields were physical chemistry, photochemistry and optical activity. He became a Fellow of the Royal Institute of Chemistry and set himself up as a consulting analytical chemist with his own laboratory in Stamford Hill. There he joined forces with a fellow German Jewish refugee, Max Sondheimer, a glue manufacturer and he, **Lehmann**, would join 'Sondal Glue' as their consulting chemist in the early 1950s, until retiring in the mid 1970s. Meanwhile **Lehmann** had become a British citizen and had made his permanent home in Epsom, where he hosted the local Jewish community and co-founded the Epsom and District Synagogue. Very interested in English history, architecture and literature, **Hans Lehmann** became a passionate, scholarly local historian, publishing *The History of Epsom Spa* (1973), *The Residential Copyholds of Epsom 1663–1925* (1987), and, with Maurice Exwood, *The Journals of William Schellink's Travels in England 1661–1663* (1993). No one could have been a more dedicated student of his adopted land.

The dashing, charismatic, internationally famous scientific star and controversial polemicist, **Professor Michael Polanyi**, FRS (1891–1976), was a complete contrast. Born into a family of secular Jews in Ukrainian Hungary, **Polanyi** had moved first to Budapest where he studied medicine and then on to Germany where he studied chemistry, actually managing to produce his Ph.D. dissertation on adsorption during a period of sick leave from the Austro-Hungarian Army's Medical Corps in the First World War. Encouraged by **Einstein**, **Polanyi** completed his doctorate from the University of Budapest in 1919. But by 1920 he left the political chaos of post-war Hungary and returned to Germany, working under Fritz Haber at the Kaiser Wilhelm Institute in Berlin. In 1923 he converted to Christianity. **Michael Polanyi** was a scientific polymath who, having already laid the mathematical foundation of fibre diffraction analysis in 1921, then also worked on chemical kinetics, X-ray diffraction, and the adsorption of gases at solid surfaces. In 1934, his application of Volterra's theory of dislocations to the plastic deformation of ductile materials was a critical insight in developing the field of solid mechanics. Given the context of the crazy inflation and Great Depression then being endured in Weimar Germany, **Polanyi** also became interested in economics. The Nazi triumph in 1933 led to his migration from Germany to the University of Manchester where he was at once offered a chair in physical chemistry. In 1944 **Polanyi** was elected a Fellow of the Royal Society and, because of his increasing concern with the sociology and philosophy of science, the University of Manchester created a new chair for him in social science in 1948. **Polanyi** was a committed anti-Marxist, accusing Marx of crude reductionism, and he totally opposed any and all central planning, whether economic or scientific, by the state.[2]

A scientist who never strayed into speculative economic or political theorising but who nevertheless was suspect for his exceptional use to applied science was the Blacklisted chemist **Dr Robert Schnurmann** (1904–1995). **Schnurmann**, born in Stuttgart, had studied mathematics and sciences in Heidelberg, Frankfurt and Goettingen before successfully completing his research on electrolytes at the latter's Institute for Physical Chemistry in 1927. He had then become one of the four assistants under Otto Stern at the University of Hamburg – until 1933 when he was dismissed on racist grounds. In 1935 he fled to Sweden, taking a post at the Stockholm Royal Higher Technical

Institute, but then moved to the Physical Chemistry Laboratory at Cambridge in 1937. From 1939 to 1945 **Schnurmann** contributed to the British war effort in several different practical areas. First he worked in the research laboratory of the London Midland and Scottish Railway Company in Derby, producing conclusions on train traction and brake wear in 1941 that are still being cited today. Next he became chief physicist at the Manchester Oil Refinery Ltd (publishing 'On the size of Gas bubbles in Liquids' in 1943) and then working at Esso Research Ltd. Finally, he taught at the department of chemical engineering at the University of Birmingham until his retirement at the age of 71, when he became an active honorary research fellow. He was also a prolific contributor to scientific journals such as *Nature* and *Engineering*.

Professor Dr Alexander Schoenberg (1892–1985), had a similarly productive life, authoring hundreds of research articles in English and German, although he did not stay in Britain but moved from the University of Edinburgh's medical faculty after 1937 to the University of Cairo. He returned in 1958 to West Germany where he was reinstated as professor emeritus of organic chemistry (retired) – after which he continued to undertake scholarly scientific research for several decades. His outstanding contribution was his *Preparative Organic Chemistry* (1958).

Quite one of the most distinguished as well as one of the oldest researchers in physical chemistry, biochemistry and colloid chemistry was **Professor Dr Isidor Traube** (1860–1943), who was aged 73 when he was driven from the personal chair that he had occupied at the University of Berlin for forty years, only to be literally locked out of his own laboratory. The University of Edinburgh, hearing of this outrage, promptly offered **Traube** a chair in physical chemistry and gave him a personal laboratory for colloid chemical research together with a place to live nearby. **Traube** worked on into his eighties and died in Edinburgh. Just one of his significant findings, among over 200 publications, concerned the purifying and disinfecting properties of hypochlorites in water treatment. He also undertook valuable research on the action of drugs on the body.[3]

The son of the outstanding Austrian writer Jacob Wassermann (author of *Mein Weg als Deutscher und Jude*, (1921) and *The Enigma of Kaspar Hauser* (1908), whose books had been banned and burned in Germany in 1933), **Albert Wassermann** (1901–1971) had already shown great promise as a young medical researcher in Germany. But in 1933, after the Nazi accession to power, he left for Britain. He worked first at University College London until 1935, then as lecturer at the University of Southampton from 1936 to 1939, being awarded the degree of doctor of science from the University of London in 1939. During the war **Wassermann** worked on secret war-related research projects for Imperial College and for the Ministry of Home Security – possibly on antidotes to poisons in the event of invasion and occupation. A forceful, somewhat eccentric personality, he would become professor of chemistry at the University of London, continuing to undertake valuable research after retirement.[4]

One of the last among the distinguished Blacklisted chemists is **Dr Gerhard Weiler** (1899–1995). A psychiatrist's son from a wealthy Jewish German family that had converted to Christianity in 1905, **Weiler** had studied chemistry. In the 1920s he and his doctor wife opened **Dr Weiler's** Diagnostic Institute in Berlin, a leading forensics laboratory, used both by hospitals and by police murder investigations, which pioneered microscopic analysis. The moment that Hitler became chancellor, however, both the **Weilers** agreed that they must emigrate and start again in Britain where there were already other family members. In 1934, Professor Robert Robinson offered **Dr Gerhard Weiler** facilities to set up a micro-analytical laboratory at the University of Oxford, since that process was not yet available in England. But first **Weiler** went back to Nazi Germany to make sure that his wife, his sister-in-law and his father got out safely. In 1940 **Weiler** was not only in the Gestapo Black Book as a *Staatsfeind* – enemy of Germany – he was also interned for several months as an 'enemy alien' by the British at Huyton Camp near Liverpool, guarded by soldiers with fixed bayonets. After his release, **Weiler** continued during the war with his forensic research work for Oxford University, and after 1945 he ran a private forensic laboratory in Oxford.

On his death in 1995 he left much of his distinguished art collection to the Ashmolean Museum. One additional fact about **Dr Gerhard Weiler** is that only in 2012 was it discovered that, unbeknownst either to himself or to Justin Welby, he was in fact a cousin of the Archbishop of Canterbury, who had had the same German Jewish great-grandparents, named Weiler.[5]

Finally, among the chemists was **Professor Dr Joseph Joshua Weiss** (1905–1972), an important but now forgotten Jewish Austrian pioneer in the field of radiation and photochemistry. In his twenties he had assisted Fritz Haber at the Kaiser Wilhelm Institute in Berlin where they discovered the Haber-Weiss reaction. **Weiss** fled Germany for Cambridge in 1933, gained his Ph.D. in 1935 from University College London, and in 1937 began teaching at King's College, Durham, which later became the University of Newcastle. There he worked on radiation biology research and was appointed professor of radiation chemistry in 1956; in 1970 he was awarded the Marie Curie Medal of the Curie Institute. The impossibility of always separating biology from chemistry is made clear in that **Weiss**'s obituary was published in the *International Journal of Radiation Biology* (October 1972).

27

Physicists, Astro-physicists, Crystallographers, Geo-physicists and Nuclear Physicists

As with the British biochemists **J. R. Marrack**, **J. B. S. Haldane**, and **Julian Huxley**, the Gestapo were almost only interested in those British-born physicists who were politically active anti-Nazis in the 1930s.

The crystallographer **J. D. Bernal**, FRS (1901–1971), although he had been born and raised as a devout Catholic in Ireland, and despite being descended from Sephardic Jews on his father's side, had become a convert to communism at Cambridge in the 1920s. Many people could not understand how he, one of the outstanding and most influential scientific thinkers of the age, proved so uncritical of Marxism, Lysenkoism[1] and even Stalinism. It seems he was someone who could not live without a vision of hope, and replaced hope for his own soul in eternity with hope for all humanity in this world. **Bernal** never gave up needing to believe that a global, socialist application of science would abolish poverty, make the deserts bloom, solve the energy problem and finally ensure world peace. In his insistence on the need for centrally organised scientific research, planned by the state to answer human needs, **Bernal** was the polar opposite of the anti-Marxist scientist and social theorist **Michael Polanyi**.

In the 1920s **Bernal** developed the methodology that enabled the X-ray crystal-structure determination of complex molecules, and his Cambridge laboratory rapidly evolved into an international research centre. He started work on the structure of water and proteins, marking the dawn of molecular biology. He and Dorothy Hodgkin took the first X-ray photographs of hydrated protein crystals 'giving one of the first glimpses of the world of molecular structure that underlies [all] living things'.[2] **Bernal** was an early influence on the founding of the European Molecular Biology Laboratory. In 1937 he became professor of physics at Birkbeck, University of London, and was made a Fellow of the Royal Society.

At the same time he had become convinced, during the Spanish Civil War, of the inevitability of a world war with fascism, and the moment that war was declared **Bernal** joined the Ministry of Home Security. His application of science to the British war effort would prove important. First he and Solly Zuckerman analysed the effects of bombing on people and buildings, demonstrating, with reference to Birmingham and Hull, that city bombing produced little ultimate disruption and that production was only affected by direct hits on factories. **Bernal** tried, unsuccessfully, to convince Lindemann and hence **Churchill** that Bomber Command's exaggerated claims for the effectiveness of the bombing of German cities would lead to a total waste of manpower and resources. He went on to work with Lord Mountbatten, Chief of Combined Operations. Most important of all, **Bernal** helped ensure that the Normandy landings would not repeat the disaster of the Dieppe raid. He achieved this by detailed mapping of the Normandy beaches without arousing German suspicions – he used library research and aerial surveys to chart every rock, mine and weak spot so reliably that tanks and trucks were able to get ashore. He himself landed on D-Day, testing the accuracy of his reports and trying to help boats floundering on the rocks.

After the war **Bernal**, together with Frederic Joliot-Curie, founded the World Peace Council, which, some think, may have influenced Krushchev during the 1962 Cuban missile crisis. **Bernal**'s influence in Britain and the United States was compromised during the Cold War by his refusal to criticise the Soviet Union, although he had to be respected for his scientific achievements. Horrified by the possibility of a nuclear war, he founded Scientists for Peace, the forerunner of CND. **Bernal**'s seminal writings include *The Social Function of Science* (1938/9) and *Science in History* (1954).[3]

Like **Bernal**, **Patrick M. Blackett**, OM, CH (1897–1974), president of the Royal Society, was not only an outstanding physicist but also a lifelong socialist. Originally from a conventional upper-middle-class home and with a training in the Royal Navy, **Blackett** was converted to left-wing politics by his friend **Kingsley Martin** in the early 1920s at Cambridge, where he studied mathematics and physics before working under Ernest Rutherford. He was a researcher for ten years in experimental physics at the Cavendish Laboratory, concentrating on particle physics and cosmic rays, and became a leading expert on anti-matter. **Blackett** was awarded the Nobel Prize for Physics in 1948 for his investigation of cosmic rays through his invention of the counter-controlled cloud chamber. Alongside his scientific work at Cambridge, Birkbeck College, the University of London and the University of Manchester, **Blackett** identified himself as a **Fabian** socialist; he campaigned for the Labour Party and was sympathetic to Soviet Russia. It would have been his socialist activism that alerted the Gestapo to Blacklist him and he in his turn did everything in his power to help ousted German Jewish scientists to start new lives in British universities.

Blackett's work in the Second World War was outstanding – 'few men did more to win the war against Nazi Germany'.[4] As early as 1935 he was arguing that resources should concentrate on the early installation of radar for air defence and in August 1940 he became scientific adviser to Anti-Aircraft Command. He also redesigned the Mark XIV bombsight, allowing bombs to be released without a level bombing run. In March 1941 he became head of Operational Research in RAF Coastal Command, where he brought about the improved survival odds of huge convoys by mapping out the radar defence of merchant ships against German U-boats in the bitter, vital 'Battle of the Atlantic', on which so much of Britain's food depended.

In December 1941 **Blackett** became chief advisor to the Admiralty on Naval Operational Research, and in early 1942 he converted the Americans to applying science to their waging of the war. As a one-man dissenting voice on the MAUD Committee in June 1941, he opposed the British production of an atomic bomb, and during

1942 and 1943 he also opposed, without success, the ineffective saturation bombing offensive by RAF Bomber Command that aimed to terrorise German cities by targeting civilians. Finally, by May 1944, **Blackett**'s strategy of targeting U-boats transiting the Bay of Biscay at last led to Allied victory in the 'Battle of the Atlantic', thus enabling D-Day. Working a seven-day week for months on end, utilising radio direction findings, Enigma decryptions, aircraft and ships' sightings, prisoner interrogations, information on individual U-boat captains' tactics, and always utilising probability theory and statistics, **Blackett** and his team of brilliant mathematicians and scientists at last won the anti-U-boat war. 'Selfless, incorruptible and absolutely determined to let the facts lead where they would ... they had an acute sense of responsibility for the injustices of the world.'[5]

After the Second World War, **Blackett** was too left-wing even for the 1945 Labour Government because of his opposition to Britain's development and possession of the H-bomb and because he advocated a neutralist foreign policy during the Cold War. He published *Fear, War, and the Bomb: the Military and Political Consequences of Atomic Energy* (1948), and, in 1956, *Atomic Weapons and East/West Relations.* In the meantime he also turned his considerable gifts to the development needs of India, believing, like **Bernal**, that it was the duty of scientists to ensure a decent life for all humanity. He advocated allocating one per cent of Britain's GDP to economic aid in order to contribute to the struggle against underdevelopment, and he co-founded the Overseas Development Institute. Eventually **Blackett** influenced Harold Wilson's creation of a Ministry of Technology in 1964 and its concentration on a revival of the British computer industry. Finally, he made an important contribution in the field of geophysics by helping to establish the existence of continental drift and tectonic plates. For all these achievements, it is fortunate that **Patrick Blackett** was not eliminated by the SS in September 1940.[6]

The two other eminent British physicists considered politically unacceptable by the Gestapo were **Sir Sidney John Chapman** and **C. P. Snow**. The geo-physicist **Chapman** (1888–1970), a pioneer of solar-terrestrial physics, had already been elected Fellow of the Royal

Society in 1919 because of his discoveries relating to the thermal diffusion of gases, the electrical conductivity of the ionosphere, the global effect of lunar tides and the morphology of storms. **Chapman** was a Christian pacifist in the First World War but in the 1930s his staunch internationalism and open revulsion at the phenomenon of Nazism caused him to renounce his pacifism. He did everything in his power to help refugee Jewish scientists find suitable posts in Britain. During the Second World War **Chapman** undertook civilian war work as well as military operational research as part of his commitment to defeat Nazism. In 1953 he resigned his Oxford chair in order to establish a research school in geophysics in Alberta, Canada and, in 1955, a High Altitude Observatory in Boulder, Colorado. He also taught at the Universities of Istanbul and Ibadan and organised the International Geophysical Year of 1957–8. **Chapman** researched indefatigably right up to his death, leaving behind a reputation for integrity, persistence and simplicity.[7]

C. P. Snow (1905–1980), later Lord Snow, CBE, was a close friend both of **J. D. Bernal** and **Patrick Blackett** throughout the 1930s and must therefore have been suspect in Gestapo eyes through his left-wing associations. He wrote admiringly on both men, on **Bernal** in his early novel *The Search* (1934) and in '**J. D. Bernal**, a personal portrait' in Goldsmith and Mackay (eds), *The Science of Science* (1966, pp. 19–31), while he used **Blackett** as one of the sources for his character Francis Getliffe in his multi-volume novel *Strangers and Brothers*, published in 1940. 'More unanimously than any other intellectual group, the scientists were anti-Nazi. [In] the thirties one had more of a sense of good and evil struggling against one another than one has today … It was as black and white as that sort of thing can be. Hitler wasn't a very nice thing.'[8]

C. P. Snow was born into a lower-middle-class home, his father a clerical worker in a Leicestershire shoe factory, and he had got to Cambridge thanks to scholarships. He had completed his Ph.D. by the age of 25 and was a postgraduate research physicist at the Cavendish Laboratory in Cambridge as well as a Fellow and (later nominal) tutor at Christ's College, Cambridge from 1930 to 1945. **Snow** became director of technical personnel for the wartime Ministry of Labour from 1942 to 1945 where he 'expedited the mobilizing of scientists for work on radar, the atomic bomb, and other high priority military technology'.[9] He became famous for his 1956 essay 'The Two Cultures', in which he deplored the unapologetic ignorance of literary intellectuals about modern science while scientists insisted, in their turn, on the special moral and social responsibility of so-called 'pure' scientists. **Snow** became a Labour peer in 1964.[10]

The two very eminent atomic physicists, both of them Nobel Prize laureates, **Sir William Lawrence Bragg** (1890–1971), and **Professor Sir George Paget Thomson**, FRS (1892–1975), would seem to have been selected for the Black List *not* for their politics, which were not notably anti-fascist, but because of the focus of their research. The Germans would have been particularly anxious to interrogate **Paget Thomson** on the progress made by British scientists in producing an atomic bomb, which he, as chairman of the MAUD Committee from 1940 to 1941, had concluded was feasible.[11] And for his part, the outstanding crystallographer **Bragg** brought about an important scientific revolution. 'Through his development and promotion of X-ray crystallography … **Bragg** transformed our understanding of the natural world: modern mineralogy, metallurgy, chemistry and molecular biology were completely reconstructed as a result of his discoveries.'[12]

The Gestapo were not omniscient; they overlooked many of the German scientists who had been dismissed and expelled after 1933 for their Jewish ancestry and then moved to Britain. Wilhelm Feldberg, Otto Frisch, Rudolf Peierls, Kurt Mendelssohn and Max Perutz, for example, are not in the Black Book, whether through sheer ignorance on the part of the German Secret Police, or because those researchers had not yet become sufficiently eminent to warrant suspicion and retribution. Nazi Germany itself did not want 'Jewish science' but it also did not wish any hostile country to reap the benefits of German education and expertise.

I shall note first the Blacklisted refugee physicists who had nothing to do with the creation of the atom bomb and then focus on those who did help create it. The extraordinary polymath **Professor**

Dr Karl Weissenberg (1893–1976) held professorships in four different sciences over his lifetime – in physics at the universities of Berlin and Southampton, in physical-chemistry at the University of Paris, in civil engineering at Columbia University, New York, and in human anatomy at the medical school of South Carolina. **Weissenberg** was the only refugee scientist for whom **Einstein** ever made an individual plea, prompted by the ***Society for the Protection of Science and Learning*** when **Weissenberg** was interned in England. Aged 47, the oldest prisoner and therefore the 'camp father', **Weissenberg** became alarmingly ill in Huyton Camp, Liverpool in or around 1940. **Einstein** then testified that **Weissenberg**, whom he had known for many years, had 'an exceptionally fine and reliable character and [was] a man of high gifts. His health seems to be seriously impaired so that prolongation of internment would endanger his life. Taking every responsibility for his loyalty to Great Britain, I appeal to you to intervene on his behalf.' **Weissenberg** was released and reapplied for naturalisation as a British citizen in March 1940. He was granted it only in 1946 when he was 53.

Who was he? Born in Vienna, **Weissenberg** studied mathematics, physics and chemistry, together with some law and medicine, at the universities of Vienna, Berlin and Jena, before gaining his Ph.D. in mathematics in 1916 and becoming professor of physics at the Kaiser Wilhelm Institute, Berlin. Having already made fundamental contributions to both theoretical and applied physics in crystallography and rheology, the study of the deformation and flow of materials, his approach to scientific research was always so interdisciplinary that the Kaiser Wilhelm Institute had needed to fund a special *professor extraordinarius* post for him. Nevertheless, he was still dismissed in 1933 for being Jewish. **Weissenberg** fled Germany, first for the Sorbonne in Paris from 1933 to 1934, before becoming guest professor in physics at Southampton University from 1934 to 1940. Among the many practical applications of his discoveries were the measurement of blood circulation in various diseases, the dosimetry of X-rays in the treatment of cancer, and the localisation by X-rays of foreign matters in the human body.

During the Second World War, **Weissenberg** worked both as liaison officer for the British Cotton Research Association in Manchester and as scientific adviser to the petroleum warfare department at Imperial College, London. After the war he became head of the mathematics division at the Rayon Research Association, and senior scientific adviser to the Ministry of Supply at Harwell, London and in Cambridge. He took up brief consultancies in the United States, working at American hospitals, universities, government departments and industries, including Shell. The papers of this phenomenal man, including articles, lectures, notes, correspondence, photographs and textile samples are held at the Churchill Archives centre, Churchill College, Cambridge.[13]

The distinguished astronomer and astro-physicist **Dr Arthur Beer** (1900–1980), was also helped by his association with **Einstein**, as well as by his distinguished German record as a tide astronomer and populariser of science. His *News from Nature and Technology* in Germany was the first science programme ever broadcast by radio. **Beer** emigrated to the UK in 1934. He carried out astrophysical research at the Cambridge Solar Physics Observatory from 1934 to 1937. He then became a seismologist at the Kew Observatory from 1941 to 1945. Until his retirement in 1967, **Beer** was senior assistant observer at Cambridge Observatories. Meanwhile, as a member of the Royal Astronomical Society and the International Astronomical Union, he edited a magisterial survey of historical and current astronomy and continued to be a successful populariser of science in English.[14]

Eugen Glueckauf, FRS (1906–1981), was an expert on the peaceful use of nuclear energy and on the problem of nuclear waste. Dismissed from his research post at the Technische Hochschule, Berlin, in 1933, he began a new life in Britain first as a research assistant at Imperial College, London, from 1934 to 1939, before moving to become research associate at the University of Durham in 1939, and then Mackinnon research student of the Royal Society from 1942 to 1944. In 1947 **Glueckauf** moved to become a researcher, first as group leader and then as branch head, at the atomic energy research establishment at Harwell. In 1961 he published his book *Atomic Energy*

Waste, which became the standard reference text on a vital subject.[15] He remained a consultant at Harwell from his official retirement until his death.

The theoretical physicist **Professor Dr Max Born**, FRS (1882–1970) (wrongly spelled **Brond** by the Gestapo in the Black Book), was a ground-breaking thinker, mathematician, and nuclear physicist who worked in quantum mechanics, optics and solid state physics. His lifelong friend **Einstein** wrote to him around 1919: 'Theoretical physics will flourish wherever you happen to be; there is no other **Born** … in Germany today.' In 1924 he was nominated for the first time (by **Einstein**) for the Nobel Prize. But in May 1933 **Born** was suspended as a Jew from his university chair at Goettingen, stripped of his doctorate and German citizenship. He fled to Britain where he published his two classics, *The Restless Universe* and *Atom Physics*. He was made a Fellow of the Royal Society in March 1939 and was 'naturalised' on 31 August 1939. He was professor of natural philosophy at the University of Edinburgh until 1952 where he promoted the teaching of mathematical physics. Up until September 1939, **Born** struggled to get as many of his endangered friends and relatives as he could out of Nazi Germany in time. He refused to take any part in the creation of the atomic bomb – the only scientist (besides Lise Meitner) to so refuse. From the first he thought it was a wicked enterprise, and indeed from the beginning of the war he had disapproved of the Allies' massive air attacks on German cities with conventional bombs. After the war his beliefs led him to be active in the movement of physicists and others to ban the use of atomic weapons.[16] In 1954, after many scientific nominations, **Max Born** was awarded the Nobel Prize for his fundamental research in quantum mechanics. In his acceptance speech **Born** declared: 'I believe that ideas such as absolute certitude … final truth, etc. are figments of the imagination … [inadmissible] in science. … [The] belief in a single truth and in being the possessor thereof is the root cause of all evil in the world.'

In 1955, aged 73, **Born** was one of the world's most distinguished scientific signatories to the **Russell-Einstein** Manifesto, warning us of the dangers posed ever since Hiroshima and Nagasaki by our new weapons of mass destruction. The manifesto called on the world's scientists and political leaders to 'Remember your humanity and forget the rest.'

Dr Herbert Froehlich, FRS (1905–1991) was 'a Picasso-like figure'[17] in the world of distinguished twentieth-century theoretical physicists. It was characteristic of him that he used the back of his letter of dismissal in 1933 to do some useful scientific calculations. His family escaped from Germany to Palestine and he then went, invited by Yakov Fraenkel, to the Physics Research Institute in Leningrad, only to be expelled at the beginning of Stalin's Great Purge. He fled to England in June 1935 where, after being granted a one-month visitor permit, he was supported for twelve months by the **Academic Assistance Council.** Interrupted by a brief period of internment as an 'enemy alien', **Froehlich** worked under Neville Mott at the University of Bristol until 1948. In 1948 **Froehlich** became professor of theoretical physics at the University of Liverpool and then, in 1973, professor of solid-state physics at the University of Salford. He was twice nominated for a Nobel Prize – in part because his thinking on dielectrics had inspired important work on superconductivity. **Fraenkel**'s pioneering work on semi-conductors 'later [dominated] every aspect of electronics and computers ... His most important legacy was the pioneering introduction of quantum field theoretical methods into condensed matter physics in 1952 which revolutionised the development of the subject.' He even discovered unexpected connections between physics and biology.[18]

Refugee Nuclear Physicists and the Bomb

Sir Francis Simon (1893–1956), was an Iron Cross First Class German officer in the First World War, having been twice wounded on the Western Front and been one of the earliest casualties of poison gas. The exact contemporary of **Karl Weissenberg**, **Francis Simon** was made associate professor *extraordinarius* of the Physical-Chemistry Institute at the University of Berlin in 1927. His special field was low temperature physics and the laws of thermodynamics. Despite his

Iron Cross and the acknowledgement of his exceptional contribution to physics in Germany, **Simon** knew he would not be able to work under the Nazis and he was recruited by Lindemann to join the Clarendon Laboratory in Oxford, early in 1933, backed by a research grant from ICI. Having bribed a fortunately corrupt customs official, **Simon** was even able to take his research equipment out of Germany and so continue his pioneering work in low temperature physics. '[It] was with one of the earliest **Simon** expansion liquefiers installed at the Clarendon Laboratory … in 1933 that helium was first liquefied in Britain.'[19]

Although he had been a naturalised British subject since 1938, and was elected a Fellow of the Royal Society during the Blitz, **Francis Simon**, as an ex-alien, was not at first able to be accepted officially for secret war work on radar. Determined, however, to combat Hitler, 'together with other refugee scientists, notably R. E. Peierls and O. R. Frisch, he became interested in the possibility of an atomic bomb and began to work on the problem before it had become an official project'.[20] Eventually, in 1940, he was commissioned by the MAUD Committee chairman, **Paget Thomson**, to investigate the feasibility of separating uranium-235 by gaseous diffusion. 'Simon's resulting conclusions on the separation of uranium isotopes were transferred to the Manhattan Project and was the basis of the process that produced sufficient U235 to make the atomic bomb.'[21] **Simon** spent the latter part of the Second World War working at Los Alamos. He died suddenly in 1956, too soon to be convinced by a younger generation of Germans that the Nazi spirit had really been exorcised.[22]

The author of the *FRS Memoir* on **Francis Simon**, **Nicholas Kurti**, CBE, FRS (1908–1998), was himself one of the most gifted experimental nuclear physics postgraduates whom **Simon** had brought with him to Oxford. He too would be 'naturalised' just before the war and would carry out valuable work on separating the isotopes of uranium before joining what came to be known as the Manhattan Project on making the atomic bomb in the USA. On his return to Oxford after the war, **Kurti** concentrated on low temperature physics. 'His crowning glory, in 1956, was the successful … demagnetisation of nuclear spins with cooling down to one millionth of a degree Kelvin.'[23] This made him world-famous and he was elected a Fellow of the Royal Society. **Kurti** was an inspiring research supervisor and played an important part in the development of cryogenics in the UK as well as contributing to the founding of the Oxford Science Park.[24]

Dr Heinrich ('Heini') Kuhn (1904–1994), was another of the outstanding physicists recruited by Lindemann in 1934 for the Clarendon Laboratory in Oxford. An expert in optics, '**Kuhn** developed a world centre for innovative high-resolution spectroscopy and laid the foundations' for Oxford's atomic and laser department'.[25] Although 'naturalised' in 1939, **Kuhn**, like **Simon**, was still regarded as too much of a security risk as an 'ex-alien' to work on radar in wartime, and so, ironically, he was made available instead to join **Simon**'s team working on isotope separation of uranium for the atom bomb. Around December 1943 to January 1944 he too went to the United States to join in work on the Manhattan Project. In 1950 **Kuhn** became the first refugee to be made a Fellow of Balliol College, Oxford and he was elected a Fellow of the Royal Society in 1954. His authoritative *Atomic Spectra* was published in 1962.[26]

Dr Heinz London, FRS (1907–1970), the son of a mathematics professor, was yet another experimental and theoretical nuclear physicist, working on superconductivity and low temperature physics. Part of the team of his mentor and professor in Germany, **Franz Simon**, **London** left Germany in 1933 to join **Simon** in Oxford. Like **Kuhn** he was interned but then released to work on the atom bomb project, in **London**'s case in Bristol and in Birmingham universities. He was 'naturalised' in 1942. His special focus was the problem of isotope separation. Like **Glueckauf**, **Heinz London** worked at the new Harwell atomic energy research establishment after the war, his achievement being to revolutionise low temperature physics.[27]

Finally, and tragically, both for himself and for the world, there was **Dr Leo Szilard** (1898–1964). Born to a prosperous, non-observant Jewish family in Budapest, and himself a convert to Protestantism, **Szilard** had graduated in civil engineering from the Technical University of Budapest because Jews could not expect a career in physics in

Hungary. He fought briefly on the losing Austro-Hungarian side in the First World War, and then found himself, a young socialist idealist, in an economically chaotic, increasingly anti-Semitic Budapest where he was beaten up more than once outside the university for being a Jew. He packed all his belongings into a suitcase, and left, ostensibly for Vienna, but arriving eventually in Berlin in January 1920. Once there, **Leo Szilard** talked his way into the Kaiser Wilhelm Institute and even into being taught statistical mechanics by **Einstein**. The two of them designed an electromagnetic pump that would, much later, be used in the cooling systems of nuclear reactors. A quite brilliant polymath, **Szilard** took courses in calculus, applied mathematics and the theory of temperature while also doing electro-technical experiments and completing his doctoral thesis, as well as writing a paper on thermodynamic equilibrium which is now considered to have been the forerunner of information theory. Living in poverty as an eternal student, '**Szilard** was a true intellectual wanderer, forever flitting from one subject to another, preoccupied with understanding life itself and devising solutions to the world's problems.'[28]

When 1933 presented the problem of triumphant Nazism in Germany, **Szilard**, influenced by a personal plea from William Beveridge, in or around 1935 left Berlin for London in order to '[throw] his energies into making contacts with people who could help [other] refugees'.[29] Having worked tirelessly to help set up the British ***Society for the Protection of Science and Learning*** in London (and having been sufficiently prominent to be included in the Black Book by the Gestapo, who believed he was still in Britain in 1939), **Szilard** had in fact left London in 1937 for the United States. There he joined other refugee scientists as a guest in the physics laboratories of Columbia University, New York.

In January 1939 the scientific world was horrified by the news that German scientists had succeeded in splitting a uranium atom in a process later known as nuclear fission. In theory a chain reaction could now be created leading to the possible construction of an atomic bomb. Otto Hahn, appalled by what he had done for humanity and personally suicidal, told Paul Rosbaud who then informed

Frank Foley, who told the British government, that the German nuclear scientists were still nowhere near able to produce an atomic bomb in the foreseeable future. Did **Robert Vansittart**, chief diplomatic adviser to the government suppress that information? Did the Foreign Office and the British government not dare to believe it? In any event, whatever the explanation, the nuclear physicists in Britain and the United States were not informed about Hahn's assurance. The refugee scientists, above all **Leo Szilard**, felt confronted by what they believed to be the imminent probability of an atom bomb being at Hitler's disposal.

In July 1939 **Szilard** conveyed his mistaken conviction to **Einstein** and in August 1939 he drafted a letter for **Einstein** to sign and send to President Roosevelt, alerting him to the military implications of the new discovery about uranium and a future nuclear chain reaction. This was then spelled out 'as a possible source of bombs with a destructiveness vastly greater than anything now known'.[30] In March 1940 **Einstein** wrote again to Roosevelt, but it was only on the eve of Pearl Harbor, December 1941, that the American government embarked on the Manhattan Project on which **Simon, Kurti** and **Kuhn** would all work.[31]

The unspeakably tragic and historic irony was that no sooner was the atom bomb nearing production in the United States than 'the scientists who had actually been engaged in the atomic project grew profoundly apprehensive about the possibility of its being used for its deadly purpose, as well as about the implications it held for the future of mankind'.[32] And no scientist was more desperately apprehensive than **Leo Szilard**: 'In March 1945 Szilard [who had himself been working on the nuclear chain reaction] … drafted a remarkably prophetic document in which he predicted the dangers of a future atomic arms race, and even discussed the role of intercontinental missiles.'[33] After Roosevelt's death there is no evidence that President Truman or the next secretary of state, James Byrnes, took on board **Leo Szilard**'s view of the danger to the world of a future nuclear arms race or his plea that the bomb be exploded as a demonstration of its force, *not* against the people of Japan, but in a desert or on some barren island. **Szilard** tried frantically to enlist the support of 150 scientists in favour of this but only 29 per cent of them gave their full agreement. At the very last minute he obtained the signatures of more than sixty scientists to a direct plea to President Truman, expressing 'opposition to the use of atomic weapons against Japan without suitable warning and without giving her an opportunity to surrender'.[34] We know what happened on 5 and 9 August, 1945. **Einstein** put his head in his hands and cried: 'O weh!'

Leo Szilard never forgave himself. He spent the last twenty years of his life trying to prevent any further military use of atomic energy, as he worked on nuclear safety and arms control. Finally, four years before his death, he founded the Council for a Liveable World, dedicated to reducing the threat of nuclear proliferation – with what success we now know. At the time of writing there are now nine nations with nuclear weapons – the US, Russia, the UK, France, China, India, Pakistan, North Korea and Israel. Together they possess between 9,220–14,000 weapons of mass destruction whose power is capable of destroying the earth many times over. Half of those nations also possess intercontinental missiles. All the nuclear-armed nations refused to attend the 2017 United Nations Conference on the abolition of nuclear weapons, giving the lie to their proclaimed belief in multilateral disarmament.

Postscript: the Guilt of the Academic Bystanders

What of all the German, non-Jewish academics, both in the humanities and in the sciences, who remained behind and, with the exception of **Otto Krayer**, profited from the racist expulsion of their former colleagues in every one of the above disciplines? In his magisterial study, *Mathematicians under the Nazis*, Sanford Segal ends by quoting the moving confession from a former colleague, Hubert Cremer, after the war. Cremer speaks for every sensitive, guilt-ridden, conscience-stricken German scholar, as he writes to the algebraist Friedrich Levi, now exiled in India:

I send you my heartiest thanks for your friendly letter, which I received yesterday. It moved me deeply through the terrible news it contained. As I so lightly sent you 'cordial greetings' I had no idea that also your poor mother and your sister were killed by those murderers' hands which have disgraced the German name forever. If the possibility had been known to me, I would never have dared to write in such a harmless fashion to you. I did not know the dead; however I had a mother and have a sister, and it is possible for me to have some feeling what such a loss in such a way must mean. And I feel myself guilty as well. To be sure we knew nothing of those horrors, however, indeed, we dimly suspected them; we had immeasurable and pitiable fear and because of this fear for our own lives, we were silent. Today I feel that we should have stood up and spoken out, even in the certainty of being murdered ourselves. At the time I silenced my conscience with the impoverished objection that such a sacrifice was indeed senseless, and with secret gifts of money to Jews in need. Even such actions were always in the fear that someone would find out and it would land us also in a concentration camp …

May I at least express to you and your wife my honest acknowledged participation in this terrible occurrence, which weighs on me heavily? And may I thank you that after such horrors you have not transferred to me only too justified feelings of hate; on the contrary, have written me such a cordial letter! It did me a great deal of good.[35]

PART SEVEN

POLITICAL TARGETS

28

The Most Dangerous British anti-Nazis in Gestapo Eyes

Almost every man and woman listed by the Gestapo as 'Most Wanted' for arrest in Britain by 1940 was a political target because they were assumed, rightly, to be hostile to Nazism. However, some were more political than others. This last section focuses on those in Britain in 1940, whether British-born or Blacklisted refugees who had applied for British citizenship, whose main concern was politics. They held leadership positions in political parties or in the trade union movement or else were political writers or activists. The Blacklisted British-born groupings include the cross-party War Cabinet, other Conservative MPs and peers, Liberal MPs and peers, Liberal activists and writers, Independent MPs, Labour MPs and peers, Labour activists and writers, Communist MPs and the communist rank and file. The refugee political targets included both government representatives in exile and those political activists who had fled Germany, Austria, Czechoslovakia or Poland, and settled in Britain.

Thus the entire political spectrum in Britain was under Gestapo surveillance with a view to its imminent dismemberment – as had been effected in Germany itself after 1933 and was now swiftly being enacted in the newly Nazi-occupied nations of Europe. Under the general heading of '*Vereinigungen*' ('Associations') the Blacklisting of *all* British political organisations, clubs or centres, large or small, in the *Sonderfahndungsliste GB* is even-handedly inclusive. We find, cheek by jowl, all the organisations that are to be searched and have their leaders and papers, including membership and address lists, seized;

they include the **Abyssinia Association**, **the Communist Party of Great Britain**, **the General Federation of Trade Unions** and the women's rights organisation the **National Council for Equal Citizenship**. (For the complete list see Appendix 5.)

The Gestapo obviously had to target Britain's wartime coalition government after the fall of **Neville Chamberlain** in May 1940, in their up-to-the-minute *Informationsheft GB* before the planned invasion. Therefore they now, on 13 May 1940, listed all thirty-five members of **Churchill**'s War Cabinet, each with his home address, many of whom had already been earmarked for arrest by March 1939, for the most part as anti-appeasers, in the *Sonderfahndungsliste GB*. Given that most of these public figures are still generally well remembered, few need further elaboration. But there are a dozen, now largely forgotten, War Cabinet members who are of special note in respect of the degree and timing of their anti-fascism. In alphabetical order they include:

A. V. Alexander MP (1885–1965), a Co-operative Socialist from a very poor home who had left school at 13. He was assessed by **Beatrice Webb** as being 'a singularly good-tempered, sane-minded, direct-speaking person'. He was also politically prescient, an anti-appeaser who had tried to warn of the Nazi danger for many years, as reported by *Hansard*. Finally, in 1937, he convinced the Parliamentary Labour Party to back Baldwin's Services Estimates Bill, which began the rearming of Britain. Between September 1939 and April 1940, **A. V. Alexander** worked to convince **Attlee** and the Labour Party Executive to support the choice of **Churchill**, not **Halifax**, for prime minister to replace **Chamberlain**. **Alexander** became First Lord of the Admiralty in the War Cabinet, doing his best for the welfare of sailors – even himself joining an Arctic Convoy in 1942. In 1944 he was the first British minister to go to France a few days after D-Day to support the troops; as a leading working-class politician he was an important figure for wartime national unity.

Ironically, and in contrast, the imperialist conservative **Leo Amery** MP (1873–1955), who was Jewish on his mother's side, had at first taken little interest in what was happening during the 1930s in

Europe and had no faith in any internationalism outside the British Empire. Even after the Munich crisis he abstained from voting and it was only in December 1938 that he finally committed himself to gearing up the country for war. In 1939 he did edit, with Richard Keane, the **Penguin** colloquium *Germany – What Next?* **Amery**'s real moment came in the debate on the Nazi invasion of Norway on 7 May 1940 when he quoted Cromwell's injunction to the Rump Parliament in 1653: 'In the name of God, go.' And **Chamberlain** went.

The non-party Independent MP for the Scottish Universities, ***Sir John Anderson*** (1882–1958), had been so brilliant a student that he was elected a Fellow of the Royal Society for his postgraduate thesis in atomic research on the chemistry of uranium. He also came first in the British Civil Service examinations, while simultaneously taking a degree in economics. During the 1930s ***Anderson*** had been out of Europe as a reformist governor of Bengal. But on his return, after being elected MP, he prepared a report on the evacuation of civilians from cities in a future war, and soon after the Munich Crisis, October 1938, he was appointed commissioner for air-raid precautions. By February 1939 the ubiquitous 'Anderson shelter' began production and mass distribution. He also organised a national register of those willing to volunteer to serve as auxiliary police, fire-fighters or nurses. Much against his will, he then had to accede to the panic-call by Conservative backbenchers, the press and the military in 1940 for mass internment of 'enemy aliens', now seen as a suspect fifth column. ***Anderson*** privately likened it to a medieval witch-hunt and favoured the release of refugees. Subsequently, when left in charge of the entire 'Home Front' throughout the war, ***Anderson*** so impressed **Churchill** with his intellect and gravitas that the latter advised the king to invite him to form a coalition government, should **Churchill** and his deputy **Eden** both die before the end of the war.[1]

The son of Queen Victoria's chaplain, Labour MP **Hugh Dalton** (1887–1962), had re-directed Labour Party policy at the end of 1937 towards *armed* deterrence and had stiffened the post-Munich national government in its opposition to Hitler. In 1940 he published a prescient tract, 'Hitler's War, before and after', in which he advocated a post-war federation of European states that would include post-Nazi Germany. Another Labour MP in the War Cabinet, **Arthur Greenwood** (1880–1954), had two moments of vital intervention regarding Britain's response to the threat from Hitler. First, on 2 September 1939, when **Attlee** was ill, it fell to **Greenwood** to demand in the House of Commons that **Chamberlain** stop wavering over Poland. How long are we 'prepared to vacillate at a time when Britain and all that Britain stands for, and human civilisation, are in peril? We must march with the French' (*Hansard*). Secondly, on 8 May 1940 it had needed **Arthur Greenwood**, together with **Attlee** and **Leo Amery**, to cast the vital Cabinet vote to *carry on* the war, electing **Churchill** as prime minister instead of **Viscount Halifax** who was considering making terms with the conquering Führer.

The Conservative ***Robert Hudson*** (1886–1957) had not been on the *Sonderfahndungsliste* but was now listed in the *Informationsheft*. Despite having had no relevant experience, he turned out to be 'by far the best minister of agriculture in either war… [He] was determined to see that farmers and landowners alike utilised every acre of soil to help keep the nation from starvation.'[2] The acreage in England and Wales of wheat was, by 1944, increased by 82 per cent, potatoes by 111 per cent, sugar beet by 24 per cent and the total area under tillage by nearly 4.75 million acres (69 per cent). In addition, ***Hudson*** enlisted the successful domestic 'Dig for Victory' campaign and greatly supported the Women's Land Army.

A clergyman's son, ***Sir William Jowitt*** (1885–1957) was a barrister who had been appointed Labour Attorney General in 1929. He was critical of appeasement and, in 1937, he called for state control of the arms industry and rapid rearmament in order to face the imminent threat from Nazism. Elected unopposed as a Labour MP in October 1939 and soon appointed solicitor general in **Churchill**'s coalition government, he also had an important role in charge of the planning for post-war reconstruction. ***Jowitt*** would, as **Attlee**'s lord chancellor in 1945, be instrumental in laying down the procedures for arraigning the top Nazi criminals at Nuremberg. Very different was **George, Lord Lloyd** (1879–1941), a Conservative imperialist who had arrested and imprisoned Gandhi and been dismissed by Labour from his colonial post in Egypt. He was sympathetic to Mussolini and to Franco, though not to Hitler, but he had no interest in Britain joining a collective security pact against the latter. Only *after* Munich did **Lord Lloyd** come to oppose appeasement, seeing a Second World War as championing Christian civilisation against atheist totalitarianism at the time of the Nazi-Soviet pact. Therefore in 1940, far from arguing for making early peace terms, **Lloyd** exhorted France to fight on.

The National Labour colonial office minister and son of Ramsay MacDonald, ***Malcolm MacDonald*** (1901–1981), was so anxious that Palestine should not become another Ireland, racked by civil war for decades, that he had produced a White Paper just before September 1939, aimed at creating a unified, independent state there, with controls on Jewish immigration. At the same time he had tried without success to find countries other than Palestine to take in the persecuted Jews. But both the US and Canada remained closed to Jews and Britain itself was increasingly reluctant to be 'overrun'. ***Macdonald***'s Palestine proposal was greeted with indignation and horror, not just by Jews in Palestine but by the League's Mandates Commission and by members of the British government, including Lloyd George, **Churchill** and the Liberal MP **Anthony James de Rothschild**, all of whom saw 'British' Palestine as the Jews' only hope of haven. The war then intervened.[3]

The National Liberal **Sir John Allsebrook Simon** (1873–1954) had been slow to face the full significance of Hitler. A leading barrister, often too aware of complexities to make up his mind, he was judged the worst Foreign Secretary (from 1931 to 1935) since Ethelred the Unready. His refusal to express an unequivocal denunciation of Japan's invasion of Manchuria at the League of Nations in 1932 constituted the first step of appeasement and haunted his reputation for life. Only on 2 September 1939, which was the very last minute, did **Simon**, then chancellor of the exchequer, lead the Cabinet in insisting that **Chamberlain** *must* declare war after Hitler's invasion of Poland. Although **Simon** had been an appeaser, **Churchill** knew that he was simply too gifted to be excluded from wartime government and made him lord chancellor.

The Liberal leader, **Sir Archibald Sinclair** (1890–1970), was a personal friend of **Churchill** who sided with him ever since 1935 in backing a dual policy of support for collective security against Hitler *and* for British rearmament, especially in the Royal Air Force. On 7–8 May 1940, **Sinclair** sided in favour of **Churchill** as against **Chamberlain** for prime minister. He was made secretary of state for air, soon abandoning his initial preference for precision bombing and endorsing strategic 'area bombing' to make the civilian population of Germany homeless. He did not admit the true nature of this bombing offensive, however, lying to the British public that German civilian deaths were an *unintended* by-product of industrial targeting.[4]

The son of a Wesleyan minister, the National Conservative ***Sir Kingsley Wood*** (1881–1943), had achieved slum clearance, a surge in council-house building, and the institution of a salaried, full-time midwifery service when he was a reformist minister of health in the 1930s. Appointed secretary of state for air after 1938, ***Wood*** raised the production figure from 80 to 546 new warplanes a month, equalling Germany by 1939 – despite his simultaneous support for **Chamberlain**'s appeasement policy, even *after* Munich. On 8 May 1940, however, he advised **Chamberlain** that he *must* resign after the German occupation of Norway and he backed **Churchill** against **Halifax** as the next prime minister. As wartime chancellor of the exchequer, ***Wood***'s economic policy was Keynesian. He introduced purchase tax on luxuries and a 100 per cent excess profits tax, while increasing both the standard rate of income tax and the top marginal rate and reducing the numbers of people exempt from tax. In this way he raised the tax revenue necessary for the war. That pill was sweetened by his announcement of post-war tax credits; ***Wood*** also laid the groundwork for PAYE before his unexpected death.

Finally, among those in the coalition War Cabinet, was the non-party, socially concerned Unitarian ***Frederick Marquis, Lord Woolton*** (1883–1964), who had spoken out for an economic boycott of Germany after Hitler's annexation of Austria in 1938. He had been reprimanded for that by **Chamberlain**. As minister of food in the War Cabinet, ***Woolton*** got the British to accept rationing as necessary and patriotic, equitable and efficient. He ensured adequate nutrition for everyone, even though it meant a simpler diet, always reassuring the public that sufficient emergency stores were in place. Putting children first, in 1942 he provided over half a million schoolchildren with free school meals and 3.5 million with free school milk. Later, as minister of reconstruction, he mediated between warring Conservative and Labour MPs about the vital White Papers on health, education, social security and employment that were behind Britain's first attempt at becoming a 'Welfare State'.

*

Only a small fraction of the more than 600 backbench MPs were in the Black Book. Why did the Gestapo single out those few? Almost all were targeted because of their stance of anti-appeasement. I shall not discuss attitudes to the appeasement of Hitler in general because this has been well covered by D. J. Dutton in his feature article 'Proponents and critics of appeasement' in the online *ODNB*. Instead, I shall focus here only on those *parliamentary* anti-appeasers whom the Gestapo saw as being among the most dangerous anti-Nazis and who would need to be made, very promptly, to 'disappear'. They came from all political parties.

Led by **Churchill** in his 'wilderness years', the Conservative anti-appeasers, although in theory in power in Baldwin's and then in **Chamberlain**'s 'national government', were in fact doomed to be isolated Cassandras until September 1939. For example **Vyvyan Adams** (1900–1951), MP for Leeds West from 1931 to 1945, already opposed the appeasement of Mussolini over Abyssinia and was one of the few Conservative MPs (with **Duff Cooper**) who opposed the Munich Agreement with Hitler in 1938. Under the pseudonym Watchman he wrote *Right Honourable Gentlemen* (1939), *What of the Night?* (1940) and *Churchill: Architect of Victory* (1940). **Adams** was also in a minority of Conservatives opposed to the death penalty and his *Times* obituary was headed 'Intellectual Honesty and Independence'.

The less straightforward **Nancy, Viscountess Astor** (1879–1964), one of the first woman MPs, was one of those few people who felt relieved to find that they had been listed in the Black Book. For as the society hostess of the 'Cliveden Set' (see p. 198) **Nancy Astor** had been very close to the Marquess of Lothian, an emissary to Hitler; and she had publicly welcomed von Ribbentrop, the Nazi German ambassador to Britain, to her home (see ***Manchester Guardian***, 14 September 1945). Her eventual inclusion on the Black List was most probably due to her finally 'dropping' Ribbentrop in March 1939 – which, as in the case of **George Ward Price**, would have seemed to the Führer like a defection and condemned her at last as being a Briton 'hostile to Germany'.

In contrast, Scotland's first woman MP, the anti-Franco, long-time *anti*-appeasing Conservative, nicknamed the 'Red' **Duchess of Atholl** (1874–1960), was actually deselected from her 'safe' Conservative seat in 1938 because of her stance over Spain and she had then lost the bye-election when standing as an Independent: 'Fifty Conservative MPS travelled north to warn that a vote for the duchess was a vote for war [against Hitler] and in a more sinister twist local landowners were alleged to have offered their tenants bonuses – or threats – on the understanding that they vote against her.'[5]

Another one of the very few consistently anti-appeasement Conservatives, even fiercer than **Churchill** on Hitler's re-occupation of the Rhineland and the Hoare-Laval pact, was **Robert, 'Bob', Boothby** (1900–1986), MP for East Aberdeenshire. Like **Churchill** and twenty-eight other Conservatives, he refused to support the government either over Munich, or after the debacle in Norway. He also joined in the doomed effort to make Stefan Lorant, editor of anti-fascist ***Picture Post***, a naturalised British citizen.[6]

Such consistency and depth of principle might not necessarily have been ascribed to the adventurer **Brendan Bracken** MP (1901–1958), whose opposition to appeasement perhaps came largely from his total loyalty to **Churchill**, whose confidant he had become in the latter's 'wilderness years'. Significantly, in May 1940, when **Chamberlain** was known to be about to resign, it was **Bracken** who convinced **Churchill** that the Labour Party would back him as wartime prime minister and therefore **Churchill** did not nominate **Viscount Halifax**. Also in 1940 **Bracken** supported the application of Lorant, the editor of ***Picture Post***, to be naturalised, writing to the minister of information: 'He is one of the best propagandists in the land, and God knows we need such people.'[7] In 1943, **Bracken** was made a successful minister of information, insisting that the British public could take much more of the truth from the heads of the armed forces than had hitherto been assumed. And it was **Bracken** who would rebuke his fellow Conservative MP, Sir Waldron Smithers, for his anti-Semitic smearing of 'aliens' – refugee German Jews – who, Smithers alleged, had infiltrated the BBC and the Ministry of Information. **Bracken** said in the Commons: 'It is a great pity that this House should be used as a sounding board for the mean campaign against decent Germans who left their country because of their opposition to Hitler, and who can and are playing a most worthy part in the war effort.'[8]

The millionaire Conservative MP for Chippenham, **Victor Cazalet** (1896–1943), was an obvious target for the Gestapo as a non-Jewish champion of Jewish refugees, an advocate for Zionism and an ally of the free Poles. Although he had supported Franco and the fascists in the Spanish Civil War in 1936, he later joined **Churchill** as an anti-appeaser and worked for the entry of the US on to the Allied side. On 22 August 1940 he spoke up in the House of Commons to denounce mass internment of anti-Nazi German Jewish refugees – 27,000 'enemy aliens' – as 'this bespattered page of our history'.[9] **Cazalet** himself was killed, together with the Polish leader **General Sikorski**, in an aeroplane crash that may have been caused by Nazi sabotage.

The Conservative MP for South Dorset, later 5th Marquess of Salisbury, and under secretary of state for foreign affairs ***Robert A. J. G. Cecil*** (1893–1972), resigned with **Eden** over Munich. (He is not to be confused with the Nobel peace laureate and Liberal peer, **Edgar Algernon Robert Cecil** (p. 65), who denounced the mass internment of 'enemy aliens' in August 1940 in the House of Lords as 'one of the most discreditable incidents in the whole history of this country'.)

A more complicated case is **Sir Edward Grigg** (1879–1955), who recognised the terrible threat of Nazi Germany ahead of most

Conservative MPs. He was not, however an anti-appeaser in parliament but was Blacklisted for his books arguing for Britain's urgent need to rearm: *The Faith of an Englishman* (1936) and *Britain Looks at Germany* (1938). Nevertheless, '[too] loyal to be a rebel, he would plead with his leaders in private but recoiled from criticising [either Baldwin or **Neville Chamberlain**] in public.'[10] Therefore he did not even abstain with some other Conservatives in the 'Munich' vote.

Harold Macmillan MP (1894–1996), however, took a much stronger public stance, already resigning the government whip when sanctions against Mussolini were dropped in June 1936; he was the only Conservative backbencher to do so. After Munich, he became a fierce anti-appeaser and in March 1939 he was already advocating a *national*, i.e. cross-party, coalition government in order to withstand Hitler. On 8 May 1940 **Macmillan** was one of the forty-three Conservative MPS who voted against **Chamberlain**, thus ending his government.[11]

In addition to those anti-Nazi Conservative MPs there was the Conservative *éminence grise* in the Foreign Office, **Sir Robert Vansittart** (1881–1957). He was understandably targeted by the Gestapo as the diplomatic chief counsellor to the government, with close links to the Secret Service – not to mention that he ran his own intelligence operation. 'More than any other Whitehall mandarin, **Vansittart** stood for rearmament and opposition to appeasement.'[12] His attempt to warn **Chamberlain** of Hitler's intention to invade Czechoslovakia, however, failed. He had a *Delenda est Carthago* ('Carthage must be destroyed' – Cato the Elder) approach to Germany, believing for his entire life that *all* Germans were evil and must be broken, and the country never allowed to industrialise again.[13] The very intensity of **Vansittart**'s blanket, racist hatred of all Germans became an embarrassment and he was 'promoted' to a peerage in 1941.[14]

This was in contrast to the pro-Nazi Conservative peers – Lords Nuffield, Londonderry and Redesdale, plus the Duke of Wellington, who were all members of the Anglo-German Fellowship of 1935–9 (p. 22). Conservative anti-appeasement peers included **Lord**

Cranborne, **Lord Derby**, co-signatory to the BBC letter to the German people, September 1939, and the bank director **Lord Henry Melchett**.

Thwarted as they often were by their leader – and leading Liberal appeaser – **Viscount Samuel**, anti-appeasement Liberals were driven to strike out ideologically for themselves, becoming ever more left wing in the process. For example, the radical, land-owning aristocrat, **Sir Richard Acland**, 15th Baronet (1906–1990), had been elected a Liberal MP, like his father, in 1935. In December 1936, however, he founded, together with **Bob Boothby**, **G. D. H. Cole** and **John Strachey**, an interparty political alliance, the popular front, in order to challenge the government's appeasement policy. Advocating closer ties with the Labour Party, including electoral cooperation with them, he did not win over his own party, but himself moved to the left. In 1942 **Acland** founded his new socialist Common Wealth Party with **J. B. Priestley**, having published *Unser Kampf* in 1940: 'I write this book because I am certain that Europe will not escape from utter destruction unless we accept entirely new ideals, and act upon them at once.' He gave his own huge Devon estates to the National Trust in 1944. In 1945 he joined the Labour Party, became a maths teacher in a London comprehensive and was soon one of the founders of the Campaign for Nuclear Disarmament.[15]

The journalist and broadcaster **Vernon Bartlett** (p. 133) was the only parliamentary candidate, who, at the suggestion of **Richard Acland**, and backed by the Liberal Party under the label of 'Independent Progressive', campaigned on a purely no-appeasement, popular front platform in 1938. He had written furiously about the betrayal of Czechoslovakia at Munich, having already warned about Hitler in his *Nazi Germany Explained* in 1933. **Bartlett** actually won the 'safe' Tory seat of Bridgwater, shocking **Neville Chamberlain**'s government.

Unlike **Bartlett**, **Megan Lloyd George** (1902–1966), was a 'hereditary Liberal' as well as a brilliant, radical orator. In 1929 she had been elected Liberal MP for Anglesey, the first ever woman MP from Wales, and she won re-election as an Independent Liberal MP in 1931 and 1935. Increasingly close to Labour, and, from 1936 the lover of **Philip Noel-Baker** (p. 68), she had opposed appeasement ever since the

Abyssinia crisis and she influenced her father's devastating speech when he pressed for **Chamberlain**'s resignation in 1940.[16]

The Liberal chief whip and deputy leader of the Liberal Party, **Sir Percy Harris, Bart.** (1876–1952) was the Liberal MP for Bethnal Green until 1945. A radical Liberal with a strong social conscience, **Sir Percy Harris** backed the Liberal leader **Sir Archie Sinclair** as an anti-appeaser, and also persuaded Sir William Beveridge, whose Welfare State plan he supported, to stand for parliament as a Liberal. Famous for introducing the Highway Code, car speed restrictions and the belisha beacon, the right-wing Liberal MP, **Leslie Hore-Belisha** (1893–1957), was almost certainly Blacklisted not as an anti-appeaser but simply on the grounds that he was a Jew. Similarly, **Barnett Janner** (1892–1982), the anti-fascist Liberal MP for Whitechapel from 1931 to 1935, of Lithuanian Jewish parentage, was 'passionately concerned with the welfare of Jews ... especially from the early days of Nazi persecution'.[17] *Hansard* reports him already on 6 April 1933 stating his anxieties about the vulnerability of German Jews and again in May 1934 about the future of Jews under the Saarland plebiscite. In addition, he tabled many motions about developing Palestine. **Janner** would have been Blacklisted primarily because of his activism on behalf of his fellow Jews. The third Blacklisted Jewish Liberal MP, the banker and race-horse owner, **James de Rothschild**, had been an appeaser until 1937, but was also a committed Zionist and became ever more anti-Nazi.

The most important of all the Liberal MPs as regards British foreign policy in the 1930s, however, was **Sir Geoffrey Mander** (1882–1962). The owner of a large family paint and varnish business and MP for Wolverhampton since 1929, **Mander** was one of the very first anti-appeasers and went on to make many dogged, eloquent appearances in *Hansard*. He warned the House against not backing the League and reacted firmly against Japan's invasion of Manchuria in 1931. He alerted the Commons to the persecution of German Jews already in April 1933, and he challenged the British government to demand of the German government whether *Mein Kampf*, 'the German Bible, was now their blueprint for an aggressively expansionist foreign policy?' (*Hansard*). He attacked Dr Goebbels' propaganda offensive, and the fact that the pro-Nazi Anglo-German League hired public venues to hold 'private meetings' in London. Of course Abyssinia, the Saarland, the Ukraine, Austria, Spain and Czechoslovakia also received **Geoffrey Mander**'s passionate anti-fascist attention at many a Question Time in the Commons and he must have been an exasperating gadfly in **Chamberlain**'s ears. And not only **Chamberlain**'s. When **Mander** spoke in support of sanctions against Italy after the invasion of Abyssinia in 1935, Mussolini fired a personal diatribe against him, and in 1938 told Italians to boycott the goods in the Milan branch of 'Fratelli Mander'. As the Liberals' backbench specialist on foreign policy between the wars, **Geoffrey Mander** was a crusader for the League of Nations and, as a believer in collective security, he opposed the absolute pacifism of the Peace Pledge Union. On 7 December 1938 he was sufficiently indignant and concerned by the imbalance of pro-Munich propaganda on Pathé cinema newsreels that he tried, in vain, to get a Private Member's Bill through the Commons, forbidding government censorship of the news. As war broke out, **Mander** 'pleaded the Jewish cause, telling Parliament in July that government immigration policy was leaving Jews with no escape from Germany "other than by illegal immigration into Palestine"'. In April 1941, he wrote in *The Jewish Standard*: 'The cause of the Jews throughout the world is the cause for which Great Britain and her allies are fighting.'[18]

Retrospectively, in 1941, **Mander** published *We Were* <u>*Not*</u> *All Wrong. The Guilty Men's Supporters say, 'Perhaps we* were *guilty; but so was* everyone' *Mr. Mander replies.*[19] In that book **Mander** reminds his readers 'How the Labour and Liberal Parties (& also the anti-Munich Tories) strove, pre-war, for the policy of collective security against aggression – with adequate armaments to make that policy effective.' And he warned, with all too much prescience:

> Municheers should never again be allowed to control our destinies. It is too ghastly to think of the same unimaginative, isolationist, naive, complacent attitude, however well meant, being adopted after the war. *Absolute national sovereignty has outlived its usefulness in the world* … [my emphasis].

In private life **Geoffrey Mander** was an enlightened employer, initiating the forty-hour week for his workers. As an early conservationist, he offered to buy William Morris's Red House for the nation and gave his own family's Whitwick Manor, together with all its post-Raphaelite art associated with Morris, to the National Trust. He joined the Labour Party in 1948.[20]

Another privileged radical was **Wilfrid Roberts** (1900–1991), the Liberal Party MP for North Cumberland from 1935, grandson of the 9th Earl of Carlisle and brother of the artist Winifred Nicholson. In his case he was so anti-fascist that he was called 'MP for Spain'. **Roberts** was secretary of the **National Joint Committee for Spanish Relief**, working with **Eleanor Rathbone** and David Grenfell, and joint secretary of the Basque Children's Committee. He supported the popular front policy with **Megan Lloyd George** and **Richard Acland**, and he was an active book selection member and anti-fascist speaker for the **Left Book Club**. **Wilfrid Roberts** supported the Beveridge Report and later he too joined the Labour Party.[21]

Finally, **Graham White** (1880–1965), the radical Liberal MP for Birkenhead, was another passionate internationalist on the executive of the **League of Nations Union**. In 1932 he resigned from office and, like the other Liberals, went into opposition to the national government. He was in favour of a popular front and collective security against the Nazi threat. In 1940 he was appointed to the executive committee of the British Council; in 1942 he campaigned on behalf of German, including Jewish German, internees in Britain, and in 1945 he was a member of the MP delegation visiting Buchenwald.

The Liberal peers of the late 1930s included the president of the Liberal Party, **Lord Meston** (1865–1943), an enlightened imperial administrator in India and co-founder of the Institute of International Affairs, **Chatham House**. He was also a prominent Freemason from 1926 – 'Grand Superintendent of the Grand Chapter of Royal Arch Masons, Berks'. Was it for his Freemasonry that he was on the Black List?[22] The **2nd Marquess of Reading**, **Gerald Isaacs** (1889–1960), was a Liberal peer from 1935 and a supporter of **Churchill**; he was Blacklisted, with his wife, **Eva**, **Marchioness of Reading**, primarily, one surmises, for being an eminent British Jew.[23] **Viscount Samuel** (1870–1963), earlier **Sir Herbert Samuel**, veteran of administering the Palestine mandate in the 1920s, and earning blame from both Zionists and Arabs, was, surprisingly, a *pro*-appeaser, despite his own Jewish background. He supported the Munich agreement – but he would not then accept a place in **Chamberlain**'s Cabinet. And, as head of the **Council for German Jewry** to fund Jewish migration from Germany, **Samuel** did appeal to the national government to allow in the *Kindertransport* children from Nazi Germany after *Kristallnacht* in November 1938. Was he Blacklisted for that or merely for being another too influential Jew?

Blacklisted Liberal political writers included **Ramsay Muir** (1872–1941) who was a Liberal Party intellectual and social economist, influenced by Keynes and Beveridge, and **Alan Pryce-Jones** (1908–2000), who was an anti-appeasing Liberal from 1937 onwards. A wealthy businessman among the male Liberals was **Neville Dixey** (1881–1947), a former Liberal MP who was chairman of Lloyds in 1934 and 1936. The Gestapo indicted him for being an anti-fascist and member of the IPC (International Peace Campaign). The Independent MP **Professor Arthur Salter**, Gladstone professor of political institutions and theory, representing Oxford University, would likewise have been suspect for his close involvement with the **League of Nations Union.**

But in addition to those men were three Blacklisted independent-minded *women* who were very active in Liberal/radical politics during these fraught, vital years. Although not herself a Liberal MP, **Violet Bonham Carter** (1887–1969), daughter of the former Liberal prime minister Asquith and president of the Women's Liberal Federation from 1939 to 1945, must be included as an eminent Liberal who was also a great (and witty) political orator on anti-appeasement platforms – with her close friend **Winston Churchill**. In 1938 she mocked **Neville Chamberlain** as the supporter of 'peace at any price, that others can be forced to pay'. She was the dynamic centre of many anti-fascist associations such as 'the Focus Group' in the 1930s, and had been one of the six British women signatories pleading to Hitler in vain for clemency for Liselotte Herrmann, the young German pacifist mother beheaded for sending abroad the evidence of Germany's military rearmament. For that alone **Violet Bonham Carter** would have earned her entry in the Black Book. A governor of the BBC during the war, she later campaigned with **Margery Fry**, **Victor Gollancz** and **Sydney Silverman** for the abolition of the death penalty in Britain, for support for the United Nations, and for Britain's entry into the Common Market.

The other Blacklisted '*Führerin der Liberalpartei*' was **Margery Corbett Ashby**, who was the president of the International Woman Suffrage Alliance from 1928 to 1946. A feminist, an internationalist and an indefatigable liberal who advocated world disarmament, colonial emancipation and the UN Charter of Human Rights, she had the honour to be Blacklisted not only by the Gestapo but also by Stalin.[24]

The Independent MP for the Northern Universities, **Eleanor Rathbone**, has already appeared in this book as a champion of persecuted Jews, a refugee rescuer and one of the twentieth-century's greatest social reformers. She was also a leading anti-appeaser and advocate in parliament of collective security that would be inspired by an international popular front of Britain, France and the Soviet Union, backed by the League of Nations. At the very last minute she published her argument *War Can Be Averted* (January 1938). It was a desperate, closely argued plea to counteract the defeatism, the absolute pacifism, and the reactionary British press hostility to communism that were now letting the fascist dictators call the tune. Possibly it was 'already too late to stop the rot'.[25] Nevertheless, she still maintained that Great Britain held the master key of the League and that a large sector of the British people could be moved to effective internationalism, as had been shown in the British 'peace ballot' and the British interventions to help Spain, for there was a British hatred of cruelty and love of liberty which, she still believed, could be organised cross party to defy threatening Nazism.

> For six years the policy of conciliating the aggressive Dictators has been tried … What effect has this policy had … ? It has

> inflamed their arrogance, encouraged their ambitions, strengthened their hold on their own subjects, shut the door of hope to thousands of unhappy victims of racial, political and religious persecution, led one nation after another to abandon democracy, lowered the prestige of the League of Great Britain and France ... War has been averted – so far, and [just] for ourselves.[26]

But **Eleanor Rathbone** knew that Hitler was set on world domination and that that would include the Nazification of Britain. Once the war began, however, she was not invited to join the all-male coalition War Cabinet but remained an indomitable outsider. A leading opponent of mass internment, she went to many of the camps, the first of them Huyton in July 1940, and promised the miserable refugee prisoners standing in the pouring rain: 'You are not forgotten ... ' One of the prisoners never forgot her saying to them:

> I shall fight in the House the policy of indiscriminate internment. It is my considered opinion that some of those people who put you here should themselves be interned and you should be let out. You are the last to be the enemies of this country, and you are the first to have a good reason to fight Nazi Germany.[27]

Eleanor Rathbone then worked indefatigably, together with Esther Simpson of the **Academic Assistance Council** and the parliamentary committee on refugees, which she had set up in December 1938, to compile lists for the Home Office of bona fide anti-Nazi internees of outstanding value to the British war effort. 'Of 4,526 cases dealt with, 1,693 applications for release from internment were submitted to the Home Office: 1,069 of these were granted and 571 were still pending [in September 1941].'[28] Government policy, influenced by liberal, eloquent, anti-fascist public opinion, including a powerful **David Low** cartoon in the *Evening Standard*, was put into reverse and only a few hundred internees were still in camps in 1942. Meanwhile, **Rathbone** tried time and again to tell Britain what was being done to the Jews. But 'Miss **Rathbone** must be refused [permission to speak]'.[29]

The Conservative and Liberal anti-appeasers had been isolated individuals testifying, against the mainstream of their respective parties, to the dictates of their own feelings, reason and conscience. The far more numerous anti-appeasement Labour MPs, however, had a long party tradition of internationalism behind them, going back to the 1890s. Composed by an Irishman in 1889, The Internationale, or 'Red Flag', hymn of the international socialist movement, encourages Labour to back not just national but international human rights. Notwithstanding that, however, Labour MPs hostile to appeasement still faced some tough opposition from within their own party – notably from **Herbert Morrison** and **Ernest Bevin**. **Bevin**, the powerful leader of the biggest union, the **TGWU**, favoured rearmament but also non-intervention against the dictators' foreign adventurism; he would not cooperate even with relief efforts for their victims if he suspected that such efforts were communist-led. How far was British anti-fascism weakened in the 1930s by the official refusal of both the Labour Party and the TUC to join, either in action or verbal protest, any political group against Hitler which they suspected to be a communist front organisation? That strategy did nothing to help the political victims of Hitler. Neither did the British Labour Party gain local grassroots backing for its refusal to respond to demands for a broad-based, united popular front against Nazism. On the contrary:

> [From] March 1933, Labour Party members began to participate in anti-fascist activities, frequently acting on their own initiative *in the absence of* [my emphasis] … an active lead from either the Labour Party or the TUC. [Anti-fascist] activity by Labour Party members in 1933 was at its most visible in opposition to Nazism – [e.g. the Relief Committee for the Victims of German Fascism].[30]

It was the eventual emergence of a staunchly anti-appeasement leader in **Clement Attlee**, denouncing 'the farce of non-intervention' in Spain after the Luftwaffe's bombing of Guernica in April 1937, that at last gave the other anti-appeasers in the Labour Party heart. 'In Spain … **Attlee** found both clarity and a cause.'[31] It is too often forgotten – or not realised – that from December 1937 it was **Attlee** who championed the International Brigade and united the Labour Party against the appeasement of Hitler, while **Churchill** was still an outsider on the issue within his own Conservative party.

Not surprisingly, many of the anti-appeasement Labour MPs in the Black Book were Jewish. **Dan Frankel** (1900–1988), mayor of Stepney, member of the London County Council for Mile End since 1931 and MP for Stepney since 1935, is reported in *Hansard* as reacting to Mussolini's aggression in Abyssinia in 1936. He protested about British fascists being allowed to march through Stepney in 1937, and as a Jew, though not as an official Zionist, he spoke up for the Jews' need to be granted refuge in Palestine. He was definitely targeted by the Gestapo for his ethnicity. So was the MP for Manchester from 1935 to 1942, **John Jagger** (1872–1942), '*Jude*' in the Black Book, who had risen through the **Co-operative Movement** and become president of the National Union of Distributive and Allied Workers. **Jagger** was a supporter of the Soviet Union, and sent a telegram to the Spanish people backing them against Franco. *Hansard* reports his dogged, anti-fascist parliamentary questions on Abyssinia in 1936, on Franco's embedded, uncritical journalists in 1937, on Basque child refugees in 1937, on the bombing of civilian targets in Spain – and on Munich in 1938.

From a quite different class was **Major Harry Louis Nathan** MP (1889–1963), later Lord Nathan, and husband of Eleanor Nathan, later chair of the London County Council. He was a social interventionist who had worked with Jewish boys' clubs in the East End. A solicitor and first a Liberal then a Labour MP from 1934 to 1935, and from 1937 to 1940, **Nathan** became a Labour peer and minister of civil aviation from 1946 to 1948.

In contrast, born in the East End, the eldest of thirteen children of a Polish tailor, **Manny Shinwell** (1884–1986) had left school at 11 to work as a machinist in a Glasgow clothing workshop. Self-educated in public libraries, art galleries, and by trade union activism, **Shinwell** became a member of the **ILP** and then a Labour MP in 1922. After 1935 he campaigned vigorously for a popular front against Franco and was fiercely anti-appeasement in the Commons, even slapping the face of a Conservative appeaser who had told him to 'go back to Poland'. **Shinwell** became minister of fuel in the post-war Labour Government when it nationalised the coal mines.

Also from a poverty-stricken Jewish background, **Sydney Silverman** (1895–1968) had made his way as a scholarship boy in Liverpool. Then, aged 19 in 1914, he served three sentences after 1916 as an 'absolutist' conscientious objector in different prisons – which was his education in the need for British penal reform. **Silverman** eventually became a poor man's lawyer and later, in 1935, a left-wing MP. As chairman of the British section of the World Jewish Congress, he wanted a national home for Jews, though not necessarily one based in Palestine. When in 1938–9 he was confronted with the choice between another world war or abandoning the European Jews, he felt bound this time to back war, although with many caveats. Despite his anti-Nazism, he strongly opposed **Churchill**'s demand for Germany's 'unconditional surrender', and he became a leading anti-nuclear weapons activist after the war. His greatest achievement, however, was his long campaign to abolish the death penalty in Britain, which finally triumphed in 1964.[32]

The Jewish millionaire **George Russell Strauss**, later **Lord Strauss** (1901–1993), was by contrast the son of a Conservative MP. Sent to Rugby public school, where he was radicalised by the bullying anti-Semitism that he encountered there, and acutely aware that his own wealth was the fruit of his family's profiteering from the metal industry in the First World War, **Strauss** became an active member of the Labour Party in 1925. He joined **G. D. H. Cole**'s Socialist League in 1931 and became MP for Lambeth North from 1934 to 1950. He financed the socialist weekly *Tribune* of **Stafford Cripps**, edited by **William Mellor**. **Strauss**'s anti-Nazism led him to join **Stafford Cripps** and Nye Bevan in advocating a cross-party, anti-fascist alliance within the Commons, as well as a popular front against Franco abroad. He visited the republican forces in Barcelona and Madrid in the winter of 1937, braving the snow-covered sierra by night and Franco's snipers by day. It was clear to him that the financial interests behind democratic Western governments preferred Franco to win. During the Second World War

Strauss was made minister of aircraft production and, after 1945, he was Labour's skilful minister of supply who steered through the nationalisation of iron and steel.[33]

The non-Jewish Labour MPs selected for immediate arrest owed their inclusion in the Black Book to their trade unionism and strong socialist commitment. For example, **Jennie Adamson** (1882–1962), daughter of a railway porter, was Blacklisted as a delegate, '*Vertreterin*' to the Second International,[34] presumably referring to 1923 when the Labour Party had merged with the IWUSP – the International Working Union of Socialist Parties – to form the Social Democratic Labour and Socialist International. She had been a member of the Workers' Union and on the Women's National Strike Committee during the 1926 General Strike. Chairman of the Labour Party from 1935 to 1936, **Jennie Adamson** 'spoke out strongly at the 1936 Labour Party conference on the fear of fascist aggression and the duty of Labour to defend peace and preserve democracy'.[35] In 1938 she became MP for Dartford and was an eloquent advocate of working-class mothers' need for family allowances and access to contraception.

Other Blacklisted Labour MPs with strong trade union connections included **Jennie Adamson**'s husband, **William Murdoch Adamson** (1881–1946), of the **ILP** and **TGWU**, as well as a number of men from the working class who had started life as exploited child workers. **George Dallas** (1878–1961), for instance, had been a miner at the age of 12, before moving up to be a coal merchant's clerk in London. In 1900 he was attacked as an anti-war 'pro-Boer' and again later as one of the few opponents of conscription in the First World War. He became a militant trade union organiser for both the Workers' Union and the National Union of Agricultural Workers, and an MP from 1929 to 1931. In the later 1930s **Dallas** rejected the movement to form a popular front with communists and anti-fascist Liberals, aligning himself instead with Labour's pro-rearmament group with **Hugh Dalton**.

The miners' leader and socialist MP **Stephen Owen Davies** (1886–1972), had also started work underground in the Welsh pits at the age of 12. Agent for the South Wales Miners' Federation, **Davies** became an ardent supporter of the Soviet Union while never joining the Communist Party. MP for Merthyr from 1934, he was an anti-appeaser, calling for a popular workers' front against fascist dictators. After 1940 he opposed the indiscriminate internment of 'enemy aliens' and the suppression of the ***Daily Worker***.[36] **Arthur Hayday** (1869–1956) had left school at 9 to work in market gardening. He had later worked as kitchen boy, chemical worker, and a stoker in the Merchant Navy. He joined Will Thorne's National Union of Gas Workers and General Workers and was victimised by employers for his trade union activism. He joined the **ILP** and became full-time union organiser, first in West Ham and then for the General Workers' Union in Nottingham. From 1918 to 1939 he was Labour MP for Nottingham West, seeing Ramsay Macdonald's national government as a betrayer of the unions.[37]

There are several more examples in the Black Book of social mobility in Britain via leadership in the trade unions and in the Labour Party. **George Hicks** (1879–1954) had started as a bricklayer. He became general secretary of the Amalgamated Union of Building Trade Workers from 1921 to 1941 and was active in the International Federation of Trade Unions. He was Labour MP for Woolwich from 1931 to 1950 and parliamentary secretary to the minister of works in the wartime coalition government. **George Alfred Isaacs** (1883–1979) was a printer who, in 1909, became general secretary of the National Society of Operative Printers and Assistants, a position he held for the next forty years. He was a Labour MP in the 1920s and again in 1939, his most important work being for workers' compensation. **George Lathan** MP (1875–1942), son of a tanner, was a railway clerk who became, via union support, MP for Sheffield South from 1921 to 1931 and from 1935 to 1942. He was president of the National Federation of Professional Workers from 1921 to 1937 and in 1938 he voiced a special claim in the House of Commons for the needs of Czech and/or Jewish refugees from the sacrificed Sudetenland.

Will Lawther (1889–1976) had started work as a trapper below ground soon after he was 12,[38] but had managed to educate himself in the Miners' Institute library and at night school, becoming active in the **ILP** and a left-wing militant in his own union, the Durham

Miners. He was a Labour MP from 1929 to 1931 and in the later 1930s an anti-appeasement anti-fascist who supported the Republicans in the Spanish Civil War. **Lawther** became vice-president of the Miners' Federation of Great Britain from 1934 to 1939. Though Blacklisted by the Gestapo in 1939 for his trade unionism, he would, in 1945, go to West Germany to assist in the post-war reconstruction of German trade unions.[39]

Once a railway clerk, **George Ridley** (1886–1944) also became a Labour MP via trade unionism. He was a fiery voice in the Commons on many humanitarian causes, from infant malnutrition to the 'barbarous and sadistic' punishment of the 'Cat' (i.e. 'Cat o'Nine Tails').[40] He was outraged by the preference of many Conservative MPs, including the prime minister, for tyranny to liberty, accusing their appeasement policy of strengthening Mussolini in Abyssinia, Franco in Spain, and Hitler in Czechoslovakia. He said that they hated an alternative to Nazism in Germany more than they did Nazism itself – all 'in the British interest'.[41] **Alexander Walkden** (1873–1951), also of the Railway Clerks' Association, was in the Black Book for his role in helping to create the *International* (my emphasis) Transport Workers' Federation in the 1930s.

Some trade union leaders were in the Black Book even though they were not MPs. They include the general secretary of the Trade Union Council, **Sir Walter Citrine** (1887–1983), a strong anti-appeaser and chair of the World Anti-Nazi Council as well as a supporter of **Churchill** on British rearmament. **Arthur Pugh** (1870–1955), who had been a smelter in an ironworks and became general secretary of the influential Iron and Steel Trades Confederation, was Blacklisted for chairing the TUC in 1926. The veteran, 80-year-old **Ben Tillett** (1860–1943), who had started work in a brickyard at 8 and eventually become a London docker, co-founding the Dockers' Union, was in the Black Book even though he had retired as an MP in 1931. Presumably he was targeted by the Gestapo because, in his seventies, he still supported the Spanish Medical Aid Committee.

(Frederick) Seymour Cocks (1882–1953) was originally a political journalist, who in 1920 had written a biography of the great anti-militarist E. D. Morel, founder of the **Union for Democratic Control of Foreign Policy (UDC)**. **Cocks** became a member of the Labour Party's advisory committee on international affairs in 1928, and from 1929 was the MP for Broxtowe, Nottinghamshire. An internationalist, anti-militarist supporter of the **UDC**, in 1927 Cocks had written the prophetic *The War Danger. Hansard* reports his many forceful interventions in the Commons on Locarno, Abyssinia, Spain and, of course, on Munich, when he always backed **Sir Geoffrey Mander** and **Eleanor Rathbone**.

As for the former naval captain **Lieutenant Commander Reginald Fletcher** (1885–1961), a veteran of the Dardanelles battles in the First World War and Labour MP for Nuneaton from 1935, he was frequently recorded in *Hansard* on the danger of German naval rearmament and on Britain's inability to police the world alone. For this reason **Fletcher** backed collective security under the League of Nations; after Munich he confessed bitterly: 'We are departing from the paths of honour' and declared 'it is time to cease running after dictators'.

There were two **Arthur Henderson** MPs in the 1930s. One was the Labour Foreign Secretary who struggled in vain for disarmament at the League of Nations Geneva Convention on disarmament before dying in 1935, and the other his barrister son (1893–1968), Labour MP for Kingswinford, Staffs (1935–50). Did the Gestapo confuse the two in 1940? Or had they registered that **Arthur Henderson** the younger was a strong anti-appeaser? For **Fred William Jowett**, aged 76 in 1940, it is worth reading **Fenner Brockway**'s homage in *Socialism over Sixty Years: The Life of Jowett of Bradford*. **Jowett** himself wrote *What Made Me a Socialist* (1941) when he opposed the inequality of the sacrifice imposed on the working class in the Second World War.[42] A similarly passionate socialist was **Jimmy Maxton** (1885–1946), a 'Red Clydesider' who had been imprisoned for a year in the First World War for sedition as a strike leader. A charismatic orator, **Maxton**'s pacifism led him at first to support appeasement and non-intervention in the Spanish Civil War, but he came around to attacking the national government for tacitly supporting the fascist side. In the

Second World War, however, he would stick to his pacifist guns, holding pacifism to be less murderous for the world's working class than was a world war.[43]

The Labour MP for Islington West, **Frederick Montague** (1876–1966), had started life as a newsboy and shop assistant. In 1935 he gave Labour's backing to **Geoffrey Mander**'s bill advocating an international police force – but with reservations. In 1937 he spoke strongly in favour of increasing Britain's air defences and balloon barrages. In 1938 he argued for increased production of Spitfires and backed **Mander** against right-wing political censorship – especially in newsreels. In 1939 he spoke on the need for improved air-raid protection. He would serve in **Churchill**'s War Coalition as parliamentary secretary to the Ministry of Transport and to the Ministry of Aircraft Production. (He was later made a Labour peer, Lord Amwell.)

From a far more privileged social background, **Harold Nicolson** (1886–1968), '*Schriftsteller und Politiker*', son of Lord Carnock, and a distinguished diplomat, spoke out early as an anti-fascist and anti-appeasement National Labour MP, from 1935 to 1941. After Munich he reproached **Chamberlain** in the Commons, saying it was in the British tradition 'not to make friends with people whose conduct is demonstrably evil'. As soon as war broke out he was commissioned to write the Penguin Special *Why Britain is at War*, explaining why it was crucial to defeat Nazism. Critical of *Mein Kampf* and spelling out Hitler's duplicity and drive to world dominance, this best-selling book went into three editions by February 1940. He and his aristocratic wife, Vita Sackville-West, like **Kingsley Martin**, **Rose Macaulay** and the **Woolfs**, were prepared to commit suicide should the Nazis invade Britain.[44]

The wealthy Liberal **F. W. Pethick-Lawrence** (1871–1961) had been converted to socialism, feminism and pacifism by his wife, the suffragette Emmeline Pethick-Lawrence. He co-founded the anti-war **UDC** and had later become a Labour MP (1923–31 and 1935–47). An anti-appeaser, he strongly deplored the Hoare-Laval pact of 1936 that ceded Abyssinia to Mussolini. **Pethick-Lawrence** ultimately renounced his long-held pacifism in favour of collective security through an armed League of Nations. Aged 70, he became leader of the opposition in the wartime coalition.[45]

Despite coming from a wealthy land-owning family, **Morgan Philips Price** (1885–1973), educated at Harrow and Cambridge, became an increasingly fierce political radical. He was against the First World War, joined the **UDC**, and then became war correspondent for the ***Manchester Guardian*** on the Eastern Front. A Russian speaker, he reported first-hand and with sympathy on the Bolshevik Revolution. Later, as ***Daily Herald*** correspondent in Germany, he interviewed Rosa Luxemburg shortly before her murder. She convinced him that Lenin was absolutely wrong to impose one-party political dictatorship on the Russian working class. An anti-appeasing MP for the Forest of Dean, **Price** spoke in the House of Commons in 1936, accusing the Nazis of 'fifteen years of gangsterism'.[46]

Appalled by the extreme poverty of his constituency, Sunderland, the barrister **Denis Nowell Pritt** (1887–1973), went even further left than **Price**, becoming an uncritical convert to Soviet communism. In 1932 **Pritt** defended Ho Chi Minh against the French. In 1933 he presided over an international enquiry into the Reichstag fire. A Stalinist ever since his 1932 **Fabian** research visit to the Soviet Union ('he swallowed the lot' wrote Margaret Cole),[47] **Pritt** even accepted the later Moscow show trials. A Labour MP from 1935, he was expelled from the party for defending the Soviet invasion of Finland in 1940. **Pritt**'s actions were better than his opinions; instead of making money as a lawyer, he 'did a mostly exemplary body of work for the labour and anti-colonial movements',[48] even, unsuccessfully, defending 'the Kenyan Six', including Kenyatta, in the 1952 Mau Mau trials.

Like **Pritt**, the Christian Socialist pacifist **Reginald Sorensen** MP (1891–1971) was a passionate anti-colonialist, leading the Commons critique of British rule in India in the 1930s. 'The operation of Imperialism in India is in essence no different from the operation of Hitlerism ... We are appalled by what is happening to the Jews in Germany, but what has been happening in India is just as bad.'[49] Despite his well-known pacifism, **Sorensen**, who had already publicly backed the Republicans in the Spanish Civil War, was so appalled by

Nazism that in September 1939 he urged his fellow pacifists not to obstruct the war effort.

The armaments manufacturer **Richard Stokes** ('Stockes' in the Black Book), is still something of an enigma. A Roman Catholic, **Stokes** was a member of the Committee for Civil and Religious Peace in Spain, as well as being a Labour MP and serving on the executive committee of the **League of Nations Union**. He has recently been accused of secret fascist sympathies[50] and charged with being a 'socialist millionaire'. **Stokes**'s most important moment in politics was his Commons speech in February 1945, denouncing the incineration of Dresden. Why was **Stokes** in the Black Book? He was, after all, *for* the appeasement of Hitler and the revision of the Versailles Treaty. Why was he a *Labour* MP in 1938? He backed **Chamberlain**. And why was he sympathetic to fascist Italy – or to Catholic Italy – despite Mussolini?

The descendant of Josiah Wedgwood, the great potter and Enlightenment thinker, **Colonel Josiah 'Jos' Wedgwood** (1872–1943), was called 'the last of the radicals'.[51] He was MP for Newcastle-under-Lyme from 1906 to 1942, first as a Liberal and after 1919 as Labour. He was an independent voice in the Commons, advocating the taxation of land ownership, refusing to support counter-revolutionary forces against the Russian Revolution and supporting independence for India. In February 1933 he had been the very first MP to react to Hitler's assumption of power, immediately challenging the Home Office to amend the Aliens Act and grant refuge to the 'persecuted victims of Nazi terrorism', likening them to the fleeing Huguenots. The first German victims to whom he referred were communists, but he quickly also focused on the desperate German Jews and advocated their right to settle in Palestine.

Wedgwood never minced words or spared his fellows in parliament from facing hard facts. After Hitler's triumph in Austria, he again urged the emendation of the Aliens Act, citing the 'bestial sadism of the SS', and illustrating it with the case of a middle-aged Jewish woman made to clean the street on her knees and with her tongue. 'We must not keep them [the Austrian Jews] out of this country.' But his Private Member's Bill was thrown out by 210 votes to 142. After Munich, **Wedgwood** became even less restrained in his defiance of the Conservative Government: 'I say that we will not be governed by those who have confidence in Herr Hitler.' After the invasion of Czechoslovakia in March 1939, he turned on **Chamberlain**: 'The Prime Minister has been blinded by his affection for dictators ... [believing it] safer to live on our knees instead of dying on our legs.'[52]

One unforgettable Blacklisted Labour firebrand in the Commons was **Ellen Wilkinson** (1891–1947), the left-wing MP who had led the Jarrow Hunger March and who had been one of the women signatories pleading to Hitler for clemency for Liselotte Herrmann. She was fiercely pro-Republican Spain, anti-fascist and anti-appeasement. 'She opposed fascism in every way open to her ... In the Second World War she worked for Civil Defence and the Fire Service, [throughout the London Blitz] spending days and nights in bomb shelters.'[53] As minister of education after 1945, **Ellen Wilkinson** raised the school leaving age to 14 and declared that she wanted 'to see more laughter in the classroom'.[54]

Although a hereditary peer, **Viscount Listowel** (1906–1997) converted to socialism on encountering the appalling poverty in Britain in the 1920s. He was later Blacklisted for his anti-Nazism, being, according to the Gestapo, a 'member of anti-German organisations'. The ex-officer of marines, **Lord Marley** (**Dudley Leigh Aman**) (1884–1952), a **Fabian** Labour MP from 1930 to 1931 and Labour peer from 1931 to 1952, wrote the introduction to *The Brown Book of the Hitler Terror and the Burning of the Reichstag*, 1933, edited by the World Committee for Victims of German Fascism (in fact, André Simon: see also p. 107). And in 1936 he supported the Co-ordinating Committee for Anti-Fascist Activities. He was chairman of the parliamentary advisory council of the ORT (supplying aid to Jews in eastern Europe) and published many articles on fascism and German refugees. '[His] humanist concerns were paramount.'[55]

The husband of **Beatrice Webb** (1858–1943), '*Presidentin*' (of the **Fabian Society**), **Lord Passfield, Sidney Webb** (1892–1943), would have been *persona non grata* because of his Fabianism and his uncritical approval of the Soviet Union in the 1920s and 1930s. (For **Lord Ponsonby** – see p. 70.)

The Labour Party leader in the House of Lords in the late 1930s, **Harry Snell, 1st Baron Snell** (1865–1944), was the son of an agricultural worker and had begun work as a farmhand at the age of 8. His strong anti-fascism and anti-appeasement convictions strengthened his Zionism: he believed that a refugee Jewish settlement in Palestine would help the Arabs by raising their standard of living. **Charles Trevelyan** (1870–1958) was *persona non grata* to the Gestapo on account of his co-founding of the **UDC**. He also fell foul of the Labour Party, being briefly expelled for supporting (with **Stafford Cripps**) a British 'popular front', that wanted to cooperate with Liberals and communists against fascism and the pro-appeasement national government in 1939.

In addition to the above members of parliament and peers, the Gestapo Blacklisted many left-wing political writers and labour activists. **Fenner Brockway** (p. 65), for example, had supported the Independent Labour Party since 1912, editing the *Labour Leader* and suffering imprisonment, including hard labour and solitary confinement, for his opposition to conscription between 1916 and 1918. He was a Labour MP in 1929 but lost his seat in 1931. A long-time dedicated anti-fascist, in October 1936 **Brockway** played a decisive role in persuading the Home Office to order Oswald Mosley to call off the march by British fascists through the East End of London, after it was confronted by a human barrier, at least 100,000 strong, assembling against the Mosley-protecting police during the 'Battle of Cable Street'. Torn between his pacifism and his anti-fascism by the Spanish Civil War, **Brockway** eventually prioritised anti-fascism until 1945.[56]

A 'lonely champion of British re-armament in the Labour Party',[57] **Richard, 'Dick' Crossman** (1897–1974) was a don and a Labour city councillor in Oxford from 1934 to 1940, as well as an assistant editor at the ***New Statesman***. In 1940 he was drafted into the propaganda side of the British war effort, attempting to undermine the impact of Goebbels on Germany. He knew that the German Service of the BBC must build the trust of the 'enemy' listener by relying on truthfulness and objectivity. In this he succeeded – as my own German grandmother, Anna Haag, who risked her life to listen to **Crossman**'s forbidden news broadcasts, testified in her secret war diary, on 4 April 1943:

> You clever, honest, humorous people – how I have come to love you! At breakfast this morning I said to my husband and daughter: 'Just imagine if they were all to be here in our kitchen one day! Lindley Fraser, Charles Richardson [i.e. Marius Goring], Hugh Carleton Greene, Gordon Walker, **Richard Crossman**, Henry English and all our friends, the best friends of our long life, who have carried us safely through these pitch-black years of dismal misery!' [58]

Quite a different character, marked by the Gestapo as a propagandist for 'Red Spain', **Charles Duff** (1894–1966) was a Northern Irishman fluent in seven languages. In 1936 he resigned from the Intelligence Division of the Foreign Office, where he was a friend of **Rowland Kenny**, on the grounds that it was supportive of fascism in Spain.[59] In 1936 he published *Spain Against the Invaders: Napoleon 1808 to Hitler and Mussolini 1936* followed by *Voice of Spain*, 1939, and *A Key to Victory: Spain* (Gollancz, 1940). **Duff**'s most influential and subversive book, however, was his Swiftian *A Handbook on Hanging* (and other forms of 'the fine art' of state execution) 1928, frequently updated by him and re-published in 1934, 1938, the 1940s and 1950s, up until 1961. It was a great weapon in the British campaign against capital punishment.

The political organiser and first International Secretary of the Labour Party (1920–44), **William Gillies** (1884–1958), was both an anti-fascist and an anti-communist. He helped to administer the Labour Party and *News Chronicle* funds for Czech relief at the end of 1938, and collaborated with **Doreen Warriner** to facilitate the last-minute evacuation of Social Democrat political refugees from Prague after the German invasion in March 1939.[60] He became a strong advocate of armed resistance to fascism.

A better known public figure was the Labour supporter and barrister **Frederick Elwyn Jones** (1909–1990). He gave legal advice to persecuted Austrian Social Democrats in 1934 and in 1936 attended political trials in Germany, Greece, Romania and Hungary as a representative of the International Association of Democratic Lawyers. He wrote three books on the threat of fascism: *Hitler's Drive to the East*; *The Battle for Peace*; and *The Attack from Within*. A Labour MP in 1945, he was asked to join the prosecuting team of the Nuremberg War Crimes Trials from 1946 to 1948.

The general secretary of the **Co-operative Union**, **R. A. Palmer**, tended not to campaign as an individual but had a huge mass-organisation behind him. Co-operative Socialism had a long history of non-Marxist, alternative socialist influence on the British Labour Party and **Palmer** was its historian, publishing *World Co-operation: A Record of International Co-operative Relations*, 1937, and *Educational Work of the Co-operative Union*, 1940, detailing the massive impact of the British **Co-operative Movement** upon its 35,000 young students, 6,757 adults and 23,871 technical workers. Co-operative educational outreach included classes in economics, sociology and citizenship. All of this was of course targeted for immediate shutdown by the Gestapo.

The indefatigable activist **Sylvia Pankhurst** (1882–1960) was not listed by the Gestapo for her past suffragette militancy, or for her pacifism, and not even because she had co-founded the **Communist Party of Great Britain** in 1921. The Gestapo targeted her as '*Sekret. Int. Frauenlig Matteotti*' – that is, for her founding of the anti-fascist pressure group the 'Women's International Matteotti Committee', after fascist thugs murdered the Italian Socialist Deputy in 1924. 'The tiresome Miss Pankhurst' (also, ironically, then under the surveillance of an exasperated MI5) became an active anti-Nazi and anti-Falangist. She went on to take up the cause of Haile Selassie's Abyssinia against its Italian occupiers in her paper *The New Times and Ethiopian News*.

Another one-person band, the autodidact **Frank Ridley** (1897–1994), a Marxist and a secularist, spoke every week at Speakers' Corner, Hyde Park between 1925 and 1964. An ex-Trotskyist, he joined the **ILP** in the 1930s and was an indefatigable humanist historian and anti-fascist writer.[61] He published *Next Year's War?* in 1936, *The Papacy and Fascism* in 1937, and *Fascism – What is it?* in 1941.

The contemporary historian **Dorothy Woodman** (*c.*1910–*c.*1990) was the anti-Nazi '*Sekretaerin d. Union d. Demokratischen Kontrolle*' (**UDC**), and the partner of **Kingsley Martin**. In 1935 she had worked in Germany for the release of Dimitrov, one of the defendants in the burning of the Reichstag case. As early as 1934 she had translated and edited Albert Schreiner's documentation of Hitler's secret preparation for war, *Hitler Rearms*, and in 1936 she supported the largely communist 'Co-ordinating Committee for Anti-Fascist Activities' in Britain. She went on to publish *China Fights On* in 1942, *An ABC of the Pacific* (a Penguin special) in 1942, and *Europe Rises: The Story of Resistance in Occupied Europe* in 1943 – and she was also under surveillance by the British SIS.[62]

By far the most important of the socialist thinkers writing in Britain in the 1930s, however, was **John Strachey** (1901–1963), '*Schriftsteller*'. Young **John Strachey** became 'the greatest populariser of socialist political economy' in twentieth-century Britain[63] – despite being the Eton- and Oxford-educated great-grandson of the reactionary 'iron-law' political economist, Nassau William Senior, begetter of the draconian 1834 New Poor Law. His father was the conservative *Spectator*'s editor, John St Loe Strachey, who considered the introduction of old age pensions to be 'Jacobinism'. **John Strachey**'s Damascene conversion had been effected in the early 1920s by his French journalist mistress (the independent-minded radical, Yvette Fouque), by the anti-militarists **Arthur Ponsonby** and **Fenner Brockway**, and by the **Fabian Webbs** and **J. A. Hobson**. During the 1926 General Strike, **Strachey** edited Birmingham's *Strike Bulletin* and was arrested for 'incitement to disaffection'. After the General Strike he backed the miners' continuing struggle and edited *The Miner*. His analysis of capitalism became increasingly Marxist and pro-communist, but he also worked on a socialist application of Keynesian economics in order to eliminate mass unemployment in Britain.

Strachey's lucid and influential writings included *The Menace of Fascism*, 1933, which argued that capitalism would lead to barbarism; *The Theory and Practice of Socialism*, 1936 – the most successful book ever produced by the **Left Book Club**, which he had co-founded with

Gollancz and **Laski** in 1936; and *Why You Should be a Socialist* (1938), which sold a quarter of a million copies in two months. In March 1934 **Strachey** became chair of the 'British Anti-War Movement' (proscribed as a communist front organisation by the Labour Party), with its monthly bulletin 'Fight War and Fascism'. In July 1934 he became secretary of the Co-ordinating Committee for Anti-Fascist Activities, and appealed to the **Co-operative Movement** and to British trade unions to push Labour to cooperate with anti-fascist activism in Britain. Whereas the Labour Party's initial response to the phenomenon of fascism focused on the threat from Mosley and the *British* Union of Fascists, **John Strachey** insisted that the most urgent task was 'to save *human civilisation* [my emphasis] from Fascism' and early in 1936 he backed the British Communist Party's distribution of a quarter of a million leaflets mainly directed at East End Jews, alerting them to the repression of Jews in Germany. (The British Union of Fascists had added 'National Socialists' to its title in 1936.) After May 1936 he concentrated on developing the **Left Book Club** in order to raise 'mass anti-fascist consciousness'.[64]

Strachey broke his connection with the Communist Party in April 1940 and articulated a patriotic socialism in *A Faith to Fight For* (1941).[65] He rejoined the Labour Party in 1943, becoming undersecretary for air under **Attlee** in 1945. After the war, however, a sadness descended on **Strachey** as the full horror of the 1930s and 1940s hit him. He wrote his great elegiac essay, 'Walter Rathenau, Dr Schacht and The German Tragedy' 1958, saying: 'The history of every great nation is tragic: but the history of Germany is more tragic than any other.'[66]

British communists were regarded with some contempt by the Gestapo for having failed to rouse the British working-class to revolution. They declared in the *Informationsheft* that this failure had been caused by the 'enormously strong position' of the conservative English trade unions. Communist Party membership had fallen to a bare 2,765 in 1931, although it was admitted by the *Informationsheft* to have climbed to nearly 18,000 by 1939. The Gestapo claimed, however, that the communists in Britain, financed from Moscow, largely operated through 'front' or 'cover ' organisations: the **National Unemployed Workers'**

Movement, for example, and the ***Rank and File Movement***, the latter said in the *Informationsheft* to boast a quarter of a million supporters.

Given that the Gestapo's original brief ever since 1933 had been to fight communism with its Group Section 1VA 1 –'Persecution of Political Opponents' – anti-communism was an essential part of their invasion plan for Britain. **Willie Gallacher**, ***J. T. Murphy***, **Harry Pollitt**, ***MacManus***, ***Tom and Harry Quelch***, **Tom Mann**, **Albert Inkpin**, **R. Palme Dutt** and ***W. Paul*** were the Communist leaders targeted in the *Informationsheft*.

The founder member of the Communist Party GB, **Willie Gallacher** (1881–1965), had been falsely convicted of sedition charges in 1916 and imprisoned for twelve months for an article criticising the First World War. He organised a strike in Glasgow in 1919 in aid of establishing a forty-hour week and was sent back to prison when the government brought in the army to break the picket. In 1925 he was imprisoned again for twelve months, with the rest of the Communist Party leadership, this time under the 1797 Incitement to Mutiny Act. In 1936, **Gallacher** supported those in the Labour Party backing an international popular front in the Spanish Civil War, and favoured a British-Soviet alliance against fascism. He was Communist MP for West Fife from 1935 to 1950 and the British 'Communist Party's most public figure'.[67]

Similarly, an early general secretary of the Communist Party GB, **Albert Inkpin** (1884–1944), was often imprisoned for 'pro-Soviet' activities and even for printing and circulating communist materials during the 1920s. He headed the Friends of the Soviet Union Society until his death, and wrote on the battle of Stalingrad.

Brought up by his impoverished parents as an idealistic young socialist, and a much warmer personality than **Inkpin**, **Harry Pollitt** (1890–1960), had started work at 12 in a weaving mill. He too served a twelve-month prison sentence in 1925 for seditious libel. He became general secretary of the British Communist Party in 1929 and was one of those whose need to believe in the Soviet Union as the world's one bulwark against fascism blinded them to the murderous totalitarianism of Stalin. However, as a passionate anti-fascist, he could not stomach the party line over the Nazi-Soviet Pact and the Nazi invasion of Poland, and he defied both the British party line and Moscow, saying '[We must] smash the fascist bastards once and for all'.[68] Once Hitler had invaded Russia, however, **Pollitt** found that he could reunite anti-fascism with his loyalty to the Soviet Union.

Among the most influential British communist thinkers, 'agitators' and trade unionists targeted by the Gestapo was **R. Palme Dutt** (1896–1974), the intellectually brilliant, privileged, half-Indian, half-Swedish theoretician of the British Communist Party and editor of its *Labour Monthly*. An influential anti-imperialist but an unswerving Stalinist, **Dutt** wrote a scathing analysis of nihilistic fascism, *Fascism and Social Revolution* (1934), and *World Politics* (1936).

A fellow writer, though not a Party apparatchik, was **Frank Jellinek** (1908–1974), who wrote his powerful *The Paris Commune of 1871* (1937) and *The Civil War in Spain* (1938) for the **Left Book Club.** Then he departed for Mexico where, as a correspondent for the ***Manchester Guardian***, he met Trotsky.

Far from being an intellectual, by contrast, **Nathan Birch** was an advocate of anti-fascist violence; he was singled out by the Gestapo as a young militant Jewish anti-fascist in East End, having written the *Mailed Fist* and having led the New World Fellowship.[69]

Among other leading young communists in the 1930s, **Ted Bramley** (1905–1970), had been born in rat-infested poverty in London, but he became a leading communist trade unionist in the Amalgamated Engineering Union (AEU), having joined the Party in 1927. He wanted to fight in Spain but the Party would not let him go. In June 1934, as secretary of the London branch of the Communist Party, **Bramley** led the large East End contingent from Stepney Green protesting against Mosley's rally at Olympia. During the war, **Bramley** spearheaded the use of the London Underground as night shelters in the Blitz; after the war he led a movement to occupy or 'squat' empty London luxury housing.

No British left-winger came from quite such a privileged, aristocratic circle as did **Lady Marian Ileene Mabel Cameron** (1895–1947), the communist daughter of the 15th Earl of Huntingdon, fox-hunting

Warner Plantagenet Hastings. The family claimed descent from the legendary Robin Hood: **Marian Cameron** certainly tried to practise taking from the rich to distribute to the poor, as did her brother, the 'Red' 16th earl, who was an assistant to the communist muralist Diego Rivera. In February 1936 she was arrested and deported from Rio de Janeiro because the Brazilian fascist dictator, Vargas, feared her exposure of the imprisonment and torture of Brazil's communist leader Luis Prestos.[70]

David Capper (1901–1974) was born to a refugee Jewish Lithuanian family and was a socialist and atheist by the age of 16. He won a scholarship to study French at King's College, London, and qualified as a teacher, but his career in education was not helped by his militant left-wing politics and trade union activism in the NUT. He managed to ensure that his humanist convictions, advocating secularism, would play a part in the NUT input into the 1944 Education Act.

A more prominent and much more influential trade unionist was the communist president of the South Wales Miners' Federation, **Arthur Horner** (1894–1968). The eldest of the seventeen children of a railway porter, only six of whom survived infancy, **Horner** became a miner in 1915, but was imprisoned in the First World War for refusing conscription because of his commitment to international working-class solidarity. He was a founder member of the **Communist Party of Great Britain** in 1921. In 1946 he was elected general secretary of the NUM and directed the union's strategy for the Miners' Charter when the industry was nationalised.[71]

The skilled engineer and leader of the National Shop Stewards movement, ***Jack Murphy*** (1888–1965), was another leading trade unionist within the British Communist Party. Imprisoned for 'seditious libel' and incitement to mutiny in 1925, ***Murphy*** was actually expelled from the Communist Party in 1932, because he could not accept 'democratic centralism'. He moved to the left-wing pressure group the Socialist League in the later 1930s.

An especially ardent young communist activist from the East End, **Abe Lazarus** (1911–1967), was listed as '*Kommunistenführer, Jude*'. First he supported the **National Unemployed Workers' Movement**. In 1933, when he was 22, he led a strike at the Firestone tyre factory, becoming South Midlands organiser for the Communist Party. A year later he was sent to organise the successful pressed steel strike at Cowley, Oxford, where he also publicised substandard local 'social housing'. In 1935 he and a companion marched on Oxford's Cutteslowe Walls – which separated middle-class homes from social housing – carrying a pickaxe in order to protest against the British middle-class attempt to impose social exclusion on the poor. (The walls were finally demolished in 1959.)[72]

Over fifty years older than **Lazarus**, aged 84 in 1940, but still an irrepressible communist activist and speaker almost to the end, was **Tom Mann** (1856–1941). At the age of 76 in 1932, he was imprisoned for refusing to keep the peace, calling for a day of action over unemployment. He was considered a phenomenon, not just in Britain but by socialists the world over and, as Chris Wrigley wrote in his *ODNB* entry on ***Mann***, 'one of the most lovable figures in the British Labour movement'.

Finally, the feminist socialist **Hilda Vernon** (fl. 1935–65), sent birthday greetings and news of the World Peace Congress in 1937 to Else Steinfurth, the widow of an assassinated German Communist MP who was herself now serving an indeterminate sentence in Moringen concentration camp.[73] **Vernon** was on the Spanish Aid committee and promoted the production of woollen garments by Hawick mills to be sent to Spain in 1936–9; she was also active in the Women's Co-operative Guild. She lived to attack the American war in Vietnam, giving lectures for the ***Daily Worker*** and supporting medical aid for Vietnam as late as 1965.

How had the Gestapo managed to learn the names, and often even the addresses, of such obscure foot-sloggers in the 1930s' British Communist Party? Clearly they must have had informers, both British and German – including 'entryist' stool pigeons[74] and fake 'refugees' in the party who were secretly enthusiastic pro-Nazis. Caroline Moorehead has given us a picture of the analogous network of informers in fascist Italy: 'By the end of the 1920s, [a] vast apparatus of surveillance had been put in place, consisting of a relatively small, tight-knit bureaucracy ... and several thousand "stringers" ... '[75] The Nazis were no doubt operating a similar structure in Britain, especially given their fantasy that Britain might be willing to cooperate with the Reich without a shot being fired.[76]

*

The Gestapo expressed special animus against 'The anti-German emigration in England' in their *Informationsheft*. They divided it, and its supporters, into Jewish, pacifist, liberal and religious organisations as well as the Labour Party and trade unions. Yet most of the foreign men and women in the Black Book who had been professional politicians in their own countries cannot be counted as would-be 'Britons' and they therefore do not form the subject of this study. For although they were refugees in danger of their lives, they never considered applying for British nationality, being now their own nations' leaders in exile in London, and living in hope of return.

From occupied Czechoslovakia, for example, came ex-president **Dr Eduard Benes** (1884–1948) and his wife **Hanna**, **Jan Masaryk** (1886–1948) the vice-president, and **Dr Jan Schramek** (1870–1956), minister president of the Czech government in exile as well as the Hapsburg **Prince Max Ernst Lobkowicz** (1903–1985), and **Dr Eduard Outraty** (fl. 1930–45), the Czech finance minister in exile, who helped the British war effort by passing on essential technical information on rifle components. **Agnes Hodina-Spurna** (1895–1963) had been a member of the Czech parliament until 1938; the Communist Party ordered her to emigrate to Britain via Poland and she became a member of the Czech state council in exile. Returning to Czechoslovakia in 1945, she was elected to the provisional national assembly as a Communist and became the first Czech woman to be vice-president of parliament. There were also the Slovak diplomat **Juraj Slavik** (1890–1969), who had reached London via Casablanca after the fall of France, and **Major General Jaroslav Vedr** (1895–1944), the Czech Chief of Staff. He had been a Czech resister to the Germans in 1938, and evacuated to Britain when he could remain in France no longer. He worked as a military diplomat for the Ministry of National Defence in London, but left Britain to fight with the Soviet Union and 1st Czech Army corps on the Eastern Front. He was killed by a mine in October 1944. **General Rudolf Viest** (1890–1945), a Slovak anti-Nazi and friend of **Benes**, also insisted on leaving London for Czechoslovakia to fight in the Slovak resistance in 1944; he died in Flossenburg concentration camp in 1945. The complex question of what was patriotism and what 'treason' in the Second World War is illustrated by **Colonel Frantiszek Moravek** (1895–1942), head of Czech intelligence, who escaped to London and helped the British Secret Intelligence Service after 1939, but who was also a full-time KGB agent after 1941, helping the Soviet Union against Nazi Germany.

It has been pointed out that most of the 13,400 Czech refugees in Britain were *not* distinguished national politicians, writers or army officers but simply workers who helped the British war effort. Just one Blacklisted example is **Albin Dick** (1913–1996), who came from a family of skilled glass-blowers and was himself a master arc-welder. **Dick** was active as a trade unionist and communist. After the German invasion of the Sudetenland, he fled to Prague, where **Doreen Warriner** of the British Committee for Refugees from Czechoslovakia and the Czech Communist Party gave him a forged British passport and visa and helped him to escape across the border. Deeply disappointed that he was not accepted to serve as a pilot in the RAF, **Dick** worked throughout the war in a munitions factory in bombed-out Coventry. After the war he refused to make his too-German name '**Dick**' more 'Czech', as demanded by the Czech authorities, choosing to live and die in communist Yugoslavia instead.

From Holland, among other Dutch political leaders, there was the former defence minister **A. Q. P. Dijkshoorn**. From Poland came the Resistance leader in exile, **General Sikorski** (1881–1943) and his deputy, **Stanislaw Mikolajczyk** (1901–1966). There was also the 80-year-old pianist **Paderewski** (1860–1941), who was on the Polish council in London, and **Wladyslaw Raczkiewicz** (1885–1947), first president of the Polish government in exile from 1940 to 1945, who would die in Wales. From France, of course, there was **General Charles de Gaulle** (1890–1970), leader of the Free French, and also **André Labarthe** (1902–1967), founder of the left-wing monthly *France Libre*, in London exile from 1940 to 1946. **Labarthe** was an opponent of the autocratic de Gaulle and possibly also a Soviet agent.

But most of the foreign political targets of the Gestapo were, of course, Austrian and German Jews, labelled 'anti-German emigrants' by the Nazis. The distinguished lawyer, economist and civil servant **Simon Abramowitz** (1887–1944), for example, had already left Germany for Britain in 1934. He worked in a London legal office and supported the exiled German Social Democrats in London before being interned in 1939 and dying in London in 1944. The Austrian Social Democrat **Heinrich Allina** reached Britain in 1939 after incarceration in Dachau and Buchenwald, only to be interned as an 'enemy alien' from 1939 to 1941. He was expelled by Austrian Social Democrats in exile in London for liaising with Austrian monarchist 'Legitimists'. Another Austrian monarchist, the Viennese doctor of law and anti-Nazi polemicist **Dr Victor Altmann**, was interned in Britain before being released to work for the BBC's wartime German service.

In 1933, the distinguished Austrian theorist of totalitarianism, **Franz Borkenau** (1900–1957), fled Germany, where he had been working at the Frankfurt Institute for Social Research. He settled first in Vienna, soon decamped to Paris and then to Panama City before arriving in London in 1936. He organised the secret German anti-Nazi movement *Neu Beginnenen* ('New Beginnings') from abroad. His best-known book was *The Spanish Cockpit* (1937), both anti-communist and anti-fascist, written after his arrest and torture in Spain. His *Austria and After* (1938), attacked the *Anschluss*, and in 1939 he tried to alert the world to Hitler's vision of world conquest, including the control of South Africa, in his *The New German Empire*. Nazi Germany *had* to aim at limitless expansionism, **Borkenau** argued, because otherwise it could not maintain its populist, totalitarian dictatorship rooted in nationalistic propaganda – plus terror – at home. During the Second World War **Borkenau** lived in London, writing for Cyril Connolly's

Horizon; after the war he moved between Germany, Paris, Rome and Zurich until his sudden death in 1957.

Among the German politicians was the former SPD MP for Franken, **Hans Dill** (1887–1973), one of the ninety-six German MPs who voted against transferring the legislative power of parliament to Hitler in March 1933. Stateless, he fled first to Czechoslovakia in 1933 and then to Britain in 1938, eventually emigrating to Canada. By contrast **Dr Curt Geyer** (1891–1963), another former leading figure in the German SPD who fled to Czechoslovakia and then France before reaching Britain, chose to remain: he became a British citizen and helped the foreign ministry during the war.

Many of the less eminent political refugees from Germany also managed to become British citizens. They included **Hans Ebeling** (1897–1968), an exiled Resistance leader of left-wing German youth. He worked for the BBC, broadcasting to Germany after the Second World War began. In 1942 he was one of the signatories of the 'Lidice Declaration' by German émigrés.[77] On the other hand the socialist **Herta Gotthelf** (1902–1963), who would become a leading figure in the women's section of West Germany's SPD after the war, was at first a stateless refugee in Britain. She supported herself as a children's maid and cleaning woman until 1943, when she found work at the BBC. In the meantime she managed to forge significant international links with other anti-Nazi refugee women from Germany, Czechoslovakia, Belgium, the Netherlands, Poland, Italy, France and Norway, all now in London. It was, she said, 'a women's international'.

The anti-Nazi Catholic socialist (and former military pilot) **Viktor Haefner** (1896–1967), had briefly been imprisoned immediately after the Nazis seized power. He fled to Paris and wrote to Rome in June 1933 warning Cardinal Pacelli, the Pope's secretary in the Vatican, of the monstrosity of Nazi anti-Semitism. He begged the Pope to excommunicate Nazi Catholics and rescind any concordat between the Nazi government and the church. **Haefner** got no reply. He fled from France to Britain in September 1939 and was stripped of his German nationality in 1942.

The German communist **Hebert Lessig** (1902–1966), was on the run from 1934 to 1942, until he was rescued by Quakers from Casablanca. In the early 1940s he volunteered for the British Army, getting his honourable discharge in 1947. He became a book binder and printer, and died in London. **Frieda Vahrenhorst** (1915–?) was another member of the socialist resistance in Germany, who, together with her youth group, had secretly circulated anti-Nazi leaflets in Hannover. She was tracked down by the Gestapo in 1936 as she tried to flee to Britain via Holland with her lover, the radical journalist **Werner Blumenberg**. Her fate is not known.

A tragic story that we do know is that of **Rudolf Olden** (1885–1940). A political journalist, lawyer and anti-Nazi activist, ***Olden*** had been one of very few Germans with sufficient moral courage to remain an outspoken supporter of human rights during the rise of Nazism. He agreed to defend the politically threatened in the German law courts before 1933, even as he saw the Nazi Party growing stronger. In 1931 he had successfully defended the pacifist leader Carl von Ossietzky. ***Olden*** addressed the last liberal/left-wing congress held in Germany, protesting against the increasing curbs on artistic liberty and freedom of speech. In February 1933 he was warned that he was now 'a wanted man', and so he fled the country with his future wife by skiing into Czechoslovakia.

After months in Prague, Geneva and Paris they reached London in November 1933, only to find it almost impossible to earn a living writing in a foreign language. They were rescued by the Greek classical scholar and Blacklisted internationalist, **Professor Gilbert Murray**, with whom they then lived in Oxford. Once there, ***Olden*** worked tirelessly as a one man anti-Nazi German pressure group. He co-founded German **PEN** in exile, lectured to Oxford University audiences and the Oxford **WEA** on the situation in Germany, and intervened on behalf of anti-Nazis still trapped in his homeland, including a failed attempt to rescue the intrepid anti-Nazi defence lawyer, Hans Litten. He also tried to arrange a Nobel laureateship for the pacifist Carl von Ossietzky.

The Gestapo were so determined to capture ***Rudolf Olden*** in Britain that they listed him several times – as lawyer, writer, secretary of International **PEN** and journalist. His correct British address is given in the *Sonderfahndungsliste* – although the Gestapo admitted to uncertainty as to whether it was in Oxford or in Cambridge. So intransigent and wide-ranging was ***Olden***'s published and spoken criticism of Nazism that he was wanted for interrogation by no fewer than five different Gestapo sections and was called 'especially notable' in the *Informationsheft*.

Olden wrote several books, including *Hitler the Pawn* (1936), *Germany a Hopeless Case?* (1940), and *The History of Liberty in Germany*, but he felt he was only another Cassandra, unable to convince the British about what they were facing. ***Olden***'s application to become 'naturalised', was actually refused by the Home Office as 'not a good one';[78] he had also been rejected by the BBC's German service. On 25 June 1940, to **Gilbert Murray's** horror, ***Rudolf Olden*** was arrested and interned as an 'enemy alien'. Despite lecturing inspiringly in the British prison camps, he soon became unwell. He was released to take up an academic post in the USA, and had to watch as a British immigration official blacked out his permission ever to return to Britain. He set sail in August 1940 and was drowned when the *City of Benares* was torpedoed by a U-boat. His wife died with him, refusing to leave him by taking a place on a lifeboat.[79] ***Rudolf Olden*** was the outstanding example of an anti-Nazi hunted by the Gestapo while simultaneously being rejected by a suspicious British Home Office.

Those German political refugees who survived but did not stay in Britain after 1945 included **Erich Ollenhauer** (1901–1963), a German SPD exile who went back in 1945 to become political leader of the SPD in Germany after Schumacher. Similarly, **Wilhelm Sander** (1895–1978), a German Social Democrat, was granted asylum in Britain in 1938, after imprisonment in 1933 and exile in Czechoslovakia and Sweden. He was active in refugee relief, editing *Socialist News* in German, and chairing the union of socialist organisations in Britain before he returned to West Germany in 1949, and became a leading SPD figure. On the far left, **Otto Beuer** had been a communist activist in Germany, who found himself imprisoned as such in Britain until 1943. After 1945 he left to live in the GDR. **Hans Schellenberger**, the communist first secretary of the refugees' free German culture league, also went to the GDR after the war, as did **Heinz Schmidt** (1906–1989), a left-wing, anti-Nazi resister, imprisoned in KZ Lichtenberg, who came to London in 1938, edited the German paper *Tribune*, and returned to East Germany in 1945.

A representative roller coaster of a trajectory for a Blacklisted German political refugee in Britain was that of **Dr Bernhard Reichenbach** (1888–1975). First an actor, then a student of literature, art history and sociology, he had been a leading figure in the youth movement of free students. As an idealistic young conscientious objector in the First World War he had served from 1915 to 1917 in the Medical Corps and had been at the Battle of Verdun. After the war he co-founded the German Communist Workers' Party and was duly on the 'Most Wanted' list for having been a German delegate to Lenin's Comintern in 1921. In 1925, still a Marxist, he joined the German Social Democrats, working as an entryist for the Communists and assuming responsibility for the needs of the prohibited '*Illegalen*'. Placed under *Berufsverbot* as a Jewish journalist and twice searched and interrogated as a left-winger by the Gestapo, **Reichenbach** fled Germany for Britain via the Netherlands in 1934. There he joined the Labour Party and worked with exiled German Social Democrat refugees. He was interned by the British as an 'enemy alien' but was promptly employed by the British government on his release, first to write anti-Nazi publications to be dropped by plane and later to edit the Foreign Office's paper for German POWs, *Die Wochenpost*. After the war **Reichenbach** became a London correspondent for West German radio and newspapers. He was decorated with the West German Federal Service Cross, First Class, in 1958 when he was 70. The most charismatic of all these left-wing German refugees was the youth-leader **Eberhard Koebel ('Tusk')** (1907–1955), a singer and writer, as well as the leader of the *Wandervoegel,* who was arrested and badly beaten up in prison in 1933. He fled to Sweden and then to London, where he joined the Free German Movement, returning to Germany (East Berlin) in 1945.

But it was not only refugee socialists and communists who were political targets of the Gestapo. **Carl August Wilhelm Weber** (1871–1957) was a banker, economist, and liberal politician. He had published *Wider [Against] den Nationalsozialismus* (Berlin, 1932), and the Gestapo pressured him to give up all his economic undertakings after 1933. He fled to Britain in 1939 and, aged 70, led the movement '*Freies Deutschland*', eventually dying in London. Meanwhile, **Gottfried Reinhold Treviranus** (1891–1971), who had been a Conservative politician under Weimar, fled in 1934 after being shot at during the anti-Roehm putsch. Castigated by the Gestapo for his work for the League of Nations – '*Sekretaer b. Fluechtlingskomitee im Voelkerbund London*', he lived in London from 1934 and then left for Canada and West Germany after 1945.

*

No one was more of a front-line political target for the Nazis than were their rivals for mass support, Germany's leading trade unionists – even after they had been forced to flee into British exile. The international trade unionist **Walter Auerbach** (1905–1975), had joined the SPD in 1923. Having completed his doctorate on 'The Press and Social Awareness', he was arrested in 1933 but managed to flee to Amsterdam where he worked for the International Federation of Trade Unions, in charge of information on fascism. Between 1939 and 1946 he was a refugee in Britain, working for the International Federation of Trade Unions in exile and organising an anti-Nazi Trade Union League. In 1939 he was stripped of his German citizenship for being a *Staatsfeind* and deprived of his doctorate. From London he broadcast calls for a European Social Democratic revolution and by 1944 was writing on how to reconstruct German trade unionism once the war was over. His hope was the ultimate formation of a world-wide association of trade unionists. He returned to Germany in 1946 (the British zone) and later worked for the Federal German Ministry of Employment.

The railway union organiser and SPD supporter **Walter Benninghaus** (1898–1947) fled Germany in 1937 for the Netherlands, the

Gestapo mistakenly believing he had gone on to Britain. Once the war started and Belgium and Holland were overrun, **Benninghaus** risked staying on in Antwerp as a British spy and anti-Nazi saboteur. He was eventually arrested and sent to the French camp at Gurs. Freed thanks to a bribe paid by a political supporter, he crossed to Spain, only to be arrested there on his way to Portugal; he finally got out and reached Lisbon in 1943. It was in October 1944 that **Benninghaus** at last reached Britain – in time to be interned as an 'enemy alien'. On his release, he worked for the headquarters of the International Federation of Trade Unions in Britain and then returned as trade union organiser to post-war Germany.[80]

Finally, the internationally renowned Dutch and international Trade Union leader **Edo Fimmen** (1881–1942) moved the whole **International Trade Union Federation** office to London in 1939. His aim, he said, was: 'not to support England and France but to oppose Hitler and his open and secret allies … The trade unions were defeated by fascism not because I gave the wrong lead but because I gave the right lead too feebly … I should have shouted.'

Felled by a stroke, **Fimmen** left Britain for Mexico, where he died.

*

London had never before been quite so cosmopolitan nor so vibrant with political argument and passion as it was during the Blitz. All the targeted refugees in this chapter, as well as many more not yet on the Gestapo's radar, added their ideas and desperate experiences to the anti-fascist discussions taking place within Britain. These refugees had been among the first Europeans to give themselves to revolutionary idealism after the First World War, all too soon followed by disillusion, the triumph of thuggish fascism, racist persecution, expulsion and exile. Not surprisingly, they were, in 1940, in the front line of those listed as 'Most Wanted' in Britain by the Gestapo. Disputing among themselves, and forced to argue continuously with their British hosts, who still hoped for the best that appeasement would work, some despaired. They had been compelled to learn *not* to wage a revolution – nor even to attempt any radical social reform – in the midst of a global economic crisis. They had then had to flee the juggernaut of Nazism and try to find asylum. Many perished.

Conclusion

We Can Fight with the Mind

Virginia Woolf, 'Notes on Peace in an Air-raid', published posthumously in *The Death of the Moth and Other Essays*, 1942

What, asks the moral philosopher Susan Neiman, can we learn from the Holocaust? We 'can learn [to] be aware of the beginnings. Be aware of racism, be aware of nationalism. The Nazis went very slowly and carefully to see what the population would accept.'[1] The Gestapo's Black Book is a terrible warning against tribalism. Yet it is also an antidote to the Nazis' 'patriotic', fascist hard-heartedness. Almost all the people selected for early elimination in a Nazi Britain were the spiritual enemies of '*Haerte*', being exceptionally humane men and women. They practised what the social reformer Jane Addams called 'the internationalism of the deed': they wanted *all* their fellow humans to have life and have it more abundantly. We should never forget that we are the heirs of **Dr Christopher Addison**, **Eleanor Rathbone**, **Frank Foley**, **F. L. Lucas**, **Margery Fry**, **Geoffrey Mander**, **Maude Royden**, ***Bishop Bell***, **Fritz Borinski** and **Herbert Sulzbach** – among many other determined rescuers, including the great scientists **Julian Huxley**, **J. D. Bernal**, **Patrick Blackett**, **Ernst Chain**, **Hugh Blashko**, **Max Born** and **Leo Szilard**.

And when, in December 1933, two little steamers chugged up the Thames bringing the Warburg Institute's wealth of art history from prehistoric times to the present, as well as their Jewish experts, from Hamburg to London, they were emblematic of the riches that are brought to their host country by every refugee. The preceding chapters have demonstrated just what a wealth of intellectual gifts the German, Austrian, Czech, Hungarian and Polish, mostly Jewish, refugees from Nazism brought with them to Britain after 1933.

Naturally, we feel relieved and thankful that all those extraordinarily gifted, humane people, both British-born and refugee, both Jewish and non-Jewish, survived. They were not, in the event, arrested, let alone shot. But for each one who survived, there were at least a hundred or more of their counterparts in Eastern Europe who suffered summary execution. 'According to its own records, [Col. Six's] Einsatzgruppe B murdered over 140,000 people by 31 March 1943, the overwhelming majority of them Jews.'[2] And '[Col. Six's] *Vorkommando* Moscow was forced to execute another 46 persons, amongst them 38 intellectual Jews who had tried to create unrest and discontent in the newly established Ghetto of Smolensk.'[3]

'How,' Jean-Michel Palmier asks, 'can one measure the impact of intellectual resistance?'[4] His answer is pessimistic. Despite all 'their courage and intelligence and ... astonishing moral sense', he claims that the anti-fascist exiles were impotent. They did not genuinely threaten fascism, because 'Europe refused to rouse itself from its slumber when the émigrés issued warning after warning ... In Italy and Germany it was *foreign* armies that brought the death of fascist regimes' (my emphasis). But Palmier does not connect the influence that the refugees' early warnings had on the eventual coming of those vital, foreign armies just six years on.

It is the contention of this book that the 'mental fight' waged over the six years from 1933 by anti-Nazi artists, publishers, writers, social reformers, political activists, businessmen, diplomats, religious leaders, university teachers and researchers, MPs and trade union leaders, whether British-born or refugee, pooling their intelligence and speaking out – until they constituted a critical mass – ultimately brought Britain to her senses. How could many of the young Spitfire pilots *not* have been influenced politically by the cartoons of **David Low**, or by the anti-fascist ***Picture Post***, or by the BBC talks of **E. M. Forster** and **J. B. Priestley**, heard by millions? And not just those among them in the Blacklisted '**left-wing movement**' – the '*sozialistische Fleigervereinigung*' ('socialist pilots' association').

But those same anti-fascists had had to struggle year after year against a very powerful will to appease Hitler. They had used graffiti, posters, books and articles, letters to *The Times* and the ***Manchester Guardian***, speeches in the Houses of Parliament, public rallies and private meetings of activists, as well as constant fundraising for the victims of fascism – the small trade union branches collecting for medical aid for Spain, the Women's Co-operative Guild branches welcoming Basque child refugees, the Quakers organising and funding the *Kindertransport*. For many years they believed themselves to be unheeded.[5] But in fact they were crucial in stiffening the nation's final determination to withstand Hitler. We should not forget that they too are part of our British DNA – although far from constituting all of it. And now it is our turn to 'stand and cover [our] stations'.[6]

Who were the most dangerous British anti-Nazis in 1940? Ask the Nazis. Quite against their intention, the Gestapo produced in their anonymous, secret 'Black Book', a great document of British history. For in it they testified to the strength and breadth of anti-fascist British resistance before and during the Second World War. How many of the rights that we still have are the fruits of that struggle? And will we champion those rights with comparable doggedness and courage?

Appendix 1

Émigré Organisations Supporting Refugees Listed in the *Informationsheft GB*

a) For émigrés in general

Committee for Mass Colonisation, Anthony de Rothschild, New Court, London EC4

Co-ordinating Committee for Refugees, Domestic Department, Mecklenburgh Square off Guildford Street, London WC1

Federation of Polish Jews in Great Britain, 24 Oldgate, London EC3

Intergovernmental Committee, Central Building, Westminster, SW1. Director: George Rublee

International Committee for Employment of Refugees (Professional Workers), 38 Primrose Hill Road, London. President: Mr Edgar Dugdale; Honorary Secretary: Miss Mary Omerod

International Student Service (ISSO), Co-operating Committee for England and Wales, 49 Gordon Square, London WC1. Chairman: Dr Tissington Tatlow; Chairman for England: Sir Walter Moberly; Treasurer: Professor Ernest Barker; Treasurer for Support Organisation: Mr Gareth Maufe; Secretary for Support Organisation: Miss Christina Ogilvy

Jewish Professional Committee, Woburn House, London. Chairman: A. J. Makower; Vice-Chairman: Sir Philip Hartog

Jewish Refugees Committee, Woburn House, London. Chairmen: Otto M. Schiff and Leonard M. Montefiore

Jewish Resettlement, Woburn House, London. Chairman: Sir Robert Waley Cohen; Director: Mayer Stephany

Refugees Co-operative Housing Scheme, 124 Westbourne Terrace, London W2

The Jewish Association for the International Protection of Jewish Girls, Women and Children, 45 Great Prescott Street, Aldgate, London E1. President: Mrs N. Charles Rothschild; Vice-Presidents: Dr Claude Montefiore, Artur R. Moro; Secretaries: Mrs L. Pyke, S. Cohen

The Society for the Protection of Science and Learning (formerly: Academic Assistance Council), 12 Clement's Inn Passage, Clare Market, London. Chairman: Lord Rutherford of Nelson

International Student Service, 3 West Castle Road, Edinburgh. Contact: J. de Gaudin

Glasgow Jewish Council for German Refugees, Queens Square, Glasgow S1

b) For German émigrés

The High Commission of the League of Nations for Refugees from Germany, 16 Northumberland Avenue, London WC2. President: Major General Sir Neill Malcolm. Representative: Lord Duncannon

British Movement for the Care of Children from Germany, 69 Great Russell Street, London WC1

Central British Fund for German Jewry, Woburn House, Upper Woburn Place, London WC1. Chairman: Sir Osmond E. d'Avigdor-Goldsmid

Central Bureau for the Settlement of German Jews in Palestine, 77 Great Russell Street, London. Division of the Jewish Agency. President: Dr Chaim Weizmann; Director of the London office: Dr Martin Rosenblüt

Council for German Jewry (Agricultural Committee), Bentinal House, 46 Southampton Row, London WC1. President: Dr Karl Kapralik, 49 Eton Place, London; Secretary: Stephany

Council for German Jewry, Woburn House, London. Chairman: Viscount Samuel of Mount Carmel

German Jewish Aid Committee, Bloomsbury House, London

Inter-Aid Committee for Children from Germany, 21 Bedford Row, London WC1. Chairman: Sir Wyndham Deedes; Secretaries: Gladys Stelton, Francis Bendet

Notgemeinschaft Deutscher Wissenschaftler im Ausland (Emergency Community of German Scientists Abroad), 12 Clement's Inn Passage, Clare Market, London. Chairman: Privy Councillor Dr Demuth

Union for Displaced German Scholars, 12 Clement's Inn Passage, Clare Market, London

Appendix 2

Jewish Organisations of Anglo-Jewry Listed in the *Informationsheft GB*

The Jewish Defence Committee, Woburn House, Upper Woburn Place, London WC1. First Secretary: Sidney Salomon

B'nai B'rith, Woburn House, Upper Woburn Place, London WC1

District Grand Lodge of Great Britain and Ireland, address as above. Grand-President: Julius Schwab; Grand Vice-President: Mrs V. Hassan and Professor S. Brodetzky; Grand Treasurer: Harry Samuels

European Committee, address as above. President: Julius Schwab, 180 Goldhurst Terrace, London NW6

Agudas Israel, 53 Queens Drive, London N16. President: Jacob Rosenheim; Treasurer: Ludwig Strauss; Political Secretary: H. Goodman; Organisation Secretary: Henry Pels

Keren Hayishuv Co. Ltd, 19 London Wall, London EC2. Chairman: J. Rosenheim; Secretary: M. L. Halpern

Freeland League for Jewish Territorial Colonisation, 69 Aberdare Gardens, London NW6. Treasurer: Dr Myer S. Nathan; Secretary: Dr I. N. Steinberg

Jewish Colonisation Association, 16 Old Broad Street, London WC2. President: Sir Osmond E. d'Avigdor-Goldsmid; Vice-President: Jules Philippson; Main Management: Dr Louis Oungre

Maccabi World Union, 37 Museum Street, London WC1. Presidents: Rt Hon. Lord Melchett, Professor S. Brodetzky; Chairman: Dr H. Lelewer; Treasurer: Dr K. F. Jacobowitz; Organisation manager: Dr W. W. Meisl

World Jewish Congress, 150 Dudden Hill Lane, London NW10. President: Marchioness of Reading; Chairman: Rev. M. L.Perlzweig; Treasurer: L. Gildesgame; Secretaries-General: N. Barou, Prof. E. Cohn

Anglo-Jewish Association, Woburn House, Upper Woburn Place, London WC1. President: Leonard J. Stein; Vice-Presidents: Sir Osmond E. d'Avigdor-Goldsmid, Rev. Dr H. I. Hertz, Lionel de Rothschild; Treasurer: Leonard G. Montefiore

Joint British Committee for the Reconstruction of East European Jewry

(Ort-Ose), Central Office: Premier House, 150 Southampton Row, London WC1. President: Lord Rothschild; Chairman: A. I. Halpern; Treasurer: I. H. Levey

ORT, address see above. Chairman: A. I. Halpern; Treasurer: S. Beloff; Secretary P. I. Rogers

Jewish Agency for Palestine (Zionist), 77 Great Russell Street, London WC1. President: Dr Chaim Weizmann; Executive Member: Prof. S. Brodetzky; Director of Information: Rev. M. L. Perlzweig; Secretary: A. Lourie (political department), Israel Cohen (information department), J. Hodes (editor of the *New Judea*), I. Linton (finance and administration)

British Section, address see above. Chairman: Lord Melchett; Secretaries-General: L. Bakstansky, A. G. Brotman

Kerem Hayesod Committee, address see above. President Gen.: Sir Osmond E. d'Avigdor-Goldsmid; President: Simon Marks; Chairman: The Marchioness of Reading; Secretaries-General: Rev. M. L. Perlzweig, L. Bakstansky; Treasurers: Dennis M. Cohn, A. Le Vay Lawrence

The World Zionist Organisation, 77 Great Russell St, London WC1. President: Dr Chaim Weizmann; Chairman of the Executive: D. Ben Gurion

Keren Kayemet Leisrael Ltd (Jewish National Fund), 65 Southampton Row, London WC1. President: Prof. Samson Wright; Treasurer: Albert van den Bergh; Secretary: Maurice Posette

The Jewish State Party, 6 Queensdown Road, Clapton, London E5. Chairman: Dr I. M. Machover; Secretary-General: E. Livny

World Mizrachi Organisation, 78 New Oxford St, London WC1. President: Dr I. H. Hertz; Vice-President: Salomon Wolfson; Chairman: S. E. Sklan; Representative Chairman: Dayn M. Gollop; Treasurer: W. N. Williams; Secretaries-General: F. N. Landau, W. Frankel

Poale Zion, 134 Goldhurst Terrace, London NW6. Secretary-General: Dr. S. Levenberg

Habonim (Zionist Youth Organisation), 65 Southampton Row, London WC1. President: Dr Nathan Morris; Vice-Presidents: J. C. Gilbert, Rev. B. Cherrick

Women's International Zionist Organisation (WIZO), 75 Great Russell St, London WC1. President General: The Viscountess Samuel; Vice-President: Mrs H. Irwell; Chairs: I. M. Sieff, Mrs Weizmann; Organisation and Propaganda Department: P. Goodman; Treasurers: H. Irwell, Olga Alman

New Zionist Organisation, 47 Finchley Road, London NW8. President: Vladimir Jabotinsky; Presidential Members: A. Abrahams, E. Ben-Horin, Dr I. Damm, Dr S. Klinger, A. Kopelowicz; Secretary-General: I. Benari

Independent Order of B'nai B'rith, 118 Great Ducie Street, Strangeways, Manchester. President General: M. Redstone; Secretary-General: D. Dolovitz

The Board of Deputies, Woburn House, Upper Woburn Place, London WC1. President: Prof. S. Brodetzky; Vice-Presidents: Sir Robert Waley Cohen, Dr

Israel Feldmann; Treasurer: Gordon Livermann; Secretary: A. C. Brotman; Syndic: Charles H. L. Emanuel

London Area Council, 43 Prescot Street, London E1. Chairman: Cyril M. Picciotto; Secretary: Councillor Henry Solomons

Sephardi World Union, Heneage Lane, Bevis Marks, London EC3. President General: Charles E. Sebag-Montefiore; President: David Vaz Nunes da Costa; Financial Secretary: David Berio

The Zionist Federation of Great Britain and Ireland, Woodside, Hinksey Hill, Oxford. President: Dr Chaim Weizmann; Vice-President: Lord Melchett; Executive: I. K. Goldbloom; Treasurer: Paul Goodman; Secretaries-General: M. L. Perlzweig, L. Bakstansky. Mrs A. Harris, 94 Clive Road, London NW2. Miss Nathan, c/o 29 Palace Road, London SW2. J. Samuel, 32 North Villas, Camden Square, London NW1. J. White, 5 King Edward's Gardens, London W13. Mrs S. W. Magnus, 55 Wolmer Gdns. J. Rosen, 24 Vaughan Ave, London NW4. A. Sheinwold, 108 Clarence Road, London E5. D. Benjamin, 367 Queen's Road, London E13. Mrs G. Karsberg, 134 Broomwood Road, London NW11. R. Gale, 220 Stamford Hill, London N16. Dr H. Capell, 121 Parkside Way, London N. Harrow. Miss J. Goldberg, 33 Wickford St, London E1. Miss S. Klein, 79 Chalkhill Rd, Wembley Park. I. J. Miller, 1 Green's Court, London W1. O. Rose, 19 Colville Road, London W11. A. Sheinwold, 108 Clarence Road, London E5

Federation of Women Zionists of Great Britain and Ireland, 75 Great Russell St, London WC1. President: Mrs I. M. Sieff; Chair: R. B. Solomon; Vice-Chair: Mrs M. D. Eder; Secretaries-General: Mrs J. Hodess, M. Liebster

New Zionist Organisation in Great Britain, 47 Finchley Road, London NW8

Brit Trumpeldor, address see above. President: Vladimir Jabotinsky; Secretary-General: M. Katz; Navy Dept: I. Helpern; Cultural Dept: I. Remba

Student Corporations, address see above

British Maccabi Association, 34 Clarendon Road, London W11. President: Lord Melchett; Chairman: I. H. Levey; Treasurer: R. R. Curtis; Secretaries: Rev. E. Levine, G. H. Gee, Hyman Cen, M. Lam, Maccabi House, 73 Compayne Gdns, London NW6. Alfred Cohen, 154 George Lane, London SE13. A. King, 83 Baston Road, London N16. M. Swerdlin, 91 Clarence Road, London E5

The Joint Foreign Committee, Woburn House, Upper Woburn Place, London WC1. Secretary: A. G. Brotman; Members of the Board of Deputies: Neville J. Laski, Sir Osmond E. d'Avigdor-Goldsmid, Israel Cohen, Lionel E. Colmen, S. Robert Waley Cohen, Barnett Janner, H. L. Nathan. Members of the Anglo-Jewish Association: Leonard Stein, Sir Philip Hartog, Leonard G. Montefiore, Sir P. Magnus

Appendix 3

British Peace Organisations Listed in the *Sonderfahndungsliste*

The Anti-Conscription League, Edinburgh
The Anti-Kriegsbewegung der Lehrer (Teachers' Anti-War Movement) (Marxist-communist) London
The British Commonwealth Peace Federation, St Stephen's House (Quaker)
The British Anti-War Movement – 'Communist'
The British Movement Against Fascism and War (BMFW), 17 Endell Street
The British Youth Peace Assembly
The China Campaign Committee
The Council of Action for Peace and Reconstruction, Horseferry House, Dean Ryle Street
The Council of Christian Pacifist Groups, 15 Victoria Street, London
The Federation Fellowship 'serves idea of Peace and European co-operation'
The Federation of Progressive Societies and Individuals ('Left-wing')
The Friends' Service Council – 'edelkommunistisch' (Quakers)
The Fellowship of Reconciliation
Internacia Esperanto Liga, London (Emigranten)
Internacia Katolika Unuigo Esperantista (London)
The International Friendship through the Churches, 1 Arundel Street
The International Peace Campaign, 18 Grosvenor Crescent Mews
The Jewish Peace Society
The League of Nations Union
The National Peace Council, 39 Victoria Street, SW1
The No More War Movement ('Leftist'), 55 Long Acre
The Peace Book Co. Ltd, St Martin's Lane – also the address for *Peace News* and The Peace Pledge Union
The Link – aiming to further German–English understanding – 230 The Strand
The Union for Democratic Control of Foreign Policy (UDC), 34 Victoria Street
'Union' – World Clubs' Union, furthering friendly relations between peoples
War Resisters International (i.e. conscientious objectors), 11 Abbey Road, Enfield, Middlesex

Women's International Congress against War and Fascism
Women's International League for Peace and Freedom (i.e. WILPF), 5 Gower Street
Women's World Committee Against War and Fascism, 39 Furnivall Street

Appendix 4

British Refugee-supporting Organisations Listed in the *Sonderfahndungsliste*

The Academic Assistance Council, 12 Clement's Inn Passage, Clare Market – '*Notgemeinschaft deutscher Wissenschaftler im Ausland*' (Emergency support for foreign scholars – works for the British Propaganda and Intelligence Services)

Austrian Emigrants in England, 9 Albert Place Mansions

Austrian Self-Aid Committee, 89 New Oxford Street; Westbourne Terrace

Austrian Centre, Emigrants' Home, Westbourne Terrace

British Committee for Refugees from Czechoslovakia

British Aid Committee for Children, 16 Russell Square

Catholic Committee for Refugees from Germany, 120 Victoria Street

Catholic Committee for Refugees from Prague, 12 Bedford Place

Central Office for Refugees, 15 Mecklenburgh Square

C of E Committee for non-Aryan children – i.e. non-Aryan Protestants, Parliament Mansions, Victoria Street

Committee for Relief of Victims of German Fascism, Anglo House, Lichfield Street, WC1

Czech Refugees Trust Fund, Colquhoun House, Broadwick Street

Czechoslovakian Emigrants' Committee, 5 Mecklenburg Square

Friends' House, Euston Road. '*Geldquelle fuer Emigranten*' ('Money source for emigrants' – i.e. refugees)

Friends of New Europe, St Stephen's House, 97 Westminster (Quaker) '*foerdert deutschfeindliche Emigrantenbestrebungen*' ('strengthens efforts for emigrants that cause hostility to Germany')

Friends of Europe, brings out a publication 'Holland/Nazi Germany and Great Britain' – 'Quaker organisation with '*stark edelkommunistischen*' ('strong noble communist aspirations') but 'Marxist'

Friends Service Council, Friends House

German Emergency Committee, Society of Friends

German Jewish Aid Committee, Bloomsbury House Palace Hotel (part Quaker *Kindertransport* administration HQ)

German Refugee Assistance Fund, Karl Knudson, Abbey House, 232 Victoria Street

German Refugee Hospitality Committee, 28 Little Russell Street (Jewish world organisation caring for non-Aryan children)

Inter-Aid Committee for Children from Germany

International Women's Congress against War and Fascism, 'Communist'

International Christian Committee for German Refugees, (Emigrants)

International Friendship through the Churches, Support for German emigrants, 1 Arundel Street, London

International Student Service, 49 Gordon Square, 'supports students' (i.e. Jewish refugee students in Britain)

Jewish Refugee Committee, Woburn House, Upper Woburn Place (Schiff)

Movement for the Care of Children from Germany (*Kindertransport*), 69 Great Russell Street

Jews' Temporary Shelter, 63 Mansell Street

National Joint Committee for Spanish Relief, 53 Marsham Street

National Christian Appeal for Refugees from Germany, Lady Bessborough, 3 Eaton Square, SW1; 46 Southampton Row

Quaeker-Vereinigung , Quaker Union, Friedens House, i.e. Friends' House, 'supporters of Aryan emigrants' '*Rote Hilfe*'- i.e. socialist

Refugee Children's Movement (*Kindertransport*)

Society of Friends, 'Quaeker' – The Society of Friends, '*betreut alle mosaischen Nichtarier*' ('looks after all Jewish non-Aryans'), Euston Road

Schriftsteller-Internationale, i.e. PEN, British Section, 59–61 New Oxford Street; 'Communist'

Society for the Protection of Science and Learning – refugee scholars, 6 Gordon Square

Relief Committee for the victims of German and Austrian fascism; 'Communist'

The High Commission of the League of Nations for Refugees from Germany, 16 Northumberland Avenue

Treetops Camp, Guildford, Surrey, 'for emigrant children'

Appendix 5

British Political Institutions, Associations, Campaigns Listed in the *Sonderfahndungsliste*

Abyssinia Association, London
Anglo-Russian Parliamentary Committee, London, 6 Buckingham Street
British Movement against Fascism and War, London, 17 Endell Street
China Campaign Committee, 34 Victoria Street
Cobden Club (Liberal), '*deutschfeindlich*', London
Communist Party of Great Britain, 16 King Street, WC2
Conservative and Unionist Central Office, Palace Chambers, Bridge Street, SW1
Cooperative Party, 56 Victoria Street, SW1
Fabian Society – '*Linksvereinigung*', 11 Dartmouth Street, SW1
For Intellectual Liberty (FIL) – Movement to resist fascism and any attack on democratic freedom, 23 Haymarket, SW1 (Secretary: Margaret Gardiner, 'Mrs Bernal')
General Federation of Trade Unions, Central House, Upper Woburn Place, WC1
Independent Labour Party (ILP), 'socialist splinter group – *Splittergruppe*', 35 St Bride Street, EC4
International Federation of Trade Unions
International Labour Defends, London
Jewish Socialist Labour Party, 27 Sandys Road, Bishopsgate, E1
Labour Book Service, 6 Catherine Street, WC2
Labour League of Youth, Transport House, Smith Square, SW1
Labour Party, 'British section of the Second International', Transport House, Smith Square, SW1
Labour Research Department, 60 Doughty Street, WC1
Left Book Service, Victor Gollancz Ltd (Aim: socialist book service), 14 Henrietta Street, WC2
Left Wing Movement, socialist pilots' association, London
Liberal National Party, 15 Old Queen Street, SW1
Liberal Party Organisation, 42 Parliament Street, SW1
Liberal Publication department, 42 Parliament Street, SW1
London Labour Party, 258–262 Westminster Bridge Road, SW1

Marx Memorial Library and Workers' School
Marxist Group – 'Trotskyist' – 25 Aubert Park, 5 Highbury
Militant Socialist International (British Section), 116 Great Titchfield Street, W1
National Committee (not Council) for Civil Liberty ('Aim: communist') – no address
National Council for Equal Citizenship (Women's Rights successor to the Suffrage Movement), Flat 5, 72 Horseferry Road
New Commonwealth (**Richard Acland**'s new party) Thorney House, Smith Square, SW1
New Fabian Research Bureau, 37 Great James Street, W1
Political and Research Dept (Secretariat of the TGWU, leader John Price) Smith Square, Westminster
Socialist League, 3 Victoria Street, SW1
Socialist Party of Great Britain, 42 Great Dover Street, SW1
The World Non-Sectarian, anti-Nazi Organisation to Secure Human Rights, London SW1
Young Communist League, King Street, WC2

Notes

Introduction: Why Resurrect These Dead?

1 The chatty, haphazard, sometimes inaccurate *The Black Book – What if Germany had Won World War II – A Chilling Glimpse into the Nazi Plans for Great Britain* by Trow, M. J. (John Blake, 2017), has no index, admits that it selects names 'at random', and mentions no more than a handful of Jewish refugees for 'reasons of space'.

2 Johnson, Eric, *Nazi Terror: The Gestapo, Jews and Ordinary Germans* (Basic Books, 1999).

3 Hansen, Randall, *Disobeying Hitler* (Faber and Faber, 2014), ch. 17.

4 In addition, there were of course the *Wehrmacht*'s plans, now held in the Bodleian Library, divided, with maps and photographs, into two parts – first the vital statistics on the British climate, industry, energy, transport, population etc., and then a strategic assessment, both overall and regarding particular regions.

5 Dams, Carsten, and Stolle, Michael, *The Gestapo: Power and Terror in the Third Reich* (OUP, 2014), p. 61. It was an electrically powered system – 'at the press of a button one man could access any one of the 500,000 cards'.

6 Copsey, Nigel, *Anti-Fascism in Britain* (Palgrave Macmillan, 2000), ch. 3. 'Never Again!' p. 81, citing Eatwell, R., *Fascism: A History* (1995), p. 14. And see Hodgson, Keith, *Fighting Fascism: The British Left and the Rise of Fascism, 1919–1939* (Manchester University Press, 2010), Introduction, p. 14.

7 Copsey, N., *Anti-Fascism in Britain*, op. cit. Introduction.

8 Webster, Wendy, *Mixing it: Diversity in World War Two Britain* (OUP, 2018), Introduction.

9 Cf. Brown, Gordon, 'The new battle for Britain? Resistance to Nigel Farage' in *The Guardian*, 30 May 2019, and Quinn, Ben, on 'Unwillingness to engage with threat of far-right groups lets them flourish', the Royal United Services Institute Report on lack of government investigation of far-right finances in *The Guardian*, 31 May 2019. For the censorship-wielding misogyny and homophobia of the far-right, worldwide, see Shafak, Eli, 'For authoritarians, stifling the arts is of a piece with demonising minorities', *Observer*, 22 September 2019.

10 For example, the murky financing of the British National Party, the English Defence League, UKIP, and the Brexit Party. And see the ongoing investigation of Arron Banks, the multi-millionaire financier of Nigel

Farage and Brexit and his possible links with Russia: 'Arron Banks and the mystery of Brexit Campaign Funds', *Financial Times*, 4 November 2018 – not to mention the mysterious financing of white supremacist 'Generation Identity' and of the anti-migrant vigilantes in 'Britain First'.

11 See Timms, Edward, *Anna Haag and her Secret Diary of the Second World War* (Peter Lang, 2015).

1. The Black Book in Context: Nazi Plans for the Invasion 1939–40

1 The American news agency Associated Press had itself had a bad record of dismissing Jews and assisting Nazi propaganda after 1935 – see Scharnberg, Harriet, 'Associated Press und die nationalsozialistische Bildpublizistik', in *Studies in Contemporary History*, vol. 13, 2016, pp. 11–37.

2 Dams and Stolle, *The Gestapo*, op. cit., ch. 4, p. 59.

3 Evans, Richard, *The Guardian*, 14 March 2015.

4 Lukas, Richard, *The Forgotten Holocaust: The Poles under German Occupation, 1939–1944*, ch. 1: published for The Polish Ministry of Information in exile, *The German New Order in Poland 1942*, Hutchinson, 1942; Piotrowski, Tadeusz, *Poland's Holocaust* (McFarland and Co., 2007).

5 Shirer, William L., *The Rise and Fall of the Third Reich: A History of Nazi Germany*, Simon and Schuster, 1960, p. 782.

6 Dams and Stolle, *The Gestapo*, op. cit., ch. 4, p. 63.

7 Webster, Wendy, *Mixing It*, op. cit., Introduction, pp. 2–8, 13.

8 Webster, *Mixing It*, op. cit., Introduction, p. 8.

9 Dams and Stolle, *The Gestapo*, op. cit., p. 182.

10 Doerries, Reinhard, *Hitler's Last Chief of Foreign Intelligence: Allied Interrogations of Walter Schellenberg* (Frank Cass, 2003) and see Hastings, Max, 'The "Good Nazi" in *The Secret War* (Collins, 2015), p. 473 et seq.

11 'Precisely who wrote the whole of this report remains unclear to this day', West, Nigel, Preface to *Invasion 1940* (St Ermin's Press, 2000).

12 **Brockway, Fenner**, *Inside the Left* (Allen and Unwin 1942), pp. 334–5.

13 Norton-Taylor, Richard, *The Guardian*, 28 February 2014. And see Willetts, Paul, 'Britain's tearoom fascists' in *BBC History Magazine*, on the anti-Semitic Nordic League and Right League during the 1930s – as well as the British Union of Fascists whose rallies attracted 20,000 followers.

14 See West, Nigel, Preface to *Invasion 1940*, op. cit., pp. xxxii–xxxiii.

15 Moorehead, Caroline, *A Bold and Dangerous Family: the Rossellis and the Fight against Mussolini* (Chatto and Windus, 2017).

16 Quoted in Caygill, Howard, *On Resistance, A Philosophy of Defiance* (Bloomsbury, 2013), p. 10.

17 Ibid., pp. 12–13 (my emphasis).

18 Ibid., op. cit., pp. 139 and 158.

19 See Dams and Stolle, *The Gestapo*, op. cit. p. 146, and Breitman, Richard,

'Historical Analysis of 20 Name Files from CIA Records', Declassified CIA records, 263, April 2001.

20 Lampe, David, *The Last Ditch: Britain's Secret Resistance and the Nazi Invasion Plans* (Greenhill Books, 1968, reprinted Skyhorse, 2007), p. 24, and see Macintyre, Ben, 'Brutal professor who would have run SS-GB,' *The Times*, 4 March 2017.

21 Breitman, Richard, Declassified CIA records.

22 Lampe, *The Last Ditch*, op. cit., p. 12.

23 Ibid., pp. 12–14 and 19.

24 Ibid., op. cit., pp. 16–18.

25 Ibid., op. cit., Preface.

2. What was wrong with Britain in Nazi Eyes? – *The Informationsheft GB*

1 Obviously the original, intended for German troops, is in German. Sixty years later an abbreviated English translation came out: *Invasion 1940: The Nazi Invasion Plan for Britain* (the author being given, mistakenly, as SS General Walter Schellenberg) with an introduction by Professor John Erickson (St Ermin's Press, 2000). I quote from the unabbreviated original, using my own translation.

2 A neighbour of the anti-Nazi resister Anna Haag in Stuttgart, quoted by Timms, Edward, in *Anna Haag and her Secret War Diary of the Second World War* (Peter Lang, 2015,) p. 108.

3 Lampe, David, *The Last Ditch*, p. 24. As well as in London, the Gestapo planned to have headquarters with *Einsatzgruppen* (execution squads) in Birmingham, Bristol, Liverpool and Manchester as well as in either Edinburgh or Glasgow.

4 Erickson, John, Introduction to *Invasion 1940*, op. cit., p. xvii.

5 Ibid., op. cit, p. xx.

6 Ibid., p. xxii.

7 All names of individuals and organisations in the *Informationsheft* are in ***bold italic.***

8 The other Oxford Pamphlet academics named here for the first time are: ***A. G. B. Fischer***, ***J. W. Brierly***, ***H. V. Hodson***, ***H. D. Henderson*** and ***G. F. Hudson***.

9 See for example the Black-listed youth leader **Eberhard Koebel** ('**Tusk**') in 'Political Targets' p. 368.

10 For the prominent individual Anglican churchmen who, the Gestapo now realised, would have to be placed at least under surveillance, if not immediately arrested, see chapter 14: The Church, pp. 200.

11 See Oldfield, Sybil, 'German Women in the Resistance to Hitler', in *Thinking Against the Current: Literature and Political Resistance* (Sussex Academic Press, 2013).

12 See Koppen, 'The anti-Masonic writings of General Erich Ludendorff' (academia.edu 2010).
13 Some German **Freemasons** were sent to concentration camps but it is not clear how many were murdered because they were **Freemasons** or because they were anti-Nazi or because they were Jews.
14 Moorehead, Caroline, *A Bold and Dangerous Family*, op. cit., p. 145.
15 See 'Freemasonry under the Nazi Regime', in the United States Holocaust Museum.
16 Scanlan, Matthew, 'Fascist Attack' in *Freemasonry Today*, 2007, pp. 25, 87, 100.
17 See **Whately, Monica,** p. 000 below.
18 See Copsey, Nigel, *Anti-Fascism in Britain*, op. cit., ch. 2, pp. 50–53 and footnote 29.
19 For discussion of these individual businessmen and financiers, see ch. 12, below.
20 Webster, Wendy, *Mixing It*, op. cit., ch. 5, 'Language, Speech, and Sound', p. 174
21 See p. 23 and 'The Secret Service', p. 159.
22 Introduction to *Invasion 1940*, p. xxviii.
23 Introduction to *Invasion 1940*, op. cit., pp. xvii–xxviii.

3. Medical Men and Women

1 Quoted in Trow, *The Black Book*, p. 76.
2 See *Immunology*, 1963, vol. 6, no. 2, 1963, and obituary in *The Times*, 27 July 1976. **J. R. Marrack** is not in the *ODNB*. Should he be?
3 Stewart, John, *The Battle for Health: A Political History of the Socialist Medical Association* (Ashgate, 1999).
4 Fyrth, Jim, *The Signal was Spain: The Spanish Aid Movement in Britain 1936–1939* (Lawrence and Wishart, 1987), p. 6.
5 In *ODNB*, no mention of Black Book, and see **Rickards'** obituary in *Lives of Fellows of the Royal College of Surgeons*, 1974–80.
6 Oldfield, Sybil, *Women Humanitarians: A Biographical Dictionary of British Women Active between 1900–1950* (Continuum, 2001), **'Janet Vaughan'**.
7 Caldecott, Leonie (ed.) *Women of Our Century* (Ariel Books, 1984), **'Janet Vaughan'**. In *ODNB*, but no mention of Black Book.
8 Stewart, *The Battle for Health*, op. cit.
9 Weindling, Paul, 'Medical Refugees and the modernisation of British medicine, 1930–1960', in *Social History of Medicine*, vol. 22, no. 3, December 2009; and see his earlier essay 'The impact of German medical scientists on British medicine: a case study of Oxford, 1933–45' in Ash and Soellner (eds), *Forced Migration and Scientific Change* (OUP, 1996).
10 Karpf, Anne, 'We've been here before', *The Guardian* 8 June 2002; and see London, Louise, *Whitehall and the Jews, 1933–1948* (CUP, 2008).
11 *Daily Mail*, 20 August 1939, quoted in Karpf, above.

12 See obituaries on **Engel** in *Annual Royal College of Surgeons*, vol. 4, 1968, p. 279 and *Journal of Clinical Pathology*, 1968, p. 420.
13 Obituary in *Paraplegia*, 17 July 1979, pp. 261–2.
14 See obituaries in *Pathology and Bacteriology*, vol. 92, no. 1, pp. 241–52, and Hide, David, 'Carl Prausnitz – father of Clinical Allergy', *Southampton Medical Journal*, vol. 8, no. 2, October 1992.
15 David Harley, obituary, *BMJ*, 1963.
16 See 'The Psychiatrists', including Professor **Willy Mayer-Gross**, p. 289.
17 See *Lives of the Fellows of the Royal College of Physicians of London*, Munk's Roll, vol. 9 (RCP, London, 1994), p. 166. Not in *ODNB*.
18 See *The Times*, 13 May 1983 and *BMJ* obit. Not in *ODNB*.
19 See *ODNB*, but no mention of Black Book.
20 Ibid.
21 **Ernst Brieger** obit in *Leprosy Review*, vol. 40, 1969, p. 256.
22 Ibid.
23 See 'Medical Researchers', p. 281.

4. Pacifists

1 Gilbert, Gustave, *Nuremberg Diary 1947* (Farrar Strauss, 1947).
2 Brinson, Charmian and Furness, N. A., '**Otto Lehmann-Russbueldt** in British Exile' in Wallace, Ian (ed.), *German-speaking Exiles in Great Britain* (The Yearbook of the Research Centre for German and Austrian Exile Studies, 1999); and see Furness, N. A., 'Otto Lehmann-Russbueldt: Forgotten prophet of a federal Europe' in Brinson, Charmian, et al., '*England? Aber wo liegt es?' Deutsche und oesterreichische Emigranten in Grossbritannien 1933–1945* (Institute of Germanic Studies Publications, 1996).
3 Miller, J. D. B., *Norman Angell and the Futility of War* (Palgrave Macmillan, 1986 and 2014).
4 See Bostridg, Mark and Berry, Paul, *Vera Brittain: A Life* (Virago, 1995).
5 'Testament to the touchstone of my life' in *The Independent*, 29 December 1993, cited in Oldfield, S., *Women Humanitarians*, op. cit., pp. 30–32.
6 Quoted in Smith, Lyn, *People Power: Fighting for Peace from the First World War to the Present* (Thames and Hudson, 2017), p. 88.
7 The Gestapo was suspicious of **Dame Adelaide** (*Leiterin [woman leader] d. brit. Graeberkommission*), for having been head of the British War Office Mission to search for the 'Missing' dead in France and Flanders after 1919 as well as for having served on the British War Graves Commission; they called her a secret agent. After the Second World War **Dame Adelaide** would become vice-president of the United Nations Association in Britain.
8 See **Ruth Fry's** obituary in *The Friend*, May 4 1962, and Oldfield, Sybil, *Women Humanitarians*, op. cit. (later reissued as *Doers of the Word*, 2006).
9 Quaker Strongrooms, Blog from Library of the Society of Friends, 23 March 2016, at WordPress.com.

10 **Howard, Elizabeth Fox**, *Memoir – Midstream.* See Quaker Strongrooms.
11 In *ODNB*, no mention of Black Book.
12 See www Next Left. 12 May 2011, 'Why **George Lansbury** wasn't Labour's great leader'.
13 'Notes in Wartime', in Jones, Raymond A., ***Arthur Ponsonby***, *A Political Life* (Christopher Helm, 1989), p. 230.
14 See Brock, Peter and Young, Nigel, *Pacifism in the Twentieth Century* (Syracuse University Press, 1999), and see *ODNB*, but no mention of Black Book.
15 '**Maude Royden**' in Oldfield, S., *Women against the Iron Fist* (Basil Blackwell, 1989), reprinted as *Alternatives to Militarism* (Edwin Mellen Press, 2000).
16 Croall, Jonathan, ***Sybil Thorndike***, *A Star of Life*, and see Oldfield, S., *Women Humanitarians*, op. cit.
17 See Morefield, Jeanne, *Covenants Without Swords: Idealistic Liberalism and the Spirit of Empire* (on **Alfred Zimmern** and **Gilbert Murray**) (Princeton University Press, 2004).
18 'Post-Munich', BBC talk, 1939, published in E. M. Forster, *Two Cheers for Democracy* (Edward Arnold, 1951).

5. Refugee Rescuers

1 Skran, Claudia, *Refugees in Inter-war Europe* (Clarendon Press, 1995), p. 2.
2 Holmes, Rose 'A Moral Business: British Quaker Work with Refugees from Fascism, 1933–39', Ph.D. thesis, University of Sussex, December 2013, p. 4
3 London, Louise, *Whitehall and the Jews 1933–1948: British Immigration Policy, Jewish Refugees and the Holocaust* (CUP, 2000).
4 Holmes, 'A Moral Business', op. cit. p. 32.
5 'Bertha Bracey' in Oldfield, S., *Women Humanitarians*, op. cit.
6 'Edith Pye' in Oldfield, S., *Women Humanitarians*, , op. cit., and *ODNB*.
7 '**Hilda Clark**' in Oldfield, S., ibid. and *ODNB*, but no mention of Black Book.
8 Wilson, Francesca, *In the Margins of Chaos: Recollections of Relief Work in and between the Wars*. (Macmillan, 1945).
9 *Who's Who 1939* and *ODNB*, but no mention of Black Book.
10 Obituary for Mora Dickson, *The Guardian*, 1 January 2002.
11 See 'The Secret Service', p. 164; Smith, Michael, ***Foley***: *the Spy who saved 10,000 Jews* (Coronet, 1999), and Smith, Lyn, *Heroes of the Holocaust* (Ebury Press, 2013).
12 Benno Cohen testifying at the Eichmann trial.
13 See Rabbi Julia Neuberger's eulogy at the unveiling of the Foreign Office plaque to their refugee-rescuing consuls in Berlin, Frankfurt and Vienna, Westminster Abbey, on the 75th anniversary of *Kristallnacht*, 10 November 2013.
14 Nicolson, Harold, *The Spectator*, January 1946.
15 Stocks, Mary, ***Eleanor Rathbone*** (Victor Gollancz, 1949), p. 259 and ch. 15.
16 **Rathbone, Eleanor**, 'A Personal View of the Refugee Problem', ***New***

Statesman 15 April 1939. **Eleanor Rathbone's** lifelong companion, **Elizabeth Macadam** (1871–1948), author of *The New Philanthropy*, the foundation text of modern social work, is also on the Black List, presumably for being **Eleanor Rathbone**'s right hand in attempting refugee rescue.

17 Ward, Stephen, 'Why the BBC ignored the Holocaust', *Independent on Sunday*, 23 September 1993; and see **'Eleanor Rathbone'** in Oldfield, S., *Women Humanitarians*, op. cit.

18 See **'Doreen Warriner'** in Oldfield, S., *Women Humanitarians*, op. cit.; Holmes, 'A Moral Business', op. cit, pp. 149–53; *AJR Journal*, April and August 2011; and Brade, Laura, and Holmes, Rose, on **Doreen Warriner** in 'Troublesome sainthood: Nicholas Winston and the contested history of child rescue in Prague, 1938–1940' in *History and Memory*, vol. 29, no. 1. 2017, pp. 3–40.

19 Stevens, Austin, *The Dispossessed: German Refugees in Britain* (Barrie and Jenkins, 1975).

20 *AJR Information*, **Schiff** obituary, December 1952 and see **'Otto Schiff** Unsung Rescuer' by Sherman, A. S. J., and Schatzkes, Pamela N., *Leo Baeck Institute Yearbook*, vol. 54, pp. 243–71, August 2009. Not in *ODNB* – should he be?

21 Oldfield, S. 'It Is Usually She', *Shofar*, vol. 23, no. 1, February 2004, pp. 57–70.

22 See Gillespie, Veronica, 'Working with the *Kindertransports*' in Oldfield, S., ed. *This Working-Day World: Women's Lives and Culture(s) in Britain, 1914–1945* (Taylor and Francis, 1994), pp. 123–32.

23 The other Jewish individual connected with refugee relief and listed in the 'Most Wanted' List was a 'Journalist' **Arnold Meyer Kaizer** or **Keyser**, general secretary of the Federation of Jewish Relief Organisations. More leading figures active in British Jewish refugee support were listed by name in the Gestapo *Informationsheft GB*, July 1940, and included **A. J. Makower**, **Sir Philip Hartog**, **Leonard Montefiore** and **Sir Robert Waley Cohen.**

24 Oldfield, S., 'Dorothy Hardisty' in *Women Humanitarians*, op. cit.

25 Ernest Rutherford, quoted in Medawar and Pyke, *Hitler's Gift: The True Story of the Scientists Expelled by the Nazi Regime* (Arcade Publishing, 2000).

26 Oldfield, S., *Women Humanitarians*, op. cit., 'Tess Simpson'.

6. Social Reformers

1 See Oldfield, S., *Women Humanitarians.* '**Margery Corbett Ashby**', and Law, Cheryl, *Women: A Modern Political Dictionary* (I.B. Tauris, 2000).

2 Stocks, Mary, entry on **Atholl** in the *ODNB*, but no mention of Black Book.

3 Jones, Enid Huws, ***Margery Fry****, The Essential Amateur* (William Sessions, 1966).

4 **'Ronald Kidd'** in **Forster, E. M.**, *Two Cheers for Democracy*, op. cit.

5 Saville, John (ed.), *Dictionary of Labour Biography*, vol. 7. and *ODNB*, but no mention of Black Book.
6 'Overturning Hitler's Military Tribunals', in *Der Spiegel (*online international) 29 June 2017.
7 ODNB entry, but no mention of Black Book.

7. Some 'Degenerate Artists'

1 See Martin, Simon, *Conscience and Conflict: British Artists and the Spanish Civil War* (Pallant House Gallery, 2004), p. 51.
2 Silber, Evelyn in *ODNB* entry on **Epstein**; no mention of Black Book.
3 In *ODNB*; no mention of Black Book.
4 Bruhns, Maike, *Kunst in der Krise, Hamburger Kunst im Dritten Reich* (Hamburg, Bd. 2: Kuenstlerlexikon, 2001), p. 41.
5 Gross, Hans Kurt in *ODNB* entry on **Charoux**; no mention of Black Book.
6 Kenneth Clark papers, **'Charoux'**, Tate Gallery Archives quoted in Bohm-Duchen, Monica (ed.), *Insiders/Outsiders: Refugees from Nazi Europe and their Contribution to British Visual Culture* (Lund Humphries, 2019), ch. 1, p. 25.
7 Bohm-Duchen, 'Accents in Art: Émigré Painters and Sculptors in Britain after 1933', in *Insiders/Outsiders,* ch. 1, p. 29.
8 Reproduced in Bohm-Duchen, *Insiders/Outsiders*, op. cit., ch. 10, p. 120.
9 Thoene, Peter, *Modern German Art* (Pelican Special, 1938).
10 Bohm-Duchen, 'Accents in Art: Émigré Painters and Sculptors in Britain after 1933', in *Insiders/Outsiders*, op. cit., ch. 1, pp. 24–6.
11 In *ODNB*; no mention of Black Book.
12 Mueller-Haerlin, Anna, 'An Unconventional Couple: Diana and **Fred Uhlman** and their Support for Exiled Artists', in Bohm-Duchen, *Insiders/ Outsiders*, op. cit., pp. 187–193.
13 Grenville, Anthony, *AJR Journal*, June 2009, and see Brinson, Charmian, *Politics by Other Means*: ***The Free German League of Culture*** (Vallentine Mitchell, 2010).
14 See Dickson, R., '"Our horizon is the barbed wire": Artistic Life in the British Internment Camps', in Bohm-Duchen, *Insiders/Outsiders*, op. cit., ch. 13.
15 Vinzent, Jutta, entry on Fred and Diana **Uhlman** in *ODNB*; no mention of Black Book.

8. Punishing the Publishers

1 *50 Penguin Years – Exhibition Catalogue* (Penguin Books, 1985); and see Hare, Stephen (ed.), *Penguin Portrait: Allen Lane and the Penguin Editors 1935–1970* (Penguin, 1995).
2 Hodges, Sheila, *Gollancz, The Story of a Publishing House 1928–1978* (Victor Gollancz, 1978).

3 Edwards, Ruth Dudley, in Stevenson, Iain, *Book Makers: British Publishing in the 20th Century* (British Library, 2010), ch.4.
4 See Nyburg, Anna, *Émigrés – The Transformation of Art Publishing in Britain* (Phaidon Press, 2014).
5 See Jackson, Julian, *France: The Dark Years 1940–1944* (Oxford University Press, 2001), ch. 13, 'Intellectuals, Artists and Entertainers'.
6 Drake, David, *Paris at War* (Harvard, 2015), p. 124.

9. Targeting Creative Writers

1 Koch, Stephen, 'The Playboy Was a Spy', *New York Times*, 13 April 2008.
2 Beauman, Nicola, '**E. M. Forster**' in *ODNB*.
3 Lago, Mary, ***E. M. Forster***, *A Literary Life* (Palgrave MacMillan, 1995), ch. 4, 'The BBC Broadcasts'.
4 Interview with Rowntree in Lago, ibid.
5 Beauman, Nicola, *Morgan: A Biography of E. M. Forster* (Knopf, 1993).
6 Ibid., and see **Forster**, 'The Menace to Freedom' (1935).
7 'Tolerance' (1941).
8 Furbank, P. N., ***E .M. Forster***: *A Life* (Faber, 1978).
9 **Forster**, BBC broadcast, 'Jew-Consciousness' (1939).
10 **E. M. Forster**, 'What I Believe', 1939 reprinted in *Two Cheers for Democracy* (Edward Arnold, 1951), pp. 84–5.
11 Lago, ***E. M. Forster***, op. cit.
12 One hundred and seventy professors and teachers at Cracow University had been arrested by the Gestapo and sent to concentration camps or shot.
13 Bedford, Sybille, *Aldous Huxley: a Biography* (Collins, 1973 and Ivan R. Dee, 2002), vol. 1.
14 Ibid.
15 **Aldous Huxley** is in the *ODNB*, but no mention of Black Book.
16 See '**Storm Jameson**' in *ODNB*.
17 **Jameson**, **Storm**, *Autobiography – Journey from the North*, vol. 1 (Virago, 1984), p. 293.
18 **Jameson**, **Storm**, *Autobiography – Journey from the North*, vol. 2 (Virago, 1984), pp. 18–19.
19 **Ould** is in *Who's Who* 1939 but not in *ODNB* – should he be?
20 Emery, Jane, *Rose Macaulay – A Writer's Life* (J. Murray, 1991).
21 **Woolf, Virginia**, *Diary*, 7 June 1940, during the Fall of France: 'Question of suicide seriously debated among the 4 of us … in the gradually darkening room. At last no light at all. This was symbolic. French are to be beaten; invasion here … [9th June]… I reflect: capitulation will mean all Jews to be given up. Concentration Camps. So to our garage.'
22 In *Who's Who 1939* and *ODNB*; no mention of Black Book, although **Naomi Mitchison** suspected already during the Second World War that she had been put on the Black List.

23 'Black Shirts', *Sunday Chronicle*, 22 October 1933.
24 'Lost Germany', ***News Chronicle***, April 1939.
25 **J. B. Priestley**, *Rain upon Gadshill* (William Heinemann Ltd, 1939).
26 'We Are All Propagandists But…', ***News Chronicle***, 24 July 1939.
27 'We are being Held to Ransom', ***News Chronicle***, 10 July 1939. All the passages of journalism here are quoted from Hanson, Neil (ed.) with Priestley, Tom, in *Priestley's Wars* (Great Northern, 2008).
28 'We Are All Propagandists But', Hawkes, Nicholas, *The Story of J. B. Priestley's Postscripts*, quoted in Hanson, op. cit., p. 199.
29 Cooper, Susan, ***J. B. Priestley***, *Portrait of an Author*, quoted in Hanson, op. cit., p. 199.
30 In *ODNB*, but no mention of Black Book.
31 Sylvia Townsend Warner is in *ODNB*, but no mention of Black Book.
32 Parrinder, Patrick, '**H. G. Wells**' in *ODNB*, but no mention of Black Book.
33 Palmier, Jean-Michel, *Weimar in Exile: The Antifascist Emigration in Europe and America* (Editions Payot, 1987; Verso, 2006), p. 293.
34 See Smith, Ali, 'Celebrating **HG Wells**' role in the creation of the UN Declaration of Human Rights', *The Guardian*, 20 November 2015.
35 See Glendinning, Victoria, *Rebecca West: a life* (Alfred A. Knopf, 1987). In ODNB, but no mention of Black Book.
36 *ODNB*, but no mention of Black Book.
37 **Woolf, Virginia**, *Diary*, 27 August 1918.
38 Ibid., *Diary,* 30 August 1924.
39 **Woolf, Virginia**, *Three Guineas* (1938).
40 *Three Guineas*, ch. 2, note 20; and see illustration from **Virginia Woolf**'s August 1935 scrapbook for *Three Guineas* (Hogarth Press, 1938), held in The Keep, Woolf archive, Brighton.
41 See Oldfield, Sybil, '**Virginia Woolf**, the Elegiac Artist' in *Women Against the Iron Fist*, and '**Virginia Woolf** and Antigone' in Oldfield, Sybil, *Thinking Against the Current*, op. cit.
42 See Lee, Hermione, *Virginia Woolf* (Vintage, 1996), ch. 37, 'Fascism', pp. 684–7 and pp. 857–8. For a comprehensive list of Virginia Woolf's signed, including jointly-signed, anti-fascist communications to the press, see Stuart N. Clarke, *Becoming a Name: Virginia Woolf's Political Reputation*, publ. Virginia Woolf Society of Great Britain, 2019, Appendix.
43 See Martin, Simon, *Conscience and Conflict: British Artists and the Spanish Civil* War, op. cit., 2014).
44 Callil, Carmen, *Bad Faith: A Forgotten History of Family and Fatherland* (Jonathan Cape, 2006), p. 309.
45 Palmier, Jean-Michel, *Weimar in Exile*, op. cit., ch. 1, and Epilogue: 'Cassandras'.
46 Ibid.
47 Ritchie, J. M., *German Exiles: British Perspectives* (Peter Lang, 1997), p. 266.

48 **Gottfurcht** in Brinson, Charmian, and Dove, Richard, *Politics by Other Means – the Freie Deutsche Kulturbund in London, 1939–1946* (Vallentine Mitchell, 2010); and see Ritchie, J. M., 'London Poems by Exile Poets in GB', in his *German Exiles*, op. cit.

49 See Ritchie, *German Exiles*, op. cit., and Dove, Richard, *Journey of No Return: Five German-speaking Literary Exiles in Britain 1933–1945* (Libris, 2000).

50 Ritchie, J. M., *German Exiles*, op. cit., ch. 6, 'Karl Otten'. Otten is not in the *ODNB*. Should he be? For all the above and for **Berthold Viertel** and **Hans Schellenberg**, see Brinson, Charmian, and Dove, Richard, *Politics by Other Means*, op. cit, and see Webster, Wendy, *Mixing It*, op. cit., p. 85.

51 **E. M. Forster** recalled **H. G. Wells** 'calling after me in his squeaky voice "Still in your ivory tower? Still on your private roundabout?"' – quoted in Smith, Zadie, 'Reading 2 – **E. M. Forster**, Middle Manager' in her *Changing My Mind* (Hamish Hamilton, 2009).

10. Shooting the Messenger – Blacklisted Journalists

1 In *ODNB*, but no mention of Black Book.

2 **Bartlett, Vernon**, *And Now Tomorrow* (Chatto and Windus, 1960).

3 *ODNB.*

4 **Cockburn** was listed twice in the Black Book, under the same London address, both as 'Cockburn' and as his pseudonym 'Frank Pitcairn'.

5 **Cockburn** is in the *ODNB*, but no mention of Black Book .

6 Voigt to **Crozier**, December 1933, in Ayerst, David, *Guardian: Biography of a Newspaper* (Collins, 1971).

7 **Crozier** is in the *ODNB*, but no mention of Black Book.

8 *Guardian* archive, obituary, April 1949. Not in *ODNB* – should he be?

9 Strachey, John, *What Are We To Do?* (Victor Gollancz, Left Book Club, 1938), ch. 12.

10 Corthorn, Paul, *In the Shadow of the Dictators: the British Left in the 1930s* (I.B. Tauris, 2006).

11 **Cummings, A. J.**, *The Press and a Changing Civilization* (Bodley Head, 1936).

12 See **Delmer**'s 2 vol. autobiography, *Trail Sinister* (Secker and Warburg, 1961); in *ODNB*, but no mention of Black Book.

13 See his *King Carol, Hitler and Madame Lupescu* (Victor Gollancz, 1942).

14 **Easterman** is not in the *ODNB* – should he be?

15 In *ODNB*, but no mention of Black Book.

16 He is in the *ODNB*, but no mention of Black Book.

17 **J. L. Garvin** is in the *ODNB*, but no mention of Black Book.

18 **Philip Gibbs** is in the *ODNB*, but no mention of Black Book.

19 See *Palgrave Dictionary of Anglo-Jewish History*. **Myer** and **Kaizer** are not in the *ODNB* and **Ivan Greenberg** is only mentioned in the *ODNB* article on his father, Leopold Greenberg, the Zionist editor of the *Jewish Chronicle* till 1931.

20 See **'Charlotte Haldane'** in *Spartacus Educational*, and **Charlotte Haldane**, *Truth Will Out* (George Weidenfeld and Nicolson, 1949).
21 See Clare Mulley, *The Spy who Loved* (Macmillan, 2012).
22 See Paul Buvarp's Ph.D. thesis for the University of St Andrews, 2016, **'Rowland Kenney** and British propaganda in Norway, 1916–1942' and **Duff, Charles**, *No Angel's Wing* (1947) for **Kenney** at the Foreign Office in the early 1930s. **Rowland Kenney** is not in the *ODNB*. Should he be?
23 See Cockett, R. B., *The Foreign Office News Department and the Struggle against Appeasement* (Institute of Historical Research, 1990; published online 2007).
24 **Lennox** is not in the *ODNB*. Should he be? See Martin Gilbert, ***Churchill*** (Hillsdale College Press, 2009), vol. 5, p. 639.
25 See Rolph, C. H., *Kingsley* (Littlehampton, 1973).
26 Spotts, Frederick (ed.), *The Letters of* ***Leonard Woolf*** (Bloomsbury, 1990).
27 **Kingsley Martin** is in the *ODNB*, but no mention of Black Book. And see his Blacklisted, anti-imperialist life partner **Dorothy Woodman**, p. 356.
28 **William Mellor** is not in the *ODNB*. Should he be?
29 Cunard, Nancy (ed.), *Authors Take Sides on the Spanish War* (Left Review, 1937).
30 **Nevinson, Henry**, *Hitler the Man* (Chapbook 1936).
31 **Jameson, Storm** *Autobiography*, vol. 1., op. cit. And see John, Angela V., *War, Journalism and the Shaping of the Twentieth Century: The Life and Times of* ***Henry W. Nevinson*** (I.B. Tauris, 2006). **Nevinson** is in the *ODNB*, but no mention of Black Book.
32 Jacobsen, Hans-Adolf, *Reporting on Hitler* (Will Wainewright, 2017).
33 'I know these Dictators', in Griffiths, Richard, *Fellow-travellers of the Right – British Enthusiasts for Nazi Germany 1933–1939* (Faber, 2011).
34 See Thurlow, Richard, 'Anti-Nazi antisemite. The Case of Douglas Reed' in *Patterns of Prejudice*, vol. 18, 1984.
35 See John, Angela V., *Turning the Tide: The Life of* ***Lady Rhondda*** (Parthian Books, 2017).
36 Beddoe, Deirdre on **Lady Rhondda** in the *ODNB*. **Lady Rhondda** is one of the few subjects in the *ODNB* whose inclusion in the Black Book *is* noted – under 'Margaret Thomas'.
37 'Praise for Women', *Sunday Times*, 13 September 1936, Hitler's speech cut and pasted into **Virginia Woolf**'s scrapbook for *Three Guineas*.
38 See *AJR Journal*, November 1981 and Glentson, George, and Pattinson, William, on the ***News Chronicle***, *The Last 'Chronicle' of Bouverie Street* (Allen and Unwin, 1963). **Segrue** is not in the *ODNB*. Should he be?
39 See Liebich, Andre, 'The anti-Semitism of **Henry Wickham Steed**' in *Patterns of Prejudice*, vol. 46, 19 April 2012. Both **Spender** and **Steed** are in the *ODNB*, but no mention of Black Book
40 Simpson, John, 'My History Hero', *BBC History Magazine*, vol. 1. no. 6, June 2010.
41 **Philip Pembroke Stephens** is not in the *ODNB*. Should he be?

42 Richards, Huw, *The Bloody Circus, the **Daily Herald** and the Left* (Pluto Press, 1997).
43 **Hannan Swaffer** is not in the *ODNB*. Should he be? See biographies of **Swaffer** by Driberg, Tom, and Andrews, Linton.
44 '**Hessell Tiltman**, from the *Daily News* and three time president of the Tokyo Foreign Correspondents' Club, became well known for covering Japan's latest outposts as its expansionist policy advanced', China Rhyming blog, on 'Marjorie Hessell Tiltman', 2015.
45 **Tiltman, H.**, *Nightmares Must End* (Jarrolds Publishers, 1940). **Tiltman** is not in *ODNB*. Should he be?
46 Gordon Young is not in the *ODNB*. Should he be?
47 See Broszat and Mehringer, *Bayern in der NS Zeit* (1983).
48 *Times* obit, 19 October 2006. Not in *ODNB*. Should he be?
49 See Wallace, Ian, *German-speaking Exiles in Great Britain*, op. cit., and Haffner, Sebastian, *Defying Hitler: A Memoir* (Weidenfeld and Nicolson, 2003).
50 See Marilyn Moos's biography, ***Siegfried Moos***, *Beaten but not Defeated, A German Anti-Nazi who Settled in Britain* (Chronos Books, 2014), and her semi-autobiographical novel *The Language of Silence*. **Moos** is not in the *ODNB*. Should he be?
51 See Bruening, Jens und Vorwort (eds), *Gabriele Tergit, Blueten der Zwanziger Jahre* (Rotation, 1984); and Bruening, *Nachwort to Gabriele Tergit,Frauen und andere Ereignisse: Publistik und Erzaehlungen von 1915–1970* (2000).
52 See Lorant, S., *I Was Hitler's Prisoner* (Gollancz, 1935, republished as a Penguin Special, 1939).
53 'For Lorant and myself the main interest was that ***Picture Post*** should be strongly political, "anti- Fascist" in the language of the time.' Hopkinson, Tom, ***Picture Post***, *1938–1950* (Chatto and Windus, 1984), Introduction, p. 9.
54 Ibid. p. 11.
55 Bohm-Duchen, *Insiders/Outsiders*, op. cit., pp. 65 and 124. And see Hallett, Michael, *Stefan Lorant: Godfather of Photojournalism* (Scarecrow Press, 2005).

11. The Secret Service

1 Smith, Michael, *Six: The real James Bonds 1909–1939* (Biteback, 2011).
2 Hastings, Max, *The Secret War, Spies, Codes and Guerrillas, 1939–45* (William Collins, 2015).
3 Volkman, E., *Spies – The Secret Agents who Changed the Course of History* (Wiley, 1994).
4 Ibid.
5 Jeffery, K., *MI6: The History of the Secret Intelligence Service 1909–1949* (Bloomsbury, 2010), p. 386.
6 Ibid.
7 Read, Anthony and Fisher, David, *Colonel Z: Life and Times of a Master of Spies* (Hodder and Stoughton, 1984).

8 Ibid.

9 Quoted in Koch, Stephen, 'The Playboy Was a Spy', *New York Times*, 13 April 2008.

10 Read and Fisher, *Colonel Z*, op. cit., ch. 25.

11 Ibid., ch. 23.

12 Smith, Michael, *Six*, ch. 20; and see West, Nigel, *MI6* (Random House, 1983).

13 See Smith, Michael, *Six*, and Smith, Michael, ***Frank Foley***, *The Spy Who Saved Ten Thousand Jews* (Hodder and Stoughton, 1999); Smith, Lyn, 'Francis **"Frank" Foley**' in *Heroes of the Holocaust*, op. cit.

14 Smith, ***Frank Foley***, in *Heroes of the Holocaust*, op. cit., p. 199.

15 See Smith, op. cit.

16 **Foley** is in the *ODNB*, but no mention of Black Book.

17 See Fry, Helen, *Spymaster: The Secret Life of Kendrick* (Marranos Press, 2014), and her *The M Room: Secret Listeners who Bugged the Nazis in WW2* (Create Space, 2012).

18 **Thomas Kendrick** is not in the *ODNB*. Should he be?

19 They include **George William Berry** in the British consulate of Vienna; **Sir Alexander Cadogan**, emphatically not a secret agent but probably Blacklisted for his doomed efforts, when head of the League of Nations Section of the Foreign Office before 1933, to work for general disarmament; **Sir George Ogilvie-Forbes**, who enabled Jews from Berlin to get out after *Kristallnacht* and who is on the British Foreign Office commemorative plaque; **G. W. Harrison**, **Henry Pomeroy**, British vice-consul in Berlin who forged passports for Jews as possibly did **Laurence Milner Robinson**, British consul-general at Danzig 1934–37 and at Hamburg 1937–9 – all of them hampered by the British ambassador **Neville Henderson**, who was under orders from the Foreign Office to appease Hitler in order to prevent war.

20 See https://www.amazon.co.uk/Spy-Tower-Untold-Joseph-Executed/dp/0750989300

21 Smith, Michael, *Six*, op. cit., ch. 13.

22 **Bruce Lockhart** is in the *ODNB*, but no mention of Black Book.

23 See West, Nigel, *Historical Dictionary of Ian Fleming's World of Intelligence: Fact and Fiction* (Rowman and Littlefield, 2009/2014); and Hirsch, Pam, *The Constant Liberal: the Life and Work of Phyllis Bottome* (who had also lived in Kitzbuehl in the 1930s) (Quartet Books, 2010).

24 Bennett, Gill, *Churchill's Man of Mystery,* ***Desmond Morton*** *and the World of Intelligence* (Whitehall Histories: Government Official History Series, Routledge, 2008).

25 Hastings, Max, *Six*, p. 13.

26 Gilman, Richard, *Behind World Revolution: The Strange Career of Nesta H. Webster* (Insights Books, 1982).

27 White, John Baker, *True Blue: An autobiography 1902–1939* (Frederick Muller, 1970).
28 Bennett, Gill, *Churchill's Man of Mystery*, op. cit., ch. 4.
29 Hollingworth, Mark, and Tremayne, Charles, *The Economic League: The Silent McCarthyism* (National Council for Civil Liberties (NCCL), 1989). The documentary film *Solidarity*, uncovering the shady workings of the Economic League and its successors in Britain, was released in October 2019 – see review in *The Guardian*, 4 October 2019.
30 McIvor, Arthur, '"A Crusade for Capitalism": The Economic League, 1919–1939', *Journal of Contemporary History*, vol. 23, 1988, pp. 631–55.
31 Hollingsworth and Tremayne, *The Economic League*, op. cit.
32 Ibid. and see Hughes, Mike, *Spies at Work* (http://www.1 in 12.com/publications/library/spies/, chs. 9 and 11.
33 See Jungk, Peter Stephan, *Die Dunkelkammern der Edith Tudor-Hart* (S. Fischer, 2015).
34 See *Graphology for Everyman*, illustrated by Gertrude Elias (Duckworth, 1957).
35 Day, Peter, *Klop, Britain's Most Ingenious Spy* (Biteback, 2014), ch. 16.
36 Ibid.
37 Ibid. 5.
38 Ibid., ch. 6 and see **Moura Budberg**, p. 175.
39 White, Dick, MI5, in Day, *Klop*, op. cit., ch. 8.
40 Wright, Peter, *Spy-catcher* (William Heinemann, 1987).
41 Day, *Klop*, op. cit., ch. 8.
42 Ibid., ch. 12.
43 McDonald, Deborah, and Dronfield, Jeremy, *A Very Dangerous Woman: The Lives, Loves and Lies of Russia's Most Seductive Spy* (Oneworld, 2015), ch. 23.
44 McDonald and Dronfield, ch. 23.
45 Smith, Michael, *Six*, op., cit., p. 363.
46 Bennett, Gill, ***Churchill**'s Man of Mystery*, op. cit., ch. 8.
47 See Nathan, Otto, and Norden, Heinz (eds), *Einstein on Peace* (Avenel Books, 1981), pp. 290–308, 'Birth of the Atomic Age 1939–1940', discussed on pp. 313–18.

12. The Army

1 Butler, Ewan, ***Mason-Mac*** (Macmillan, 1972); in *ODNB*, but no mention of Black Book.
2 Egremont, Max, on **Spears**, *ODNB*, but no mention of Black Book.
3 See **Strong, K. W. D**, *Men of Intelligence* (1970), and *ODNB* entry, but no mention of Black Book.
4 See Roskill, Stephen, ***Churchill** and the Admirals* (William Morrow, 1978).
5 See *Hansard* (1938).
6 Ivor Bulmer-Thomas on Fletcher in *ODNB*, but no mention of Black Book.

7 See **Doreen Warriner**, 'Refugee Rescuers, p. 84, and *AJR Journal*, April and August 2011.
8 Another Blacklisted pioneering civil aviation pilot was **Captain H. S. Robertson.**
9 Philip Mellinger on **Salmond** in the *ODNB*, but no mention of Black Book; and see Williams, Charles, *Max Beaverbrook: Not Quite a Gentleman* (Biteback, 2019).
10 Ross, John F., *Enduring Courage: Ace Pilot Eddie Rickenbacker and the Age of Speed* (St Martin's Press, 2014).
11 Vincent Orange on **Trenchard** in *ODNB*, but no mention of Black Book.
12 Ditto.
13 *Informationsheft GB*, section on Freemasonry in Britain.

13. Business and Industry – Friend or Foe to Nazi Germany?

1 Yergin, Daniel, *The Prize: the Epic Quest for Oil, Money & Power* (Free Press, Simon and Schuster, 1991).
2 Kenny, Angela, 'Andrew Agnew' in *ODNB*, but no mention of Black Book.
3 see Howarth, Stephen, *A Century in Oil: The* ***'Shell' Transport and Trading Company*** *1897–1997* (Weidenfeld and Nicolson, 1997).
4 **J. B. A. Kessler**, **H. W. Malcolm**, and **Bertram A. Smith** were also Blacklisted for their work for **Shell Transport and Trading** and in **Smith**'s case for Burmah Oil.
5 Even 83-year-old **Sir Hugh Shakespear Barnes** (1857–1941), 'old India hand', banker and company director with interests in **Anglo-Persian Oil**, was not too old to be Blacklisted. See *ODNB*, but no mention of Black Book.
6 Torrens, H. S. **'John Cadman'** in *ODNB*, but no mention of Black Book.
7 Yergin, *The Prize*, op. cit., p. 271.
8 Torrens, H. S., **'John Cadman'** in *ODNB*.
9 Other important Blacklisted figures at **Unilever** included the future chairman of ICI, Britain's largest manufacturer, **Geoffrey Heyworth** (1894–1974), **R. H. Muir**, **J. L. Simpson**, and **C. E. Tatlow**, as well as the advisory director, the counselling chemist and patent law expert **Horatio Ballantyne** (1871–1956) and the company secretary **L. V. Fildes**.
10 See p. 71 and Fletcher, Sheila, ***Maude Royden*** (Wiley-Blackwell, 1999).
11 Murphy, Phillip, *ODNB* article on **Oliver Lyttelton**, but no mention of Black Book.
12 Ditto.
13 See Aichinger, Hans, **Richard Merton** (Stephen Verlag Waldemar Kramer, 1970). **Israel Richard Merton** is in the *Sonderfahndungsliste*, described as *Kaufmann, Emigrant, Jude* (British Metall Corporation)'.
14 See articles on **Strakosch** and **Gregory** in *ODNB*, but no mention of Black Book. **Sir Theodore Emmanuel Gugenheim Gregory** (1890–1970), an economics graduate from LSE, was professor of economics at the

University of London from 1927 to 1937 and author of *Gold, Unemployment and Capitalism* (1933).

15 *Informationsheft.* **Sir Isidore Salmon,** as well as being Conservative MP for Harrow, was chairman of J. Lyons and Co. and chairman of the Westminster Technical School for training chefs and waiters. From 1938 to 1941 he was honorary catering adviser to the British Army, forming a specialised Army Catering Corps to improve food standards.

16 See Foot, M. R. D. on **C. J. Hambro** in *ODNB*, but no mention of Black Book.

17 *Invasion 1940*, op. cit., p. 97.

18 Orbell, John on **Japhet** in *ODNB*, but no mention of Black Book. '**Saemy Japhet** was a great supporter of the Jewish community in Britain and [an advocate for a] Jewish State in Palestine.'

19 See Roberts, Richard, and King, John, on **d'Erlangers**, **Emile** and **Leo**, in the *ODNB*, but no mention of Black Book.

20 See Macksey, Kenneth on **Sir Albert Stern** in *ODNB*, but no mention of Black Book.

21 **Stern** had also been co-developer of the first British armed tank in the First World War as well as of tank models in the Second World War.

22 All are in the *ODNB*, but no mention of Black Book.

23 See Souhami, Diana, in *ODNB* entry for the **Glucksteins**' sister, the painter Hannah Gluck.

24 In *ODNB*, but no mention of Black Book.

25 In *ODNB*, but no mention of Black Book.

26 All the above financial figures have entries in the *ODNB*.

27 See Wenden, D. J. on **Montagu** in *ODNB*, but no mention of Black Book; see also British Film Institute papers and ***Ivor Montagu*** papers in the British Communist Party archive.

28 See Wedell, George, on **Sidney Bernstein** in *ODNB*, but no mention of Black Book; and see British Film Institute papers on ***Bernstein***.

29 *Sidney Bernstein, a biography* (Jonathan Cape, 1984), ch. 5, 'Politics in the 1930s'.

30 See Moorehead, Caroline, *A Bold and Dangerous Family*, op. cit., ch. 7, 'The Propaganda War'.

31 See Murphy, Robert, on **Isidore, Mark** and **Maurice Ostrer** in *ODNB*, but no mention of Black Book.

32 See Eyles, Allen, entry on **Oscar Deutsch** in *ODNB*, but no mention of Black Book.

33 Pugh, Martin, *'Hurrah for the Blackshirts!' Fascists and Fascism in Britain Between the Wars* (Jonathan Cape, 2005), pp. 270–71.

34 See Lord Londonderry writing to Goering, 1936, quoted in German *Wikipedia* article: 'Anglo-German Fellowship'.

35 Kershaw, Ian, *Making Friends with Hitler: Lord Londonderry, the Nazis and the Road to World War II* (Allen Lane/Penguin Press, 2004), p. 174.

36 Norton-Taylor, Richard, *The Guardian*, 28 February 2014.

14. The Church

1 For Count Galen's denunciation of the Nazis' 'mercy killing' of 'the unfit' see p. 00 and William Shirer, *The Rise and Fall of the Third Reich*, op. cit., pp. 238–40.

2 Bonhoeffer would be stripped naked and slowly hanged in Flossenburg concentration camp, 9 April 1945.

3 See Jasper, Ronald, ***George Bell, Bishop of Chichester***, ch. 8, 'The Refugees' (OUP, 1967).

4 See Siegele-Wenschkewitz, Leonore, 'Christians against Nazis: the German Confessing Church' in *Christian History*, issue 9, 1986, 'Heritage of Freedom'.

5 See Steinmetz, Susan, 'Die Deutschen Evangelistischen Gemeinden in GB und die "Nicht-Arischen" Fluechtlinge' in Brinson and Dove (ed), *England? Aber wo liegt es? Deutsche und Oesterreichische Emigranten in Gross Britannien 1933–1945*, Institute of Germanic Studies Publications, vol. 64, 1996. And Dell'Omo, Augusta Lynn, 'Tending the flock: German Lutherans, reconstruction, and prisoners of war', http://doi.org/10.1080/14682745. 2019.

6 See Bonhoeffer, Dietrich, *Works*, vol. 15, *Theological Education Underground 1937–1940* (Fortress Press, 2014).

7 Zasloff, T., *A Rescuer's Story: Pastor Pierre-Charles Trouveille in Vichy France* (University of Wisconsin Press, 2003).

8 *Irish Times*, 23 April 1997.

9 Lucien Wolf Memorial Lecture to the Jewish Historical Society, 'Humanity and the Refugees', 1 February 1939, quoted in Jasper, Ronald, ***George Bell***, op. cit., ch. 8, 'The Refugees'.

10 Helen Roberts of the **Church of England Committee for Non-Aryan Christians**, quoted in Bohm-Duchen, *Insiders/Outsiders*, op. cit., pp. 196–7.

11 Jasper, ***George Bell***, op. cit., ch. 8, 'The Refugees', and Chandler, Andrew, *George Bell Bishop of Chichester: Church, State, and Resistance in the Age of Dictatorship* (William B. Eerdmans, 2016), chs. 5–8.

12 Chandler, Andrew, entry on ***Bell*** in *ODNB*.

13 ***Bell***'s sister-in-law reporting from Germany 1937–8, quoted in Jasper, ***George Bell***, op. cit., ch. 8.

14 See Chandler, Andrew, 'George Bell and the Art of Refugees from Totalitarian Europe' in Bohm-Duchen, *Insiders/Outsiders*, op. cit., ch. 19.

15 Ibid.

16 *Hansard*, and quoted in Jasper, Ronald, ***George Bell***, op. cit.

17 Chandler, Andrew, entry on ***Bell*** in the *ODNB*, but no mention of Black Book.

18 Martin, Hugh, entry on ***Tatlow*** in *ODNB*, but no mention of Black Book.

19 **Hertz** is in *ODNB*, but no mention of Black Book.

15. Art Historians and Musicologists

1 See Medawar and Pyke, op. cit., *Hitler's Gift* (Piatkus, 2001), ch. 2 for refugee scientists; and Crawford, Sally, Ulmschneider, Katharina, and Elsner, Jas, *Ark of Civilization: Refugee Scholars and Oxford University, 1930–1945* (OUP, 2017), for some refugee scholars in the humanities.

2 Perutz, Max, foreword to Medawar and Pyke, *Hitler's Gift*, op. cit. And see Oldfield, S., op. cit., *Women Humanitarians*, for the Society for the Protection of Science and Learning's all-important Secretary, Tess Simpson.

3 McEwan, Dorothea, 'A Tale of One Institute and Two Cities: The Warburg Institute', in Wallace, Ian (ed.), *German-speaking Exiles in Great Britain*, op. cit. And for a revisionist view see Hoenes, Hans Christian, 'A Very Specialised Subject: Art History in Britain', in Bohm-Duchen, op. cit., ch. 7.

4 Hoenes, 'A Very Specialised Subject', op. cit., ch. 7, p. 100.

5 See *A Heritage of Images*, posthumous edition of *A Selection of* ***Saxl****'s Lectures* (Penguin, 1970), and entry on **Saxl** by **Gertrud Bing** in *ODNB*, but no mention of Black Book.

6 See 'In Memoriam **Gertrud Bing**', *Journal of the Warburg and Courtauld Institutes*, vol. 27, 1964, pp. 1–2.

7 See article on **Antal** by Anthony Blunt in *ODNB*, but no mention of Black Book.

8 See article on **Wind** by Ben Thomas in *ODNB*, but no mention of Black Book.

9 See article on **Wittkower** by Howard Hibbard in *ODNB*, but no mention of Black Book.

10 '**Dr Alfred Scharf**. Obituary', in *Burlington Magazine*, vol. 108, 1966, pp. 201–202.

11 Gordon Higgott, '**Helen Rosenau** 1900–1984' in *Journal of Jewish Art*, vol. 11, 1985, pp. 79–80, and see Pollock, Griselda, 'Making Feminist Memories', lecture, 2014. Not in *ODNB*. Should she be?

12 Hoenes, Hans Christian, 'A Very Specialised Subject', in Bohm-Duchen, op. cit., p. 99.

13 *Ham & High*, 22 October 2015.

14 See '**Mosco Carner**, Musicologist': his obituary in the *New York Times*, 7 August 1985.

15 See Sue Carole De Vale: '"Intrusions": 'A Remembrance of **Klaus Wachsmann** (1907–1984)', *Ethnomusicology*, vol. 29, no. 2, 1985, pp. 272–82.

16. Attacking Ancient Classicists

1 **E. R. Dodds**, *Missing Persons* (Clarendon Press, 1977)

2 Ibid. p. 144.

3 Ibid. No mention of Black Book in Hugh Lloyd-Jones' *ODNB* entry on **E. R. Dodds.**

4 Lloyd-Jones, Hugh, obituary on **Fraenkel** in *Gnomon*, 43, vol. 1971,

pp. 634–40. No mention of Black Book in Hugh Lloyd-Jones' *ODNB* entry on **Fraenkel.**

5 Honore, Toby, entry on **Daube** in *ODNB*, but no mention of Black Book.

6 See Lawrence, K. S., in Metzger, Ernest (ed.) *Law for All Times: Essays in Memory of David Daube* (Roman Law Society of America, 2004).

7 See Vermes, Geza, *Jesus the Jew* (Fortress Press, 1973); Carmichael, Calum (ed.), *Essays on Law and Religion: The Berkeley and Oxford Symposia in Honour of* ***David Daube***, University of California and Berkeley, 1993; and Rodger, Alan, **'David Daube'** in Beatson and Zimmermann, *Jurists Uprooted: German-speaking émigré Lawyers in Twentieth-century Britain* (OUP, 2004).

8 *ODNB* and see obituaries in *The Independent*, 5 March 1999, and *The Guardian*, 12 March 1999.

9 See article on **Kantorowicz** in *Encyclopaedia Britannica*.

10 Curran, Vivian Grosswald, 'Re-thinking **Hermann Kantorowicz'** in Ries, Anneliese (ed.), *Re-thinking the Masters of Comparative Law* (Hart Publishing, 2001).

11 See Friedmann Renee, **'Elise J. Baumgaertel'** in Cohen and Joukopwsky (eds), *Breaking Ground: Pioneering Women Archeologists* (University of Michigan Press, 2006).

12 See Kelly, W. A., *Librarians in Exile,* ***Dr. Erich Langstadt***, German Studies Library Group, 1991.

17. Economists of All Kinds – but not All Economists

1 www. Rastafari-in-motion.org/Abyssinia association.html. **George Paish** is in the *ODNB* but no mention of Black Book.

2 *The Journal of Economic Literature*, vol. 38, no. 3, 2000, pp. 614–26.

3 Hagemann, H., in *Journal of the History of Economic Thought*, vol. 27, no. 4, 2005, pp. 405–20.

4 Clavin, Patricia, 'A Wandering Scholar in Britain and the USA, 1933–1945', in Grenville, Anthony (ed.), *Refugees from the Third Reich in Britain*. (Rodopi, 2003), pp. 27–42.

5 Hagemann, Harald, **'Burchardt, Fritz'** in Glaser, David (ed.), *Business Cycles and Depressions: An Encyclopaedia* (2013), p. 59 et seq.

6 Worswick, G. D.N., entry on **Burchardt** in *ODNB*, but no mention of Black Book.

7 See Hagemann, H. 'German-speaking Economists in British Exile 1933–1945', *Journal of the History of Economic Thought*.

8 Green, John, *A Political Family: The Kuczynskis, Fascism, Espionage and the Cold War* (Routledge, 2017). And see Green, John, laudatory article on **Kuczynski** in *ODNB*, but no mention of Black Book.

9 Oakley, Ann, 'Legacies of Altruism: Richard Titmuss, **Marie [Dessauer] Meinhardt**, and Health Policy Research in the 1940s' in *Social Policy and Society*, vol. 18, no. 3, 2019, pp. 383–92.

10 Personal information.
11 Hagemann, H., 2005.
12 Hammond, Richard, review of *The West African Shipping Trade 1909–1959* in *Journal of Economic History*, vol. 24, no. 1, March 1964, pp. 107–108, published online (CUP, 2011). And see Dickmann and Schoeck-Quinteros, *Zuflucht Exil? Juedische Wissenschaftlererinnen in der Emigration 1933–45* (Bremen, 2005), vol. 9.
13 *Collected Writings of J. M. Keynes* (CUP, 1978), vol. 20, p. 191.
14 Personal information.
15 See Jolly, Richard, entry on **Singer** in *ODNB*, but no mention of Black Book.

18. Down with Humane Educationists

1 Goldman, L., *Dons and Workers: Oxford and Adult Education Since 1850* (OUP, 1995).
2 McCullough, Gary, in *ODNB*, but no mention of Black Book.
3 See Harrison, J. C. B., *Learning and Living, 1790–1960* (Routledge, 1961/2013), ch. 8.
4 See Elsey, Barry, 'R. H. Tawney, patron saint of adult education' in Jarvis, Peter (ed.), *Twentieth Century Thinkers in Adult and Continuing Education* (Routledge, 1987).
5 Stocks, Mary, *The Workers' Educational Association: The First Fifty Years* (George Allen and Unwin, 1953), p. 115.
6 **Elisabeth Blochmann**'s mystifying personal attachment to the morally compromised Nazi apologist Martin Heidegger was revealed in Storck, J. (ed.), *Martin Heidegger – Elisabeth Blochmann. Briefwechsel 1918–1969* (Marbach, 1989).
7 See Mayne, Richard, *In Victory, Magnanimity In Peace, Goodwill: A History of Wilton Park*, Whitehall Histories (Routledge, 2003; Taylor and Francis, 2014).
8 See Olbrich, Josef, **'Fritz Borinski** – Vita und Werk von der Praxis zur Wissenschaft der Erwachsenbildung' in Jelisch und Hausmann (eds), *Fritz Borinski, Zwischen Paedaogik und Politik.* (Recklingshausen, 2000), pp. 11–33.
9 9 *AJR – Association of Jewish Refugees*, Journal, February 2007.
10 Self-Pierson, Rob, ' Is there a point in Town-twinning?' *The Guardian*, 30 April 2008.
11 Feidel-Metz, Hildegard (ed.), *Schulen im Exil* (Rowohlt, 1983).

19. Erasing Some Historians

1 Leventhal, F. M., *The Last Dissenter: H. N. Brailsford and His World* (OUP, 1985), p. 269.
2 In *ODNB*, but no mention of Black Book.
3 In *ODNB*, but no mention of Black Book.
4 See article on **R.C.K. Ensor** in *History Today*, vol. 37, 1 January 1987.
5 In *ODNB*, but no mention of Black Book.

6 In *ODNB*, but no mention of Black Book.
7 In *ODNB*, but no mention of Black Book.
8 In *ODNB*, but no mention of Black Book. And see Berg, Maxine, 'Eileen Power' in Shils, Edward and Blacker, Carmen (eds.), *Cambridge Women: Twelve Portraits* (CUP, 1996).
9 In *ODNB*, but no mention of Black Book.
10 In *ODNB*, but no mention of Black Book. See obituary article in *Labour Monthly*, March 1975.
11 See Honigsheim, Paul, '**Veit Valentin** (1885–1947): Der Weg eines deutschen Historikers zum Pazifismus', *Die Friedens-Warte [Peace-Watch]*, vol. 47, no. 4/5, 1947, p. 274; and 'National History or Social History? Zwei Aussenseiter der deutschen Historkierzunft: Veit Valentin und Ludwig Quidde', in Wehler and Berding (eds), *Vom Staat of the Ancien Regime zur modernen Parteienstaat* (Oldenburg, 1978), pp. 349–68; and Bauer, H., '**Veit Valentin**' in Halperin, S. W. (ed.), *Some 20th-Century Historians* (Chicago University Press, 1961), pp. 103–141.

20. Masters of the Word: Some Linguists and Literary Critics

1 *The Führer and the People* (Fontana, 1975); and cf. Ugresic, Dubravka, on the toxicity of words in *The Culture of Lies – Anti-political Essays* (Weidenfeld and Nicolson, 1998), citing the media's racist hate speak that stirred up the recent ethnic wars in the Balkans.
2 *Critical Thoughts in Critical Days* (Allen and Unwin, 1942).
3 During the Second World War **Loewenson** worked on the preparation of a Russian–English military dictionary for the War Office; the SSEES library holds his substantial Russian archive including mss. materials. See *Slavonic and East European Review*, vol. 47, no. 108, 1969, pp. 2–5.
4 See Stone, Dan, '"The *Mein Kampf* Ramp": **Emily Overend Lorimer** and Hitler Translations in Britain', *German History*, vol. 26, no. 4., 2008, pp. 504–19. She is a footnote in the *ODNB* entry on her diplomat husband, David Lockhart Robertson Lorimer, but no mention of Black Book.
5 **Trend, J. B.**, *A Picture of Modern Spain, Men and Music* (1921; republ. Becker Press, 2009).
6 See the Australian *Dictionary of Biography.*
7 See Bawden, Charles, R., '**Ernst Julius Walter Simon**, CBE, FBA', in *Proceedings of the British Academy*, vol. 67, 1981, pp. 459–77.
8 See Cohen, R. H. L. and Pottle, Mark, entry on **F. L. Lucas** in *ODNB*, but no mention of Black Book.
9 *The Delights of Dictatorship* (Heffer and Sons, 1938.)
10 See Judith Kerr's autobiographical trilogy, *When Hitler Stole Pink Rabbit*; *The Other Way Round*; and *A Small Person Far Away.*
11 **Alfred Kerr**'s son, Michael Kerr, would become a High Court judge – the first foreign-born British judge in 800 years – and his daughter, Judith

Kerr, a beloved author/artist of children's books as well as an outstanding autobiographer of childhood. **Alfred Kerr's** grandson is the writer Matthew Kneale.

12 See the important, too little known essay by Goldstein, Cora, 'Purges, Exclusions and Works of Art: politics of the OMGUS [Occupation Military Government in Germany US] 1933–1949' (Cultural Policy Center, University of Chicago, after 1998).

21. Philosophers and Socio-Political Theorists

1 See **Ernest Barker's** memoir, *Age and Youth* (OUP, 1953) and Stapleton, Julia, *Englishness and the Study of Politics: The Social and Political Thought of Ernest Barker* (CUP, 1994). In *ODNB*, but no mention of Black Book.

2 See **Cohen**'s *Almost an Autobiography: Confessions of a Freethinker* (1940) and Royle, E., entry on **Cohen** in *ODNB*, but no mention of Black Book.

3 Newman, Michael, entry on **Laski** in *ODNB*, but no mention of Black Book.

4 Davis, John, entry on **Beatrice Webb** in *ODNB*, but no mention of Black Book.

5 See Eppel, E. M , 'Address on **Morris Ginsberg**', given at the University of Jerusalem, April 1991, printed in *Wikipedia.*

6 Halsey, A. H., in *ODNB*, but no mention of Black Book.

7 See Engler and Hasenjuergen (eds), ***Marie Jahoda***, *Ich Habe die Welt nicht veraendert: Lebenserinnerungen einer Pioneerin der Sozialforschung. [I have not changed the world: Memories of a pioneer in social research]* (Campus Verlag, 1997).

8 Platt, Jennifer, in *The Palgrave Handbook of Sociology in Britain* (2014), p. 8; and see Whitty, Geoff on **'Karl Mannheim'** in the *ODNB*, but no mention of Black Book.

9 See Grygier, T., Jones, H., Spencer J. (eds), *Criminology in Transition: Essays in Honour of* ***Hermann Mannheim*** (Tavistock, 1965).

10 See Melossi, Dario , **'Georg Rusche**, a biographical essay' in *Crime and Social Justice*, no. 14, Winter 1980, pp. 55–63.

22. Some Mathematicians

1 Mestel, Leon,' **Sergei Brodetsky'** in *ODNB*, but no mention of Black Book.

2 Ditto.

3 Personal information.

4 Cohn, P. M. entry in *ODNB*, but no mention of Black Book.

5 Ibid. and see **'Professor A. H. Heilbronn'**, in *Memoirs FRS*, vol. 22, 1976.

6 Rogers, C. Ambrose, entry in *ODNB*, but no mention of Black Book. And see *Memoirs FRS*, 31, 1997.

7 See Praeger, C. E., *Memoirs FRS*, vol. 56, 2010.

8 **Hirsch** is not in the *ODNB*.

23. Jewish Inventors in the Material Sciences

1 Wittenberg, Guenter, obituary on **Eisler** in *The Independent*, 29 October 1992.

2 Ibid.

3 Medawar and Pyke, *Hitler's Gift*, op. cit., p. 93. And see Paul Eisler, *My Life with the Printed Circuit* (Lehigh University Press, 1989).

4 See *Journal of the Institute of Fuel*, vol. 18, 1945, pp. 53–9.

5 **Schallamach**'s findings were published in *Rubber Chemistry and Technology*, vols 41 and 83.

24. Biochemists and Other Medical Researchers

1 Kronberg, Arthur, *For the Love of Enzymes: The Odyssey of a Biochemist* (Harvard University Press, 1989.)

2 Medawar and Pyke, *Hitler's Gift*, op. cit., pp. 105–106.

3 Not in *ODNB*.

4 Not in *ODNB*.

5 Not in *ODNB*.

6 Medawar and Pyke, *Hitler's Gift*, op.cit., pp. 114–20; and Abrahams, Edward, **'Ernst Boris Chain'** in *Memoirs FRS*, 1983. In *ODNB*, no mention of Black Book.

7 Medawar and Pyke, *Hitler's Gift*, p.100.

8 *Memoirs FRS*, 1994.

9 Not in *ODNB*.

10 In *ODNB*, but no mention of Black Book.

11 **Ellinger** is not in the *ODNB*.

12 See Lever, J. D., 'In Memoriam Prof. **Fritz Jacoby**', *Journal of Anatomy*, April 1992 p. 180; (pt. 2) pp. 347–9. **Jacoby** is not in the *ODNB*. Should he be?

13 *British Medical Journal* obituary, 23 May 1987.

14 *British Medical Journal* obituary, 30 August 1980.

15 *British Medical Journal*, 1961. **William Mayer-Gross** is in the *ODNB*, no mention of Black Book.

16 Erich Wittkower is not in the *ODNB*.

17 Prince, Raymond, 'Origins of ... trans-cultural psychiatry' in *World Cultural Psychiatry Research Review*, December 2005.

18 See the journal, *Trans-cultural Psychiatry*, and Delille, Emmanuel, **'Eric Wittkower** and the Foundation of Montreal's Trans-cultural Psychiatry Research Unit after the Second World War' in *History of Psychiatry*, 27 March 2018.

25. Biologists – including Physiologists, Geneticists and Zoologists

1 In *ODNB*, but no mention of Black Book.

2 In ODNB, but no mention of Black Book.

3 In *ODNB*, but no mention of Black Book.

4 See *Biographical Memoir*, National Academy of Sciences, 1990. Not in *ODNB*
5 See Lewis and Hunt, '**Hans Grueneberg**', *Memoirs FRS*, vol. 30, 1984. Not in *ODNB.*
6 Ruerip and Schuering, *KWI Memoirs.* In *ODNB*, but no mention of Black Book.
7 See Otto Lowenstein, '**Dr H. D. S. Honigmann**, in *Nature*, vol. 153, 1944, p. 74.
8 Obituary in *Medical Microbiology*, vol. 22, 1986.
9 See Finlayson, L. H., obituary on **Professor Otto Loewenstein**, *The Independent*, 22 February 1999.
10 See *Jewish Women's Archive Encylopaedia* entry.

26. Chemists

1 See K. C. Ludema, '**Jacob Joseph Bikerman**, Friction and Adhesion' in *Wear*, vol. 53, 1979, pp. 1–8.
2 See Wigner and Hodgkin, '**Michael Polanyi**', *Memoirs FRS*, vol. 23, 1977.
3 See John Edsall, '**Isidor Traube**, Physical Chemist, Biochemist, Colloid Chemist and Controversialist' in *Proceedings of the Am. Philos. Society*, December 1985, pp. 371–406.
4 See *Times* obituary '**Albert Wassermann**', 8 October 1971.
5 See **Gerhard Weiler**'s privately published memoir and diaries 1928–1995 held in the Wiener Library Holocaust collection, London, and *Daily Telegraph*, 2 December 2012. Not in *ODNB*.

27. Physicists, Astro-physicists, Crystallographers, Geo-physicists and Nuclear Physicists

1 Lysenkoism was a Stalinist Soviet political campaign rejecting natural selection and asserting that environmentally induced traits could be inherited.
2 Olby, Robert, *ODNB* entry on **Bernal**, but no mention of Black Book.
3 And see Hodgkin, Dorothy, on **Bernal** in *Memoirs FRS*, vol. 28, 1980, and Brown, Andrew, ***J. D. Bernal:*** *the Sage of Science* (OUP, 2005).
4 Budiansky, Stephen, *Blackett's War: The Men Who Defeated the Nazi U-boats and Brought Science to the Art of Warfare* (Alfred A. Knopf, 2013).
5 See Hore, Peter, *Patrick Blackett: Sailor, Scientist, Socialist* (Routledge, 2002).
6 See Lovell, Bernard, '**Patrick Blackett**' in *Memoirs FRS*, 1975, and Mary Jo Nye, *Blackett: Physics, War and Politics in the Twentieth Century* (Harvard University Press, 2004). In *ODNB*, but no mention of Black Book.
7 See Cowling, T. G. on **Chapman**, *Memoirs FRS* 1971. In *ODNB*, but no mention of Black Book.
8 Halperin, J., *C. P. Snow: An Oral Biography* (Branch Line, 1983).
9 Weintraub, Stanley, author of entry on Snow in *ODNB*.
10 No Black Book in Snow's entry in the *ODNB*.

11 Mason, P.B. on **George Paget Thomson** in *ODNB*, but no mention of Black Book.
12 Phillips, D., *Memoirs FRS*, vol. 25 on **Bragg**. In *ODNB*, but no mention of Black Book.
13 **Karl Weissenberg** is not in *ODNB*. Should he be?
14 *Times* obituary, 23 October 1980, p. 18. Not in *ODNB*. Should he be?
15 See Everett, D. H., *Memoirs FRS*, vol. 30, 1984. Not in *ODNB*. Should he be?
16 Medawar and Pyke, *Hitler's Gift*, op. cit., p. 96.
17 Hyland and Rowlands, *Herbert Froehlich FRS: A Physicist Ahead of his Time* (University of Liverpool, 2006).
18 Ibid. In *ODNB*, but no mention of Black Book.
19 **Kurti, Nicholas** entry on **Francis Simon** in the *ODNB*.
20 Ibid.
21 Medawar and Pyke, *Hitler's Gift*, op. cit. p. 221.
22 See **Kurti**, 'Sir **Francis Simon**' in *Memoirs FRS*, vol. 4, 1958. **Simon**'s entry in the *ODNB*, but no mention of Black Book.
23 *ODNB*, but no mention of Black Book.
24 See obituary on **Kurti** in *The Independent*, 1998 and *Memoirs FRS*, vol. 46, 2000.
25 Sandars, Patrick, obituary on **Kuhn,** *The Independent*, 2 September 1994.
26 See Bleaney, B., '**Heinrich Kuhn**' in *Memoirs FRS*, vol. 42, 1996. In *ODNB*, but no mention of Black Book.
27 Shoenberg, D. M, '**Heinz London**', *Memoirs FRS*, vol. 17, 1971; in *ODNB*, but no mention of Black Book.
28 Medawar and Pyke, *Hitler's Gift*, op. cit. p. 53.
29 Ibid., p. 53.
30 Advisory Committee on Uranium's Report to Roosevelt, November, 1939, in Nathan, Otto, and Norden, Heinz (eds.), *Einstein on Peace* (Avenel Books, 1981), p. 297 et seq.
31 Nathan, Otto, et al., *Einstein on Peace*, op. cit. p. 302
32 Ibid., p. 303.
33 Ibid., p. 305.
34 Ibid., p. 307.
35 Sanford L. Segal, *Mathematicians under the Nazis* (Princeton University Press, 2003), p. 492.

28. The Most Dangerous British anti-Nazis in Gestapo Eyes

1 See Wheeler-Bennett, J. W. ,*John Anderson, Viscount Waverley* (Macmillan, 1962).
2 Earl Winterton, *Orders of the Day* (Cassell, 1953), p. 272.
3 The historian and retired civil servant **Albert Montefiore Hyamson** (1875–1954), although not in the War Cabinet and a spiritual rather than a political Zionist, had served as chief immigration officer in the British

Mandate of Palestine from 1921 until 1934 and had struggled indefatigably to find a viable solution for both Arabs and Jews, proposing in *c.* 1940 that each community have autonomy and all citizens have equal rights. However, in May 1937 he had acknowledged in a letter to *The Times*: '[It] may be that the Palestine problem is insoluble.'

4 See Grayling, A. C., *Among the Dead Cities: Is the Targeting of Civilians in War ever Justified?* (Bloomsbury, 2006), and see Addison, Paul, in *ODNB* entry on **Sinclair**, but no mention of Black Book.

5 See Sutherland, Duncan in *ODNB* entry on **Atholl**, but no mention of Black Book.

6 Webster, Wendy, *Mixing It*, op. cit., ch. 1, p. 42.

7 Hallett, Michael, *Stefan Lorant – Godfather of Photojournalism* (Scarecrow Press, 2006).

8 Quoted by Briggs, Asa, *The War of Words 1939–1945 – The History of Broadcasting in the United Kingdom*, vol. 3 (OUP, 1970), p. 634, fn. 2.

9 Webster, W., *Mixing It*, op. cit., ch. 1. '1940', p. 63.

10 Rose, Kenneth, in *ODNB* entry on **Grigg**, but no mention of Black Book.

11 The above-mentioned were the only Conservative MPs named by the Gestapo. For other Conservative anti-appeasement MPs see D. J. Dutton, 'Proponents and critics of appeasement', feature essay in online *ODNB*.

12 Andrew, Christopher, *The Defence of the Realm: The Authorized History of MI5* (Allen Lane, 2009).

13 See **Vansittart, R.**, *Black Record: Germans Past and Present* (Hamish Hamilton, 1941).

14 Rose, Norman, ***Vansittart**: The Study of a Diplomat* (Holmes and Meier, 1978).

15 See Thompson, A. F. in *ODNB* entry on **Acland**, but no mention of Black Book.

16 See Morgan, Kenneth O., in *ODNB* entry on **Megan Lloyd George**, but no mention of Black Book.

17 *Times* obituary, May 1982.

18 Mander, Nicholas, 'Sir **Geoffrey Mander** – the last of the Midland Radicals', *Journal of Liberal History*, vol. 57, Winter, 2006–2007. And see Parker, R. A. C., on **Mander** in Parker, ***Chamberlain** and Appeasement* (Red Globe Press, 1993).

19 Victory Books, no. 12 (Victor Gollancz, 1941), 4th edn.

20 See Mander, Nicholas, op.cit. Not in ***ODNB***. Shouldn't he be?

21 Not in *ODNB*. Shouldn't he be?

22 In *ODNB*, but no mention of Black Book.

23 Not in *ODNB*.

24 See Oldfield. S., entry on **Margery Corbett-Ashby** in *Women Humanitarians*, op. cit., and Law, Cheryl, *Women: A Modern Political Dictionary* (I. B. Tauris, 2000).

25 **Rathbone, E.**, *War Can Be Averted: The Achievability of Collective Security* (Victor Gollancz, Victory Books, 1938), p. 153.

26 Ibid., pp. 192–3.
27 Quoted in Cohen, Susan, *Rescue the Perishing: **Eleanor Rathbone** and the Refugees* (Vallentine Mitchell, 2010), ch. 6, p. 144.
28 Ibid., pp. 151–2.
29 BBC Director General, 17 November 1943, quoted in Stephen Ward, 'Why the BBC ignored the Holocaust', *Independent on Sunday*, 22 August 1993. And see Oldfield, S., on **Eleanor Rathbone** in *Women Humanitarians*, op. cit.
30 See Copsey, Nigel, *Anti-Fascism in Britain*, op. cit., ch. 1, pp. 16–20.
31 Bew, John, *Citizen Clem* (Riverrun/Quercus, 2017), p.217.
32 In *ODNB*, but no mention of Black Book.
33 Dalyell, Tam, obituary on **Strauss** in *The Independent*, 9 June 1993.
34 In 1923 the Social Democrat Labour and Socialist International had been formed.
35 Neild, Barbara, in Bellamy and Saville (eds), *Dictionary of Labour Biography*, vol. 4. And see Law, Cheryl, *Women: A Modern Political Dictionary* (I.B. Tauris, 2000).
36 See Saville and Bellamy, *Dictionary of Labour Biography*; and *ODNB*, op. cit., but no mention of Black Book.
37 In *ODNB*, but no mention of Black Book.
38 To clear the mines of gas, a child 'trapper' would sit underground opening and closing trapdoors to ventilate and allow coal trucks through.
39 Saville and Bellamy, *Dictionary of Labour Biography*, op. cit., vol. 7.
40 The 'Cat' was used as severe punishment in the Royal Navy, the British Army (until 1870), and in British prisons. Judicial corporal punishment was only removed from the Statute Book in 1948.
41 *Hansard*, 1936–8.
42 See *ODNB* , but no mention of Black Book; and see vol. 9 of Saville and Bellamy, *Dictionary of Labour Biography*, op. cit.
43 See Brown, Gordon, *Maxton*. 2002. In *ODNB*, but no mention of Black Book.
44 **Virginia Woolf**, *Diary*, 7 June 1940. 'Up till 1.30 this morning, **Kingsley** [**Martin**] diffusing his soft charcoal gloom. Question of suicide seriously debated among the 4 us – **R. Macaulay** the other in the gradually darkening room. At last no light at all.' The full quotation is in ch. 9, above, endnote 21. **Woolf** is in *ODNB*, but no mention of Black Book.
45 In *ODNB* , but no mention of Black Book.
46 See **Philips Price, Morgan**, *My Three Revolutions* (Allen and Unwin, 1970).
47 Quoted by Morgan, Kevin in *ODNB* entry on **Pritt**, but no mention of Black Book.
48 Morgan, Kevin, in *ODNB* entry on **Pritt**.
49 *Yorkshire Post*, 7 October 1933.
50 See *Spartacus Educational* biography of **Stokes**'s and Crowcroft, R., on **Stokes**'s anti-militarism and anti-Stalinism, in 'What is Happening in

Europe, **Richard Stokes**, Fascism and the Anti-War Movement in the British Labour Party during WW2', in *History*, 14 October 2008.

51 Wedgwood, C. V., *The Last of the Radicals: Josiah Clement Wedgwood* (Cape, 1951).

52 *Hansard;* in *ODNB*, but no mention of Black Book.

53 Harrison, Brian, *ODNB* entry on **Wilkinson**, but no mention of Black Book.

54 Vernon, Betty, ***Ellen Wilkinson*** *1891–1947* (Croom Helm, 1982).

55 Bittner, Donald, in *DNB* entry on **Marley**, but no mention of Black Book.

56 See Copsey, Nigel, *Anti-Fascism in Britain*, op. cit., ch. 1, pp. 57, 59–60; and **Brockway**, **Fenner**, *Inside the Left: Thirty Years of Platform, Press, Prison and Parliament* (Allen and Unwin, 1942).

57 Howard, Anthony in *DNB* entry on **Crossman**.

58 Timms, Edward, *Anna Haag and her Secret Diary of the Second World War*, op. cit., pp. 103–104. And see Briggs, Asa, *The War of Words*, op. cit., pp. 182 and 176, and Burchell, Andrew, online article, 'Crossman and Psychological Warfare', University of Warwick Modern Records Centre, August 2012.

59 See **Duff**'s memoir *No Angel's Wing*, 1947.

60 See Brade, Laura E., and Holmes, Rose, 'Troublesome Sainthood: Nicholas Winton and the contested history of child rescue in Prague, 1938–1940' in *History and Memory*, vol. 29, no. 1, pp. 3–40.

61 Morrell, Robert, *The Gentle Revolutionary: The Life and Work of* ***Frank Ridley*** (Freethought History Review, 2003). And see **Ridley**'s obituary in *The Independent*, 4 May 1994. Not in *DNB*. Should he be?

62 Not in *DNB*. Should she be?

63 Noel Thompson in Saville, *Dictionary of Labour Biography*, vol. 10.

64 Copsey, Nigel, *Anti-Fascism in Britain*, op. cit., p. 45 and chs. 1 and 2, passim.

65 In *Who's Who*, *DNB*, but no mention of Black Book.

66 Published in **Strachey**, **John**, *The Strangled Cry* (Bodley Head, 1962).

67 Duncan, Robert, *ODNB* entry on **Gallacher**; no mention of Black Book.

68 Morgan, Kevin, *ODNB* entry on **Pollitt**; no mention of Black Book.

69 See Hann, Dave, and Tilzey, Steve, *No Retreat: The Secret War Between Britain's Anti-fascists and the Far Right* (Milo Books, 2003); and Hann, Dave, *Physical Resistance: A Hundred Years of Anti-Fascism* (Zero Books, 2013).

70 See Hastings, Selina, *The Red Earl* (Bloomsbury, 2014).

71 See Horner, Arthur, *Incorrigible Rebel* (MacGibbon and Kee, 1960), and Fishman, N., *Arthur Horner: A Political Biography* (Lawrence and Wishart, 2010).

72 Lisle, Nicola, 'And the walls came tumbling down', *Oxford Times*, 9 March 2009; Stevenson, Geoff, 'Abe Lazarus and the lost world of British Communism', *History Workshop Journal*, 1 April 2017; and Samuels, R., *The Lost World of British Communism* (Verso, 2006). **Lazarus** is not in *DNB* – should he be?

73 **Monica Whately**, *Women behind Nazi Bars* (publ. unknown, 1935), and

1938 British Non-Sectarian Anti-Nazi Council to Champion Human Rights. And see Bruley, Sue, *Leninism, Stalinism and the Women's Movement in Britain 1920–1939* (Routledge, 2014).

74 See **John Baker White** in 'The Secret Agents' p. 170.

75 Moorehead, *A Bold and Dangerous Family*, op. cit., ch. 15, p .273.

76 See Trow, M. J., on the *Ausland* organisation strengthening the Reich's ties with Germans abroad – including London, Birmingham, Liverpool, Glasgow and Belfast branches in his *The Black Book*, op. cit., pp. 89–90.

77 The (originally) Polish Jewish Dr Barnett Strauss (1899–1967), Labour MP after 1945, founded the campaign 'Lidice shall live' in 1942 – see *Finchleystrasse: German Artists in Exile 1933–45* (German Embassy, 2018), p. 36. The Gestapo had overlooked him for inclusion in the Black Book in 1940.

78 Webster, Wendy, *Mixing It*, op. cit., p. 42.

79 See Brinson and Malet, 'Rudolf Olden in Oxford' in Crawford, Ulmschneider and Elsner, *Ark of Civilization – Refugee Scholars and Oxford University 1930–1945* (OUP, 2017), pp. 208–19.

80 Among many other persecuted trade unionists seeking refuge in Britain and listed by the Gestapo for arrest are: the German, and later international, trade union leader **Hans Gottfurcht** (1896–1982), who was arrested by Gestapo in 1937 for illegal trade union organising. Being Jewish, he fled Germany for Britain where he founded an organisation for exiled German trade unionists. He broadcast in German for the BBC and planned post-war TU activity for Germany. The SPD and trade union organiser **Josef Lampersberger** (1912–?), worked as a waiter on long-distance trains. He was made stateless in Germany in 1939, went to Britain, and gained British nationality in 1946. **Kurt Weckel** (1877–195?) was a teacher, trade unionist and a supporter of the SPD. Stripped of German citizenship in 1937 while in Prague, he emigrated to Britain in 1939. Part of the SPD leadership in exile, he too helped to map out future trade union organisation in a post-war Germany. After 1945 he returned to East Germany, but then left five years later for the Bundesrepublik. The Luxembourgian women's trade union leader **Lily Becker Krier** (1898–1981) was a feminist syndicalist who became a refugee in London just before the war, together with her husband, the socialist minister **Pierre Krier**. The mechanic and trade union organiser **Alfred Ziehm** (1896–?) fled to Czechoslovakia where he organised the SPD in exile for anti-fascist resistance. In 1939 he reached Britain, only to be interned as an enemy alien in 1940; he later worked as a mechanic. His date and place of death are unknown.

29. Conclusion: 'We Can Fight with the Mind'

1 *Guardian Review*, 14 September 2019.

2 Dams and Stolle, *The Gestapo*, op. cit., p. 146.

3 Breitman, Richard, 'Historical Analysis of 20 Name Files from CIA Records', Declassified CIA records, 263, April 2001.
4 Palmier, Jean-Michel, *Weimar in Exile*, 'Epilogue: Cassandras', p. 648.
5 Ibid., pp. 653–6.
6 Milton, '[It] shall require firm hearts in sound bodies to stand and cover their stations', *Apology for Smectymnus* (1654).

List of Illustrations

15. Klaus Wachsmann recording in Uganda, 1940. Image courtesy of the British Library. Photo © Philipp Wachsmann & Katrine Adler
16. 'The Happy Elephants', *Picture Post*, 15 October 1938. Image © Picture Post Historical Archive/Gale, Cengage Company
17. 'Back to the Middle Ages', *Picture Post*, 26 November 1938. Image © Picture Post Historical Archive/Gale, Cengage Company
18. A typical classroom in the Germany of 1939, *Picture Post*, 1 July 1939. Image © Picture Post Historical Archive/Gale, Cengage Company
19. Portrait of Dr David Daube, unknown photographer. Photo © Berkeley Law School
20. Portait of Gabriele Tergit, *c.* 1920s. Photo © INTERFOTO/Alamy Stock Photo
21. Virginia Woolf, photographed by Man Ray, *c.* 1930s. Photo © Granger Historical Picture Archive/Alamy Stock Photo
22. Portrait of Frank Laurence (F. L) Lucas, 7 July 1957. Photo © Caius & Gonville College, Cambridge
23. Portrait of Dr Marie Jahoda. Photo © University of Graz
24. Dr Ernst Chain sitting at his desk, *c.* 1944. Photo © Bettmann/Getty Images
25. Portrait of Dr Hugh Blaschko. Photo © The Royal Society
26. English Physicist Patrick Blackett (1897–1974), *c.* 1935. Photo © Howard Coster/Hulton Archive/Getty Images
27. German physicist Max Born (1882–1970), *c.* 1931. Photo © ullstein bild/Getty Images
28. Albert Einstein and Leo Szilard, 1946. Photo © The LIFE Picture Collection/Getty Images
29. English politician Josiah Clement Wedgwood (1872–1943), First Baron Wedgwood. Photo © Hulton Archive/Stringer/Getty Images
30. Photograph of John Strachey by Stuart Heydinger, courtesy of the *Observer*, published in *The Strangled Cry and Other Unparliamentary Papers*. Photo © The Bodley Head, 1962
31. English Liberal politician Lady Violet Bonham Carter, *c.* 1941. Photo © Pictorial Press Ltd/Alamy Stock Photo
32. Portrait of Rudolf Olden. Photo © National Library of Germany

While every effort has been made to contact copyright-holders of illustrations, the author and publishers would be grateful for information about any illustrations where they have been unable to trace them, and would be glad to make amendments in further editions.

Names Index

S

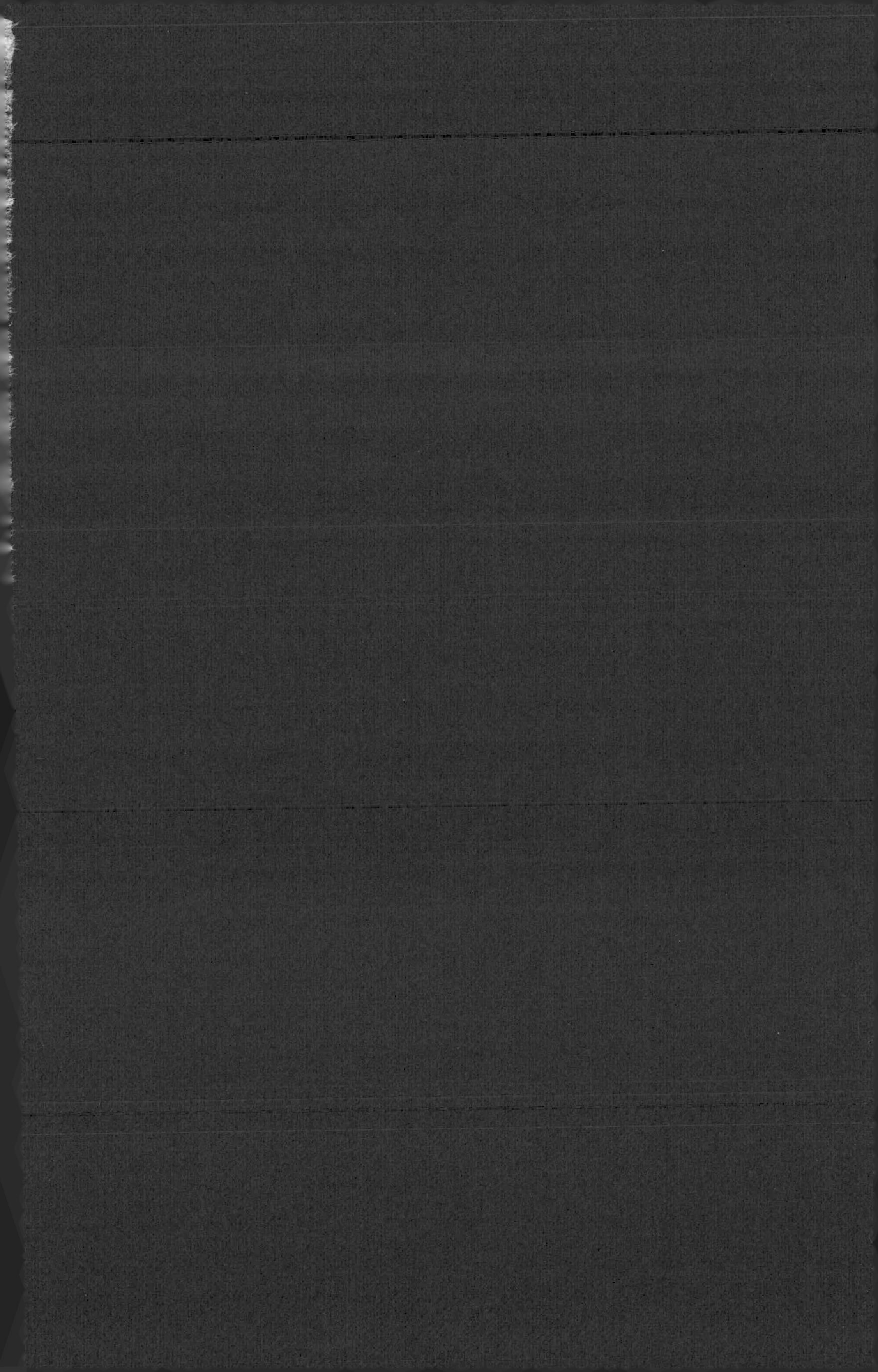

n 5. George Bell, Bishop of Chichester 6. Richard Rapier Stokes 7. Eleanor Rathbo
. The National Council of Women 16. The Navy League 17. The Public Record Office
e World Union of Progressive Judaism 25. YMCA 26. J. B. Priestley 27. Left Book C
. Dr Lee Billard 39. Werner Lehmann 40. Lina Wertheimer 41. Richard Israel Merton
50. Professor W. J. Reddaway 51. Dr Alexander Boswell 52. Dr Kenneth Edwards 53. Dr
lain 63. Lord Hankey 64. Lord Halifax 65. Anthony Eden 66. Oliver Stanley 67. Duff
l Council for Civil Liberties 77. The Quaker Friends of Europe 78. Transport and G
ographic Printers and Artists 85. Bookbinders 86. Cigar Makers 87. Textile Worke
rt Stern 97. Peter Montefiore-Samuel 98. Viscount Bearstead 99. E. L. Franklin 1
oldsmid MP 109. Rothschild family 110. Lord Swaythling 111. B. Maisel 112. Johanna
ry Strakosch 122. Lord Beaverbrook 123. Mark Ostrer 124. Maurice Ostrer 125. Oscar
an Engel 134. Dr Alfred Leeser 135. Dr Lorenz Michaelis 136. 'Laury' Michaelis 13
uttmann 145. Franz Bergel 146. Dr Ernst Brieger 147. Otto Lehmann-Russbueldt 148. Alo
lfred Einstein 157. William Ravenscroft Hughes 158. Friends Service Council 159. Ruth
aude Royden 169. Sybil Thorndike 170. Ellen Wilkinson 171. Violet Bonham-Carter 1
d Refugees 178. Rev. Henry Carter 179. Alec Dickson 180. Captain Frank Foley 181.
89. Professor Sir Ernest Barker 190. Nettie Adler 191. Margery Corbett-Ashby 192.
aret Dorothea Layton 200. Sir Walter Layton 201. Leah Manning 202. Ernest Thurtle
. Professor Julian Huxley 213. Rose Macaulay 214. Naomi Mitchinson 215. H. W. Nevi
rnthal 224. Siegfried Charoux 225. Margarethe Charoux 226. John Heartfield 227.
Collins 238. News Chronicle 239. Ruth Gollancz 240. Linksbuch-Clubs 241. 14 H
250. Hutchinson and Co 251. Felstead's 252. Leo Amery 253. Rich and Cowan Ltd
Townsend Warner 263. For Intellectual Liberty 264. Karl Doberer 265. Hans Flesch-
Lambert 275. John Russell Scott 276. H. W. Nichols 277. Israel Cohen 278. A. J
Philip Gibbs 288. C. E. M. Joad 289. Ivan Marion Greenberg 290. Morris Myer 291.
Douglas Reed 300. Margaret Haig Mackworth, Viscountess 301. John Chrysostom Segru
Francis, 'Frank' Williams 312. Lord Southwood 313. Franz Aenderl 314. Fritz Beer
Payne Best 324. Major Richard Stevens 325. Lionel Louis Loewe 326. Alaeddin Jusuf
Norman Dewhurst 338. David Footman 339. Walter Charles Rudolph Aue 340. Lieutenan
sling 347. Emil Strankmueller 348. Oldrich Tichy 349. Colonel Moravec 350. Wolfgan
tain Leslie Remvik Grant 360. Major Mac Harper 361. Colonel Haywood 362. Captain J
aham 370. Admiral Sir Reginald Hall 371. Franz von Rintelen 372. Colonel Frank No
379. Leonard Kirkpatrick 380. Captain Richard Shelley 381. H. N. Stoddart 382.
89. Warsop Petrol Drill and Tools 390. John Paterson 391. Rover 392. Standard Mo
r Co 400. Sir Andrew Agnew 401. Frederick Godber 402. Sir George Barstow 403. Jo
e John van den Bergh 410. Sidney van den Bergh 411. Lord David Davies 412. Nevil
Erlanger 422. Julius Sommer 423. L. Silkin 424. Sir Percy Simmons 425. L. S
Rothschild 435. Chaim Weizmann 436. Ben Gurion 437. The Marchioness of Reading
Julius Rieger 448. Pastor Martin Boeckheler 449. Dr Adolf Freudenberg 450. Fra
458. Professor E. F. Jacob 459. Bishop Harold Jocelyn Buxton 460. Church Sociali
469. Rabbi Joseph Hertz 470. Rabbi Israel Mattuck 471. Agudas Israel 472.
Dr Frederick Antal 480. Dr Otto Kurz 481. Dr Richard Salomon 482. Dr Martin
Hermann Meyer 491. Dr Klaus Wachsmann 492. Eduard Fraenkel 493. David Daube
Paish 502. Vyvyan Adams MP 503. Adolf Loewe 504. Hermann Levy 505. Maur
ard Rosenbaum 514. Dr Charlotte Leubuscher 515. Kurt Mandelbaum, later Kurt
Brailsford 524. G. D. H. Cole 525. C. A. Macartney 526. G. P. Gooch 527.
535. Otto Kahn-Freund 536. Professor Dr Gustav Mayer 537. Georg Schwarzenber
al 546. Dr Richard Samuel 547. Professor Ernst Julius Walter Simon 548. Jo
r Karl Mannheim 559. Hermann Mannheim 560. Dr Georg Rusche 561. Professor
Dr Kurt Hirsch 570. Paul Eisler 571. Hans Gerhardt Lubszynski